YOUR, MY, OUR HISTORY

NAMES FROM HISTORY LISTED ALPHABETICALLY
FROM ENGLISH INTO CHINESE

FOREST LEIGH LITTKE

YOUR, MY, OUR HISTORY
NAMES FROM HISTORY LISTED ALPHABETICALLY FROM ENGLISH INTO CHINESE

iUniverse books may be ordered through booksellers or by contacting:

iUniverse
1663 Liberty Drive
Bloomington, IN 47403
www.iuniverse.com
844-349-9409

Because of the dynamic nature of the Internet, any web addresses or links contained in this book may have changed since publication and may no longer be valid. The views expressed in this work are solely those of the author and do not necessarily reflect the views of the publisher, and the publisher hereby disclaims any responsibility for them.

Any people depicted in stock imagery provided by Getty Images are models, and such images are being used for illustrative purposes only.
Certain stock imagery © Getty Images.

ISBN: 978-1-6632-0028-0 (sc)
ISBN: 978-1-6632-0029-7 (e)

Print information available on the last page.

iUniverse rev. date: 10/26/2020

FOREST LEIGH LITTKE

~

Forest ~ FU RUI SI TE

福									
瑞									
斯									
特									

~

~To Ponder~

You can not open a book without learning
不学不开书.
CONFUCIUS孔夫子kong fu zi

~

"Writing is perhaps the greatest of human invention. Binding together people ... who never knew one another."

"写作也许是人类最伟大的发明.把人们绑在一起…他们从来都不认识."

Carl SAGAN萨根sa gen

In honor of

Sir Thomas Francis Wade

~

Herbert allen giles

~

Zhou youguang

Three people bridging two languages together

The collecting of surnames
~THREE sources where used~

C2C radio interviews, Wikipedia
AND BING

[hence]

Frigyes karinthy

introduced the concept of

six degrees oF separation!

CIRCA 1929

~

**In one way or another … we are all connected
in this world.**

CONTENTS

SECTION

FROM THE BEGINNING

PART A

Since the dawn of our species, language is the basis of our communication between two individuals. If we follow the historical account of the Biblical records, then language was first used between big G or God and Adam. In certain circles it is called the A-da-mic tongue! However, their are no written records to prove that it actually existed!

We only know what is recorded in the KJV of the bible as it is written in Genesis chapter 11:1..."and the whole earth was of one language, and of one speech.[1]

As time passed and the earths population grew, the bible would record later in chapter 11 verse 7: "Go to, let us go down, and there confound their language, that they may not understand one another's speech.[2] At this moment, "ethnogue"[3] informs us that we have about 7000 languages on Earth.

Thus, written language (painted or engraved) began with the ancient Egyptian heiroglyphs and perhaps other locations scattered around the globe. Gobeklitepe, has engravings going far far back in time and memorial. Ancient pictograms from which the Chinese began its baby steps in relation to these. It is also known as the "Logographic" writing system.[4]

In ancient China, we learn that words were carved into dried bones, then onto strips of bamboo (tiles), and perhaps animal skins etc until paper was developed!

I have lived in main land China from 2010 to 2018 and was an oral English teacher. In my free time, I would catch the occasional movie in English but the subscript was always in Chinese. Gradually you get to match the Chinese script character with the spoken words and ... you begin to understand the phonetic approach.

During a dinner function in 2010, I came across my English name written in Chinese phonetics... thus Forest transforms into 福瑞斯特 （fu rui si te … as it is in Pin Yin). Zhou You Guang understood the existing problem of his time and made great efforts to standardize the system. This is how the older generation come to grips with the PHONETICS of English words. However, you MUST stretch your imagination to connect the dots so-to-speak. Todays' students do not need to rely on this system completely. However, some students will playfully call me FO-RE-S TAH. You must not take the Chinese words literally as 福 (fu) equals "fortune", 瑞 (rui) equals "lucky", 斯 (si) "is a filler sound", and 特 (te) equals "special".

This book 'our History' with the subtitle "福瑞斯特" is to be seen as a collection of historic people from our past. I have one large written dictionary and one ipad dictionary and of course the internet format "Wikipedia". Even with three sources to choose from, it was difficult to get a "complete" match on many names. In odd cases, three sources would not agree and so I could not locate a name and simply had to fill in with my phonetic knowledge.

At the beginning of this book I give full recognition to the work of Wade, Giles and Zhou. They are the forerunners to today's Chinese languages for foreigners.

Here-in the focus will be on the SURNAME, followed by a common name as is the Chinese custom! As well, I will include Chinese names in the second portion of historic note as it may be of interest. Over 7 billion people live on Mother Earth, however the list of surnames seems endless displayed here in! Learn, Discover and Enjoy!

PART B

Written versus spoken words
An overview

It should be noted that this collection leans heavily towards the HISTORIC figures of ACEDEMIA. Some figures who are not in the fore mentioned group but still play a dominant role in history will also be visited here and in a follow- up within Entertainment and Sports (issues being planned).

This article is devoted to the diversity found within English as well as Chinese. Language can seem so simple to the person who grows up and speaks ONLY his native tongue. We accept without reservation the linguistics that our forebears used as our language matured through the prior centuries. New words are added or created as our civilization becomes more civilized so-to-speak. We jumped from Phonetician to Greek to Latin, thus todays English is a hoshposh or transliteration of these forerunner languages.

As a child going to grade school, I would ask mom … "why does the word phone have a "F" sound instead of PH?" Her reply was "it just does son!" and so "phonetics" is not spoken as P-honetics, etc. I felt English was a no-win language and you just had to learn what Mrs. Williams*4 taught us in school. Thus you had to take these "twists" in your native language, put it on the "back burner" of your brain and use the words at the appropriate time within grammar. So easy ….NOT!

The Chinese do use the 4 tone system with their spoken language in main land China. It can seem complicated from the get go as you try to master it. However, Pin Yin was introduced so that the English speaking world could adopt and speak "pu tong hua" (普通话) which is the bridge to speaking Chinese without the need to read Chinese. For me, Pin Yin is an absolute nightmare as one sound could give you a dozen different meanings when you try to speak Chinese. "shi" is a common pin yin sound, but can correspond to "是，时，事，市，石". Each has a separate distinct meaning but all sound like "sh". So, if you can step away from the pin yin and learn the character (modern or historical) in and of its self ... you will find Chinese simple and easy! This book will show you back to back the English word, then the true character and the phonetic sound. Most sounds do duplicate the English and are only a "ball park" phonetic sound and you really have to stretch your imagination to understand. So, you will see many of these "stretches"as you gander through this book. Bethune is the prime example.. Since I am Canadian and was living in China, most older Chinese would ask where I am from, my response of course is Canada! They immediately put on a smile and shake my hand and say "Bai qiu en", which is their equivalent of Bethune, the popular Canadian doctor who served in China healing their soldiers. So, all people who come from Canada are warmly welcomed because of Norman Bethune.

You will discover who coined new terms and how double standards came in vogue as phrases such as "catch-22", "doublethink" and "alternative medicine" would be become standardized etymology of our modern era.

The six degree of separation (Karinthy) came into clear perspective as I researched the people and found patterns of who Knew who! Wikipedia and Bing often will include several names linked with the person. Who was suing who among the inventors for pending patent wars! Each influenced the world in their own way.

My search engine for this work included "BaiDu" (China's Google), Wikipedia -"the Free library to the world" and Han-ping dictionary for translation services to verify accuracy. Bing often centered on one person but was not always the rule. Often, no name is attached to a photo and so I did not want to be proven wrong for choosing a photo that did not belong to a new entry. At present, there is NO dictionary or encyclopedia in the WORLD that is all inclusive. Why???? Because language evolve's as the SPECIES evolves intellectually! My collection is merely a glance at "1500 +" surnames that ought to be remembered "Lest we forget". In the very very early stages of collecting a name list, it ONLY looked like the "In Brief" page. Just a Surname ~ Chinese ~ phonetic!!!! For the academic minded person, it might not be enough to "chew on"... and FYI was born. So my "encyclopedia of surnames" grew! A wide cross section alphabetically. Please note, that a Chinese person with no formal education can not pronounce a Foreign Surname easily, and this book is prepared and researched in larger measure for the Chinese. In their schools, YOUR first name becomes your SURNAME! Forest Littke hence becomes Mr. Fu Rui Si Te ~ 福瑞斯特.

Out side of the Chinese culture, I have no idea how many Surnames exist in the world. Names with "Q" or "X" are difficult to find and I must search eccentric ethnic groups. I wish to note as well that the Tibetans do not carry a family name ... Tai-ring or 才 is given to all members of that society! I had a student from Tibet and thus added the pieces together.

This all began as a curiosity and I hope the public will join me for this journey of discovery and a willingness to get a hint of Chinese along this journey of learning.

You will find a Memorial page within this book ~ several groups will be mentioned. The S.S. Edmund Fitzgerald and the RMS Titanic to name a few.

Some names came as a surprise to me as in the event called 'Woodstock Music and Arts Fair". MAX YASGUR the dairy farmer who allowed the organizers to hold a three day music weekend on his farm. I discovered his name by watching the PBS program 'Woodstock' and felt this man earned the right to be in this collection and conclude this finite collection.

I hope this collection will be warmly welcomed into the classroom or home or office waiting room. My apologies if I have missed a person that you may favor!

~ IN BRIEF~

The People who Molded my Character and my way of thinking.

Bell~Blanc~Burton~Diefenbaker~Gorbachev~Harvey~Hawking~Homme~ Joyce ~Kurtzman~Kasem~Massey~McConkie-Mclean~Oeming~Rockwell~ Roddenberry~Rooney~ Sagan~Sterling~Ustinov~ Welk~

>ASSIMOV艾斯麻 ai si mo: Writer; Fehrenheit 451

>BELL 贝尔 bei er: Radio personality ~ C2C radio

>BLANC 布兰科 bu lan ke: TV voice actor~Man of a thousand voices

>BURTON 伯顿 bu dan: Writer and documentary: Voice of Canada

>DIEFENBAKER 迪芬贝克 di fen ba ka: A Canadian politician

>GORBACHEV 戈尔巴乔夫 ge er ba qiao fu: 1931- USSR Russian leader

>HARVEY 哈维 ha wei: Radio Icon~The rest of the story.

>HAWKING 霍金 huo jin: Phyisist ~Thinking out side of the Box

>HOMME 侯马hou ma: The Friendly Giant ~ a soft voice

>JOYCE 乔伊斯 qiao yi si: Writer "Ulysses"~ my first novel

>KASEM 初步 chu bu: Radio personality; Weekly Top 100 count down

>KURTZMAN 库茨曼 ku ci man: publisher of MAD magazine

>MASSEY 梅西 mei xi: Academic professor *Massey Lecture Series

>MCCONKIE 麦康基 mai kang ji *Jesus The Christ~ L.D.S.

>MCLEAN 麦克林 mai ke lin: Radio personality; The humor of Daily Life.

>OEMING 奥命 ao ming: Philanthropist~ Alberta Game Farm

>ROCKWELL 罗克韦尔 luo ke wei er: Painter

>RODDENBERRY罗登贝瑞 luo deng bei rui: Writer and director

>ROONEY 如尼 ru ni: TV personality

>SAGAN撒干 sa gan: Professor of astronomy; TV personality "Cosmos"

>STERLING 斯特林 si te lin: Writer and director "The Night Gallery"

>USTINOV 鸟斯季诺夫 niao si ji nuo fu: Writer-TV personality

>WELK 威尔克 wei er ke: TV personality and musician.

Ask your self!

WHO

has molded MY thoughts as I finger through this book!

~ETYMOLOGY~GLOSSARY~

These words are mentioned briefly as they pop up occasionally in the mini- bio's that I have provided.

Aphorist: short expression with quirky meaning;

Anabaptist: baptism first and foremost before being allowed to belong to a society. [~ammann-simons-hutter:anabaptist]

BIOSPHERE: where life is contained; [chakan-Suess]

CCGS: Canadian Coast Guard Ship; Amundsen

CMHF: Canadian Medical Hall of Fame; Best

Elocution: is the study of formal speaking in pronunciation, grammar, style and tone.

Ephemarides: Latin for Journal or Diary

Eponymous: named after a person [Gregg]

Etymology: the study of words or their history

Lexicography: making dictionaries

NEO-Latin: is reference to new Latin post renaissance.

NWMP: North Western Mounted Police

O.C.: Order of Canada

Olympic: the name is derived from a small Greek town.

Orthonym: GREEK for ones true name.ONOMATOLOGY

Pseudonym: pen names, nickname, A.K.A. (also known as)

Portmanteau: a linguistic blend of names ie: Mattel

Polymath: a person knowledgeable in multiple languages or fields of study.

Renaissance: a rebirth of humanism ie: Erasmus

Thesaurus: Latin for Treasure Storehouse. ie: Roget's Thesaurus.

Transliteration: phonetic transcription of a name from one language to a separate language.

纪念~ji nian: in memorial

查看~cha kan: search and see

年 or nian beside the year and sometimes followed by 月month，日day.

THE ANATOMY OF A LISTED NAME

*Historically Surname's are derived from ancient birth rights, cities from whence you are born, occupation, as well as enforced (adopted) by slavery! (Phonetic Surname encyclopedia)

Line one: Surname 姓名> Chinese 中文 > yin yue 音韵.
*The phonetic sound will always be in GREEN.

Line two: the foreign name always in BLACK.

Line three: Time line; 生人~ 年 refers to the years of existence.

Line four: FYI; Era & aka is included with High lite info
*sources include but are not limited to Wikipedia, IMDb, Nobelprize.org, Massey lectures, C2Cam, Sparticus Educational and others. Quotes are also included to give perspective of the persons thoughts. So a sample quote of a person mentioned in each section and is seen at the top of each alphabet. As well, at the end of this book is a small collection and practice unit. In the future, I will have a book that is centered on quotes and will be called 'Voices from the Past'.

Line five: *史实:~The Chinese translation. *史传，史实，all equal FYI or "sher sher". All Chinese is written in RED. It is the symbolic color for China.

In addition to the names we are given at birth, their is the added issue or problem of the "initial" or middle name. As with Forest L. Littke, the collecting of a name with the Initial causes a small head ache. It is to represent a name of importance to the parent, but seldom does the name have significance to the individual. Even after 60 years (2019) I have no idea why mother gave me the middle name of "Leigh". To put a dot (.) beside it only shows the abbreviated form. While developing this book

I simply put a [~@~] as a filler. In a Sr., Jr., or child as all share the main name...the middle initial is all that gives evidence of a change. In the Chinese section they do not share this common problem. Their are NO initials in the Chinese Language. Their is ancient Chinese verses contemporary modern written characters, but their is no way to shorten a given name in their culture.

The majority of people collected are from an academic setting. [a&e] Arts and entertainment, [S] sports are mentioned as specialized areas.

Memorial Wall will be included at the end of the book.

**This book should be viewed as a work book for self education.

The longest name in my research:

*Bernhard Friedrich Aberhard Leopold Julius Kurt Carl Gottfried Peter Graff von Biesterfeld (birth name) 12 given names for one person.

~

**Because of 'online copyright' restrictions, I was unable to get specific photos such as 'The Red Baron' or 'Therese of Lisieux' and many more. Thus my photos came from schools, historic sites and local government with permission to enter and photograph images. Breton Museum, John Walter Museum and the near by Ukrainian Village in Alberta and private monies. Names that we commonly ignore in our day to day rush, are remembered here.

A

教育不是你完成的事情
"education isn't something you finish.~"
Isaac ASIMOV啊阿斯嘛a si ma

ABBOTT艾博特ai bo te

[SIR] John Abbott

生人1821 ~ 1893年 》72

FYI: 4th Canadian pm. c.1892

史传: 加拿大曾经首相四号~ 1892

courtesy Alberta Legislation building

ABERHART阿布赫特a bu he ta

William Aberhart

生人1878 ~ 1943年 》64

FYI: Premier of Alberta:1935-43. Aberhart Medical Centre (Edmonton).

史传: 艾伯特主席 年1935-43，阿布赫特义务中心

photo from Adair Park.
Photo courtesy of Forest L. ~福瑞斯特

ADAIR阿代尔a dai er
Joseph Woods and Dorothy Trembley Adair
生人1877～1960年 》83; 生人1887～1960年 》73
FYI: Both were prominent members of Garneau community within the city of Edmonton.
[See ~ Garneau]
史传: 他们都是埃德蒙顿市的加纳社区的杰出成员.

ADAIR阿代尔a dai er
Red Neal Adair
生人1915～2004年 》89
FYI: Oil Well firefighter: "Hellfighter's" c.1968 is based on his life.
史传: 油井小伙; "Hellfighters's 顷1968 是他生活

ADAMS亚当ya dang
John Adams
生人1735～1826年 》91
FYI: 2nd President of United States c 1797-1801
史实: 第二总统 U.S.

ADLER啊德勒a de le

Alfred*W*Adler

生人1870 ~ 1937年 》 67

FYI: Renouned psychologist: [Understanding Human Nature]

史实: 心理学: [明白人性]

Photo courtesy of Forest L. ~福瑞斯特

ADULYADEJ阿杜亚德a du ya de

Bhumibol Adulyadej

生人1927 ~ 2016年 》89

FYI: KING of Thailand. His reign was 9 June 1946 – 13 October 2016. His reign lasted 70 years and 126 days.

史实: 泰国国王.他的统治时间是1946年6月9日至2016年10月13日.他的统治持续了70年126天.

AESCHYLUS埃斯库罗斯ai si ku luo si

Aeschylus

生人c.524 ~ 455Bc年 》67

FYI: The Greek Father of tragedy. Robert Kennedy quoted Aeschylus the day M.L.King was assassinated. April 4 1968

史实: 希腊悲剧之父.

AESOP伊索yi suo

Aesop

生人620 ~ 560 年BC 》80

FYI: Story teller of ancient times.

史实: 古代故事平话

AGRICOLA 阿格里奥拉a ge li ao la

Georgius Agricola

生人1494 ~ 1555年 》61

FYI: "Father of mineralogy". Coined the term "fossil fuel" c1556.

史实: "矿物学之父".创造了术语"化石燃料" C1556.

Used with permission. Harry Ainley school

Photo courtesy of Forest L. ~福瑞斯特

AINLEY埃恩雷ai en lei

Harry Dean Ainley

生人1887年1月3日~ 1970年3月12日 》83

FYI: Canadian educator, politician and mayor of Edmonton c1944-1949. Harry Ainley High School in his honor.

史实: 加拿大教育家,政治家,埃德蒙顿市市长C1944-1949.为了纪念哈里·安利高中.

ALASKEY啊拉斯卡起a la si ke qi

Joseph Frances "Joe" Alaskey

生人1952 ~ 2016年 》63

FYI: [a&e] Voice actor of Bugs Bunny and others.

史实: 口吻义人 "Bugs Bunny".

Statue and stain glass courtesy of Albert Government.

Photo courtesy of Forest L. ~福瑞斯特

ALBERTA哎波塔ai bo ta

Louise Caroline Alberta Windsor ~ Duchess of Argyll

生人1848年3月18日~ 1939年12月3日 》91

FYI: Lake Louise, Mt Alberta, Province of Alberta named in her honor and was chosen to honor her father. * 4th daughter of Queen Victoria. House of Windsor. The province of Alberta was established on 1905 Sept. 1. The stain window seen only in the 'upper chambers' represents the grain of the prairies, morning sun rise in the East, Saskatchewan river, Northern lights, all seen within the province.

史实： 路易丝湖，阿尔伯塔山，阿尔伯塔省，以她的名字命名，并被选为尊重她的父亲.*维多利亚女王的第四个女儿.温莎之家.阿尔伯塔省成立于1905年9月1日.只在"上层房间"看到的污点窗口代表了大草原的谷粒,东部日出,萨斯喀彻温河,北极光,这些都是在该省看到的.

ALDRIN奥尔德林ao er de lin
Buzz Aldrin

生人1930年1月20日~ active

FYI: aka: Edwin Eugene Aldrin jr.; Second astronaut to set foot on the moon [1969.07.21;03:15:16]. His sisters would mispronounce the word brother by calling him "buzzer", hence his Nickname of "Buzz"and used it legally as his first name c.1977. *My first inclination is to be a bit skeptical about the claims that human-produced carbon dioxide is the direct contributor to global warming.

史实： 第二位宇航员踏上月球[1969.07.21; 03：15：16].他的姐妹们将"兄弟"一词称为"蜂鸣器",因此发音不清.因此,他的昵称为"蜂鸣器",并在1977年被合法地用作他的名字.*我的第一个倾向是对人为产生的二氧化碳是导致全球变暖的直接原因的说法有些怀疑.

ALEIXANDRE阿莱克桑德雷a lai ke sang de lei
Vicente Aleixandre

生人1898 ~ 1984年 》86

FYI: Awarded the Nobel for Literature: poetry 1894. [Nobelprize.org]

史实： 诺贝尔 1894年为了式著作

ALEXANDER亚历山大ya li shan da
Stephen Alexander

生人1806 ~ 1883年 》77

FYI: Astronomer and educator. [Physical Phenom as per Solar Eclipses]

史实: 天文学家和教育家.

ALLINGHAM阿玲哈a ling ha
Henry William Allingham

生人1896 ~ 2009年 》113

FYI: Supercenturian for the oldest living man circa 2007. "cigarettes, whisky and wild women...give longevity!"

史实: 顷2007: 世纪113 "吸烟威士忌

ALTGENS阿格恩斯a ge en si

James William "Ike" Altgens

生人1919 ~ 1995年 》76

FYI: Press photographer during JFK assassination

史实: JFK凶杀。报界

ALVAREZ阿尔瓦雷茨a er wa lei ci

Luis Walter Alvarez

生人1911 ~ 1988年 》76

FYI: American nuclear physicist who designed the trigger switch for the Hiroshima bomb. Discovered the K electron. Awarded the Nobel for physics in 1968. [*Nobelprize.org]

史实: 美国物理学家设计师总开关广岛原子弹.发现K电子.奖赏诺贝尔在物理学顷1968.

ALZHEIMER阿兹海默a zi hai mo

Alois Alzheimer

生人1864 ~ 1915年 》51

FYI: aka: Aloysius "Alois" Alzheimer. German psychiatrist and neuropathologist.

史实: 德国人心里学家.神经病.

AMBER安珀an po

Amber Rene Hagerman

生人1986年11月25日~ 1996年1月17日 》10

FYI: The AMBER Alert was first created in 1996 following her abduction.The name has been changed to an acronym for Americas Missing: Broadcast Emergency Response. Now is a world wide protocol for any missing child.

史实: 》AMBER警报《 是在她被绑架后于1996年创建的.这个名字已经改为"失踪的美洲人:广播紧急响应" 的首字母缩写.现在是一个世界范围内的任何失踪儿童的协议.

AMONTONS阿蒙顿a meng dun

Guillaume Amontons

生人1663 ~ 1705年 》48

FYI: invented the barometer scale. [see Kelvin, Celsius, F, Romer]

史实: 创作者气压表

AMMANN阿曼a man

Jakob Amman

生人1644 ~ 1714年 》70

FYI: The Founder of the Amish religion. [see~ ammann- simons- hutter: anabaptist]

史实: 阿米什教的创始人.

AMPERE安培an pei

Andre-Marie Ampere

生人1775 ~ 1836年 》61

FYI: The Amp or (A) is the base unit of electricity named after him. *His name appears among the 72 names on the base of the Eiffel Tower. [NW13] >1/72

史实: 安（A）基础单位电子以人名命名.新元史上埃菲尔铁塔.

Photo courtesy of Forest L. ~福瑞斯特

AMUNDSEN啊阿曼森a man sen

Roald Engelbregt Agravning Amundsen

生人1872 ~ 1928年 》56

FYI: A Norwegian explorer who was the first to reach BOTH poles. CCGS Amundsen and Mt. Amundsen in his honor. The CCGS Amundsen is also pictured on the back of the Canadian 50 bill.

*Adventure is just bad planning.

史实: 第一个到达两极的挪威探险家.为纪念阿蒙森和阿蒙森山.CCGS阿蒙森号也在加拿大50号法案的背面.*冒险只是不好的计划.

ANDERS安德斯an de si

Ernst Rudolf Anders

生人?~ 1937年5月6日 》[memorial纪念]

FYI: Passenger; LX - Hindenburg

史实：乘客惨变·兴登堡

ANDERSON安德森 an de sen

Abraham Anderson

生人1829 ~ 1915年 》86

FYI: Co-founder of Campbell Soup c1869.

史实：合资 Campbell*汤

ANDERSON安德森an de sen

Micheal Phillip Anderson

生人1959 ~ 2003年 》 [memorial纪念]

FYI: NASA astronaut: Columbia Accident 2003 Feb 1

史实：太空人2003年 02月1日

ANDERSON安德森an de sen

Thomas Anderson

FYI: co-invented the"Band-Aid"with Earle Dickson for johnson*johnson c1920

史实：共同发明了 "创可贴" 与Earle Dickson为约翰逊*约翰逊C1920 [看- Dickson]

ANDERSSON安德森an de sen

Johan Gunnar Andersson

生人1874 ~ 1960年 》86 [memorial纪念]

FYI: Archaeologist. **co-discovery of Peking man c1926.

史实：墓坑航土层 1926年.

ANDRE安德烈an de lie

Fabian Andre

生人1910 ~ 1960年 》50

FYI: [a&e] Composer, "Dream a little dream of me". Made famous by Mama Cass Eliot

史实：作曲家，《梦一个小梦我》由卡丝•艾略特妈妈演唱

ANDREWS安德鲁斯an de lu si

Thomas Andrews jr

生人1873 ~ 1912年 》38 [memorial纪念]

FYI: 1912 April 15; Chief builder of the TITANIC.

史实:1912年4月15日 泰坦尼克号的首席建造者.

ANGELOU安杰鲁an jie lu

Maya Angelou

生人1928年4月4日~ 2014年5月28日 》86

FYI: aka: Marguerite Annie Johnson; Acclaimed author and poet. (Maya means "mya sister").*I've learned that people will forget what you said, people will forget what you did, but people will never forget how you made them feel.

史实: 著名作家和诗人.（玛雅的意思是"玛雅姐姐".）*我了解到人们会忘记你说的话, 人们会忘记你的所作所为, 但是人们永远不会忘记你如何表达自己的感受.

ANTHEIL安太尔an tai er

George Johann Carl Antheil

生人1900 ~ 1959年 》58

FYI: [a&e] Composer, writer. co-inventor of band width jamming with Heidi Lemarr.

史实: 作曲家作者.造频段拥塞帮助 [看~ heidi_lemarr]

ANTOINETTE安托瓦妮特an tuo wa ni te

Marie Antoinette

生人1755 ~ 1793年 》37

FYI: aka: Maria Antonia Josepha Johanna; last Queen of France 1792

史实: 法国王后.1792年

ANTONY安通义an tong yi

Mark Antony

生人83 ~ 30BC年 》53

FYI: Roman politician and General.

史实: 罗马将和政界

APPLETON阿普尔顿a pu er dun

[Sir] Edward Victor Appleton

生人1892 ~ 1965年 》72

FYI: He was a Pioneer in radio physics ~ discovered the ionosphere.

史实：射电先导~ 所发现电离层

ARAFAT啊拉法特a la fa te

Yasser Arafat

生人1929年8月24日~ 2004年 》75

FYI: aka: Mohammed Yasser Abdel Rahman Abdel Raouf Arafat Al-qudwa; PLO leader. *Peace, for us, is an asset and in our interest. It is an absolute human asset that allows an individual to freely develop his individuality unbound by any regional, religious, or ethnic fetters.

史实：民放走将. *对我们而言, 和平是一项资产, 符合我们的利益.这是一项绝对的人力资产, 可以使个人自由地发展自己的个性, 不受任何区域, 宗教或种族束缚的束缚.

ARAGO阿拉戈a la ge

Dominique Francoise Jean Arago

生人1786 ~ 1853年 》67

FYI: physicist, astronomer. His name appears among the 72 names on the Eiffel Tower. [SE16] 2/72

史实：物理学家天文学家.新元史上埃菲尔铁塔.

ARISTOTLE亚里士多德ya li shi duo de

Aristotle

生人384 ~ 322BC年

FYI: Greek philosopher wrote papers on biology, zoology, metaphysics, poetry, linguistics, ethics, music etc.

史实：古希腊语写关于生物学动物学形上旧时语言学道德音乐.

ARISTOPHANES阿里斯托芬a li si tuo fen

Aristophanes

生人c446 ~ 385年 BC

FYI: Greek scholar and grammarian. The Tones of words....rising, dropping etc.

史实: 希腊学者和语法学家.语调……上升,下降等.

ARMAGOST啊马格斯特a ma ga si te

Micheal~E~Armagost

生人1938 ~ 1975年 》37 》 [memorial纪念]

FYI: *SS Edmund Fitzgerald~Lake Superior 10 Nov 1975

史实: S.S. 埃德蒙*菲茨杰拉德 湖高强1975年 11月10日

Public Archives of Edmonton.
Photo courtesy of Forest L. ~福瑞斯特

ARMSTRONG阿姆斯特朗a mu si te lang

George Seale Armstrong

生人1867年5月16日~ 1947年6月9日 》80

FYI: Mayor of Edmonton from 1910~1912. Canadian business man and politician.

史实: 1910年至1912年任埃德蒙顿市长.加拿大商人和政治家.

ARMSTRONG阿姆斯特朗a mu si te lang

Neil Alden Armstrong

生人1930年8月5日~ 2012年8月25日 》82

FYI: American astronaut, aeronautical engineer, naval aviator, test pilot, and university professor. First to set foot on the moon.1969 July 21, 2:56 UTC. An American hero and international legend.

"That is one small step for man, one giant leap for mankind!" (Q)

史实: 美国宇航员和航空工程师, 海军飞行员, 试飞员, 大学教授.第一次踏上月球.1969年7月21日, 2:56 UTC《这是人类的一小步, 是人类的一大飞跃! 》

ARMSTRONG阿姆斯特朗a mu si te lang

Louis Armstrong

生人1901 ~ 1971年 》70

FYI: [a&e] renouned Trumpet player and singer

史实: 出喇叭歌唱

ARNOLD阿诺德a nuo de

Kenneth~A~Arnold

生人1915 ~ 1984年 》69

FYI: Infamous 1947 UFO sighted

史实: 1947年 幽浮一见如故

ARROW阿罗a luo

Kenneth Joseph "Ken" Arrow

FYI: Economist. 'Arrow's Impossibility Theorem'

史实: 经济学家 [箭的不可能理论]

ASHEVAK阿舍瓦克a she wa ke

Kenojuak Ashevak

生人1927年10月3日 ~ 2013年1月8日 》76

FYI: As a former Inuit artist, she is regarded as one of the most notable indigenous pioneers of modern Inuit art. 2016 she is featured in 'A Canadian Heritage Minute.'
*There is no word for art. We say it is to transfer something from the real to the unreal. I am an owl, and I am a happy owl. I like to make people happy and everything happy. I am the light of happiness and I am a dancing owl.

史实: 作为前因纽特人艺术家, 她被认为是现代因纽特人艺术中最著名的本土先驱之一.2016年, 她被选为 "加拿大传统分钟".*艺术是没有字的.我们说这是将某些东西从真实转移到虚幻.我是猫头鹰, 也是快乐的猫头鹰.我喜欢让人们开心, 让一切都开心.我是幸福之光, 我是跳舞的猫头鹰.

ASIMOV艾斯麻a si ma

Isaac Asimov

生人1920年1月2日 ～ 1992年4月6日 》72

FYI: aka: Isaak Ozimov; Professor of biochemistry and writer. Science fiction writer. *Education isn't something you finish.*

史实: 教授生活,文章.科学文章. *教育不是你完成的事情

ASTBURY阿斯特伯里a si te bo li

William Thomas Astbury

生人1898 ～ 1961年 》63

FYI: Discovered the Alpha helix, forerunner to the DNA 51 moment.

史实: 发现双链核算,先行者 DNA 51.

ASTOR阿斯特a si te

John Jacob "Jack" Astor IV

生人1864 ～ 1912年 》47 》 [memorial纪念]

FYI: Businessman *Est Ntw: 87M(1912), 1514 people died aboard the Titanic.

史实: 商业人,1514 人死者上Titanic 1912年

ATKINS阿特金a te jin

Dr. Robert Coleman Atkins

生人1930 ～ 2003年 》72

FYI: Cardiologist who developed the 'Atkins Diet' to help people loose weight.

史实: 心脏病专家,他开发了"阿特金斯饮食"来帮助人们减肥.

ATTENBOROUGH爱登堡ai deng bao

[SIR] Richard Samuel Attenborough

生人1923 ～ 2014年 》90

FYI: Actor (Jurassic Park), filmmaker (Gandhi:1983), voice actor, entrepreneur, and politician. *I passionately believe in heroes, but I think the world has changed its criteria in determining who it describes as a hero.*

史实: 演员（侏罗纪公园），导演（甘地:1983），配音演员,企业家和政治家. *我充满激情地相信英雄,但我认为世界已经改变了确定英雄人物德标准.

AUBREY奥帕瑞ao pa rui

John Aubrey

生人1626～1697年 》71

FYI: Pioneer Archaeologists, toponym.

史实: 先导考古学家,地名 [see - Aubrey*holes-stonehenge].

AUSTIN奥斯汀ao si ting

Jane Austin

生人1775～1817年 》41

FYI: English novelist; Pride and Prejudice, Sense and Sensibility.

史实: 小说家 傲慢与偏见, 理智与情感.

AVERY埃弗里ai fu li

Oswald Theodore Avery jr.

生人1877～1955年 》77

FYI: molecular biologist, forerunner to the [DNA 51 slide]

史实: 分子生物学.DNA 51

AYRES艾尔斯ai er si

Thomas Almond Ayres

生人1816～1858年

FYI: *c.1855 sketch of Yosemite valley.

史实: 1855年 Yosemite 山沟

AYTOUN艾同ai tong

Robert Aytoun

生人1570～1638年 》68

FYI: A poet of the 16th century. He had penned a very short version of 'Old Long Syne', therefore it is likely that Burns extended the verses.

史实: 16世纪的诗人.他写了一个很短的版本的"古老的长诗",因此很可能伯恩斯延长了诗句. 《Old Long Syne》 (古代) [~Burns]

From Group "A" you can pick one person or up to ten and write their Surname in Chinese. You may try HORIZONTAL or VERTICAL in the traditional Chinese form.

B

《有比焚书更为恶劣的犯罪，其中之一就
是不读书》
"There are worse crimes then burning
books. One of them is not reading them."
Ray BRADBURY吧如大步以ba ru da bu yi

BACH巴赫ba he

Johann Sebastian Bach

生人1685 ~ 1750年 》65

FYI: German composer of the Baroque period. *"I play the notes as they are written, but it is God who makes the music."

史实: 德国作曲家巴洛克. *我按字面上的音符演奏，但这是上帝创造的音乐."

BACKSTER巴戈斯特ba ge si te

Grover Cleveland "Cleve" Backster jr.

生人1924 ~ 2013年 》89

FYI: CIA Interrogation specialist. Theory of Primary Perception ie ESP as it related to plants feeling pain.

史实: CIA 审讯专家.理论基础卉感通 [看- J*D*bose]

BACON培根pei gen

Roger Bacon

生人1219 ~ 1292年 》73

FYI: Scholastic scientist; was the first to record how gun powder was made.

史实: 是第一个记录火药是如何制成的.

BACON培根pei gen

[SIR] Francis Bacon

生人1561 ~ 1626年 》65

FYI: Renaissance philosopher, statesman, author, orator. Is known for "opus majus". *In order for the light to shine so brightly, the darkness must be present.

史实: 文艺复兴哲学家，政治家，雄辩家.《opus majus》.*为了使光线如此明亮地发光，必须在黑暗.

BAKER贝克bei ke

George Herman Baker

生人1923 ~ 2003年7月23日 》79

FYI: Pte. Baker served in the second world war and was among the Canadian troupes to be deployed on Juno beach. A camera crew was filming the troupes as they readied to leave the U-boats and Baker was in close range of the camera when he was padded on the back and looked back briefly. From the still of the archive footage a coin now has his image for all Canadians to see. A real person, a soldier who served his country. He survived that fateful day and returned to Canada to raise a family.

史实：Pte.贝克曾在第二次世界大战中服役，是将在朱诺海滩上部署的加拿大剧团之一.摄制组正在准备离开U型艇时，正在摄制摄制组，贝克背靠后背并短暂回头，贝克就在摄制机的近距离内.从档案片段的静止图像中，一枚硬币现在有他的画像，供所有加拿大人观看.一个真实的人，为他的国家服务的士兵.他度过了这一天，并返回加拿大抚养了一个家庭.

BALCH包车ba che
Emily Greene Balch
生人1867 ~ 1961年 》94
FYI: Awarded the Nobel in 1946 for Peace Movement
史实：年1946 授予诺贝尔I为了平安. [Nobelprize.org]

BANHOLZER班后勒泽ban hou le zer
Walter Banholzer
生人1908 ~ 1937年 》29 》[memorial纪念]
FYI: Engine mechanic aboard the Hindenburg, died from burns.
史实：机械师为了LZ- 兴登堡, 死亡为了烧伤

BANNISTER班尼斯特ban ni si te
[SIR] Roger Gilbert Bannister
生人1929 ~ 2018年 》89
FYI: [S] Distinguished British neurologist was the first amateur athlete to run under 4 minute mile [3:59:4] on 6 May 1954
史实：英国神经性医生.首次级选手下四分钟mile [5:59:4] 1954年月6日

photo by Forest L. ~福瑞斯特

BANTING班廷ban ting

[SIR] Frederick Grant Banting

生人1891 ~ 1941年 》49

FYI: Awarded the Nobel in physiology for Insulin with Dr. Charles Best *knighted by King George V c1934. The Insulin image is seen on the back of the Canadian 100 bill. [Nobelprize.org]

史实: 获得了诺贝尔胰岛素生理学奖, 由国王乔治五世授予查尔斯·贝斯特*爵士.胰岛素图像出现在加拿大100元钞票的背面 [~ Best]

BARBERA巴伯拉ba bo la

Joseph Roland "Joe" Barbera

生人1911 ~ 2006年 》95

FYI: [a&e] co-animator with Hanna-Barbera. Produced such childrens programs of the 60's and 70's such as 'The Flintstones and Jetsons.

史实: 与汉娜芭芭拉合作动画师.制作了60年代和70年代的儿童节目, 如《燧石》和《杰森一家》. [~ Hanna]

BARNUM巴尔纳吗ba er na ma

Phineas Taylor "P. T." Barnum

生人1810 ~ 1891年 》81

FYI: American Circus owner. (The life of P.T. Barnum)

史实: 美国马戏团

BARRAL巴拉勒ba la le

Jean-Augustan Barral

生人1819 ~ 1884年 》65

FYI: He was an agronomist by profession. His name is among the 72 names on the Eiffel Tower. [SW07] >3/72

史实: 农业民事.新元史上埃菲尔铁塔单名 *barret

BARROW巴罗ba luo

Clyde Chestnut Barrow

FYI: c1934 'Bonnie and Clyde' . Renouned bank robbers and killers in America during the dirty 30's

史实: 美国银行劫匪 顷1934

BARTHOLDI巴托尔迪ba tuo er di

Frederic Auguste Bartholdi

生人1834 ~ 1904年 》70

FYI: French sculptor who designed the 'Statue of Liberty'. The face is modeled after his own mother.

史实: 设计 "自由女神像" 的法国雕塑家.这张脸是模仿他自己的母亲做的.

BARSANTI巴尔叁弟ba er san di

Eugenio Barsanti

生人1821 ~ 1864年 》43

FYI: first combustion engine (1853~patent).*Felice Matteucci co-invent.

史实: 内燃机 顷1853

Courtesy Forest L. ~ 福瑞斯特

BAUDOUIN博杜安bo du an

King Baudouin of Belgium

生人7 September 1930 – 31 July 1993年 》62

FYI: aka Baudouin Albert Charles Leopold Axel Marie Gustave. The king of the Belgians. He ascended the throne and became King of the Belgians upon taking the constitutional oath on 17 July 1951. He
and his wife appear on the 50 Frank note.

史实: 比利时国王.他于1951年7月17日宣誓立宪, 即位比利时国王.
和他的妻子出现在50弗兰克纸币上.

BAUDRILLARD鲍德里亚bao de li ya

Jean Baudrillard

生人1929 ~ 2007年 》77

FYI: French theorist- philosopher- sociologist. *We live in a world where there is more and more information, and less and less meaning.*The only thing worse than being bored is being boring.

史实: 理论家, 哲理, 社会学. *我们生活在一个信息越多. *含义越来越少的世界.

BAUM鲍姆bao mu

Lyman Frank Baum

生人1856 ~ 1919年 》62

FYI: Author and writer best known for "The Wizard of Oz" [1939]

史实: 作者 "绿野仙踪" 顷1939 [看~bolger-lahr-haley-]

BAUM鲍姆bao mu

Gregory Baum

生人1927 ~ 2017年 》90

FYI: aka: Gerhard Albert Baum; Massey Lectures Series 1987: "Compassion and Solidarity".

史实:顷1987马赛教程;讲演系列

BAYER拜尔bai er

Friedrich Bayer

生人1825 ~ 1880年 》55

FYI: Founder of BAYER aspirin~c.1863 [created by Charles Frederick Gerhardt]

史实: 顷1863拜尔阿司匹林

BAYNES贝恩斯bei en si

Thomas Spencer Baynes

生人1823 ~ 1887年 》64

FYI: Philosopher; Supervised 9th edition of Encyclopedia Britannica.

史实: 哲学家; 管理辞书大不列颠

BEAVER比费bi fei

[SIR] Hugh Eyre Campbell Beaver

FYI: English-South African engineer, industrialist, and founder of the Guinness World Records. He started the Guinness book of records .c1951.

史实: 英国南非工程师, 实业家, 吉尼斯世界纪录的创始人.他创立了吉尼斯世界纪录. [~ Guinness]

BECQUEREL贝克勒尔bei ke le er

Antoine Cesar Becquerel

生人1788 ~ 1878年

FYI: French scientist of Electrophenomina. His name is among the 72 names at the base of the Eiffel Tower. [SW12-] >4/72

史实: 电磁理论科学家.新元史上埃菲尔铁塔单名

BECQUEREL贝克勒尔bei ke le er

Antoine Henri Becquerel

生人1852 ~ 1908年 》56

FYI: Awarded the Nobel for the Becquerel model for discovery of radioactivity [Bq] 1896. [Nobelprize.org]

史实: 授予诺贝尔 顷1896 为了发觉放楔形或 [BQ]

BEECHER比彻bi che

Henry Knowles Beecher

生人1904 ~ 1976年 》72

FYI: aka: Harry Unangst; Anesthesiologist "the powerful placebo"

史实: 麻醉状态, "强假药" (安慰剂）

BEER比尔bi er

Anthony Stafford Beer

生人1926 ~ 2002年 》76

FYI: British theorist~cybernetics."Designing Freedom". Massey Lecture Series c1973

史实: 顷1973, 马赛教程讲演系列, 控制论

BEERNAERT比纳特bi nei te

Auguste Marie Francois Beernaert

生人1829 ~ 1912年 》83

FYI: Awarded the Nobel prize in 1909 for Peace Movement.

史实: 顷1909 年- 授予诺贝尔I安平将.[Nobelprize.org]

BEETCHER比彻bi che

Frederick~J~Beecher

生人1919 ~ 1975年 》56 》 [memorial纪念]

FYI: *SS Edmund Fitzgerald~Lake Superior 10 Nov 1975

史实: [感念]S.S. 埃德蒙*菲茨杰拉德 湖高强1975年 11月10日

BEETHOVEN贝多芬bei duo fen

Ludwig Van Beethoven

生人1770 ~ 1827年 》56

FYI: [a&e] German composer, musician. 9 symphonies. 5 concertos. Perhaps the most recognized rhythm in the world [da da da daaah]

*Music is the one incorporeal entrance into the higher world of knowledge which comprehends mankind but which mankind cannot comprehend.

史实: 撰写 九交响.五协奏曲.多半辨认旋律在世界. *音乐是进入人类的高等知识世界的唯一入口.人类无发理解.

BEGIN贝京bei jing

Menachem Begin

生人1913 ~ 1992年 》78

FYI: 6 pm of Israel. Joint peace prize with Sadat. *Peace is the beauty of life. It is sunshine. It is the smile of a child, the love of a mother, the joy of a father, the togetherness of a family. It is the advancement of man, the victory of a just cause, the triumph of truth.[Nobelprize.org]

史实: 以色列首相六号.授予诺贝尔安平将. *和平是生命之美.是阳光.它是孩子的微笑, 母亲的爱, 父亲的喜悦, 家庭的团聚.这是人的进步, 正义事业的胜利, 真理的胜利.

BELANGER贝朗贝bei lang ge

Jean-Baptised Charles Joseph Belanger

生人1790 ~ 1874年 》84

FYI: He studied applied Hydraulics and hydrodynamics. His name appears on the Eiffel Tower. [NW07] >5/72

史实: 使用水利工程.新元史上埃菲尔铁塔.

BELGRAND贝格安bei ge an

Eugene Belgrand

生人1810 ~ 1878年 》68

FYI: French engineer who modernized Paris by developing the SEWER system. His name appears on the base of the Eiffel Tower along with 72 names [SE02] >6/72

史实: 工程给巴黎粪尿.新元史上埃菲尔铁塔单名.

BELL贝尔bei er

Joseph~G~Bell

1912 ~ [memorial纪念]

FYI: Chief Engineer aboard the SS Titanic.

史实: SS Titanic 张机械师

BELL贝尔bei er

[Sir] Charles Bell

生人1774 ~ 1842年 》68

FYI: Scottish surgeon, anatomist, physiologist and neurologist. Most noted for discovering the difference between sensory and motor nerves. "Bell palsy" is a motor muscle dysfunction or sagging of one side of the face.

史实: 再造咒术,人体解剖,生理学,神经学.Bell 麻痹.

courtesy Ukrainian Village
Photo courtesy of Forest L. ~福瑞斯特

BELL贝尔bei er

Alexander Graham Bell

生人184 7年3月3日 ～ 1922年8月2日 》75

FYI: American inventor, scientist, and teacher of the deaf. 1876 was issued the patent for the telephone. 1885 founded the American Telephone and Telegraph. *Before anything else, preparation is the key to success.

史实: 美国发明家、科学家和聋人教师.1876年被授予电话专利.1885年成立了美国电话电报公司.*除此之外, 准备是成功的关键.

BELL贝尔bei er

Arthur William Bell III

生人1945年6月17日~ 2018年4月13日 》73

FYI: Author (Day after Tomorrow) and Icon American broadcaster. At thirteen he got his license to be an amateur radio operator. After leaving military service in Vietnam, he was recognized by Guinness World records for being on the air for 116 hours fifteen minutes which served as a 'fund raiser' to rescue orphans from Saigon. Later he founded the internet radio station of Coast to Coast am.com * "The greatest question of all is whether our experience on this planet is "it" or whether there is something else. Things in the supernatural realm give support, strangely perhaps, to the things we take on faith."(Coasttocoast AM.com)

史实: 作者（后天）和偶像美国广播公司.十三岁时，他获得了业余无线电操作员的执照.在越南服役后，他因在空中飞行116小时15分钟而获得吉尼斯世界纪录的认可，这是一个从西贡拯救孤儿的"募捐者".后来他创立了Coast to Coast AM.com的互联网广播电台* "最大的问题是我们在这个星球上的经历是"它"还是其他什么东西.奇怪的是，超自然领域的事物可能会支持我们信仰的事物."

BELLMAN贝尔曼bei er man

Richard Ernest Bellman

生人1920 ~ 1984年 》63

FYI: mathematician (Bellman equation) Dynamic Programming.

史实: 数学家贝尔曼于东返程.

BENSON本森ben sen

Oscar Herman Benson

生人1875 ~ 1951年 》76

FYI: is credited for the development of the 4-H emblem.

史实: 开展4-H 徽章 [~ O.E.Hall]

BENSON本森bin sen

Ezra Taft Benson

生人1899 ~ 1994年 》95

FYI: Government official, 15th president of LDS church. *f you really want to receive joy and happiness, then serve others with all your heart. Lift their burden, and your own burden will be lighter.

史实: 政府官,官耶稣基督后期圣徒教会官 15 号. *如果您真的想获得快乐和幸福，那就全心全意为他人服务。减轻他们的负担，您自己的负担就会减轻.

BENT曲qu

Josiah Bent

FYI: c 1801 coined the term "cracker". The cracker was made for the troupes over seas. The phonetic is 本特 (ben te) "qu" is the literal meaning of "bent".

史实: 顷1801年 给名字饼干. 音位是本特（本特）"qu"是"bent"的字面意思.

BENTLEY宾利bin li

Walter Owen Bentley

生人1888 ~ 1971年 》82

FYI: car designer; Bentley Motors.

史实: 车外观射进 [宾利]

BENTSEN奔特森ben te sen

Thomas~D~Bentsen

生人1952 ~ 1975年 》23 》 [memorial纪念]

FYI: *SS Edmund Fitzgerald~Lake Superior 10 Nov 1975

史实: 1975年 11月10日S.S. 埃德蒙*菲茨杰拉德 湖高强

BENNETT班尼特ban ni te

Richard Bedford Bennett

生人1870 ~ 1947年 》77

FYI: Canadian lawyer, businessman, and politician. The founder of The Bank of Canada and the founder of Canadian Broadcasting Corporation, 11th Prime Minister of Canada from 1930~1935.

史实: 加拿大律师,商人和政治家.1930～1935年加拿大银行创始人,加拿大广播公司创始人,加拿大第11任总理.

BENZ奔驰ben chi

Carl Frederich Benz

生人1844 ~ 1929年 》85

FYI: aka: Karl Friedrich Micheal Valliant; Benz patent motorcar c.1885, the first practical automobile.

史实: 奔车 顷1885年. 第一辆实用汽车.

BERGEN卑尔根bei er gen

Edger Bergen

生人1903 ~ 1978年 》75

FYI: [a&e] Ventriloquism ~ with Charlie McCarthy. Radio hall of fame.

史实: 口技,收音机丁高名. (charlie*Mccarthy)

BERGER伯格bo ge

Hans Berger

生人1873年5月21日 》6月1日68

FYI: German Psychologist best known for inventing the EEG [electroencephalagraphy] He coined "brain waves" 1924. Alpha waves ie: Berger waves. Alpha-8~12Hz. Beta 12-34Hz, Gamma 34-100Hz [~ Heinrich Hertz]

史实: 心里医生, 高明为了造EEG [脑电图] 顷1924脑波.

BERGMAN伯格曼bo ge man

Jeffrey Allen Bergman

生人1960 ~ active

FYI: voice actor of Pillsbury c1986-2013; Bugs Bunny- George Jetson- DaffDuck [~ Frees-Cerny]

史实: 出声[Pillsbury] 顷1986. Bugs_ Bunny, Daffy_Duck.

BERKELEY柏克莱bai ke lai

George Berkeley

生人1685 ~ 1753年 》 67

FYI: British philosopher; University of Berkeley is named in his honour. *Truth is the cry of all, but the game of few.

史实: 英国哲学.柏克莱大学. *真理是所有人的呐喊, 但很少有人参与.

BERLE比丽bi li

Milton Berle

生人1908年7月12日 ~ 2002年3月27日 》93

FYI: [a&e]aka: Mendel Beringer; was known warmly as "uncle Miltie".* If opportunity doesn't knock, build a door.

史实: 高明是叔叔"Miltie'.搞笑片. *如果机会没有敲门, 那就盖一扇门.

BERLIN伯林bo lin

[SIR] Isaiah Berlin

生人1909年6月6日 ~ 1997年11月5日 》88

FYI: Philosopher and historian of ideas. "the world's greatest talker".*1958 "Two concepts of Liberty". [see ~Ignatieff]

史实: 哲学家,历史,哲学,世界上最伟大的健谈者顷1958 "自由的两个概念."

BERLINER伯林爱尔bo lin ai er

Emile Berliner

FYI: inventor of the vinyl disc for music c.1888 and the Gramophone. The "Grammy" award is named after it.

史实: 1888年发明音乐用乙烯基唱片和留声机."格莱美"奖是以它命名的.

BERNAYS伯内斯bo nei si

Edward Louis James Bernays

生人1891～1995年 》103

FYI: "The Father of Public Relations". Supercentenial.

史实: "公共关系之父".超世纪的.

BERNERS-LEE伯纳斯里 bo na si li

[SIR] Timothy John Berners-Lee

生人1955年6月8日 ～ active.

FYI: co-creator World Wide Web. (HTTP~hypertext Transfer Protocol) along withe the URL (Uniform Resource Locator) 2004~KNIGHTED. "Turing award":2016

史实: 共同创建万维网.(http~超文本传输协议)以及URL(统一资源定位器)2004~爵士."图灵奖" 2016.

prince BERNHARD [高]本汉 [gao] ben han

FYI: [prince-gao] Chairman~ Bilderberg Group.> prince Bernhard of lippe ~2004;

*1.bernhard 2.friedrich 3.eberhard 4.leopold 5.julius 6.kurt 7.carl 8.gottfried 9.peter 10.graff [11.von biesterfeld]Family name plus 10.~1911-2004

*中文名字: 1本汉 2福利德力西 3阿比哈德 4刘泊德 5 乔刘斯 6哭特 7卡 8格特飞 9b比德 10图呀 11比斯特费尔德

*音韵: 1ben han. 2.fu li de li xi 3. e bi ha de 4. liu po de 5. qiao liu si 6. ku te 7. ka 8. ge te fe i9. bide 10.tu ya [11.bi si te fei e de ~ family name.]

史实: 主席高本汉 比尔德伯格集团

BERNHARDT布尔那哈德特bu er na ha de te

Alfred Bernhardt

生人1905～1937年 》32 [memorial纪念]

FYI: Helmsman on the LZ - Hindenburg.

史实: LZ- 兴登堡 舵手

BERNOULLI贝努力 bei nu li

Johann Bernoulli

生人1667 ~ 1748年 》81

FYI: Swiss Mathematical family~Johann and [Daniel]

史实: 瑞士数学家

BERRA贝拉 bei la

Lawrence Peter "Yogi" Berra

生人1925年5月12日 ~ 2015年9月22日 》 90

FYI: [S] Baseball Hall of Fame ~ New York Yankees.*90 percent of baseball is mental; the other half is physical.

史实: 棒球名人堂~纽约洋基队.*90%的棒球是精神上的, 另一半是身体上的.

BERRILL贝尔里 bei er li

Roland Berrill

FYI: co- started Mensa in 1946 with Dr. Lancelot Ware. The term Mensa is Latin for "table", hence *All good thoughts should be shared around the table! [see-ware]

史实: 门萨 顷1946.拉丁~圆桌. '表里如一在拉丁' "所有好的想法都应该在桌子周围分享! "

BERTHIER怕瑞尔 pai rui er

Pierre Berthier

生人1782 ~ 1861年 》79

FYI: French geologist and mining engineer. His name is included with all 72 names at the base of the Eiffel Tower. [Eiffel: SW06] #7/72

史实: 法国人,地质学家,矿业.新元史上埃菲尔铁塔.

BERTON布特 bu te

Pierre Frances de Marigny Berton

生人1920年7月12日 ~ 2004年11月3日 》84

FYI: Prolific Canadian writer and voice commentator. Author: My Country. O.C.~1974. *I only write books about dead people. They can't sue.

史实: 高明加拿大作者和声解说员.作者 [我的国家] . *我只写有关死者的书.他们不能起诉.

Photo courtesy of Forest L. ~福瑞斯特

BEST贝斯特bei si te

Charles Herbert Best

生人1899 年2月27日 ～ 1978年3月31日 》79

FYI: Co-discover of insulin. 1994 inducted into the Medical Hall of Fame. c 1967, O.C.~1967, CMHF~1994. The image of insulin is seen on the reverse of the Canadian 100 bill.[-see Banting] [Nobelprize.org]

史实: 共同发现胰岛素.1994年入选医学名人堂.1967年, O.C.~1967年, CMHF~1994年.胰岛素的形象出现在加拿大100元钞票的背面.

Chinese medical outlet in Edmonton
Photo courtesy of Forest L. ～ 福瑞斯特

BETHUNE白求恩bai qiu en

Norman Henry Bethune

生人1890年3月3日 ～ 1939年11月12日 》49

FYI: First prominent Canadian in Chinese history served as a medical doctor saving Chinese soldiers. Dr. Bethune effectively brought modern medicine to rural China and often treated sick villagers as much as wounded soldiers. NORMAN BETHUNE MEDAL: China. Canadian Medical Hall of Fame:1998

史实: 中国历史上第一位显赫的加拿大人是一名救兵的医生.白求恩医生有效地把现代医学带到了中国农村,经常像对待受伤士兵一样对待生病的村民.白求恩勋章:中国.加拿大医学名人堂:1998年.

BEVEL北瓦bei wa

James Luther Bevel

生人1936 ~ 2008年 》72

FYI: Civil rights activist. Minister.

史实: 公民权利活跃分子, 新教.

BIALAS比利斯bi li si

Rudi Bialas [memorial纪念]

FYI: Engine mechanic: LZ - Hindenburg 1937 may 6.

史实: LZ-兴登堡机械师.

BIBB比吧bi ba

[major] John Jack Bibb

[unknown-1884]

FYI: Kentucky attorney and horticulturalist "Bibb lettuce~Kentucky".

史实: 高明蜘蛛.

BICHAT比沙bi sha

Marie Francois Xavier Bichat

生人1771 ~ 1802年 》31

FYI: The Father of histology; anatomist and pathologist. Is included with the 72 names on the Eiffel tower. [NE14] #8/72

史实: 高明组织学,解剖,病理学家.新元史上埃菲尔铁塔.

BIELSKI比厄斯克bi e si ki

Tuvia Bielski

生人1906 ~ 1987年 》81

FYI: Set up a Jewish camp running from the German armies of WWII. With his brothers, they saved over 1000 from the Ghettos. They made their home in the Forest's of Naliboki. After the war he moved to America. Movie: Defiance.

史实: 建立一个犹太营地,躲避二战德国军队.他们和他的兄弟们一起从贫民区救出了1000多人.他们在纳利博基的森林里安家.战后他搬到了美国.电影:挑衅.

BINCK宾客bin ge
Birger Binck [memorial纪念]
FYI: Passenger, LZ Hindenburg 1937 may 6.
史实: 记:乘客上兴登堡.

BINDON彬德安bin de an
Edward~F~Bindon
生人1928 ~ 1975年 》47 》[memorial纪念]
FYI: First Assistant Engineer.*SS Edmund Fitzgerald~Lake Superior 10 Nov 1975
史实:S.S. 埃德蒙*菲茨杰拉德 湖高强1975年11月10日

BINET宾阿bin a
Alfred Binet
生人1857 ~ 1911年 》64
FYI: French psychologist devised the Binet-Simon I Q test c1904 [intelligence quotient]
史实: 顷1904 Binet-Simon -智商. [查看- theodore_simon]

BINGHAM宾厄姆bin e mu
Hiram Bingham III
生人1875 ~ 1956年 》81
FYI: American academic and explorer. The first to photograph Machu Picchu which gave it much press for National Geographic in the 1900;s * three other groups claim to have found it prior to Bingham.
史实: 美国探,首次照片Machu*Picchu 顷1900.

BINGHAM宾厄姆bin e mu
Eugene Cook Bingham
生人1878 ~ 1945年 》67
FYI: Professor of chemistry c1920 'rheology'. The Society of Rheology: Bingham medal. [see- Reiner]
史实: 顷1920: 教受化学在流变学 [~ Reiner]

BIRD比尔德bi er de

Mary Brave Bird

玛丽勇敢的鸟[ma li yong gan de niao]

生人September 26, 1954 ~ February 14, 2013年 》58

FYI: Also known by Mary Brave Woman Olguin, Mary Crow Dog. A Lakota writer and activist who was a member of the American Indian Movement during the 1970s. She was an active participant in 'Native causes' which included the Wounded Knee Incident in 1970.

She authored two memoirs; Lakota Woman ~1990, and Ohitika Woman ~ 1993. *The thing to keep in mind is that laws are framed by those who happen to be in power and for the purpose of keeping them in power.

史实: 玛丽也知道勇敢的女人奥尔金, 玛丽乌鸦狗.拉科塔作家和活动家, 1970年代是美国印第安运动的一员.她积极参与了包括1970年受伤膝盖事件在内的"本土事业".她写了两本回忆录:Lakota Women~1990和Ohitika Women~1993. *要牢记的是,法律是由那些掌权的人制定的. 目的是使其保持执政的目的.

BISHOP比绍普bi shao pu

[SIR] Henry Rowly Bishop

生人1786 ~ 1855年 》69

FYI: "Bishop mark c.1661" first postage stamp mark for mail. Composer "Home! sweet Home!"

史实:顷1661 "比绍普印", 首次邮票.音乐'甜蜜的家.'

BISMARCK俾斯麦bi si mai

Otto Eduard Leopold von Bismarck

生人1815 ~ 1898年 》83

FYI: Former German chancellor WWII. History records that he created the first 'welfare state' in the modern world. He was always mindful of the struggle of his people. * Politics is the art of the possible.

史实: 德国前总理二战.历史记载他创造了现代世界第一个"福利国家".他总是关心人民的斗争.*政治是可能的艺术.

BLACK布莱克bu lai ke

James Whyte Black

生人1924 ~ 2010年 》86

FYI: Scottish physician and pharmacologist. He developed propronel to be used on the heart. Received the Nobel prize in medicine for propranolol and cimetidine. [Nobelprize.com]

史实: 医生药理学.嘉将诺贝尔:propranolol, cimetidine. 心医药

BLACK布莱克bu lai ke

Davidson Black

生人1884 ~ 1934年 》49

FYI: Palaeontologist ~ Homo erectus pekinensis;

史实: 古脊椎动物学, 直立人北京猿人 [~ Andersson/ zdansky.]

BLAKE布里克bu li ke

William Blake

生人1757 ~ 1827年 》70

FYI: British poet and printmaker of the romantic period.

史实: 英国式,列印 顷浪漫主义.

BLANC布兰报嘉bu lan bao jia

Melvin Jerome "Mel" Blanc

生人1908 ~ 1989年 》81

FYI: [a&e] Voice actor of 1000 voices: "That's All Folks"; Bugs Bunny, Daffy Duck, Tweety Bird, Marvin the Martian, Wile_ E_ Coyeti, Speedy Gonzales, Road Runner, Yosemite Sam.

史实: 口声 1000 发声: 《全是这样的人》更多动画片.

city of Edmonton public archives
Photo courtesy of Forest L. ~ 福瑞斯特

BLATCHFORD布拉奇福德bu li ke fu de

Kenneth Alexander Blatchford

生人1882 ~ 1933年 》51

FYI: Served as Mayor of Edmonton from 1923~1926. A Canadian career politician.

史实: 1923~1926年任埃德蒙顿市市长.加拿大职业政治家.

BLINCOE布兰科bu lan ke

Robert Blincoe

生人1797 ~ 1860年 》63

FYI: British author ~1860 "Oliver Twist" is based on his life.

史实: 英国作者 》Oliver Twist《顷1860

BLOCH布洛赫bu luo he

Felix Bloch

生人1905 ~ 1983年 》77

FYI: awarded the Nobel prize in 1952 for the Bloch equation in Physics / magnetism. [Nobelprize.org]

史实:顷1952 嘉奖诺贝尔为了布洛赫 运动方程和磁.

BOEING波音bo yin

William Edward Boeing

生人1881年10月1日 ~ 1956年9月28日 》 74

FYI: American Industrialist founded "Boeing company"c. 1917

史实: 美国企业家 成立 波音 顷1917

BOHLIN博林bo lin

Anders Birger Bohlin

生人1898 ~ 1990年 》92

FYI:Swedish Palaeontologist. c1950 Homo erectus confirmed.

史实: 古脊椎动物学, 直立人北京猿人.顷1950.

BOHM博米bo mi

David Joseph Bohm

生人1917 ~ 1992年 》75

FYI: Professor of Theoretical physics

史实: 理论物理教授.

BOLGER博哥尔bo ge er

Raymond Wallace Bolger

生人1904 ~ 1987年 》83

FYI: [a&e] Actor famous for playing the "Scarecrow~ Wizard of Oz".

史实: 高明艺人: Scarecrow, Wizard of Oz.

[~ bolger- lahr- haley-]

BONO博弄bo nong

Salvortore Philip Sonny Bono

生人1935 ~ 1998年 》63

FYI: [a&e] entertainer, politician. Spouse; Cher. * *Don't cling to fame. You're just borrowing it. It's like money. You're going to die, and somebody else is going to get it.*

史实: 高明艺人, 政客.*不要固守名气.您只是在借钱.就像钱.你会死的, 其他人会死的.

BORDA博大bo da

Jean-Charles de Borda

生人1733 ~ 1799年 》46

FYI: physicist and sailor. Cape Borda is named in his honor, as well, he is among the 72 names listed on the Eiffel tower. [SE12] 09/72

史实: 水手,地岬博大在名的.新元史上埃菲尔铁塔单名.

Photo courtesy of Forest L. ~ 福瑞斯特

BORDEN波登bo deng

[SIR] Robert Laird Borden

生人1854年6月26日~ 1937年6月10日 》83

FYI: 8th Prime Minister of Canada and image appears on the $100.bill.

史实: 八号先首相加拿大,他照片是上一个100 钱.

BORGESON乔根森qiao gen sen

Thomas~D~Borgeson

生人1934 ~ 1975年 》41 》[memorial纪念]

FYI: *SS Edmund Fitzgerald~Lake Superior 10 Nov 1975

史实: S.S. 埃德蒙*菲茨杰拉德 湖高强1975年 11月10日

BORGLUM博格勤姆bo ge qin mu

John Gutzon de la Mothe Borglum

生人1867 ~ 1941年 》74

FYI: Sculptor~mt Rushmore.

史实: 他雕琢山拉什莫尔 [~ Rushmore]

BORODIN鲍罗丁bao luo ding

Alexander Borodin

生人1883 ~ 1887年 》53

FYI: Russian composer and chemist.

史实: 哦语作曲,化学家.

BOSE博斯bo si

[SIR] Jagadis Chandra Bose

生人1858 ~ 1937年 》79

FYI: Regarded as the greatest mind of his time in studying electromagnetism.

史实: 被认为是他那个时代学习电磁学的最伟大的思想。

BOSTON波斯顿bo si dun

Ralph Harold Boston

生人1939年5月3日~ active

FYI:[S] American athlete. *NB: was the first athlete to break the 27 foot marker in Long Jump c.1963 at 27 feet 1/2 inch (Nine yards). Nine yards is now the common expression meaning the Full Distance or "Whole Nine Yards". The phrase was intermittent until then.

史实: 美国运动员.*NB:是第一个在跳远中打破27英尺标志的运动员, 大约1963年, 身高27英尺1/2英寸（9码).九码是现在常用的表达方式, 意思是全程或 "整个九码".这句话在那之前是断断续续的.

BOOLE布勒bu le

George Boole

生人1815 ~ 1864年 》49

FYI: Mathematician. Author, "The Laws of thought"~1854 ~"The Information Age"

史实: 数学家 》思想规律《 顷1854

BOURNE博恩bo en

William Bourne

生人1535 ~ 1582年 》47

FYI: English mathematician who designed the written forerunner logbook for today's nautical log book. He also designed the "time glass: Tempus fugit"[time flies] for measuring speed in 30 second. [bartolomeau*crescencio]

史实:　　　英国数学家, 为今天航海航海日志设计了先行航海日志.他还设计了》时间玻璃:TEMPUS FugIT《（时间飞逝）在30秒内测量速度.

BOURSEUL布瑟尔bu se er

Charles Bourseul

生人1829 ~ 1912年 》83

FYI: "make and break" evolution of the telephone c.1856. The meaning of make and break refers to the disturbance of a signal to create a LETTER to form a word.

史实: 电话的 "接通和断开" 演变c.1856.接通和断开的意思是指干扰信号来产生一个字母来构成一个单词.

BOWELL布尔bu er

[SIR] Mackenzie Bowell

生人1823年12月27日~ 1917年12月10日 》94

FYI: Canadian Newspaper publisher and politician. 6th pm of Canada [1894-1896].

史实: 曾经先首相加拿大6号, 报刊和党员.

BOYLE波义耳bo yi er

Willard~S~Boyle

生人1924 ~ 2011年 》97

FYI: Received the Nobel in 2009 for Physics, CCD sensor [Nobelprize.org]

史实: 嘉奖诺贝尔 顷2009 在物理学;CCD 检测仪.

BOYSEN博森bo sen

Charles Rudolf Boysen

生人1895 ~ 1950年 》55

FYI: American horticulturalist who created the Boysenberry: blackberries, raspberries and loganberries

史实: 园艺发展波森梅; 黑莓, 木魅, logan 梅.[~ Knott]

BOXHALL巴斯赫ba si he

Joseph Groves Boxhall

生人1884 ~ 1967年 》83

FYI: Fourth officer SS Titanic.[survived]

史实: 四副党卫军泰坦尼克号- 幸存

BRADBURY吧如大步以ba ru da bu yi

Ray Douglas Bradbury

生人1920年8月22日 ~ 2012年6月5日 》92

FYI: author and screen writer.* Fahrenheit 451 c1953

New York Time: "the writer most responsible for bringing modern science fiction into the literary mainstream." There are worse crimes then burning books. One of them is not reading them.

*Everything is generated through your own will power.

史实: 作者和屏幕作者.*华氏451 c1953纽约时报: "最有责任将现代科幻小说带入文学主流的作家. *有比焚书更为恶劣的犯罪, 其中之一就是不读书.*一切都是通过自己的意志力产生的.

BRADLEY吧达义ba da yi

Milton Bradley

生人1836 ~ 1911年 》74

FYI: Game pioneer and publisher. Toy Industry Hall of Fame.

史实: 桌游奠基人.玩意展馆.

BRAGG布拉格bu la gei

[SIR] William Lawrence Bragg

生人1890 ~ 1971年 》81

FYI: Bragg's Law of X-ray refraction. Forerunner to the DNA 51 slide.

史实: 布拉格法 X-ray 折光.

BRAHMS勃拉姆斯bo la mu si

Johannes Brahms

生人1833年5月7日 ～ 1897年4月3日 》64

FYI: [a&e] German composer, pianist and conductor of the Romantic period. Known as one of the 'Three B's'. *Q ~ If there is anyone here who I have not insulted, I beg his pardon.

史实: 德国作曲家,钢琴家和浪漫时期的指挥家.被称为 "三个B" 之一.*问:如果这里有我没有侮辱过的人, 请原谅.

Photo courtesy of Forest L. ~ 福瑞斯特

BRAILLE布莱尔bu lai er

Louis Braille

生人1809年1月4日~ 1852年1月6日 》43

FYI: Inventor of the Braille system or "alphabet for the blind."

史实: 布莱尔字母表为了目盲人"盲人字母表." [~ f_h_HALL]

BRANDO比任都bi ren dou

Marlon Brando

生人1924 ~ 2004年　》80

FYI:[a&e] American Icon Actor. Superman, God Father series.

史实: 高明演员.超人爸爸.

BRANDT勃兰特bo lan te

Willy Herbert Karl Brandt

生人1913 ~ 1992年　》79

FYI: aka: Herbert Ernst Karl Frahm; German politician. *Massey Lecture Series- 1981
"Dangers and Options.

史实: 德国政治家.马赛教程顷1981《危险和选择》

BRAUN布芳恩bu fang en

Karl Ferdinand Braun

生人1850年6月6日~ 1918年5月20日 》　67

FYI: German physicist and inventor. *1897 developed the first (CRD) cathode-ray tube.

史实: 德国物理学家造的.顷1897 CRD

BRECHT布莱希特bu lai xi te

Eugene Bertolt Friedrich Brecht

生人1898 ~ 1956年　》58

FYI: German poet.

史实: 德国诗坛

BREGUET布勤盖bu qin gai

Abraham Louis Breguet

生人1747 ~ 1823年　》76

FYI: Was a Horologist; "Horologists" is from the Greek. The study of time. "hora>hour>time".

史实: 他学习季节>几点？"hora>小时>时间".

BRESSE布雷斯bu lei si

Jacque Antoine Charles Bresse

生人1822 ~ 1883年　》61

FYI: French civil engineer with hydraulics. His name is listed among the 72 names on the Eiffel tower. [NW05] >10/72

史实: 法国水利工程.新元史上埃菲尔铁塔单名.

BREQUET不可特bu ke te

Louis Francois Clement Brequet

生人1804 ~ 1883年 》79

FYI: French physicist and watch maker. Was a pioneer on Telegraphy. He is named among the 72 listed on the Eiffel tower. [NE08] >11/72

史实: 法国物理学家.他是先导在发电. 新元史上埃菲尔铁塔单名

BREZHNEV勃列日泥夫bo lie r nie fu

Leonid Llyich Brezhnev

生人1906 ~ 1982年 》76

FYI: General Secretary of the USSR c 1964-1982.

史实: 顷1964-1982 总书记USSR

BRIDE巴让德ba rang de

Harold Sydney Bride

生人1890 ~ 1956年 》66

FYI: SS Titanic junior wireless operator. c1912 April 14; 11:40 pm *Bride survived the accident of 1912

史实: 顷1912 SS Titanic 无线操作员.他幸存.

BRITTEN布里顿bu li dun

Benjamin Britten

生人1913 ~ 1976年 》63

FYI: aka: Edward Benjamin Britten; English composer.

史实: 英国撰写者

BROCA布罗卡bu luo ka

[Dr.] Pierre Paul Broca

生人1824 ~ 1880年 》56

FYI: French anatomist.*"Broca's -area" (frontal lobe) is named in his honor. His name is listed among the 72 names on the Eiffel tower. [SW11] >11/72

史实: 法国解剖学 "布洛卡区-额叶" 新元史上埃菲尔铁塔单名

BRODIE布罗迪bu luo di

Fawn Mckay Brodie

生人1915 ~ 1981年 》66

FYI: First female prof of UCLA. Biographer.

史实: 先导女儿教授 UCLA

BRONTE勃良特bo liang te

Charlotte Bronte

生人1816 ~ 1855年 》39

FYI: author of mystery and romance novels. Books: Jane Eyre, Villette.

史实: 作者神秘.书: Jane*Eyre

BROWN布朗bu lang

David McDowell Brown

生人1956 ~ 2003年 》46 》[memorial纪念]

FYI: NASA astronaut. Challenger accident 2003 Feb 1

史实:纪念 NASA 顷2003 年月2日1 挑战者号

BRUNEL布鲁内尔bu ru nei er

Isambard Kingdom Brunel

生人1806 ~ 1859年

FYI: English mechanical engineer. Is ranked second on Britons Top 100 most famous. Ranked first was Churchill.

史实: 英国工程.英国二号高明.第一次式丘吉尔.

BRYAN布兰bu lan

William Jennings Bryan

生人1860 ~ 1925年 》65

FYI: American Orator and politician. In the Wizard of Oz, he is Depicted as the Cowardly Lion by L. F. Braun. [see- Hearst-Bryan-Haley]

史实: 美国口政客.

BRYANT布兰特bu lan te

William Cullen Bryant

生人1794 ~ 1878年 》84

FYI: American romantic poet and journalist. Known as one of the "Fireside Poets ie: Bryant, Longfellow, Holmes, Wittier, Lowell."

史实:美国式.炉边式

BRYNNER比任热bi ren re

Yuliy Borissovich Brynner

生人1920 ~ 1985年 》65

FYI: [a&e] Icon of Hollywood actors: King and I, Ten Commandments and Anastasia. *When I am dead and buried, on my tombstone I would like to have it written, 'I have arrived.' Because when you feel that you have arrived, you are dead.

史实: 好莱坞演员的偶像:国王和我,十诚和安娜斯塔西娅. *当我死后被埋葬时, 我想在墓碑上写下"我已经到了".因为当您感觉到自己已经抵达时, 您已经死了.

BUCKLEY布克利bu ke li

William Knapp Buckley

FYI: Canadian cold medicine. c1919~ "it tastes awful and it works".

* Frank Buckley is the son of William and became company spokesperson.

史实: 拿大感冒药.C1919 ~ "味道很难吃,而且很管用". *弗兰克•巴克利是威廉的儿子,后来成为公司发言人.

BUICK别克bie ke

David Dunbar Buick

FYI: Founder of "Buick" c1899

史实: 顷1899 先导别克

BUISSON布义森bu yi sen

Ferdinand Edouard Buisson

生人1841 ~ 1932年 》91

FYI: Awarded the Nobel prize c 1927 peace movement; League for Human Rights. [*Nobelprize.org]

史实: 嘉奖诺贝尔顷1927为了安静;人权

BUKOWSKI步卡噢实bu ka o shi

Henry Charles Bukowski

生人1920 ~ 1994年 》74

FYI: German-American poet, novelist and short story writer.

史实: 德国-美国式, 作者

sitting-BULL坐的牛zuo de nuo

Sitting~ Bull

生人1831 ~ 1890年 》59

FYI: North American Indian leader c.19th Century.

史实: 顷19th 世纪北美印第安

BUNKER巴克ba ke

Chang & Eng Bunker

生人1811 ~ 1874年 》63

FYI: Thai- American conjoined twins. Siamese Twins: The Kingdom of Siam (todays' Thailand). They adopted the surname of Bunker when living in America. They fathered 21 children with two American wife's.

史实: 泰国爽男;连体婴.他们有二十一孩子们.

BUNSEN本生ben sheng

Robert Wilhelm Aberhard Abunsen

生人1811 ~ 1899年 》88

FYI: German chemist. Developed the Bunsen burner.

史实: 德国化学家.先导本生灯.

BURK帕克pa ke

Dean Burk

生人1904 ~ 1988年 》84

FYI: co-Discovered Biotin with Hans Lineweaver

史实:先导biotin [维生素]

BURKE怕克pa ke

Billie Burke

生人1884 ~ 1970年 》85

FYI: [a&e] AKA Mary William Ethelbert Appleton "Billie" Burke. "Glinda the GOOD witch of the South" Wizard of Oz. She represented the metaphor of the honest politician.

史实: 绿野仙踪 [魔棒] (www~USA gold)

BURNS伯恩斯bo en si

Robert Burns

生人1759 ~ 1796年 》37

FYI: Lyrics "Auld Lang Syne" 1878 [old long since] Regarded as the end of the year "song [Hogmanay]*.

史实: 顷1878 年底歌 [看- Aytoun]

BURNS步任斯bu ren si

George Burns

生人1896年1月20日 ~ 1996年3月9日 》100

FYI: [a&e] aka; Nathan Birnbaum. Centenarian plus 6 weeks. Stand up Icon of Stage and Television. *Too bad that all the people who know how to run the country are busy driving taxicabs and cutting hair.*

史实: 高明搞笑片. 百年岁六星期 ;). *可惜的是，所有知道如何管理这个国家的人都忙着开出出租和剪头发。

BURSON博森bu sen

Greg Burson

生人1949 ~ 2008年 》58

FYI: voice over actor

史实: 口声搞笑片

City of Edmonton public archive
Photo courtesy of Forest L. ~ 福瑞斯特

BURY伯里bo li

Ambrose Upton Gledstanes Bury

生人1869 ~ 1951年 》84

FYI: A practicing lawyer he served as the 18th mayor of Edmonton 1926~1929. As well he was a member of the House of Commons in Canada.

史实: 1926~1929年任埃德蒙顿市第18任市长.他也是加拿大下议院的成员.

BUSH布实bu shi

Vannevar Bush

生人1890 ~ 1974年 》84

FYI: Engineer, Inventor. Essay~"As we may think"

史实: 先导,工程.散文 《而思索》

BUTTLER巴斯勒ba si le

Samuel Buttler

生人1835 ~ 1902年 》77

FYI: British author "The Way of all Flesh".

史实: 英国作者《人情市古》

BYLES拜尔斯bai er si

Thomas Roussel Davids Byles [memorial纪念]

生人1870年2月26日 ～ 1912年4月15日 》42 》

FYI: English Catholic Priest: Titanic 1912

史实: 纪念 Titanic 1912年; 牧师

BYRD怕德pa de

Richard Evelyn Byrd jr.

生人1888 ～ 1957年 》68

FYI: Reputed to be first to fly to the North and South pole. Author: The Hollow Earth.

史实: 飞机北南几点.作者:中空大地

BYRON拜伦bai lun

[Lord] George Gordon Byron

生人1788年1月22日 ～ 1824年4月19日 》36

FYI: was a nobleman, poet, politician. Famous works is "Don Juan".

史实: 式,政治家.撰写《唐胡安》

From Group "B" you can pick one person or up to ten Surnames and write their Surname in Chinese. You may try HORIZONTAL or VERTICAL in the traditional Chinese form.

C

不要只是教你的孩子阅读···教他们质疑他们所读的内容.教他们质疑一切!

"Don't just teach your children to read …
teach them to question what they read.
Teach them to question everything!"
- CARLIN卡林ka lin

CADILLAC卡迪拉克ka di la ke

Antoine de la Mothe Cadillac

生人1658 ~ 1730年 》72

FYI: The Cadillac ~ named after the French explorer. The founder of the city of Detroit [Fort Pontchartrain] c1701

史实: 高名车[凯地拉克] 法国人名字.

CADBURY凯德布尔kai de bu er

John Cadbury

生人1801 ~ 1889年 》88

FYI: Founder of Cadbury chocolates. c1824

史实: 顷1824 凯德布尔 巧克力先导

CAESAR凯撒kai sa

Gaius Julius Caesar

生人100 ~ 42年 B.C 》38

FYI: Roman Emperor

史实: 罗马皇帝

CAIL科勒ke le

Jean-Francois Cail

生人1804 ~ 1871年 》67

FYI: French industrialist; his name is mentioned with the 72 names on the Eiffel Tower face.[SW14] >13~72

史实: 法国工程人.新元史上埃菲尔铁塔单名.

CALVIN加尔文 jia er wen

John Calvin

生人1509年7月10日 ~ 1564年3月27日 》55

FYI: AKA John Jehan Cauvin; french protestant reformer who founded the Calvinist movement.

史实: 法国先导加尔文 (加尔文）教

CAMPBELL坎贝尔kan bei er

Joseph Albert Campbell

生人1817 ~ 1900年 》83

FYI: c1869 founded Campbell Soup.

史实: 顷1869 先导 [坎贝尔唐][查看- Abraham_ Anderson]

CAMPBELL坎贝尔kan bei er

Joseph John Campbell

生人1904 ~ 1987年 》83

FYI: American Mythologist, writer and lecturer. "Follow your Bliss."

史实: 美国神话, 作者, 讲课 《天赐之福》.[继你的快乐]

CAMSELL坎赛尔kan sai er

Charles Camsell

生人1876年2月8日 ~ 1958年12月19日 》82

FYI: Canadian Geologist and commissioner of the NWT. *1946 Charles Camsell Hospital. Now permanently closed.

史实: 加拿大地理.他名字是上查尔斯 坎塞尔 [医院]

CAPONE卡珀ca po

Alphonse Gabriel Capone

生人1899 ~ 1947年 》48

FYI: Notorious gangster of the 20th century. Public enemy #1

史实:美国臭名昭著匪徒 20世纪.

CARLIN卡林ka lin

George Denis Patrick Carlin

生人1937年5月12日 ~ 2008年6月22日 》71

FYI: [a&e] American comedian, author, critic. *"Seven Words you can not say on TV" . Mark Twain Prize for American Humor"[2008] "Black Comedy". "Don't just teach your children to read … teach them to question what they read. Teach them to question everything!"

史实: 美国人作者, 批评家, 搞笑片." 禁止七言词"*不要只是教你的孩子阅读···教他们质疑他们所读的内容.教他们质疑一切!

CARNEGIE卡内基ka nei ji

Andrew Carnegie

生人1835年11月25日 ～ 1919年18月11日 》83

FYI: steel giant and philanthropist. *sources state he was the wealthiest in America. [*wiki]

史实: 钢铁工业, 善心.

CARNEGIE卡内基ka nei ji

Dale Harbison Carnegie

生人1888年11月23日 ～ 1955年11月1日 》67

FYI: Writer and lecturer, and the developer of the now famous self improvement books, salesmanship, cooperate training, public training and personal relationship training know through out the world. 'How to Win Friends and Influence People.'1936. *Talk to someone about themselves and they'll listen for hours.

史实: 作家和讲师, 以及现在著名的自我完善书籍,销售技巧,合作培训,公共培训和人际关系培训的开发者, 全世界都知道."如何赢得朋友和影响他人."1936年. *与某人谈论他们自己, 他们会听几个小时.

CARNOT卡诺ka nuo

Lazare Nicholas Marguerite Carnot

生人1753 ～ 1823年 》70

FYI: Politician, mathematician and engineer; his name appears with the list of 72 names on the Eiffel tower: [NE17] 14/72

史实:工程人, 新元史上埃菲尔铁塔单名.

CARPENTER卡溢特ke pen te

Karen Anne Carpenter

生人1950年3月2日 ～ 1983年2月4日 》32

FYI: [a&e] The Carpenters; singer, drummer, writer. Top 100's "We've Only Just Begun".

史实: 口哥,演奏者, 作者.《我们才刚刚开始》

CARRINGTON卡林屯ka lin tun

Richard Christopher Carrington

生人1826年5月26日 ～ 1875年11月27日 》49

FYI: British Astronomer, 1859~solar flares [Carrington Event], 1863 solar differential rotation discovered.

史实: 英国天文学家:卡林屯事件 (卡林屯事件)

CARSON卡森ka sen

Johnny William Carson

生人1925年 ～ 2005年 》79

FYI: [a&e] stand up comedian re: "Johnny Carson show".

史实: 笑人.《约翰尼·卡森秀》

CARTER卡特ka te

Henry Vandyke "H. V. " Carter

FYI: Gray's Anatomy; illustrated by Carter M.D.

史实: 医学家书说明

The 1984 one dollar coin depicts Cartier as he arrives at the new land.

Photo by Forest L. ~ 福瑞斯特.

CARTIER卡莱亚ka lai ya

Jacque Cartier

生人1491 ～ 1557年 》65

FYI: A French Seaman who traveled to North America and to the very fertile land that the Iroquois called "Kanata" but he misunderstood and called it Canada. c1534 [* Susan Monroe]

史实: 一个法国海员, 他去了北美, 来到了易洛魁人称之为 "卡纳塔" 的肥沃土地上, 但他误解了, 并称之为加拿大.C1535

$10 bill Photo by Forest L. ~ 福瑞斯特.

CARTIER卡莱亚ka lai ya

[Sir] George-Etienne Cartier

生人1814 ~ 1873年 》58

FYI: A practicing lawyer. At the time of the formation of the dominion of Canada, he was asked to serve as Minister of Militia and Defence by PM MacDonald. His image appears on the Canadian 10 dollar bill of 2017 [150 edition] along with Sir John A. MacDonald, Agnus Macphail and James Gladstone.

史实: 执业律师.在加拿大领土形成之时,麦克唐纳总理要求他担任民兵和国防部长.他的形象出现在加拿大2017年10美元钞票上（150版）,还有约翰•麦克唐纳爵士,阿格努斯•麦克费尔和詹姆斯•格莱斯顿.

CARVER卡威ka wei

George Washington Carver

生人1864 ~ 1943年 》79

FYI: American scientist, farmer, botanist and teacher. Peanut connoisseur of over 200 products.

史实: 美国人科学家和老师.先导跟多200 花生

CASANOVA卡萨诺瓦ka sa nuo wa

Giacomo Girolamo Casanova

生人1725 ~ 1798年 》73

FYI: famous "womanizer". Italian adventurer.

史实: 高名好色之徒著名的《女性主义者》

CASEY凯西kai xi

William Joseph "Bill" Casey

生人1913 ~ 1987年 》74

FYI: Director of Center Intelligence Agency 1981-1987.

史实: C.I.A. 主任

CASH卡实ka shi

Johnny Cash

生人1932 ~ 2003年 》71

FYI [a&e] American singer and song writer. [Man In Black] "Ring of Fire, I walk the Line". As a Morse Code interceptor in Germany during WW2, he was the first American to hear of the death of Joseph Stalin. His songs had gained great popularity among men in prison. *Well, you wonder why I always dress in black, Why you never see bright colors on my back, And why does my appearance seem to have a somber tone. Well, there's a reason for the things that I have on. I wear the black for the poor and the beaten down, Livin' in the hopeless, hungry side of town, I wear it for the prisoner who has long paid for his crime.

史实: 美国歌手和歌曲作家.[穿黑衣服的人] "火之环, 我在排队".作为第二次世界大战期间德国的莫尔斯密码拦截者, 他是第一个听说约瑟夫•斯大林之死的美国人.他的歌在监狱里的人中很受欢迎. *好吧, 你想知道为什么我总是穿黑色衣服, 为什么你永远看不到我的背上明亮的色彩, 为什么我的外表看起来有些阴沉.好吧, 我拥有这些东西是有原因的.我为穷人和被殴打的人穿黑色的衣服, 在小镇绝望, 饥饿的一面生活, 为长期为他的罪行付出代价的囚犯戴上黑色的衣服.

CASSEGRAIN卡塞格伦ka sai ge lun

Laurent Cassegrain

生人1629 ~ 1693年 》64

FYI: A Catholic priest who designed a two-fold reflecting mirror.
[see -bernard Schmidt]

史实: 天主教徒司铎道两个反射竞争 [查看- bernard _Schmidt]

CASSIDY卡西迪ka xi de

Theodore Crawford "Ted" Cassidy

生人1932 ~ 1979年 》46

FYI: [a&e] American actor of radio, television and film and voice artist. He was one of the tallest actors at 6 feet 9 inches in Hollywood and would go on to play in several movies and serials including Star Trek, Butch Cassidy and Addams family. He is affectionately known as "Lurch" in The Addams Family. "You rang?"

史实: 美国广播,电视,电影和声音艺术家演员.他是好莱坞最高的演员之一, 身高6英尺9英寸, 还将继续出演几部电影和连续剧, 包括《星际迷航》,《布奇·卡西迪》和《亚当斯家族》.他在亚当斯家族中被亲切地称为"潜伏者"."你打电话了?"

CASSIN卡心ka xin
Rene Cassin

生人1887～1976年 》89

FYI: Received the Noble in 1968 for Human Rights. The Father of the Declaration of Human Rights. *"All human beings are born free and equal in dignity and rights."(Q) [Nobleprize.org]

史实: 顷1968 为了人权.人权斗士.《人人生而自由, 在尊严和权利上一律平等.》

CASTORIADIS卡斯托里亚迪ka si tuo li ya di
Cornelius Castoriadis

生人1922～1997年 》75

FYI: named after Cornelius the centurion Acts 10.; he was a Greek -french philosopher and social critic

史实: 显哲学人.他是希腊-法国的哲学家和社会评论家.

CASTRO卡斯特罗ka si te luo
Fidel Alejandro Castro Ruz

生人1959～2017年 》58

FYI: Cuban revolutionary leader. *Victory has thousands father but failure always find itself an orphan.

史实: 古巴革命党. *胜利有成千上万的父亲, 但失败总是使自己成为孤儿.

CATHERINE II凯瑟琳kai se lin
Catherine the Great

生人1729～1796年 》67

FYI: aka: Princes Sophia of Anhalt-Zerbst. Empress of Russia

史实: 俄罗斯奴黄

CAUCHY柯西ke xi

Augistine Louis Cauchy

生人1789 ~ 1857年 》68

FYI: mathematician and physicist who focused on Complex Analysis. He is named among the 72 people listed on the Eiffel tower face.[SE01] >15/72 insert*

史实: 物理学家.新元史上埃菲尔铁塔单名.

City of Edmonton public archives; Photo by Forest L. ~ 福瑞斯特

CAVANAGH卡瓦纳ka wen na

Terry Cavanagh

生人1926 ~ 2017年 》91

FYI: Served as 29th mayor of Edmonton. He also served as an Alderman in Edmonton. His private life was an instructor at various schools through out Edmonton in purchasing management as well as a business man.

史实: 曾任埃德蒙顿市第29任市长.他还担任埃德蒙顿市的议员.他的私生活是从埃德蒙顿到各个学校的采购管理讲师,同时也是一名商人.

CAYCE凯西kai xi

Edgar Cayce

生人1877 ~ 1945年 》67

FYI: 'The Sleeping Prophet'. American Christian mystic and clairvoyant

史实: 《睡先知》美国基督怪米和千里眼

CELCIUS厕力斯ce li si

Anders Celcius

生人1701年11月27日 ～ 1744年4月24日 》 43

FYI: Swedish meteorologist invented the current temp scale. [see F, Kelvin, Romer, Amontons]

史实: 高名瑞典气象人员先导文标.

CERF塞尔夫sai er fu

Bennett Alfred Cerf

生人1898 ～ 1971年 》73

FYI: co-founder of Random House with Donald Klopfer- c1925 *We just said we were going to publish a few books on the side at random" thus Random House was born.

史实: 先导Random*House (出版) 刊物.

CERNAN塞尔南sai er nan

Eugene Andrew Cernan

生人1934 ～ 2017年 》82

FYI: NASA astronaut was the last man on the moon ～ Apollo 17 [1972]

史实: NASA 太空人最后人上月 顷1972.

CHADWICK查德威克cha de wei ke (insert jpg 826)

Roy Chadwick

生人1893 ～ 1947年 》54

FYI: Designed the Avro Lancaster bomber for WWII

史实: 企划兰开斯特轰炸机 顷WWII.

CHAFFEE霞飞xia fei

Roger Bruce Chaffee

生人1935 年2月15日～ 1967年1月27日 》32 》[memorial纪念]

FYI: Astronaut, Apollo 1 fire.

史实:纪念太空人死在火顷1967.

CHAMPEAU钱普qian pu

Oliver~J~Champeau

生人1934 ~ 1975年 》41 》[memorial纪念]

FYI: S.S. Edmund Fitzgerald~ Third Assistant Engineer 10 Nov 1975:

史实: 纪念 SS 埃德蒙航-第三助理工程师.

CHANCELLOR差那斯勒cha na si le

Connie Chancellor

FYI: aka ANN LANDERS [1955] interim advice columnist. [see~ Crowley~ Friedman]

史实: 临时建议专栏作家.

CHANEL香奈儿xiang nai er

Gabrielle Bonheur "Coco" Chanel

生人1883 ~ 1971年 》87

FYI: French fashion designer, Nazi spy and businesswoman. The founder and namesake of the Chanel brand. * In order to be irreplaceable, one must always be different.

史实: 法国时装设计师, 纳粹间谍和女商人.香奈儿品牌的创始人和同名品牌.*为了不可替代, 一个人必须始终保持不同.

CHAPLIN卓别林zhuo bie lin

[Sir] Charles Spencer Chaplin

生人1905 ~ 1978年 》73

FYI: [a&e] Icon of the early days of the silent films era. He was married 4 times, fathered 8 children with his 4th wife Oona. *A day without laughter is a day wasted.

史实: 无声电影时代初期的标志.他已婚4次, 与第4任妻子Oona育有8个孩子.*没有欢笑的一天是没有意义的.

CHAPTAL徐普尔xu pu er

Jean-Antoine Chaptal

FYI: Agronomist and chemist . Listed on the Eiffel tower [NW18] >16/72

史实: 化学家.新元史上埃菲尔铁塔单名.

CHARCOT沙尔科sha er ke

Jean-Martin Charcot

生人1825 ~ 1893年 》68

FYI: French neurologist. ALS

史实: 法国神经性, 先导ALS

CHARGOFF贾格夫jia ge fu

Erwin Chargoff

生人1905 ~ 2002年 》96

FYI: Established the 2 rules of the DNA, fore runner of the DNA 51 slide.

史实: 两个章程为了DNA.

CHASLES沙勒sha la

Michel Floreal Chasles

生人1793 ~ 1880年 》88

FYI: French mathematician; he is among 72 names on the Eiffel

Tower face. [NW11] >17/72

史实: 法国数学.新元史上埃菲尔铁塔单名.

CHATELIER查特勒cha te le

Louis Le Chatelier

FYI: Engineer who produced aluminum from bauxite. Is listed on the Eiffel Tower [SW05] 18/72

史实: 法国工程.新元史上埃菲尔铁塔单名.

CHAUCER乔叟qiao sou

Geoffrey Chaucer

生人1343 ~ 1400年 》57

FYI: Poet and English author. Canterbury Tales and "The House of Fame". *Nothing Ventured, Nothing Gained.*

史实: 诗人和英国作家.坎特伯雷故事和"名人堂".*不入虎穴, 焉得虎子.

CHAWLA乔拉qiao la

Kalpana Chawla

生人1962 ~ 2003年 》41 》[memorial纪念]

FYI: East Indian- American astronaut: Challenger 2003 Feb 1

史实: 太空人 挑战者

CHENNAULT陈纳德chen na de

Claire Lee Chennault

生人1893年9月6日 ~ 1958年 》66

FYI: "old leather face" was leader of the 'Flying Tigers' for the Republic of China Air Force: WWII.

史实: 飞虎中华人民共和国空军WWII [看-陈香梅, 将周泰]

CHERNYSHEVSKY车尔尼雪夫斯基 cha er ni xue fu si ji

Nikolai Chernyshevsky

生人1828 ~ 1889年 》61

FYI: Author and Philosophy. 'What is to be done?' [c1905] Is now known as a Russian classic, written while he was in prison.

史实: 作者, 哲学 《要做什么》 (怎么办？) 顷1905. 俄罗斯古典.

CHEVREUL谢弗勒尔xie fu le er

Michel Eugene Chevreul

生人1786年8月31日 ~ 1889年 》103

FYI: Chemist; Is named among the 72 names on the Eiffel tower. [NW14] >18/72

史实: 化学家.新元史上埃菲尔铁塔单名.

CHEVROLET雪佛兰xue fo lan

Louis Joseph Chevrolet

生人1878年12月25日 ~ 1941年 》63

FYI: Swiss race car driver and founder of Chevrolet c.1911

史实: 高名雪佛兰, 瑞士人开车. 先导 顷1911 Chevrolet.

CHOPIN肖邦xiao bang

Frederic Francois Chopin

生人1810 ~ 1849年 》39

FYI: [a&e] Polish composer and renouned pianist.

史实: 高名钢琴师, 撰写者

CHRISTIANSEN克里新琴森ke li xin qin sen

Ole Kirk Christiansen

生人1891 ~ 1958年 》67

FYI: First started in business in 1932 during the great depression. He chose the name "Lego" from the Danish "leg gotd"~ meaning play well. He started making toys from wood carvings then switched in 1949 experimenting with plastic. Today we now have Lego cities and Lego the Movie.

史实: 顷1932; Lego（乐高）商业,《leg gotd》 意思玩儿. 今我们有乐高市和乐高电影.

CHRISTIE克里斯蒂ke li si di

[DAME] Agatha Christie

生人1890年9月15日 ~ 1976年1月12日 》86

FYI: aka Agatha Mary Clarissa Christie. She was a prolific author of her era writing 66 detective novels and 14 short stories. 'And then their was None' voted the best of her writing.*I have sometimes been wildly, despairingly, acutely miserable, racked with sorrow, but through it all I still know quite certainly that just to be alive is a grand thing.

史实: 她是一位多产的作家她的时代写了66部侦探小说和14部短

小说.'然后他们没有 "被选为她写作中的佼佼者".*我有时候经历了狂

绝望, 极度悲惨, 悲痛欲绝, 但通过这一切, 我仍然很清楚地知道,

活着是一件大事.

CHRISTIE克里斯蒂ke li si di

William Mellis Christie

生人1829年1月5日 ~ 1900年6月14日 》71

FYI: Trained as a baker, he would go on to establish "Christie" with the slogan : Mr. Christie, you make good cookies. Nabisco [national biscuit company] is part of the product line.

史实: 受过面包师培训, 他会继续用口号建立 "佳士得" :佳士得先生, 你做的饼干不错.纳比斯科[全国饼干公司]是生产线的一部分.

CHRYSLER克莱斯勒ke lai si le

Walter Percy Chrysler

生人1875 ~ 1940年 》65

FYI: The founder of Chrysler c.1925 Chrysler motors.

史实: 克莱斯勒先导1925年.

CHURCH丘吉qiu ji

Nolan~S~Church

生人1920 ~ 1975年 》 55 》[memorial纪念]

FYI: *SS Edmund Fitzgerald~Lake Superior 10 Nov 1975

史实: S.S. 埃德蒙*菲茨杰拉德 湖高强1975年 11月10日

CHURCH丘吉qiu ji

Austin Church

生人1799 ~ 1879年 》80

FYI: American physician and business manufacture: Arm and Hammer baking soda

史实: 美国医生和商业:手臂和武器小苏打.

CHURCHILL丘吉尔qiu ji er

[SIR] Winston Leonard Spencer-Churchill

生人1874年11月30日 ~ 1965年1月24日 》91

FYI: United Kingdom politician and Prime Minister during WWII. He is named in the top 100 Britons as number one. 1953 received the Nobel prize in Literature. *Let us brace ourselves to our duties and so bear ourselves that, if the British Empire and its Commonwealth last for a thousand years, men will still say 'This was their finest hour' ."

史实: 二战期间的英国政治家和首相.他在英国前100名中名列第一.1953年获得诺贝尔文学奖.*让我们振作起来履行我们的职责,并承担起自己的责任,这样,如果大英帝国及其英联邦持续一千年,人们仍然会说'这是他们最美好的时刻'."

CICERO西塞罗xi sai luo

Marcus Tullius Cicero

生人106 ~ 43 BC年

FYI: Considered one of Romes greatest Orator. lawyer / politician.

史实: 他是罗马最高明的演说者之一.律师和政治家.

CLAPEYRON克拉培龙ke la pei long (insert jpg 4)

Benoit Paul Emile Clapeyron

生人1799 ~ 1864年 》65

FYI: french engineer and physicist. Founder of thermodynamics. He is among the 72 names on the Eiffel tower. [NE11] > 19/72

史实: 法国工程师和物理学家.新元史上埃菲尔铁塔单名.

CLARK克拉克ke la ke

Laurel Blair Salton Clark

生人1961 ~ 2003年 》42》[memorial纪念]

FYI: American medical doctor, United States Navy Captain, NASA astronaut and Space Shuttle mission specialist. NASA: Columbia disaster 2003 Feb 1

史实: 美国医学博士, 美国海军上尉, 美国宇航局宇航员和航天飞机任务专家.美国航天局:哥伦比亚灾难2003年2月1日.

CLARK克拉克ke la ke

Arthur Charles Clark

生人1917年12月16日 ~ 2008年3月19日 》91

FYI: Author, fiction writer and futurist. Is most renouned for "2001: Space Odyssey."(1968).*The limits of the possible can only be defined by going beyond them into the impossible.*

史实: 作家,小说作家和未来学家.最著名的是"2001:太空漫游".

（1968).*可能性的极限只能通过超越不可能的极限来定义.

City of Edmonton public archives; Photo by Forest L. ~ 福瑞斯特

CLARKE克拉克ke li ke

Joseph Andrew Clarke

生人1917年12月16日 ～ 2008年3月19日 》91

FYI: Politician and lawyer, he served twice as Mayor of Edmonton; 1918~1920, 1934~1937. Clarke stadium in Edmonton bears his name.

史实: 政治家和律师, 曾两次担任埃德蒙顿市长;1918年至1920年, 1934年至1937年.埃德蒙顿的克拉克体育场以他的名字命名.

CLARKE克拉克ke li ke

Wallace H. Clarke

生人1924 ～ 1997年 》73

FYI: Skin pathologist and dermatologist. He is best known for devising the "Clark's level", which consists of 5 levels for classifying the seriousness of a malignant melanoma skin cancer based on its microscopic appearance.

史实: 皮肤病理学家和皮肤病学家.他最著名的是设计了"克拉克水平", 这包括5个水平, 根据恶性黑色素瘤皮肤癌的微观外观对其严重性进行分类.

CLANCY克兰西ke lan xi

Thomas Leo Clancy jr.

生人1947 ～ 2013年 》66

FYI: American novelist best known for espionage story lines.

史实:美国作者高名为了间谍情节.

CLAUSIUS克修斯ke xiu si

Rudolf Julius Emanuel Clausius

生人1822 ～ 1888年 》66

FYI: Founder of thermodynamics.

史实: 奠基人热力学.

CLEOPATRA克里奥佩特拉ke li ao pei te la

Cleopatra

生人70 ～ 30年 B.C. 》40

FYI: aka: Cleopatra VII Philopator; Queen of Egypt

史实: 埃及艳后; 埃及女王.

COASE孔斯ko si
Ronald Harry Coase

生人1910～2013年 》103

FYI: Awarded the Nobel in c1991 for economic science. [Nobelprize.org]

史实:1999年诺贝尔经济学奖.

CODY科迪kedi
William Frederick "Buffalo Bill" Cody

生人1846～1917年 》70

FYI: Army scout, Pony Express, showman.

史实:兵役, 非常快马, 演讲者.

COFFIN卡芬ka fen
Levi Coffin

生人1798～1877年 》79

FYI: Was a Quaker and an abolitionist, was considered to be in charge of the "underground railroad" freeing black slaves from the white supremist of his era.

史实: '火车地下为了'把黑人奴隶从他那个时代的白人统治下解放出来.

COHEN科恩ke en
Leonard Norman Cohen

生人1934～2016年 》82

FYI:[a&e] A Canadian poet, writer, singer, musician. O.C.; Canadian Music Hall of Fame. *There is a crack in everything.That's how the light gets in.

史实:一个加拿大诗人, 作家, 歌手, 音乐家.*一切都有裂缝. 这就是光线的进入方式.

COLE口勒kou le
George~W~Cole

FYI: along with J. Noah H. Slee inventor of "3 in one" oil c.1894

史实: 顷1894 先导 《三在一》

COLE科尔ke er
Nathaniel Adams "King" Cole

生人1919～1965年 》45

FYI: [a&e] Singer, entertainer, pianist, actor.

史实: 高名人歌, 艺人, 钢琴家.

COLEMAN科尔曼ke er man

Patrick Vincent Coleman

生人1872 ~ 1917年12月6日》75

FYI: A Canadian hero, was a train dispatcher with CPR. Just before 8:45 a.m. he sent his last message before the Halifax explosion made history. The story is retold in 'A Heritage Minute'. *Hold up the train. Ammunition ship afire in harbour making for Pier 6 and will explode. Guess this will be my last message. Good-bye boys.

史实: 一个加拿大英雄, 是一个有心肺复苏术的火车调度员.就在早上8点45分, 他在哈利法克斯爆炸成为历史之前发出了最后一条信息.故事在《遗产时刻》中重演. '停下火车.弹药船在港口起火, 驶向6号码头, 将爆炸.我想这是我最后的留言了.再见, 孩子们.'

COLGATE高露洁gao lu jie

William Colgate

生人1783 ~ 1857年 》74

FYI: Founder of COLGATE SOAP~toothpaste~1873

史实: 先导《高露洁肥皂》- 牙膏 顷 1873年

COLUMBUS哥伦布ge lu bu

Christopher Columbus

生人1451 ~ 1506年 》55

FYI: Explorer. Queen Victoria named British Columbia in honor of Columbus.

史实: 探险家.维多利亚王后叫 不列颠哥伦比亚 在荣誉格鲁布.

COMBES古姆斯gu mu si

Charles Pierre Mathieu Combes

生人1801 ~ 1872年 》71

FYI: French engineer and metallurgist. Listed among the 72 names on the Eiffel Tower [SE14] >20/72

史实: 新元史上埃菲尔铁塔单名

CONNORS康内斯kang nei si

Charles Thomas "Stomping Tom" Connors

生人1936 ~ 2013年 》77

FYI: Canadian Icon and folk singer-song writer. During every stage performance, he would always 'stomp' his foot to help him keep his timing while playing the guitar, earning the name "Stomping Tom". Awarded the Order of Canada.

史实: 加拿大偶像和民歌歌手兼歌曲作家.在每一场舞台表演中, 他总是 "踩脚" 来帮助他在弹吉他的时候保持时间, 从而获得 "踩脚汤姆" 的称号.授予加拿大订单. [see Messer]

CONSTANTINE康斯但丁kang si dan ding

Flavius Valerius Constantine I

生人280 ~ 337年 A.D.

FYI: known as "The Great" was the first Christian Roman Emperor. The Nicene Creed was conducted at his request in 325 AD.

史实: 一个大, 是第一次基督罗马王人."尼西亚信条 " 顷325 A.D.

COOK库克ku ke

Thomas Cook

生人1808 ~ 1892年 》84

FYI: Cook Travel Agency: explorer and preacher.

史实:游泳和累.

COOMBS苦吗斯ju ma si

"Ernie" Arthur Coombs

生人1927年11月26日 ~ 2001年9月18日 》73

FYI: Coombs came to be known as "Mr. Dress up" a children's program in Canada and featured two lovable puppets know as Casey and Finnegan respectfully. O.C. 1996

史实: 加拿大谁他是《打扮先生》加拿大的儿童节目, 有两个可爱的木偶.

COOPER库帕尔ku pa er

Charlotte Cooper

生人1870 ~ 1966年 》96

FYI: [s] First woman to win in the 1900 Olympics in tennis.

史实: 第一个在奥林匹克网球项目获胜的女人.

COOPER库帕尔ku pa er

Leroy Gordon Cooper jr.

生人1927 ~ 2007年 》90

FYI: Astronaut and mercury project

史实:太空人和水星计划.

COOPER库帕ku pa

Milton William "Bill" Cooper

生人1943 ~ 2001年 》58

FYI: American conspiracy theorist, radio broadcaster and author.

史实: 美国人阴谋论的, 联播, 作者.

COORS库尔斯ku er si

Adolf Herman Joseph Coors

生人1847 ~ 1929年 》82

FYI: aka: KURS; Co founder Coors beer c.1873. First to change to aluminum cans~1959.

史实:先导喝一杯啤酒 顷1873 [看: Molson-Coors-Labatt]

CORIOLIS科里奥利ke li ao li

Gaspard-Gustave de Coriolis

生人1792 ~ 1843年 》51

FYI: engineer and scientist. The first to coin the term "work" in the process of moving an object. His name appears among the 72 names listed on the Eiffel Tower. [SW13] > 21/72

史实: 工程人，新元史上埃菲尔铁塔单名.

CORPERINICUS卡帕尼克斯ke pa ni ke si

Nicholas Corpernicus

生人1473 ~ 1543年 》70

FYI: Astronomer during the renaissance. Put to death for his theory that the Earth went around the Sun.

史实: 他是一个物理学家之际文艺复兴.因为他的地球绕太阳转的理论而被处死.

CORRY卡瑞ka rui

James Alexander Corry

生人1899～1985年 》86

FYI: Academic Canadian Prof. * "The Power of the Law" Massey Lectures Series 1971.O.C.1968

史实: 加拿大教授.顷1971,《法律的力量》教程.

CORNELIUS科尼利厄斯ke ni li a si

CORNELIUS

FYI: The Centurion Acts: 10

史实: 使徒行传十.

CORNWALLIS康沃利斯kang wo li si

Edward Cornwallis

生人1713～1776年 》63

FYI: Lieutenant General of British Empire. Nova Scotia has many buildings and streets named in his honor.

史实: 英国曾经中将.新斯科舍有跟多名字尊重他.

CORSO科索ke suo

[COL] Philip James Corso

生人1915～1998年 》83

FYI: USA army, Author: The Day After Roswell: Colonel Corso.

史实: 作者 '罗斯威尔事件后的岁月' 陆军上校柯索.

CORTES考特斯kao te si

Cortes Hernando

生人1485～1547年 》82

FYI: Spanish explorer who exploited the Aztec.

史实: 西班探险盘剥阿芝特克语.

COSELL口测kou ce

Howard William Cosell

生人1918年3月25日 ～1995年4月23日 》77

FYI: [a&e] American renouned sports announcer for CBS. *What's right isn't always popular. What's popular isn't always right.*

史实: 高名美国报告员为了 CBS. *正确的方法并开总是受欢迎.流行并不总是正确的.

COULOMB库伦ku lun

Charles- Augistin de Coulomb

生人1736 ~ 1806年 》70

FYI: Physicist known for the "Coulomb Law" the theory of electromagnetism. His name is listed among the 72 names on the Eiffel tower. [SE08] >22/72

史实:《库伦法》... 电磁理论.新元史上埃菲尔铁塔单名.

COUSTEAU哭思头ku si tou

Jacque-Yves Cousteau

生人1910 ~ 1997年 》87

FYI: French renouned oceanographer, author and inventor. He invented the Aqualung to breath in deep ocean. His famed boat 'Calypso' was the title of a song by the same name in 1975 by his personal friend and singer -song writer John Denver.*The sea is the universal sewer.

史实: 法国著名的海洋学家,作家和发明家.他发明了深海呼吸的水肺.他著名的船 "卡利普索" 是1975年由他的私人朋友和歌手-歌曲作家约翰丹佛同名的歌曲的标题.*大还是通用的下道.

CRAM卡冉ka ran

Donald James Cram

生人1919 ~ 2001年 》82

FYI: 1987 awarded the Nobel in organic chemistry. Best known for synthesize crown ethers. [Nobleprize.org]史实: 顷1987 嘉佳诺贝尔为了化学家.乙醚. [看- c*j*pedersen, JMLehn]

CRASSUS克拉苏ke la su

Marcus Licinius Crassus

生人c.53 B.C. 》?

FYI: Roman general.

史实: 罗马将军.

CRAZY HORSE疯马(*)feng ma

生人1840 ~ 1877年 》37

FYI: leader of the Lakota tribe. In Chinese the meaning of crazy horse is "*feng ma".
Is the literal meaning.

史实: 他是疯马将军Lakota 部族.

CRICK卡尔可ka er ke

Francis Crick

生人1916 ~ 2004年 》88

FYI: DNA co-discover 1953.*I had discovered the gossip test—what you are really
interested in is what you gossip about. [see Watson]

史实: 顷1953 DNA 先导. *我发现了八卦测试-您真正感兴趣的是您八卦.

CRIPPS克里普斯ke li pu si

[SIR] Richard Stafford Cripps

生人1889 ~ 1952年 》63

FYI: UK politician.

史实: 英国政治家.

CROCE克罗新ke luo xin

James Joseph Croce

生人1943 ~ 1973年 》30

FYI: [a&e] Singer, song writer. Billboard 100 list "Time in a Bottle".

史实: 高名音乐家《瓶子里的时间》

CROCKER克罗克尔ke luo ke er

William~G~Crocker

FYI: His name was chosen for the Crocker brand of Betty Crocker as he was associated
with the flour milling industry. Betty is a 'fictional person'. Several ladies have portrayed
her on radio and television.

史实: 他名字评选为了克罗克尔高名磨子商业. Betty 是一个犬夜叉。Betty 克罗
克尔帕子.

CROCKET 克罗克特 ke luo ke te

David "Davy" Crocket

生人1786 ~ 1836年 》50

FYI: 19th century folk hero, frontiersman, politician. Known as "The King of the Wild Frontier."

史实: 19 世纪民间传说，政治家.

CROHN 克罗恩 ke luo en

[DR.] Burril Bernard Crohn

生人1884 ~ 1983年 》99

FYI: Was a scientist and medical doctor. Crohn's disease; a disease of the intestine and absorption problems.

史实: 是一名科学家和医学博士.克罗恩病;肠道疾病和吸收问题.

CROMWELL 克伦威尔 ke lun wei er

Thomas Cromwell

生人1485 ~ 1540年 》55

FYI: Kings court~lawyer.

史实: 王律师.

CRONKITE 克朗凯特 ka liang kai te

Walter Leland Cronkite Jr.

生人1916年11月4日 ~ 2009年07月17日 》93

FYI: Television news anchor in America. Known as 'The most trusted man in America.' Famous for his closing remarks "and that's the way it is!" Voice actor for A&E dinosaurs.

史实: 美国新闻,声艺人为了《就是这样! 》A&E 恐龙类.

CROOK 克鲁克 ke lu ke

George~R~Crook

生人1830 ~ 1890年 》60

FYI: U.S. Military against the Native American Indians~c19th century.

史实: 19世纪, 军杀印第安.

CROSBY克劳新贝ke lao xin bei

Harris Lillis Bing Crosby jr.

生人1903 ~ 1977年 》74.

FYI: [a&e] Icon of the early 19th century music and movies. "White Christmas" was his signature song. Irving Berlin; White Christmas

史实: 19世纪高名,音乐,电影.

cereal package photo by Forest L. Photo by Forest L. ~ 福瑞斯特

CROWELL克威尔ke wei er

Henry Parsons Crowell

生人1855 ~ 1944年 》89

FYI: He bought Quaker Oates from Seymour and Heston c1877

史实: 他卖商业...Seymour 和 Heston 顷1877

Courtesy of Alberta Government Photo by Forest L. ~ 福瑞斯特

CROWFOOT生人1830 ~ 1890年 》60

FYI: A warrior within early Canada, he served as Chief of the Siksika First Nations of Canada. His ancestry name is Isapo-muxika which is translated as 'Crowfoot'. His statue is now visible within the Alberta Legislature building.

史实: 他是加拿大早期的一名战士, 曾担任加拿大锡卡第一民族的首领。他的祖名是伊萨波·穆西卡, 译为 "乌鸦脚".他的雕像现在可以在阿尔伯塔省的立法大楼内看.

CROWLEY克劳莱ke lao li

Ruth Crowley

FYI: The original Ann Landers (pseudonym)-c.1943-1955. Ruth was a professional nurse and wrote for the newspaper only as a part time job. [see~Chancellor~Friedman]

史实: 原本亲爱的Ann_Landers

CUNDY昆弟kun di

Ransom~E~Cundy

生人1922 ~ 1975年 》53 》[memorial纪念]

FYI: *SS Edmund Fitzgerald~Lake Superior 10 Nov 1975

史实: 纪念S.S.埃德蒙*菲茨杰拉德 湖高强1975年 11月10日

CURIE 居礼 ju li

Pierre Curie

生人1859 ~ 1906年 》67

FYI: Studied Magnetism, radioactivity and other fields. "Curie temperature" is when lava temperature drops and becomes magnetized. Awarded the Nobel in nuclear physics..

史实: 他学习放谢性活度.顷1903 嘉将诺贝尔.

CURIE 居礼 ju li

Marie Curie

生人1867 ~ 1934年 》67

FYI: Scientist awarded a Nobel in Physics 1903, Chemistry 1911. Discovered Radium-Polonium. [nee- sklodowska][Nobelprize.org]

史实:学习放谢性活度.顷1903/1911 嘉将诺贝尔.

CURRIE 库尔义 ku er yi

[SIR] Arthur William Currie

生人1875 ~ 1933年 》58

FYI: Senior officer in the Canadian Military c WWI [see-Hahn]

史实: 加拿大陆军一战高级军官.

CURTIS 柯带斯 ke dai si

Heber Doust Curtis

生人1872 ~ 1942年 》70

FYI: American Astronomer. Discovered the [polar jet-messier 87-1918]

史实: 美国天文学家. 所发现两积分.

CURTIUS 柯带斯 ke dai si

Philippe Curtius

生人1741 ~ 1794年 》53

FYI: Swiss Physician and Wax expert. *Master teacher of "Madame Tussaud".

史实: 蜡像馆老师 "杜莎夫人蜡像馆" 的老师.

CUSTER卡斯特ka si te

George Armstrong Custer

生人1839年12月5日 ~ 1876年6月25日 》37

FYI: A military general and genius in military affairs. "Custer Last Stand" is a famous American story of his army against the Indian braves at Little Big Horn c1876.

史实: 军事将领和军事天才 "最后一个 "看台" 是一个著名的美国故事, 讲述了他的军队对抗印第安人的故事.勇敢地面对小小的大角 C1876.

CUVIER居维叶ju wei ye

Jean Leopold Nicolace Frederic "Georges" Cuvier

生人1769 ~ 1832年 》63

FYI: Naturalist and zoologist; the 'Father of palaeontology'. Name appears with the 72 on the Eiffel tower [NW08] >23/72

史实: 先导在古生物学.新元史上埃菲尔铁塔单名.

From Group "C" you can pick one person or up to ten Surnames and write their Surname in Chinese. You may try HORIZONTAL or VERTICAL in the traditional Chinese form.

D

《变老是必须的，但成长是可以选择的》
"growing old is mandatory, but growing up
is optional."
Walt DISNEY 迪斯尼di si ni

Cultural Tip:

In the French language, "de or DE" plays a significant role in their heritage as it pertains to the village whence they come from. As it refers to "of" or "from" depending on the grammar. Some families choose to drop it at their discretion.

Other cultures such as the Germans have similar traits.

DAGUERRE达盖尔da gai er

Louis -Jacque Mande Daguerre

生人1787 ~ 1851年 》64

FYI: [a&e] artist and photographer~ known for his panoramic paintings. His name appears with the 72 names on the Eiffel tower. [NE22] >24/72

史实: 艺术家,摄影家.高名为了丹青全景.新元史上埃菲尔铁塔单名.

DALAMBRE达拉贝da la bei

Jean Baptiste Joseph Dalambre

生人1749 ~ 1822年 》73

FYI: [a&e] French Astronomer, was director of Paris Observatory. His name appears with the 72 names on the Eiffel tower. [NE06] >25/72

史实: 高名法国天文学家.新元史上埃菲尔铁塔单名.

DALTON道尔顿dao er dun

John Dalton

生人1766 ~ 1844年 》78

FYI: [a&e] Chemist, physicist. "Daltonism"-color blindness.

史实: 物理学家,化学家 "Daltonsim" (道尔顿的) 》色盲.

DANGERFIELD丹戈菲尔德dan ge fei er de

Roger Dangerfield

生人1921 ~ 2004年 》83

FYI: [a&e] aka: Jacob Cohen. American stand-up comedian, writer, director. Catch phrase "I get no respect".

史实: 高名美国人.悲喜剧,作者,指导. 《我没有宗师! 》

DANGI唐吉tang

Chandra Bahadur Dangi

生人1839 ~ 2015年 》76

FYI: smallest man according to Guinness until his death. 57 cm.

史实: 最小的男人，直到死.57厘米. [*Guinness.org]

DANSEREAU丹赛罗dan sai luo

Pierre Dansereau

生人1911 ~ 2011年 》100 Super-centennial

FYI: Father of Ecology; 'Inscape and Landscape' Massey Lecture Series 1972.

史实: 生态学老师.内景与景观》马赛教程.1972年

DANTE但丁dan ding

Dante Alighieri

生人1265 ~ 1321年 》56

FYI: Italian poet of the early renaissance period. Is considered the "Father of the Italian language". Noted for "The Divine Comedy".

史实: 意大利式.智者意大利语《神曲》.

City of Edmonton public archives; Photo by Forest L. ~ 福瑞斯特

DANTZER丹泽dan ze

Vincent Martin Danzer

生人1923 ~ 2001年 》78

FYI: Served as a Canadian lawyer, economist and politician in Edmonton. Mayor of Edmonton from 1965~68. Dantzer' Hill in Edmonton bears his name.

史实: 曾在埃德蒙顿担任加拿大律师,经济学家和政治家.1965~68年任埃德蒙顿市长.埃德蒙顿的丹泽尔山以他的名字命名.

DART达特da te

Raymond Arthur Dart

生人1893 ~ 1988年 》96

FYI: Australian anatomist and anthropologist. 1924 discovery of the first fossil of extinct hominin.

史实: 澳大利亚解剖学家和人类学家.1924发现了灭绝的人类基因的第一个化石.

DARWIN达尔文da er wen

Charles Robert Darwin

生人1809 ~ 1882年 》73

FYI: English Scientist, naturalist and author of " Origin of Species"1859. *A man who dares to waste one hour of time has not discovered the value of life.

史实:英国自然主义,作者.《物种起源》顷1859. *一个敢于浪费一个小时时间的人并没有发现生命的价值.

Photo by Forest L. ~ 福瑞斯特

DAVIDSON达威森da wei sen

Arthur Davidson

生人1881 ~ 1950年 》69

FYI: Arthur was co-founder of Harley-Davidson *total of 4 men namely Walter Davidson Sr., William, Arthur and William S. Harley.

Arthur and William were childhood friends who shared the dream of producing a motorized bicycle. Arthur's older brothers, Walter and William would provide mechanical support to make the dream come true and form the new trade name of Harley-Davidson.

史实: 亚瑟是哈雷戴维森的联合创始人*共有4个人, 即沃尔特戴维森, 威廉, 亚瑟和威廉S 哈雷.亚瑟和威廉是儿时的朋友, 他们共同梦想着生产一辆摩托车.亚瑟的哥哥沃尔特和威廉将提供机械支持, 使梦想成真, 并形成哈雷戴维森的新商标.

[~ Harley]

DAVIS戴维斯dai wei si

[SIR] Colin Rex Davis

生人1927 ~ 2013年 》86

FYI: was a conductor with the London Symphony Orchestra.

史实: 伦敦交响乐团指挥.

DAVIS戴维斯dai wei si

Bette Davis

生人1908 ~ 1989年 》81

FYI: [a&e] aka: Ruth Elizabeth Davis; Actress and singer of the early days of cinema.

史实: 电影早期的演员和歌手.

DAVIS戴维斯dai wei si

Raymond Davis jr.

生人1947 ~ 2006年 》59

FYI: Awarded the Nobel Prize for neutrino astrophysics c2002

史实: 顷2002 嘉奖 诺贝尔在星星物理学家 [*Nobelprize.org]

DAVIS戴维斯dai wei si

Jacob ~W~ Davis

生人1831 ~ 1908年 》79

FYI: aka: Jacob Youphes; he added rivets to denim jeans in 1870. He joined Levi Strauss and the modern jeans were born. [see Strauss]

史实:他加铆钉到牛仔裤,他在一起Levi*Strauss 1870年.[~ Strauss]

da VINCI达芬奇da fen qi

Leonardo da Vinci

FYI: Italian painter; the name "Mona" as Mona Lisa*蒙娜丽莎was added in by present custom.

史实: 意大利画家 - 蒙娜丽莎, 威图威.[~ Mona-Lisa, Vitruvias]

DAVITT大卫特da wei te

Lt. William Francis Davitt

生人1886 ~ 1918年 》32

FYI: Father William Francis Davitt is historically regarded as the last officer to be killed in WWII prior to the Armistice of 1918, the armistice was to be signed at 11:00 on Nov. 11, [eleventh hour of the eleventh day of the eleventh month] of 1918. However, Davitt was killed @ 9:45 a.m. on Nov. 11, 1918.The first officer to die in WWII is recorded as Lt. William Fitzimons.

史实: 威廉·弗朗西斯·戴维特神父历来被认为是1918年停战前第二次世界大战中死亡的最后一名军官,该停战协定将于1918年11月11日11:00(11月11日11:00)签署.然而,大卫于1918年11月11日上午9时45分被杀.第一个在二战中死亡的军官被记录为威廉·菲茨蒙斯中尉.

DAVY大卫da wei

[SIR] Humphrey Davy

生人1778 ~ 1829年 》51

FYI: chemist discovered: sodium, potassium, calcium and electrolysis.

史实: 化学家高明为了纳,钾,钙,点解.

DAWSON道森dao sen

[Honourable Reverend] Peter Dawson

生人1892 ~ 1963年 》70

FYI: Canadian minister and politician. Speaker of the "Assembly " for 26 years. The first to receive a State funeral in Alberta, Canada.

史实: 高名加拿大人.训导职务和政治家.国会议长为了26年之久: 国葬. [see- MacEwan]

DEAN得能dei neng

James Dean

生人1931 ~ 1955年 》24

FYI: [a&e] Renouned actor of the twentieth century. *Dream as if you'll live forever. Live as if you'll die today.*

史实: 高名艺人,电影.*梦想, 就像你将永远活着.生活就好像你今天要死.

De BROGLIE德布罗息de bu luo

Louis- Victor- Pierre- Raymond de Broglie

生人1892 ~ 1987年 》95

FYI: French physicist who concentrated on quantum theory. Awarded the Nobel prize in 1929 for physics. [Nobelprize.org]

史实: 法国物理学家, 嘉奖诺贝尔 1929年为了物理.

De CHARDIN德查丁de cha ding

Pierre Teilhard de Chardin

生人1881 ~ 1955年 》74

FYI: French philosopher and Jesuit priest; trained as a paleontologist and geologist. Notable works: "The Phenomenon of Man." >Peking man project.

史实: 法国哲学和耶稣会.学的旧石器时代 ""人的现象".

DeCHANCOURTOIS德尚古尔多阿de shang gu er duo a

Alejandra-Emile Beguyer de Chancourtois

FYI: French geologist and mineralogist: As the Father of the periodic table c.1862 he assigned all the minerals by weight. Small to Large

史实: 法国地质学家和矿物学家:作为周期表C.1862的父亲, 他按重量分配了所有的矿物.小到大 [~ Mendeleev]

City of Edmonton public archive; Photo by Forest L. ~ 福瑞斯特

DECORE德克尔de ke er

Laurence George Decore

生人1940年6月28日 ～ 1999年11月6日 》59

FYI: aka Lavrently Dikur was a Canadian lawyer. Also served as 31st Mayor of Edmonton [1983-1988] and Leader of the Alberta Liberal Party. Decore 'look out' over looks the South bank of South Edmonton.

史实: 是一名加拿大律师.曾任埃德蒙顿市第31任市长（1983-1988年），阿尔伯塔自由党领袖.装饰"小心"看南埃德蒙顿南岸. [Wiki]

de DION迪迪安di di an

Earl Henry de Dion

生人1878 ～ 1928年 》50

FYI: French engineer noted for assisting with the Eiffel tower; listed among the 72 names on the Eiffel tower [SW08]

>26/72

史实: 发箍工程帮埃菲尔.新元史上埃菲尔铁塔单名.

DEE德义de yi

John Dee

生人1527 ~ 1609年 》82

FYI: Mathematician, astronomer and occult philosopher. Adviser to Queen Elizabeth I. Coined the phrase "British Empire".

史实: 数学家,天文学家和哲学.生造"大英帝国 ".

DEERE德尔de er

60John Deere

生人1804 ~ 1886年 》82

FYI: Black smith and inventor of machine implements - farming tractors and small machines.

史实: 黑人史密斯和机械工具的发明者-农业拖拉机和小型机械.

DeFOE得福de fu

Daniel Defoe

生人1660 ~ 1731年 》70

FYI: writer of Robinson Crusoe

史实: 作者,写Robinson*Crusoe.

De FOREST帝福瑞斯特di fu rui si te

Lee de Forest

生人1873 ~ 1961年 》87

FYI: "Father of Radio". Was the first to develop the "Audion vacuum tube" for practical amplification such as loud speakers or headphones.

史实: "收音机之父".是第一个开发用于实际放大的"音频真空管",如扬声器或耳机.

De FOREST帝福瑞斯特di fu rui si te

Lockwood de Forest

FYI: wood, glass, artist

史实: 木,璃,涂家.

De GAULLE戴高乐dai gao le

Charles Dandre Joseph Marie de Gaulle

生人1890 ~ 1970年 》80

FYI: French general during WW 2

史实: 法国将军,顷WWII

De HAVILLAND德哈维兰de ha wei lan

Olivia Mary de Havilland

生人1916年7月16日 ~ 103 ~ active

FYI: Actress who appeared in 49 feature films of the 'Golden age' of Hollywood. She played Melanie in 'Gone with the Wind' being her most memorable role.

史实:　曾出演过49部好莱坞黄金时代电影的女演员.她在《飘》中扮演梅兰妮是她最难忘的角色.

De la RENTA得拉仁特dai la ren te

Oscar de la Renta

生人1932 ~ 2014年 》82

FYI: Fashion designer

史实: 时装设计师.

DELAUNAY德落内de lau nei

Charles Eugene Delaunay

生人1816 ~ 1872年 》56

FYI: French Astronomer, his name is listed among the 72 names on the Eiffel tower: [SE11] >28/72 insert

史实: 法国天文学家.新元史上埃菲尔铁塔单名.

de LEON德利昂de li ang

Juan Ponce de Leon

生人1474 ~ 1521年 》47

FYI: Spanish explorer and conquistador; searched for the Fountain of Youth for most of his life.

史实:探险家.他查看为了"喷泉青春" 万古长青!

De LILLE德里尔de li er

Elaine de Lille

生人c1125 ~ 1202年 》77

FYI: aka: Alan of Lille. A French theologian and poet. "all roads lead to Rome".

史实: 法国教人,式.《条条大路通罗马》

DEMIKHOV德米科霍夫de mi ke huo fu

[Dr.] Vladimir Petrovich Demikhov

生人1916 ~ 1998年 》82

FYI: heart transplant pioneer; coined the term tranplantology. 1937- First artificial heart transplant.

史实: 先导心脏移植.1937年 第一次心脏移植.

DEMILLE德米尔de mi er

Cecil Blount Demille

生人1881 ~ 1959年 》77

FYI: Father of Cinema in America for Silent and Sound films. (DeMille award).*The Ten Commandments.

史实:高名先导电影,安静和声电影. "十诫"

DEMING德明de ming

William Edwards Deming

生人1900 ~ 1993年 》93

FYI: He was the inspiration behind the "Japanese post -war economic miracle". Plan-Do-Study-Act.

史实: 他是 "日本战后经济奇迹" 背后的灵感来源.计划-做-研究-行动.

DEMOCRITUS德魔卡它死de mo ka ta si

Democritus

生人460 ~ 370年BC 》100

FYI: Greek philosopher."Atomic Theory of the Universe."

史实: 希腊哲学:原子论在宇宙.

DENT得恩特de en te

Ivor Graham Dent

生人1924年2月7日 ~ 2009年3月29日 》85

FYI: Former mayor of Edmonton 1968-1974, candidate for the House of Commons and the Legislature Assembly of Alberta.[bing]

史实: 1968-1974年埃德蒙顿的前市长,下议院和阿尔伯塔省议会的候选人.

De PRONY德怕若尼de po ruo ni

Gaspard Clair Francois Marie Niche de Prony

生人1755 ~ 1839年 》84

FYI: French engineer; he developed the "Prony" brake to measure "torque". He is listed among the 72 names on the Eiffel tower.

[SE05] >29/72 insert

史实: 法国工程.先导定标.新元史上埃菲尔铁塔单名.

DESCARTES笛卡特di ka er

Rene Descartes

生人1596 ~ 1650年 》53

FYI: aka L[renataus] French mathematician, philosopher and scientist. As with Shakespear, he coined the phrase "Cogito, ergo sum ~ I think, therefore I am." from his writings adapted from Principles of philosophy.

史实: 法国数学家,哲学家和科学家.和莎士比亚一样,他根据他的著作改编自哲学原理,创造了一个短语"cogito, ergo sum~我想, 因此我就是".

$10 Canadian Photo by Forest L. ~ 福瑞斯特

DESMOND德斯莫德de si mo de

Viola Irene Desmond

生人1914 ~ 1965年 》51

FYI: Canadian black lady who challenged the government for equal rights for black citizens in Canada. From 2018 she will appear on the new $10.00 bill.

史实: 加拿大黑人，平等的法律地位 2018年她照片是上加拿大 十钱 [see J.A. MacDonald]

DEWAR杜瓦尔de wa er

[SIR] Thomas~R~Dewar

FYI: Scottish Whisky distiller. Shared his wealth and his name to many groups ie: "Dewar trophy" for automobile excellence.

史实:苏格兰人威士忌焦化."德瓦尔 锦标" 纪念奖.

DIANA戴安娜dai an na

Princess Diana

生人1 July 1961 – 31 August 1997年 》36

FYI: aka: Dianna Frances Spencer. She is described as the world's most photographed woman. Once married to Prince Charles, but later divorced. She was known for her many humanitarian works. Several memorials bear her name. *Carry out a random act of kindness, with no expectation of reward, safe in the knowledge that one day someone might do the same for you.

史实: 戴安娜•弗朗西斯•斯宾塞.她被称为世界上摄影最多的女人.曾经和查尔斯王子结婚,但后来离婚了.她因许多人道主义工作而闻名.几座纪念馆上刻着她的名字.*在知道某人天可能会为您做同样的事情的情况下。请放心递进一次不带回报的随意的善举.

DICKENS狄更斯 di geng si

Charles John Huffam Dickens

生人1812 ~ 1870年 》58

FYI: English novelist: A Christmas Carol, Oliver Twist.

史实:高名英国人*A_Christmas_Carol- 圣诞宋, Oliver*Twist.

DICKENSON得肯森de ken sen

Emily Dickenson

生人1830 ~ 1886年 》56

FYI: American Poet

史实:美国人式.

DICKSON迪克森di ke sen

Earle Dickson

生人1892 ~ 1961年 》69

FYI: co-invented the "Band-Aid" with Thomas Anderson for johnson*johnson c1920. Earle made the band-aid for his wife.

史实: 先导绷带顷1920. [johnson*johnson]

DIDON迪动di dong

Henri Didon

生人1840 ~ 1900年 》60

FYI: Writer, educator and French Dominican Preacher. He coined the Olympic motto: Citius, altius, fortius; Latin for faster-higher-stronger. c1894 games.

史实: 法国人作者,老师,教.生道 "奥林匹克:快-高-强"

[see Fredy*Coubertin]

DIEFENBAKER迪芬贝克di fen ba ka

John George Diefenbaker

生人1895年10月18日 ~ 1979年8月16日 》84

FYI: Canadian lawyer and politician. 13 PM. of Canada. He introduced the first female to the house of commons. As well he introduced voting to the First Nations. *The Liberals are the flying saucers of politics. No one can make head nor tail of them and they never are seen twice in the same place. [see-Fairclough]

史实: 加拿大政治家.曾经首相 十三号.引进第一次女服直辖渥太华,引进印度人到投票.*自由主义者是政治的飞碟.没有人能制造它们的头和尾, 在同一个地方它们从来没有两次被看见过.

DIEMER迪默di mo

Walter~E~Diemer

生人1904 ~ 1998年 》94

FYI: Inventor of Double Bubble gum c.1928

史实: 先导泡泡口香糖顷1928 [查看- f*FLEER]

DILLER迪乐di le

Phyllis Ada Driver Diller

生人1917 ~ 2012年 》95

FYI: [a&e] Icon in humor. Funniest comedian twentieth century.*A smile is a curve that sets everything straight.*

史实: 高名女强人, 高谐谈人. *微笑是一条曲线, 可以使所有事物变得笔直.

DIMMLER迪马尔di ma er

Wilhelm Dimmler

生人1937 may 6: 》[memorial纪念]

FYI: engineering officer LZ Hindenburg

史实: 工程人, LZ- 兴登堡.

DIOPHANTUS刁番图diao fan tu

Diophantus

生人3rd century AD.

FYI: Greek mathematician

史实: 希腊数.

DISNEY迪斯尼di si ni

Walt Elias Disney

生人1901年12月5日 ~ 1966年12月15日 》65

FYI: Animator; Disneyland~ introduced Mickey mouse to the world. *Growing old is mandatory, but growing up is optional.*

史实: 高名动画片迪斯尼地介绍 Mickey*mouse. *变老是必须的, 但成长是可以选择的.

DODGE道奇dao qi

[Colonel] Richard Irving Dodge

生人1827 ~ 1895年 》65

FYI: Discovered "Devils Tower": Devils Tower National Monument c.1902

史实:寻出 Devils塔国宝.

DOEHNER 德内尔 de ni er

Hermann Doehner

1937 may 6 》[memorial 纪念]

FYI: LZ- Hindenburg

史实: 1937年LZ- 兴登堡.

DOLAN 多轮 duo lun

Burtis John Dolan

1937 may 6 [memorial 纪念]

FYI: LZ- Hindenburg

史实:1937年 LZ- 兴登堡.

DOLBY 得比 de bi

Ray Milton Dolby

生人1933～2013年 》80

FYI: American engineer who developed the DOLBY NS -noise reduction system and started Dolby Laboratories.

史实: 美国工程.他先导德比*[NS] 声下

DONNE 多恩 duo en

John Donne

生人1572～1631年 》69

FYI: English poet and clerk~ famous for 'No man is an Island'

史实: 英国式,《无男是一个岛》.

DONOHUE 德那乎 de na hu

Jerry Donohue

生人1920～1985年 》65

FYI: Hydrogen bonding theory. Pioneer to discovering DNA. [see Watson and Crick]

史实: 氢键定理DNA

DOOHAN都汉du han

James Montgomery Doohan

生人1920 ~ 2005年 [memorial]

FYI: Canadian and American actor. Star Trek fame "Engineer Scotty"

史实: 加拿大和美国演员.《星际迷航》的名气 "斯科蒂工程师".

DOPPLER多普勒duo pu le

Christian Johann Doppler

生人1803 ~ 1853年 》49

FYI: He discovered that the stars and galaxies are in motion. The 'doppler affect' refers to movement of the galaxies.

史实: 他寻出全星星, 恒星系在运行*多普勒效应.

DORGAN都尔格恩do er ge en

Thomas Aloysis Dorgan

生人1877 ~ 1929年 》54

FYI: The first illustrator who coined the phrase " hot dog" at a base ball game.

史实: 生道 Hot*dog, 广告为了棒坛.

DOYLE道尔dao er

[SIR] Arthur Conan Doyle

生人1859 ~ 1930年 》71

FYI: writer and author of "Sherlock Holmes." *When you have eliminated the impossible, whatever remains, however improbable, must be the truth.*

史实: 作者神探 "歇洛克福尔摩斯".*当您消除了不可能的事情之后, 无论多么不可能的事情, 剩下的都是事实.

DOUBLEDAY独步代du bu dai

Frank Nelson Doubleday

生人1862 ~ 1934年 》72

FYI: Founded Doubleday books in 1897

史实: 先导[独步代书] 1897年.

DOUGLAS杜格拉斯du ge la si

Edward Douglas

1937 may 6 》[memorial纪念]

FYI: LZ- Hindenburg

史实:纪念 1937年LZ- Hindenburg.

DOUGLAS杜格拉斯du ge la si

Thomas Clement "Tommy" Douglas

生人1904年10月20日 ~ 1986年 2月24日》84

FYI: Trained as a Baptist minister before entering politics. Served as Premier of Saskatchewan from 1944 to 1961. Introduced Universal Health Care within Canada. 2004 was voted the *Most Important Canadian in Canadian history. *I don't mind being a symbol but I don't want to become a monument. There are monuments all over the Parliament Buildings and I've seen what the pigeons do to them.

史实: 在进入政界之前受训成为浸礼会牧师.作为1944年至1961年
任萨斯喀彻温省总理.介绍通用加拿大境内的医疗保健.2004年被评为
最重要的加拿大历史上的加拿大人.*我不介意成为象征，但我不想成
为纪念碑.国会大厦上遍布着纪念碑，我已经看到了鸽子对它们的作
用.

City of Edmonton public archives; Photo by Forest L. ~ 福瑞斯特

DOUGLAS道格拉斯da ke li si

James McCrie Douglas

生人1867 ~ 1950年 》83

FYI: Canadian politician and served as Mayor of Edmonton from 1930~31. James Mccrie Douglas park in West Edmonton.

史实:　　加拿大政治家,1930~31年任埃德蒙顿市长.西埃德蒙顿的詹姆斯•麦克里•道格拉斯公园.

DOUGLASS杜格拉斯du ge la si

Frederick Douglass

生人1818 ~ 1895年 》77

FYI: aka Frederick Augustus Washington Bailey; American social reformer and slave abolitionist.

史实: 黑美国人,奴废除在美国.

DOWN都按dou an

John Langdon Down

生人1828 ~ 1896年 》68

FYI: Literal translation. 23 levels of 2 chromosomes for healthy people, however level 21 has 3 chromosomes instead of the normal 2. c1961 was renamed "Trisomy 21 Anomoly". (Down-syndrome)

史实:健康人有二十三小组两有染色体."都按人"有三个在二十一级
"先天愚型21"1961年.

DRAKE德雷克de lei ke

Frank Donald Drake

生人1930年5月28日 ~ active

FYI: Astronomer and physicist. SETI. >drake equation

史实: SETI 》德雷克方程.天文学家.

DRESSLAR德雷斯勒de lei si le

Elmer "Len" Dresslar jr.

生人1925 ~ 2005年 》80

FYI: American voice actor. He was the voice of the Jolly Green Giant: HoHoHo"; as well, he was highly sought after for singing "jingles" for many companies。

史实: 美国人口艺人.Jolly_Green_Giant: "HO HO HO". [快乐绿巨人

DRUCKER德鲁克de lu ke

Mort Drucker

生人1929年3月22日 ~ active

FYI: illustrator for MAD magazine since 1956

史实: 1956年到今年画插图者为了MAD周报.

DUDEK杜德克du de ke

Louis Dudek

生人1918 ~ 2001年 》83

FYI: Canadian Poet and academic giant. Order of Canada. *A critic at best is a waiter at the great table of literature.

史实: 加拿大诗人和学术巨人.加拿大订单.*评论家充其量不过是文学大舞台上的诗应生.

DUDO杜都du do

Dudo

生人C 965 ~ 1043年 》78

FYI: aka Dudon. Was a Norman historian during the Normans time period. He, historically joins the ranks of Josephus and Mormon.

史实: 是诺曼时代的一位诺曼历史学家.他，历史上加入了约瑟夫和摩门教的行列.

City of Edmonton public archives;Photo by Forest L. ~ 福瑞斯特

DUGGAN达根da gen

David Milwyn Duggan

生人1785 ~ 1838年 》53

FYI: Mayor of Edmonton from 1920~1923. He founded Duggan Investments. Duggan community in South Edmonton is in honor of his services.

史实: 1920年至1923年任埃德蒙顿市长.他创立了杜根投资公司.南埃德蒙顿的杜根社区对他的服务表示敬意.

DULONG都龙du long

Pierre Louis Dulong

生人1785 ~ 1838年 》53

FYI: French chemist who studied heat on gases. His name appears among the 72 names listed on the Eiffel tower. [NW10] >28/72

史实: 法国化学家,他学汽暖.新元史上埃菲尔铁塔单名.

DUMAS杜马斯du ma si

Jean Baptiste Andre Dumas

生人1800 ~ 1884年 》84

FYI: A french chemist who put atomic weights into relative atomic masses. He is listed on the Eiffel tower. [NE 10]>30 /72

史实: 法国化学家,他整理质量数. 新元史上埃菲尔铁塔单名.

DUNANT杜南特 du nan te

Henry Dunant

生人1828 ~ 1910年 》92

FYI: Founder of the Red Cross, Nobel Prize for peace c.1901

史实: 先导 "RED CROSS" ~ 红十字.1901年 诺贝尔为了安.

[*Nobelprize.org]

DuPont杜邦du bang

Eleuthere Irenee DuPont

FYI: French American chemist and founder of duPONT paint ~1802

史实: 先导杜邦画1802年.法国化学家. [看/see lavoisier]

DUPREE都普义du pu yi

[prof] Louis Dupree

生人1925 ~ 1989年 》64

FYI: Archeologist of Kabul university. Author "Afghanistan".

史实: 喀布尔大学.他写" 阿富汗"~阿富汗.

DURAS都拉斯du la si

Marguerite Duras [pseudonym]

生人1914 ~ 1996年 》82

FYI: aka Marguerite Donnadeau was a French novelist, playwright, screen writer and essayist. *Compared with your past beautiful outlooking, I love your nowaday tortured face more.*

史实: 法国小说家,剧作家,银幕作家和散文家.*与你过去美丽的外表相比,我更爱你现在扭曲的脸.

DURR都尔du er

Ludwig Durr

生人1878 ~ 1956年 》72

FYI: The designer of the LZ- Hindenburg

史实: 图案为了 LZ 兴登堡.

DYER迪尔di er

Wayne Walter Dyer

生人1940 ~ 2015年 》75

FYI: American philosopher, motivational speaker. Your Erroneous Zone [1976] Father of Motivation.

史实: 美国人哲学, 激励人口.Your Erroneous Zone:1976 年.

DYSON蒂宋di song

Freeman John Dyson

生人1923 ~ Active

FYI: Theoretical physicists and mathematician. Known for the Dyson sphere ie: completely enclosing the sun and capturing all of its electromagnetic energy.

史实: 理论物理学家和数学家.以戴森球而闻名, 即:完全包围太阳并捕获太阳的所有电磁能量.

D'YOUVILLE蒂尤维勒di you wei le

Saint Marguerite d'Youville

生人October 15, 1701 – December 23, 1771年 》70

FYI: born Marie-Marguerite Dufrost de Lajemmerais. As a widow she founded The Order of Sisters of Charity of Montreal and poor houses. As well, hospitals and schools bear her name in Canada and in particular in Alberta.

史实: 出生于Marie-Marguerite Dufrost de Lajemmerais.作为寡妇, 她创立了蒙特利尔慈善修女会和贫民窟.同样, 医院和学校在加拿大, 特别是在艾伯塔省也以她的名字命名.

From Group D" you can pick one person or up to ten Surnames and write their Surname in Chinese. You may try HORIZONTAL or VERTICAL in the traditional Chinese form.

E

《我学的越多，就越意识到自己不知道的东西有多少.》

"The more I learn, the more I realize how much I don't know."

Albert EINSTEIN爱斯特坦ai si te an

EARHART鳄和特e he te

Amelia Mary Earhart

生人1897 ~ 1937年 》40

FYI: First female aviator to fly solo across the Atlantic ocean. Was the 16th female to be issued a pilots license in that era. She was co-founder of the "ninety-nine" group.

史实: 高名女人驾驶员做独奏横断Atlantic海.》》不见.

EARP尔普er pu

Wyatt Berry Stapp Earp

生人1848 ~ 1929年 》80

FYI: deputy sherrif ~ early Wild America.

史实: 早美国,人民警察 [see ~ Holliday]

EASTMAN伊斯曼yi si man

George Eastman

生人1854 ~ 1932年 》88

FYI: co-founder of Kodak c.1888. The name 'Kodak' was strictly generic in nature "pulled from the air".

史实: 先导为了柯达顷1888. "柯达" 这个名字在自然界中是严格通用的, "从空气中提取". [-h a strong]

EBELMEN埃布尔曼a bu er man

Jacque-Joseph Ebelmen

生人1814 ~ 1852年 》38

FYI: Ebelmen was a renouned chemist and is listed among the 72 people noted on the Eiffel tower. [SE07] >31/72

史实: 高名化学家.新元史上埃菲尔铁塔单名.

EBERT义布尔特yi bu er te

Roger Joseph Ebert

生人1942 ~ 2013年 》71

FYI: American film critic, historian, journalist and author. Siskel and Ebert was a weekly commentary about new movie releases. *I learned to be a critic by reading 'Mad magazine.

史实: 美国电影评论家,历史学家,记者和作家.西克尔和埃伯特每周都会对新电影的发行进行评论. "我通过阅读《疯狂杂志》学会了成为一名评论家."

EDDINGTON艾丁顿ai ding dun

[SIR] Arthur Stanley Eddington

生人1882年12月28日~ 1944年11月22日 》61

FYI: Astronomer [Eddington luminosity] foremost on the study of the Sun energy.

史实: 天文学家[埃丁顿光度]最重要的研究太阳能量.

EDISON爱迪生ai di sheng

Thomas Edison

生人1847年2月11日 ~ 1931年10月18日 》84

FYI: inventor and businessman. He held 1093 US patents. *Our greatest weakness lies in giving up. The most certain way to succeed is always to try just one more time.*

史实:商业和发明.他有1093专利权.*我们最大的弱点在于放弃.成功的最确定的方法是总是再尝试一次.

public archives Photo by Forest L. ~ 福瑞斯特

EDMISTON埃德米斯顿ai de mi si dun

William Somerville Edmiston

生人1857 ~ 1903年 》46 》[memorial纪念]

FYI: Architect and politician in Alberta, serving twice a Mayor of Edmonton.

史实: 阿尔伯塔的建筑师和政治家, 曾两次担任埃德蒙顿市长.

EDWARDS艾德沃斯ai de wo si

Thomas ~E~ Edwards

生人1925～1975年 》50 》[memorial纪念]

FYI: S.S.*Edmund Fitzgerald ~ Second Assistant Engineer

史实: 他是第二次工程:S.S.*Edmund Fitzgerald.

with permission of Alberta Legislature. Park sign courtesy of Forest L.

EDWARDS艾德沃斯ai de wo si

Henrietta Muir Edwards

生人1849～1931年 》82

FYI: She was one of The Famous Five in Canadian history demanding that any woman is to be recognized as a person. She was the first female cabinet member in Alberta. A park in Edmonton is named in her honor.

史实: 她是加拿大历史上著名的五人之一，要求任何女人都要被承认为一个人.她是阿尔伯塔省第一位女内阁成员.埃德蒙顿的一个公园以她的名字命名. [see Murphy]

EDWARDS艾德沃斯ai de wo si

Robert ~G~ Edwards

生人1925～2013年 》88

FYI: was awarded the Nobel prize in c.2010. for Medicine: Vitro Fertilization

史实: 嘉奖诺贝尔在医学 2010年.体外受精. [Nobelprize.org]

EHMAN埃曼ai man

Jerry~R~Ehman

FYI: The Astronomer Ehman discovered the signal while reviewing data from the "Big Ear". It was focused on the Sagittarius constellation. 1977:72 sec "wow! signal"

史实: 高名为了: 大耳《哇哦! 线》信号.1977年72秒钟

courtesy of Rebecca E. Littke

EIFFEL埃菲尔ai fei er
Alexandrie Gustave Eiffel
生人1832年12月15日 ～ 1923年12月27日 》91
FYI: civil engineer and designer of the Eiffel Tower. *72 names are engraved at the base of his tower. On the four faces, their are no female names mentioned.
史实: 法国工程和设计和命名埃菲尔铁.七十二名字上四个面它没有女人名的新元史上埃菲尔铁塔单名.

EICHELMANN艾克尔曼ai ke er man
Franz Eichelmann
生人1937年5月6日 》[memorial纪念]
FYI: radio operator LZ - Hindenburg. 1937 may 6
史实: 报务员LZ - 兴登堡.1937 may 6

EICHMANN爱可曼ai ke man
Karl Adolf Eichmann
生人1906 ～ 1962年 》56

FYI: The Third Reich; hanged for his services with Hitler.

**Third Reich refers to "Third Realm or Third Empire"

史实: 第三蒂国:他是绞溢为了帮希腊特. [看- Hitler] [**NG]

EINSTEIN爱因斯坦ai yin si tan

Albert Einstein

生人1879年3月14日 ~ 1955年4月18日 》76

FYI: Renouned physicist of the 19th century ~(E=Mc2) Awarded the Nobel in 1921 for services to Theoretical physics. *Life is like riding a bicycle. To keep your balance, you must keep moving.

史实: 高名物理学家:E= Mc 2. 1921年嘉奖诺贝尔为了相对论.*生活就像骑自行车.为了保持平衡, 您必须继续前进.

EISENHOWER艾森豪威尔ai sen hao wei er

Dwight David Eisenhower

生人1890年10月14日 ~ 1969年3月18日 》79

FYI: *US army general of WW2; politician, US President 1953-1961. *Plans are nothing; planning is everything.

史实: 美国将 WWII, 政治家.美国总统 1953年到1961年. *计划无济于事; 规划就是一切.

ELION厄里恩e li en

Gertrude Belle Elion

生人1918 ~ 1999年 》81

FYI: American biochemist and pharmacist. Awarded the Nobel in 1988 for physiology in medicine. [Nobelprize.org]

史实: 美国药剂师.嘉奖诺贝尔1988年为了生理.

Photo by Forest L. ~ 福瑞斯特

ELIZABETH伊莉萨佰yi li sa bai II

QUEEN Elizabeth II of England

生人1926年4月21日 ~ active. Elizabeth Alexandria Mary Windsor.

FYI: Since 1952 her image appears on the Canadian $20 and the abverse of Canadian coinage.*current Monarch: D.G.Regina [Dei Gratia Regina] God Save the Queen

史实: 1926年4月21日:君主1952年到今.她照片上加拿大钱,每铸币有她形象.帝就援王后.

ELLIOT埃里森ai li sen

Cass Elliot

生人1941 ~ 1974年 》33

FYI: [a&e] aka Ellen Naomi Cohen. Singer, writer of the 60 era. Sang with the Mama's and the Papa's.

史实: 歌手, 60年代的作家.和妈妈和爸爸一起唱歌.

ELLIOT埃里森ai li sen

Thomas Sterns Elliot

生人1888 ~ 1965年 》77

FYI: British Essayist, publisher and social critic. 1922- "Waste Land" is regarded as one of his many great works. *1948 Nobel Prize in Literature. [see -Cawein] [Nobelprize.org]

史实: 英国作者出版者, 评论家.嘉奖诺尔贝1948 为了文艺[查看- Cawein]

ELVEHJEM埃尔维纳姆ai er wei na mu

Conrad Arnold Elvehjem

生人1901 ~ 1962年 》61

FYI: American Biochemist discovered Niacin in 1937

史实: 1937年 药剂师Niacin.

EMERSON爱默生ai mo sheng

Ralph Waldo Emerson

生人1803 ~ 1882年 》79

FYI: Lecturer, essayist, poet. Abe Lincoln called him the "American Confucius". *For every minute you are angry you lose sixty seconds of happiness.

史实: 讲师,散文家,诗人.林肯称他为 "美国孔子". *每生气一分钟, 就会失去六十秒的幸福.

ENGALS恩格斯en ge si

Friedrich Engals

FYI: philosopher, co-authored "The Communist Manifesto".

史实: 哲学家, 合著了《共产党宣言》. [查看- Marx]

ERAMUS而阿姆斯er a mu si

Desiderus Eramus Roterodamus

生人1466～1536年 》70

FYI: Dutch born with a back ground in renaissance humanism

史实: 生于文艺复兴时期的荷兰人.

ERDMANN尔达曼er da man

Fritz Erdmann

生人1937年5月6日 》[memorial纪念]

FYI: Colonel Fritz Erdmann was a passenger and died on the LZ- Hindenburg 1937 may 6 while docking.

史实: 他死了上 兴登堡.

ESTERBROOK埃斯特布鲁克ai si te bu lu ke

Richard Esterbrook

生人1812～1895年 》83

FYI: Developed today's fountain pen.

史实: 开发了今天的自来水笔.

EUCLID欧氏ou shi

Euclid

生人c300 B.C.

FYI: Greek mathematician and Father of geometry.

史实: 希腊数学家, 几何学之父.

EURIPIDES欧里比得斯ou li bi de si

Euripides

生人480～406年 B.C. 》74

FYI: Greek author. * Question everything. Learn something. Answer nothing.

史实: 希腊文作者.*质疑一切.学点东西.什么都不要回答.

City of Edmonton public archives; Photo by Forest L. ~ 福瑞斯特

EVANS埃文斯ai wen si
Harry Marshall Erskine Evans

生人1876 ~ 1973年 》97

FYI: Business man and politician in Canada, served as Mayor of Edmonton 1917~1918. Both Evansburg and Evansdale bear his name.

史实: 加拿大商人,政治家, 1917~1918年任埃德蒙顿市长.埃文斯堡和埃文斯代尔都有他的名字.

EVEREST额菲尔士e fei er shi
George Everest

生人1790年7月4日 ~ 1866年12月1日 》76

FYI: SIR Everest was a Colonel and British surveyor; Mt Everest in his honor. *8848 meters

史实: 埃佛勒斯特爵士是一名上校和英国测量员;埃佛勒斯特山是为了纪念他.*8848米

From Group "E" you can pick one person or up to ten Surnames and write their Surname in Chinese. You may try HORIZONTAL or VERTICAL in the traditional Chinese form.

F

《教育的目的是鼓励和引导人作为一个有意识的, 思考和感知存在的人这是我的荣幸....》

"The purpose of education is to encourage and guide man as a conscious, thinking and perceiving being..."

Friedrich Wilhelm August FROBEL福禄贝尔fu lu bei er

FAHRENHEIT飞轮海fei lun hai

Daniel Gabriel Fahrenheit

生人1686年5月24日 ~ 1736年9月16日 》50

FYI: German physicist. The Fahrenheit mercury scale [1714] was used until the 1960's and replaced by the Celsius scale in most countries.

史实: 德国物理学家.华氏水银温标[1714]一直使用到1960年代, 在大多数国家被摄氏温标取代.

[- Amontons, Celsius, Kelvin, Romer]

FAIRCLOUGH发尔卡奥fa er ka ao

Ellen Louks Fairclough

生人1905 ~ 2004年 》99

FYI: First female allowed into the House of Commons in Canada. [1950-1963CHC] O.C.

史实: 第一次女服 在加拿大仪院 顷1950

[~ Diefenbaker]

FAIRBAIRN费本fe ben

William Ewart Fairbairn

生人1885 ~ 1960年 》75

FYI: British Royal Marines WW2, trained American and British officers to be expert in sabotage and guerrilla warfare.

史实: 英国皇家海军陆战队二战, 训练美国和英国军官成为破坏和游击战专家.

[Churchill's Ministry of Ungentlemanly Warfare~ G. Milton]

FARADAY法拉第fa la di

Michael Faraday

生人1791年9月22日 ~ 1867年8月25日 》76

FYI: Father of electro - magnetism~ [faraday cage]. Your micro-wave oven is a faraday cage.

史实: 高名为了电磁学 [法拉第笼子].你的微波炉是法拉第笼子.

FARNSWORTH范斯沃斯住fan si wo si zhu

Philo Taylor Farnsworth

生人1906 ~ 1971年 》65

FYI: inventor and entrepreneur; Television pioneer who developed the first working B/W in c1927.

史实: 发明家和企业家;电视先驱，他在1927年发明了第一个工作软件.

FAWKES福克斯fu ke si

Guy Fawkes

生人1570 ~ 1606年 》36

FYI: 05 November 'Guy Fawkes day' in Great Britain.

史实: 11月5日火桐木哦.

FEIBUSCH费布什fei bu shi

Moritz Feibusch

生人1937 年5月 6日 》[memorial纪念]

FYI: LX- Hindenburg 1937 may 6

史实: LX- 兴登堡.

FENN芬恩fen en

John~B~Fenn

生人1917 ~ 2010年 》93

FYI: awarded the Nobel c 2002 in chemistry: analysis of biological micromolecules. [Nobelprize.org]

史实: 2002年嘉将诺贝尔 在化学家.

FERBER菲伯fei bo

Edna Ferber

生人August 15, 1885 – April 16, 1968年 》83

FYI: An American novelist, short story writer and playwright. All of her books and plays showed a strong female protagonist in the early twentieth century *It's terrible to realize you don't learn how to live until you're ready to die, and then it's too late. ~ Christmas isn't a season. It's a feeling.

史实: 美国小说家,短篇小说作家和剧作家.她所有的书和戏剧都展示了20世纪早期一位强大的女性主角*很难意识到, 在你准备好死亡之前, 你不会学会如何生活, 然后就太晚了.**圣诞节不是一个季节.这是一种感觉.

FERDINAND斐迪南fei di nan

[ARCHDUKE] Franz Ferdinand Carl Ludwig Joseph Maria

生人1863 ~ 1914年 》52

FYI: his assassination by Gavrilo Princip began the setting for WW1

史实: 一战开始什么时候他是死了.

FERMI费米fei mi

Enrico Fermi

生人1901 ~ 1954年 》53

FYI: Italian physicist, awarded the Nobel 1938. Fermi Paradox "where is everybody？", Fermi Gamma-ray Space Telescope named in his honor. Architect the nuclear age.

史实:1938年嘉奖诺贝尔在物理学家.设计师核轰炸Fermi Paradox "哪里大家"　[查看-Oppenheimer~ Drake]

FERNANDEZ费尔南德丝fei er nan de si

Emilio "El Indio" Fernandez

生人1904 ~ 1986年 》82

FYI: aka: Emilio Fernandez Romo. Writer and director in Mexico, Fernandez is the model for today's Oscar award.

史实: 墨西哥作者经理.他是Oscar 模特人.

FERRERO费利罗fei li luo

Michele Ferrero

生人1929 ~ 2015年 》86

FYI: Italian Confectioner of sweets ie: Tic Tac mints, Rocher, nutella

史实: 意大利糖分为了Rocher.

FIESER菲泽fei ze

Louis Frederick Fieser

生人1899 ~ 1977年 》78

FYI: Chemist who invented the "napalm" bombs of the Vietnam era.1972~Vietnam-Trang bang-PHUC.

史实: 化学家谁造 "Napalm" 1972年 [查看- PHUC]

FIRESTONE费尔斯通fei er si tong

Harvey Samuel Firestone

生人1868年 ~ 1938年 》70

FYI: American business man and founder of Firestone Tires and Rubber company.

史实: 美国商业 [火石,车带]

FISH费事fei shi

Marjorie Eleanor Fish

生人1932 ~ 2013年 》80

FYI: She interviewed and gathered the data for "The Betty Hill Star Map".

史实: 她采访并收集了 "贝蒂山星图" 的数据, 星星图书. [see HILL]

FISHER费什尔fei shen er

Carrie Frances Fisher

生人1956年12月15日 ~ 2017年12月27日 》61

FYI: aka: Carrie Reynolds Fisher; "Princes Lei~Star Wars".

史实: Lei公主

[-see Reynolds]

FITZGERALD菲茨杰拉德fei ci jie la de

Ella Jane Fitzgerald

生人1917 ~ 1999年 》82

FYI:[a&e] Soul singer of the Twentieth century

史实: 二十世纪的灵魂歌唱家.

FITZIMONS

Lt. William T.Fitzimons

生人1889 ~ 1917年 》28

FYI: A United States Army officer in World War I, he was killed in a German air raid on September 4, 1917 and is considered the first American officer killed in the war.

[see Davitts]

史实: 1917年9月4日, 他在德国空袭中丧生, 被认为是第一位在战争中丧生的美国军官.

FIZEAU飞速fei song

Armand Hippolyte Louis Fizeau

生人1819 ~ 1896年 》77

FYI: French physicist, who measured the speed of light within water is known as the "Fizeau Experiment". Listed among the 72 names on the Eiffel tower: [SW03] >32/72

史实: 高名法国物理学家 "飞速式" 光内水. 新元史上埃菲尔铁塔单名.

FLACHAT法拉查特fa la cha te

Eugene Flachat

生人1802 ~ 1873年 》71

FYI: French civil engineer. He started the first railroad station in Paris. Is listed among the 72 names on the Eiffel tower。[NW15] >32/72

史实: 工程，第一次火车站.新元史上埃菲尔铁塔单名.

FLACKUS弗兰克fe lan ke

Fritz Flackus

生人1937年5月6日 》[memorial纪念]

FYI: Cook's assistant LZ- Hindenburg

史实: 炊事员LZ- 兴登堡.

FLEER菲勒尔fei le er

Frank Henry Fleer

生人1860 ~ 1921年 》61

FYI: Fleer was the first manufacturer of chewing gum and baseball cards c.1885 gumball

史实: 美国第一次口香糖和棒坛卡. [查看- w.diemer]

FLEET非异特fei yi te

Frederick Fleet

生人1887 ~ 1965年 》77 》[memorial纪念]

FYI: SS Titanic "look out" seamen. The first to spot the Iceberg.

史实: 他是第一次人查看冰山为了泰坦尼克.

FLEMING弗莱明fu lai ming

[SIR] Alexander Fleming

生人1881 ~ 1955年 》74

FYI: Biologist who developed their first successful penicillin~1928. *One sometimes finds what one is not looking for.*

史实: 高名化学家先导青霉素 1928年.*有时候, 人们会找到不想要的东西.

[看- Fleming- Chain- Florey]

FLEMING弗莱明fu lai ming

[SIR] Sanford Fleming

生人1827 ~ 1915年 》88

FYI: Canadian engineer and inventor. He was the first to suggest a Worldwide Standard Time scale for all countries. Began with the Railways of CANADA in 1883. Knighted 1897. GMT is the first zone: Greenwich [England] Mean Time.

史实: 加拿大工程和先导.倡议世纪表春点.开始在火车站的 1883年.开始在格林尼治标准时间.格林尼治平均时间.

FORAY费雷fei lei

June Foray

生人1917年 ~ 2017年 》100

FYI: [a&e] aka: June Lucille Forer; voice of Rocky the flying squirrel and many other voices. Looney Tune series

史实: 洛基的声音,飞鼠和许多其他的声音.鲁尼曲调系列

FORD福特fu te

Henry Ford

生人1863 ~ 1947年 》84

FYI: Patented pending; The first industrialist to start wide spread production of the car. *The object of education is not to fill a man's mind with facts; it is to teach him how to use his mind in thinking.

史实: 第一个开始广泛生产汽车的工业家.*教育的目的不是要用事实充实一个人的思想, 而是要教他如何在思想中运用自己的思想.

FORGIONE福希奥内fu xi ao nei

Franceseco Forgione

生人1887 ~ 1968年 》81

FYI: aka: Padre Pio; Friar, priest, stigmatist, and mystict.

史实: 修士,牧师,污名主义者和神秘主义者.

FORREST福瑞斯特fu rui si te

Nathan Bedford Forrest

生人1821 ~ 1877年 》56

FYI: Member of the "KU KLUX KLAN" >kuklux is Greek>kyklos is Latin for Circle; in the current context of "Klan" is equal to "兄弟~brother's". Circle of Brothers.

史实: "ku klux klan" 的成员 ">ku klux是希腊语>kyklos是拉丁语, 表示圆;在当前的 "klan" 上下文中, 等于 "brother's".兄弟圈.《周兄弟》.

FOUCAULT博科bo ke

Jean Bernard Leon Foucault

生人1819 ~ 1868年 》49

FYI: French physicist; known for the gyroscope and the Foucault pendulum and discovered "Eddy currents" [closed loop of electricity]. Eiffel tower: [SE10] >34/72

史实: 法国物理学家;以陀螺仪和福柯摆闻名, 发现了 "涡流" （电流闭环）.

FOURIER博拉叶bo la ye

Jean Baptiste Joseph Fourier

生人1768 ~ 1830年 》62

FYI: physicist is credited for the "green house" effect.
He is named along with the 72 names on the Eiffel tower.
[NE13] >35/72
史实: 物理学家被誉为"温室效应".他和埃菲尔铁塔上的72个名一起被命名.

FOX福克斯fu ke si
George Fox
生人1624 ~ 1694年 》70
FYI: Founder of Religious Society of Friends "Quakers".
史实: 先导为了Quaker 社

FOX福克斯fu ke si
Terrance Stanley "Terry" Fox
生人1958年8月28日 ~ 1981年7月28日 》23
FYI: "Terry Fox Run" c.1981 began the fight against cancer - Osteosarcoma.*I've said to people before that I'm going to do my very best to make it, and I'm not going to give up. And that's true. But I might not make it. And if I don't make it, the Marathon of Hope better continue.
史实: 1981年战斗癌 特里*福克斯*跑. *我之前已经对人们说过, 我会尽力做到这一点, 并且我不会放弃.没错.但是我可能做不到.如果我没有做到, 希望马拉松最好继续.

FOX福克斯fu ke si
William Fox
生人1879 ~ 1952年 》73
FYI: aka: Vilmost fried; build the first "Nickelodeon~ c.1905, than founded Twentieth Century Fox circa 1915.
史实:商业为了镍镍合金1905年,艺人电影1915年.

FRANK富兰克fu lan ke
Anne Frank
生人1929年6月~ 1945年 》16
FYI: aka: Annielies Maria "Ann" Frank; Anne Frank Diaries. Her struggles as child during WWII. "The Diary of a Young Girl".
史实: 安弗兰克日记之际WWII.

FRANKLIN富兰克林fu lan ke lin

Rosalind Elsie Franklin

生人1921 ~ 1958年 》37

FYI: X-ray crystallographer ~DNA slide 51~12 members

史实: X光照片子. [查看-51]

FREDY弗雷迪fei lei di

Pierre de Fredy

生人1863 ~ 1937年 》70

FYI: aka Pierre de Coubertin; Founder of the modern International Olympic Committee and instituting of the 5 rings**. c1894. The Coubertin Medal.

史实: 先导为了奥林匹克运动会和确立五环会徽 [查看-see Didon]

FREES法里兹fa li zi

Paul Frees

生人1920 ~ 1986年 》66

FYI: aka: Solomon Hersh Fees; He was the first of three Voices of the Pillsbury Dough-boy; many other credits. [see -j Bergman-j Cerny] insert

史实: Pillsbury*Dough-boy 发声和更多发声.

FRESNEL福瑞奈fu rui nai

Augustin Jean Fresnel

生人1788 ~ 1827年 》39

FYI: Engineer and physicist who's research in OPTICS began "wave light theory". He invented the catadioptric lens used in Light Houses. His name is among the 72 listed on the Eiffel tower [SE04] >34/72

史实: 工程和物理学家介绍光波长.介绍岸标透镜.新元史上埃菲尔 塔单名.

FREUD佛洛伊德fo luo yi de

Sigmund Schlomo Freud

生人1856年5月6日 ~ 1939年9月23日 》83

FYI: Austrian~neurologist and author. Founder of psychoanalyst.*From error to error, one discovers the entire truth.

史实: 奥地利神经学家和作家.心理分析师创始人.*从错误到错误，人们发现了全部真相.

FRIEDMAN弗里德曼fu li de man

Esther Pauline Friedman

生人1918 ~ 2002年 》84

FYI: aka "Eppi" Lederer; Ann Landers and Dear Abby were fictional advice columnist. However, Esther and Pauline were twin sisters. The first Ann L. was Ruth Crowley until her passing. *The naked truth is always better than the best dressed lie.

史实: 安•兰德斯和亲爱的艾比是虚构的咨询专栏作家.然而, 以斯和波琳是双胞胎姐妹。第一个安•L•是露丝•克劳利, 直到她去世.
*赤裸裸的事实总是比装腔作势的谎言好. [see Pauline]

FRIEDMAN弗里德曼fu li de man

Pauline Esther Friedman

生人1918 ~ 2013年 》95

FYI: aka "Popo" Phillips; Dear Abby and Ann were fictional advice columnist. However, Pauline and Esther were twin sisters. Originally the name was "Abigail Van Buren" then shortened to Abby.

史实: 亲爱的 "Abby" 曾经"阿比盖尔范布伦 "[see e.p.Friedman]

FRISCH费里斯fei li si

Ragnar Anton Kittil Frisch

生人1895 ~ 1973年 》78

FYI: Norwegian economist ~"FRISCH" Award is named in his honor.

史实:挪威人,经济学家."FRISCH" 将.

FROBEL弗罗贝尔fu luo bei er

Friedrich Wilhelm August Frobel

生人1782年4月21日 ~ 1852年6月21日 》70

FYI: Father of Kindergarten. He coined the word "Kindergarten" and is translated as "Garden for the Children." *The purpose of education is to encourage and guide man as a conscious, thinking and perceiving being...

史实: 幼儿园夫子先导.生道 "幼儿园" 它是翻译是花园为了孩子们.
《教育的目的是鼓励和引导人作为一个有意识的, 思考和感知存在的人这是我的荣幸....》

FROBISHER弗罗比合fu luo bi he

[SIR] Martin Frobisher

生人1539 ~ 1594年 》55

FYI: English seaman and pirate. FROBISHER BAY (Canada) is named in his honor.

史实: 海员.加拿大有" 弗罗比合" 海湾.

FROST弗罗斯特fu luo si te

[SIR] David Paradine Frost

生人1939 ~ 2013年 》74

FYI: Journalist, television host. Media personality in England

史实:高名在英国,主持人,新闻记者.

FROST弗罗斯特fu luo si te

Robert Lee Frost

生人1874 ~ 1963年 》89

FYI: American poet: The Road not Take.

史实:美国式:末路.

FRUM弗尔姆fu er mu

Barbara Frum

生人1937 ~ 1992年 》54

FYI: aka: Barbara Frum Roseberg; Canadian Journalist~CBC radio: "As it Happens".

史实: 加拿大人记者:CBC "正巧".

city of Edmonton public archives; Photo by Forest L. ~ 福瑞斯特

FRY弗莱fu lai

John Wesley Fry

生人1876～1946年 》88

FYI: Teacher, realtor, politician and mayor of Edmonton 1937~1945.
John Fry park in Edmonton bears his name.

史实: 仅供参考:1937~1945年埃德蒙顿的教师,房地产经纪人,政治家和市长.埃德蒙顿的约翰•弗莱公园以他的名字命名.

FRYE弗莱fu lai

Herman Northrop Frye

生人1912～1991年 》78

FYI: was a Canadian Literary critic. Author of "Fearful Symmetry-1947. Massey Lecture Series: The Educated Imagination c1962

史实: 作者,,梅西教程.

FULLER富勒fu le

Alfred Carl Fuller

生人1885～1973年 》88

FYI: the original Fuller Brush Man. c.1906 he started his own company after working for Somerville Brush and mops.

史实: 先导富勒刷工 1906 年.

FULLER富勒fu le

Richard Buckminister "Bucky" Fuller

生人1895～1983年 》87

FYI: he coined "Spaceship Earth", synergetic. Creator of the Geodesic Dome. *You can't learn less.

史实: 生道 "太空船". *你不能少学.

FUNK冯卡feng ka

Casimir Funk

生人1884～1967年 》83

FYI: First to coin the word "vitamin"from vital amines and discovered B3 [niacin]

史实: 生道 "维生素".

FURCHGOTT弗奇戈特fu qi ge te

Robert Frances Furchgott

生人1916～2009年 》93

FYI: awarded the Nobel in 1998 for pharmacology~ how nitric oxide is used in the body.

史实:诺贝尔1998年 为了化学家. [Nobelprize.org:]

~

**FYI: [Fredy] inset The Five rings and colors is derived from the 5 continents: Europe, Asia, Africa, Australia, Americas. [blue-yellow-black-green-red]

From Group "F" you can pick one person or up to ten Surnames and write their Surname in Chinese. You may try HORIZONTAL or VERTICAL in the traditional Chinese form.

G

《圣帝没有宗教》
"God has no religion."
mahatma GANDHI 甘地gan di

GABE加布jia bu

Frances Gabe

生人1915 ~ 2016年 》101

FYI: aka: Frances Grace Arnholtz; Developed the "self cleaning house". Supercenturian

史实: 介绍自己干净方

GABOR嘉柏jia bo

Zsa Zsa Gabor

生人1917 ~ 2016年 》99

FYI: [a&e] An Hungarian- American icon actress of the 19th century.

史实: 19世纪匈牙利裔美国偶像女演员.

GADDAFI卡扎菲ka zha fei

Muammar Mohammed Abu Minyar Gaddafi

生人1943 ~ 2011年 》68

FYI: Politician, political theorist and Libyan leader.

史实: 政治家,政治理论家和利比亚领导人.

GAGARIN加加林jia jia lin

Yuri Alekseyevich Gagarin

生人1934 ~ 1968年 》34

FYI: c.1961 first human in space. "Hero of the Soviet Union".*I looked and looked but I didn't see God.

史实: 先导第一次人太空人.苏联好汉.*我看了又看, 但没看见上帝.

GALILEO伽利格jia li ge

Galileo Galilei

生人1564 ~ 1642年 》78

FYI: Italian astronomer. He discovered the "Law of the Pendulum" and is how clock time is set. c1619 he coined the term "Aurora Borealis": Aurora is Latin for dawn from the Roman goddess of the Dawn.

史实: 意大利天文学家.生道 "北极光",法语为了钟摆.

Used with permission; archives City of Edmonton; Photo by Forest L. ~ 福瑞斯特

GALLAGHER加拉赫ja li he

Cornelius Gallagher

生人1854 ~ 1932年 》78 》memorial

FYI: Operated a meat processing business and also served as an Alderman then as the third Mayor of Edmonton [1896-1896]. Gallagher park in Edmonton bears his name and is the location of the annual jazz festival each summer in Edmonton.

史实: 经营着一家肉类加工企业,当时还担任埃德蒙顿市第三任市长。埃德蒙顿的加拉赫公园以他的名字命名,是每年夏天埃德蒙顿爵士音乐节的举办地。

GALLUP高勒普gao le pu

George Gallup

生人1901 ~ 1984年 》83

FYI: the "Gallup poll" is named after him as he aided many companies to determine the success rate of their product. American Institute of Public Opinion.

史实: "盖洛普民意测验"是以他的名字命名的,因为他帮助许多公司确定了他们产品的成功率.美国舆论研究所.

GALTON高尔顿gao er dun

[SIR] Frances Galton

生人1822 ~ 1911年 》89

FYI: he coined the phrase "eugenics". As well, he founded psychometrics. He is most noted for developing a method for recognizing fingerprints for forensics.

史实: 生道 "优生学",先导为了指纹.

GAMBLE甘波尔gan bo er

James Gamble

生人1806 ~ 1891年 》85

FYI: Co founder of Proctor & Gamble founded c1837 [see Proctor]

史实: 1837年先导为了 "白洁公司".

with permission St. Laurent Catholic school.

GANDHI甘地gan di

Mahatma Gandhi

生人1869 ~ 1948年 》79

FYI: aka; Mohandas Karamchand Gandhi~ Lawyer and peace activist. Public assassination. "Mahatma" is an honorific title of respect given by India in 1914. *God has no religion.

史实: 律师和和平活动家.公众暗杀. "圣雄主义" 是印度在1914年授予的尊称.*圣帝没有宗教

GANDHI甘地 gan di

Indira Pryadarshini Gandhi

生人1917 ~ 1984年 》67

FYI: First female prime minister of India until her assassination. Not related to Mahatma.

史实: 第一次女子印度洋总理.

GARLAND加兰jia lan

Judy Garland

生人1926 ~ 1969年 》43

FYI: [a&e] aka: Frances Ethel Gumm; "Dorothy" in the Wizard of Oz. Dorothy represented the individual ideal of the American people. Noted child star of early cinema. *Always be a first-rate version of yourself, instead of a second - rate version of somebody else.

史实: 绿野仙踪中的"多萝西".多萝西代表了美国人民的个人理想.早期电影院的著名儿童明星.*永远是自己的一流版本,而不是别人的一流版本. (*USA gold).

Laurent and Eleanor Garneau in their Sunday best with

Garneau Park Edmonton.

GARNEAU

Laurent Garneau

生人1840 ~ 1921年 》81

FYI: He was born to a French fur trader and a Ojibway mother of the First Nations. For the era, he assisted with the Metis and was directly involved with Louis Riel and the uprising of 1869. The photo taken at Garneau park in Edmonton, is next door to the Garneau school and movie theatre.

史实:他出生于一个法国皮草商和一个第一民族的奥吉比韦母亲.在那个时代,他协助梅蒂斯,直接参与了路易•瑞尔和1869年的起义.这张照片摄于埃德蒙顿的加诺公园,紧挨着加诺学校和电影院.

GATLING加特林 jia te lin

Richard Jordan Gatling

生人1818 ~ 1903年 》85

FYI: forerunner of the machine gun; the Gatling Gun

史实:曾经一个机枪.

GAYETTY盖蒂gai di

Joseph~C~Gayetty

FYI: first patent for Toilet paper. Circa 1860.

史实:造专利为了草纸.

GAY-LUSSAC盖-吕萨克gai-lv sa ke

Joseph Louis Gay-Lussac

生人1778 ~ 1850年 》72

FYI: Chemist and physicist; discovered that water is made of two components- namely two parts hydrogen and one part oxygen. H_2/O_1. he is among the 72 names on the Eiffel tower: [SW02] >37/72

史实:物理学家,所发现氧气.氢化学家.新元史上埃菲塔名.

GEHRIG各日工ge ri gong

Henry Louis "Lou" Gehrig

生人1903 ~ 1941年 》38

FYI: [S] was number 3 for the New York Yankees. 1939, he removed himself from baseball as a result of an unknown ailment ie: "amyotrophic lateral sclrosis "ALS. Aka Lou Gehrig disease." Hall of Fame 1939. *There is no room in baseball for discrimination. It is our national pastime and a game for all.

史实: 是纽约洋基队的第三名.1939年, 他因一种未知的疾病, 即 "肌萎缩性侧索硬化症" 退出了棒球比赛.又名Lou Gehrig疾病〉,《名人堂》,1939年.*棒球中没有歧视的余地.这是我们的民族消遣,也是所有人的游戏.

Courtesy Government of Alberta ~ portrait on upper floor Legislation building

GEORGE 'V'乔治qiao zhi

George Frederick Ernest Albert House of Marlborough

生人1865 ~ 1936年 》70

FYI: King of the United Kingdom 1910~1936. Grand Father of Elizabeth the future Queen of England.

史实: 1910~1936年英国国王.伊丽莎白的祖父, 未来的英格兰女王.

GEORGE乔治qiao zhi

Henry George

生人1839 ~ 1897年 》58

FYI: Economist and writer "Progress & Poverty"-1879

史实: 经济学家和作家 "进步与贫穷" -1879.

GERBER格尔布ge er bu

Daniel Frank Gerber

生人1898 ~ 1974年 》75

FYI: Founder of Gerber Products Company

史实: 格尔布宝贝吃饭.

GERHARDT格哈德ge ha de

Charles Frederick Gerhardt

生人1816 ~ 1856年 》40

FYI: chemist, while working for Bayer discovered the formulation for aspirin c.1853

史实: 化学家,巴尔: 阿斯匹林.

GERMAIN 姖尔曼ju er man

Marie-Sophie Germain

生人1776 ~ 1831年 》55

FYI: mathematician and physicist. He developed the Elasticity theory, Sophie Germain Prize is in her honor.

史实: 先导弹力理论.

GERONIMO杰罗尼莫jie luo ni mo

Geronimo

生人1829 ~ 1909年 》79

FYI: "the one who yawns", was an Historical Apache Indian who played a valuable part in American history.

史实: "打哈欠的人",是一个历史悠久的阿帕奇印第安人,在美国历史上发挥了重要作用.

GERSTNER郭士内 guo shi ni

Frantisek Josef Gerstner

生人1756 ~ 1832年 》76

FYI: physicist & engineer. "Theory of Wave" (Gerstner-wave), applied mathematics and hydrodynamics. Trochoidal effect.

史实: 工程和物理学家."定理".

GERVAIS杰维斯 jie wei si

Paul Gervais

生人1816 ~ 1879年 》63

FYI: aka: Francois Louis Paul Gervais; French palaeontologist and entomologist (insects)

史实: 古生物学家,昆虫学.

GESNER格斯拗ge si ne

Conrad Gesner

生人1516 ~ 1565年 》49

FYI: Father of modern zoology and botany.

史实: 夫子为了动物学.

GIFFARD古福gu fu

Baptist Jules Henri Jacques Giffard

生人1825 ~ 1882年 》57

FYI: French engineer who invented the steam injector. His name is with the 72 on the Eiffel tower. Noted for the Giffard airship. [SW16] >36/72

史实: 古福飞机,新元史上埃菲尔铁塔单名.

GILBERT吉伯特ji bo te

Augustin Nicolas Gilbert

生人1858 ~ 1927年 》69

FYI: French physician. Known for Gilbert syndrome, a mild generic liver disorder.

史实: 法国医生.以吉尔伯特综合征 (Gilbert syndrome) 而闻名,是一种轻微的普通性肝病.

GILES翟理斯zhai li si

Herbert Allen Giles

生人1845 ~ 1935年 》89

FYI: Sinology-Linguist: Chinese Romanization system. Also known as Pin Yin (Wade-Giles)

史实: 汉语罗马化.又称针阴.

GILLETT舌列she lie

King Camp Gillett

生人1855 ~ 1932年 》77

FYI: inventor of Gillett razor and businessman.

史实: 吉列剃刀的发明者和商人.

GILMAN格勒曼ge le man

Alfred Goodman Gilman

生人1941 ~ 2015年 》74

FYI: American pharmacologist. 1994 Nobel in physiology for medicine.

史实: 药理学家. 1994诺贝尔生理学. [Nobelprize.org]

GINZBURG金茨堡jin ci bao

Vitaly Lazarevich Ginszburg

生人1916 ~ 2009年 》93

FYI: awarded the Nobel in 2003 for condensed matter physics.

史实: 2003年诺贝尔为了物理学家. [Nobelprize.org]

Photo by Forest L.

GLADSTONE格拉德斯通ge la de si tong

James Gladstone

生人1887 ~1971年 》84

FYI: Trained as a printer for the Calgary Herald he also worked as an interpreter between the Blackfoot's and the English. He was the first status Indian to be elected to the Senate within Ottawa. The book 'The Gentle Persuader' is a bio of his life by H. Dempsey. 2017 his image appeared on a commemorative Canadian $10 alongside Sir John A. Macdonald, Sir George-Étienne Cartier, and Agnes Macphail.

史实: 他曾为卡尔加里先驱报当过印刷员, 也曾在黑脚怪和英国人之间做过翻译.他是第一个被选入渥太华参议院的印度人.《温柔的劝说者》是他一生的写照.2017年, 他的照片出现在一个纪念加拿大10美元的网站上, 旁边还有约翰·A·麦克唐纳爵士,乔治·蒂安·卡地亚爵士和阿格尼斯·麦克费尔爵士.

GLENN格伦ge lun

John Herschel Glenn jr.

生人1921年7月18日 ～ 2016年12月8日 》95

FYI: pilot, astronaut, congressman. mercury flight c.1962

史实: 水星飞行1962年,太空人,政治家.

GODEL哥德尔ge de er

Kurt Friedrich Godel

生人1906 ～ 1978年 》72

FYI: World renouned Mathematician, logician, philosopher.

史实: 数老师,哲学,后勤.

GOEBBELS戈培尔ge pei er

Paul Joseph Goebbels

生人1897 ～ 1945年 》48

FYI: Hitlers propaganda minister. He held a Doctorate in philosophy. Known for his public speaking abilities. Member of the Third Reich. *Third Reich refers to "Third Realm or Third Empire". The First Reich was the Roman empire [962-1806] and the Second Reich was the Hohenzollern empire [Germany 1871-1919].*...the rank and file are usually much more primitive than we imagine. Propaganda must therefore always be essentially simple and repetitious.

史实: 高名侃侃而谈,希特勒文宣部.三次帝国第一帝国是罗马帝国[962-1806],第二帝国是赫亨佐勒帝国[德国] 1871-1919]. * ……等级和档案通常比我们想象的要原始得多.因此, 宣传必须始终本质上是简单而重复的.

GOETHE哥德ge de

Johann Wolfgang von Goethe

生人1749 ～ 1832年 》83

FYI: Poet, Novelist. "Wilhelm Meister's apprenticeship" (GOETHE awards). *A man should hear a little music, read a little poetry, and see a fine picture every day of his life, in order that worldly cares may not obliterate the sense of the beautiful which God has implanted in the human soul.

史实: 诗人, 小说家."威廉•梅斯特的学徒生涯".*一个人应该每天听一点音乐, 读一点诗歌, 看一幅精美的图画, 以免世俗的关心不能抹杀上帝植入人心中的美丽感.

GOLD金 jin

[Dr.] Thomas Gold

生人1920 ~ 2004年 》84

FYI: Austrian Astrophysicist who introduced the concept that the earth creates oil on a continuous basis. [The Deep Hot Bioshphere ~Abiotic oil.] *In choosing a hypothesis there is no virtue in being timid. I clearly would have been burned at the stake in another age.

史实: 他介绍意思,地球继续制由.A-生物群由. *选择一个假设，没有胆怯的美德.我显然会在另一个时代被火刑柱烧死.

GOLDBERG戈登伯格ge deng bo ge

Reuben Barrett Lucius Goldberg

生人1883 ~ 1970年 》87

FYI: cartoonist,sculptor, author, engineer, and inventor. Awarded the REUBEN award.

史实: 漫画家,雕塑家,作家,工程师和发明家.获得鲁本奖.

GOLDFISH戈法实ge fa shi (insert jpg 15)

Samuel Goldfish

FYI: aka: Samuel Goldwyn; film producer and co-founder of "Goldwyn"(MGM).

史实: 先导电影: MGM.

GOODYEAR古德伊尔gu de yi er

Charles Goodyear

生人1800 ~ 1860年 》60

FYI: Self taught chemist and engineer. Learned how to make rubber and developed it into tires and shoes.

史实: 先导车带商业.学会了如何制造橡胶,并把它发展成轮胎和鞋子.

GORMSSON戈姆森ge mu sen

Harald 'Blatand' Gormsson

生人940 ~ 981年 》41

FYI: He was a Viking King of Denmark who brought two warring communities together. His nickname [Blatand] was Anglicized to read 'Blue-tooth' as a tooth was discolored. Japp Haartsen felt that the story of 'HB' was good symbolism of bringing together two separate industries, the PC and cellular industries and decided to use the Latin symbol to create today's 'Blue-tooth' logo. The logo is created by an H which resembles an 'X' with a vertical line through it. The 'B' over lays it to create the logo. [*thoughtCo]

史实: 他是丹麦的一位维京国王,他把两个交战的社区聚集在一起.他的绰号(blatand)被英国化为"蓝牙",因为牙齿变色了.贾普·哈特森认为"HB"的故事是将两个独立的行业,个人电脑和手机行业结合在一起的一个很好的象征,并决定用拉丁符号来创造今天的"蓝牙"标志。这个标志是由一个H创建的,它类似于一个"X",中间有一条垂直线."B"将其覆盖以创建徽标.

GOSLING高斯林gao si lin
Raymond George Gosling
生人1926 ~ 2015年 》88 》memorial
FYI: x-ray diffraction of photo 51 of the double Helix. [see- Roslind Franklin]
史实: X-光.五十一照片.

GOTTLIEB戈斯利布ge si li bu
Robert Adams Gottlieb
FYI: Editor-in-chief; Simon and Shuster.
史实: 编辑 西蒙·舒斯特.

GOUIN狗恩gou en
Ernest Gouin
生人1815 ~ 1885年 》70
FYI: A French civil engineer; built locomotives and bridges.Name appears on Eiffel tower. [SW09] >39/72
史实: 工程,火车头.新元史上埃菲尔铁塔单名.

GRAHAM 格拉汉姆ge la han mu
Albert Belmount Graham
生人1868 ~ 1960年 》92
FYI: A school master whom is considered the founder of the 4H club c1902.
史实: 4-H 为了孩子们 [看-hall-Shambaugh]

GRAHAM格拉汉姆ge la han mu

William Franklin "Billy" Graham.

生人1918 ~ 2018年 》99

FYI: Former Fuller Brush salesman, Evangelist, TV personality, author.

史实: 前富勒刷推销员,福音传道者,电视个性,作家.

GRANGER格兰杰ge lan jie

Walter Willis Granger

FYI: c1921 began the Initial excavation of zhou kou dian near Beijing.

史实:C1921在北京附近开始了周口店的初步挖掘. [see Anderson]

GRAUMAN格劳曼ge lao man

Sidney Pat~rick Grauman

生人1879 - 1950年 》70

FYI: American Showman (Grauman Chinese Theater~ Hollywood.)

史实: 美国艺人"格劳曼中国剧院".

GRAY格雷ge lei

[DR.] John Edward Gray

生人1800 ~ 1875年 》75

FYI: British Zoologist [mulluscs]. First known stamp collector c.1840.01.05

史实: 动物园.第一个已知的邮票收藏家C.1840.01.05

GRAY格雷ge lei

[DR.] Henry Gray

生人1827 ~ 1861年 》34

FYI: English anatomist and surgeon. Medical Text book: Gray's Anatomy

史实: 解剖学.医科书;医书[格雷解剖学]

GRAY格雷ge lei

Elisha Gray

生人1835 ~ 1901年 》66

FYI: Electrical engineer; forerunner of the telephone [Father of the music synthesizer]

史实: 电气工程师;电话先驱 [音乐合成器之父]

photo by Forest L.

GRAY 格雷 ge lei
George Kruger Gray

生人1880 ~ 1943年 》63

FYI: British artist, best remembered for his designs of coinage and stained glass windows. He designed the Canadian 5 cent coin with the Beaver [national animal] on the reverse. Depending on the year, the Monarch can be seen with or without a crown on the opposing side. Please see miscellaneous.

史实: 英国艺术家, 因其对硬币和彩色玻璃窗的设计而闻名.他设计了加拿大5美分硬币, 背面是海狸 (国家动物).根据年份的不同, 君主可以戴皇冠也可以不戴皇冠.请参阅杂项.

GRAY 格雷 ge lei
Barry Gray

生人1916 ~ 1996年 》80

FYI: aka Bernard Yaroslaw; know as the Father of Talk Radio.

史实: 夫子为了广播节目.

GRAY 格雷 ge lei
William "Bill" Mason Gray

生人1929 ~ 2016年 》87

FYI: Atmospheric Science: Colorado State U. Noted for discovering the cycles of Tropical Storm forecasting.

史实: 热带风暴天气预报.

GREGG格雷戈ge lei ga

John Robert Gregg

生人1867 ~ 1948年 》61

FYI: Educator, publisher and inventor of the eponymous "shorthand" system. Gregg Shorthand system published Light-line phonograph c1888.

史实: 学府,作者和发明,速记 "格雷格*速记系统 ".[see- I.PITMAN] [*wiki.]

photo by Forest L.

GREEN格林ge lin

Nancy Green

生人1834 ~ 1923年 》89

FYI: story teller, cook, activist and FIRST African-American to model as "Aunt Jamima" for Davis Milling.

史实: 格林一个黑女,评化,厨师," 贾玛妈"是一个牌子.

GREENE格林ge lin

Lorne Hyman Greene

生人1915 ~ 1987年 》72

FYI: [a&e] aka Lyon Himan Green; Canadian-American actor known for several films. He was the host of 'New Wilderness'.

史实: 加拿大裔美国演员,因几部电影而出名.他是 "新荒野" 的主人.

GREGORY XIII格雷果里 ge lei guo li十三

Pope Gregory XIII

生人1502 -~ 1585年 》83

FYI: aka Ugo Boncompagni introduced the Gregorina Calender: circa.1582 and replaced the Julian. 01 Jan ~ 31 Dec.

史实: 介绍了格雷戈里纳日历:大约1582年，并取代朱利安.1月1日至12月31日.

City of Edmonton public archive

GRIESBACH格里斯巴赫ge li si ba he

William Antrobus Griesbach

生人1878 ~ 1945年 》67

FYI: Major General Griesbach, decorated soldier, politician, and youngest Mayor in Edmonton's history. Edmonton military barracks named in his honor.

史实: 格里斯巴赫少将，被授予勋章的士兵,政治家和埃德蒙顿历史上最年轻的市长.埃德蒙顿军营以他的名字命名.

GRIFFIN格里芬ge li fen

Merv Griffin

生人1925 ~ 2007年 》82

FYI: aka: Mervin Edward "Merv" Griffin jr.; Television personality and game show creator.

史实: 艺人.电视个性和游戏节目创作者.

GRIFFITH格里菲恩ge li fei en

Frederick Griffith

生人1879 ~ 1941年 》62

FYI: Pioneer of observing cells transforming into a new strain ie; DNA replication circa 1928. [DNA strand]

史实: 1928 年去氧核糖核酸.

GRIGG格里戈ge li ge

Charles Leiper Grigg

生人1868 ~ 1940年 》72

FYI: Chemist and entrepreneur who developed the 7up brand. It originally was called Lithiated Lemon-Lime soda. The LITHIUM contained in the drink had a standard chemical number of [6.94] hence 7 up.

史实: 化学家,企业家.反应为了7up 饮料.

GRISSOM格里森ge li sen

Virgil Ivan "Gus" Grissom

生人1926 ~ 1967年 》41 》[memorial纪念]

FYI: NASA Astronaut, test pilot, engineer. Apollo 1 fire.

史实: NASA 太空人,工程.火死. [see- E.White, R.Chaffee]

GROVE归入沃gui ru wo

[SIR] William Robert Grove

生人1811 ~ 1896年 》85

FYI: Physical scientist; invented the Grove Voltaic cell

史实: 发明 "归入我点子伏".

GUATAMA寡头吗 gua tou ma

Siddhartha Guatama [Buddha]

生人563 ~ 483年BC

FYI: The word "Buddha" is the equivalent of a Great Prophet or Sage or "awakened one". *There is nothing more dreadful than the habit of doubt.

史实: "佛" 这个词相当于伟大的先知或圣人或 "觉醒者".*没有比怀疑习惯更可怕的东西了.

GUILEY吉利gui li
Rosemary Ellen Guiley
生人1950~ 2019年 》69
FYI: American writer on supernatural, radio host, trained hypnotist. 'The Encyclopedia of Saints'~ 2001. "True healing must come first at the Soul level... prayer aligns our souls with God... By aligning ourselves with God - this highest possible state of unconditional love, joy, and wholeness - we can overcome anything, be healed of all afflictions."

史实: 美国超自然作家, 电台主持人, 训练有素的催眠师.《圣徒百科全书》~2001年. "真正的疗愈必须在灵魂层面首先出现…祈祷使我们的灵魂与上帝保持一致…通过使我们自己与上帝保持一致——这是无条件的爱,快乐和完整的最高境界——我们可以克服任何事情, 治愈所有的痛苦."

GUILLOTINE给利题恩gei li ti en
Joseph- Ignance Guillotine
生人1738 ~ 1814年 》76
FYI: French physician, politician. c1789 proposed a method for the death penalty. The "guillotine" was named after his suggestions. [see- a.Louis]
史实: 法国医生."给力特恩" 为了死人. [看- a.Louis]

GUINNESS古尼斯gu ni si
Arthur Guinness
生人1725 ~ 1803年 》78
FYI: Irish brewer and entrepreneur. His name would be used for the Guinness book of World Records by Beaver. [see - Beaver]
史实: 啤酒厂.他名字为了世纪.

GUTENBERG古登堡 gu deng bao
Johannes Gensfleich zur Laden zum Gutenberg
生人1400 ~ 1468年 》68
FYI: Blacksmith, goldsmith, printer and publisher. Inventor in Europe of the printing press. The Gutenberg bible was known as the 42 line Bible.
史实: 印刷所*发表.曾经四十二拍.

GUTENBERG古登堡 gu deng bao

Beno Gutenberg

生人1889 ~ 1960年 》71

FYI: co inventor of the Richter Scale. [see Richter- Wadati]

史实: 造"李希特量表" ~ 尺度.

GYORGY乔治qiao zhi

Paul Gyorgy

生人1893 ~ 1976年 》82

FYI: Biochemist who isolated Riboflavin, B6 and Bioton.

史实: 分离核黄素,B6和生物素的生化学家.

GZOWSKY给做斯卡 gei zuo si ke

Peter John Gzowsky

生人1934 ~ 2002年 》68

FYI: radio personality and host for CBC: Morning Side. He was nicknamed "Captain Canada".

史实: 加拿大高名, 广播家目人.他绰号 "加拿大船长".

From Group "G" you can pick one person or up to ten Surnames and write their Surname in Chinese. You may try HORIZONTAL or VERTICAL in the traditional Chinese form.

《没有乐趣的生活是悲惨的》
"Life would be tragic if it weren't funny!"
Stephen HAWKING霍金huo jin

* Often in Chinese when they translate from Foreign to Chinese the letter "H" is given the "xi (she)" sound.

HAGAMAN哈嘎慢ha ga man
Allen Orlando Hagaman
生人1937年5月6日 ~ mem
FYI: civilian linesman. LZ- Hindenburg . [see M. Wall]
史实: 普通人死了.

photo by Forest L.

HAHN哈恩ha en
Emanuel Otto Hahn
生人1881 ~ 1957年 》75
FYI: German Canadian sculptor and coin designer of the Canadian dime. Since 1922 it is the smallest coin. The ship was the Bluenose.
He also drew the design for the Canadian quarter of the caribou.
史实: 加拿大一角硬币的德国-加拿大雕塑家和硬币设计师.自1922年以来, 它是最小的硬币.船是蓝鼻子. [A.Currie]

HAINES海恩斯hai en si
William Lister Haines
生人September 17, 1908 - November 18, 1989年 》81
FYI: An American author, screenwriter, and playwright. *Limits exist only in the soul's of Those who don't dream.
史实: 美国作家,编剧和剧作家.*限制只存在于那些不做梦的人的灵魂中.

HALE 海尔 hai er

George Ellery Hale

生人1868 ~ 1938年 》70

FYI: Solar Astronomer: discovery of magnetic fields on the sun: spectroheliograph. [查看- E.Rutherford, W.Huggins, N.Lockyer,]

史实: 天文学家, 磁场上太阳.

HALL 哈勒 ha le

Frank Haven Hall

生人1841 ~ 1911年 》70

FYI: American inventor and essayist who helped improve the Braille reading system for the blind; Hall -Braille writer. The system allows for 256 possible configurations of 8 dots each.

史实: 他改善布莱尔文风启用八圈点.二百五十六位形[看- Braille]

HALL 哈雷 ha lei

Otis~E~Hall

FYI: wrote the "4H pledge". Head, Heart, Hands, Health. 4-H motto: to make the best better.

史实: 他写四H发誓:头, 心, 手, 健康。最好最好好

[看 a.b.Graham, JF Shambaug

HALL 哈雷 ha lei

Joyce Clyde Hall

生人1891 ~ 1982年 》91

FYI: founder of Hallmark Cards

史实: 先导哈雷卡.

HALL 哈罗 ha luo

[SIR] Benjamin Hall

生人1802 ~ 1867年 》65

FYI: Welsh civil engineer and politician. The Big Ben bell in the London Tower was nicknamed in his honor.

史实:工程, 政治家.《Big Ben》 伦敦英国 [看- Pugin]

HALL哈罗ha luo

Monty Hall

生人1924 ~ 2017年 》96

FYI: [a&e] aka Monte Halparin. Game show host [Lets make a deal] and philanthropist.

史实: 游戏节目主持人[让我们做个交易]和慈善家.

HALEY哈雷ha lei

John Joseph "Jack" Haley jr.

生人1897 ~ 1979年 》82

FYI: [a&e] stage, radio and film, best known for playing "Tin Man" in Wizard of Oz. He represented "the Iron workers of America"

史实: 舞台,广播和电影, 最著名的是在《绿野仙踪》中扮演 "铁人".他代表 "美国的钢铁工人". [查看~ bolger- lahr- haley-]

HALEY哈雷ha lei

Alexander Murray Palmer Haley

生人1921 ~ 1992年 》71

FYI: American writer and author of 1976 book "Roots" a genealogical book of a Black-American family.

史实: 美国作家, 1976年《根》一书的作者, 该书是美国黑人家庭的家谱书.

HALLEY哈雷ha lei

Edmund Halley

生人1656 ~ 1742年 》86

FYI: Discovered the motions of the great Halley comet.

史实: 发现了哈雷彗星的运动.

HARBURG哈尔堡ha er bao

Edgar Yipsil "Yip" Harburg

生人1896 ~ 1981年 》84

FYI: American popular song lyrist. "Over the Rainbow: Wizard of Oz" [see-Baum]

史实: 美国流行歌曲抒情诗人.歌写:在桑彩虹.

HARDISTY哈蒂斯题ha di si ti

Richard Charles Hardisty

生人1831 ~ 1889年 》58

FYI: Early fur trader, politician and Parliament senator. Town of Hardisty in Alberta Canada is named in his honor.

(Senator Hardisty's Prairies - jg_MacGregor)

史实:早加拿大贸易, 政治家.哈蒂斯特市 艾伯特,加拿大

[*parliament of Canada]

HARINGTON哈林顿ha lin dun

[SIR] John Harington

FYI: author, first to invent the FLUSH Toilet..post 1560.

史实: 作者, 先导WC 1560

HARLAND哈兰德ha lan de

[SIR] Edward James Harland

生人1831 ~ 1895年 》62

FYI: politician~shipbuilder (SS Titanic)

史实:政治家, 航 SS Titanic

Edmonton South Division ~ photo by Forest L.

HARLEY哈雷ha lei

William Sylvester Harley

生人1880 ~ 1943年 》63

FYI: co founder of Harley-Davidson. First designed for use on a peddle bike frame becoming a 'power bike' or 'motor bicycle'. Arthur and his two brothers William D. and Walter D. assisted until the first prototype was ready on 1904 Sept 8. ready for the Milwaukee motor cycle race, placing 4th. [see- Arthur Davidson]

史实 哈雷戴维森联合创始人.首先设计用于步行自行车车架,成为"电动自行车"或"机动自行车".亚瑟和他的两个兄弟威廉和沃尔特D.一直在帮助他,直到1904年9月8日第一个原型完成。准备好参加密尔沃基摩托车赛,排名第四.

HART哈特ha te

Stewart Edward Hart

生人1915 ~ 2003年 》88

FYI: Canadian Icon in professional wrestling and co-founder of Stampede Wrestling~ Calgary Canada. 2000~ "Order of Canada"

史实: 专业搏击;先导 《踩踏摔跤》卡尔加里*艾伯特.

HARTLEY哈特利 ha te li

Wallace Henry Hartley

生人1878 ~ 1915年 》37 》[memorial纪念]

FYI: Titanic 1915: Bandleader on the RMS Titanic.

史实: 乐团皇家邮轮泰坦尼克号上的乐队指挥.

HARVARD哈佛ha fo

John Harvard

生人1607年11月26日 ~ 1638年 》31

FYI: Pastor and educator. Harvard University is named in his honor.

史实: 牧师和教育家.哈佛大学以他的名字命名.《哈佛大学》

HARVEY哈维ha wei

Paul Harvey Aurandt

生人1918 ~ 2009年 》90

FYI: Icon in American radio broadcasting. His program, "and now you know The Rest of the Story."

史实: 高名美国广播节目."现在你知道故事"

HASSENFELD海森福尔德hai sen fu er de

* three brothers: Herman, Hillel and Henry

FYI: started HASBRO c 1923

史实: 开始:哈斯兄弟商业.

HAMILTON哈米尔顿 ha mi er tun

Margaret Brainard Hamilton

生人1902～1985年 》82

FYI: [a&e] The Wizard of Oz: Wicked Witch of the West. She represented the Money brokers of Western America. She was the Top-ranked female villain of her era.

史实:高名最好反派 "邪恶女巫". 早电影. (*USA gold).

HAMNER汉姆纳han mu na

Earl Hamner Jr.

生人1924年7月10日～2016年 》92

FYI: prolific writer and producer of such shows as "The Walton's"

史实: 美国人作者和出品人.

HANCOCK哈那克ha na ke

John Hancock

生人1937～1793年 》56

FYI: Merchant and Statesman. John Hancock became the synonym for "a large signature" hence the Declaration of Independence.

史实: 商业, 政治家. "大下款"为了独立宣言.

HANDLER韩德勒尔han de le er

Elliot and Ruth Handler

生人1916～2011年 》95

FYI: with Harold Matt Matson co founder of *Mattel c1945; Ruth introduced the "Barbie doll" from Barbara after their daughter.

史实:*Mattel 商业. Elliott 女儿是 "芭比娃娃 ".

HANNA汉纳han na

William Denby "Bill" Hanna

生人1910 ~ 2001年 》91

FYI: Animator with Hanna- Barbera. (Flintstones, Jetsons)

史实: 高名动画. [see -Barbera]

HARVEY哈维ha wei

Paul Harvey

生人1943 ~ 2001年 》58

FYI: akan Paul Harvey Aurant; was an American broadcaster. He had on radio, three sound bytes each day about the inside scoop on people both famous and nonfamous. At the end of each story he would add "and now you know The Rest of the Story."

史实: 是个美国广播公司.他在收音机里每天播放三个关于名人和非名人的内幕消息.在每个故事的结尾, 他都会加上.《现在你知道故事》

HARRISON哈若森ha rui sen

George Harrison

生人1943 ~ 2001年 》58

FYI: He is the second of the Beatles to pass away. He is known as the quiet Beetle before playing with other groups.[see- Lennon]

史实: 他是披头士中第二个去世的.在和其他乐队一起演奏之前, 他被称为 "安静的披头士".

HASEK哈塞克ha se ka

Jaroslav Hasek

生人1883 ~ 1923年 》40

FYI: was a Czech writer best known for "the Good Soldier Svejk"

史实: 作者 "好士兵Svejk" [捷克].

HAUY或衣huo yi

Rene Just Hauy

FYI: renouned mineralogist. Named among the 72 listed on the Eiffel tower. [SE13]> 40/72 insert

史实: 法国矿物学.新元史上埃菲尔铁塔单名.

HASKELL哈克尔ha ke er

Russel~G~Haskell

生人1935 ~ 1975年 》40 》[memorial纪念]

FYI: SS Edmund Fitzgerald~Lake Superior 10 Nov 1975

史实: S.S. 埃德蒙*菲茨杰拉德 湖高强1975年 11月10日

HAWKING霍金huo jin

[Prof.] Stephen William Hawking

生人1942年1月8日 ~ 2018年3月14日 》76

FYI: World renouned British physicist. 'A Brief History of Time. The Universe in a Nutshell'. Prof. Hawking held 12 honorary degrees. His disease was ALS. *Life would be tragic if it weren't funny!

史实: 世界著名的英国物理学家."时间简史.简言之，宇宙.霍金教授获得12个荣誉学位.他的病是ALS.《没有乐趣的生活是悲惨的》

Public archive and Hawrelak Park Edmonton

HAWRELAK霍若拉克huo ru la ke

William Hawrelak

生人1915 ~ 1975年 》60

FYI: Canadian politician and longest serving Mayor in Edmonton Alberta Canada. Hawrelak Park in Edmonton is named in his honor.

史实: 加拿大政治家和在加拿大埃德蒙顿阿尔伯塔任职时间最长的市长.埃德蒙顿的霍雷拉克公园以他的名字命名.

HAWTHORNE霍桑huo sang

Nathaniel Hawthorne

生人1804 ~1864年 》62

FYI: American novelist and short story writer.

史实: 美国小说家和短篇小说作家.

HAY海hai

Louise Lynn Hay

生人1926 ~ 2017年 》91

FYI: American motivational speaker and founder of Hay House publishing. *It's okay to learn from every experience, and it's okay to make mistakes.

史实: 美国励志演说家和 Hay House出版社.*可以从各种经验中习, 他可以犯错误.

HAYDN海德恩hai de en

Joseph Haydn

生人1732 ~ 1809年 》77

FYI: Austrian composer of the classical period. Is considered the "Father of the Symphony".

史实: 奥地利古典时期的作曲家.被认为是《交响乐之父》

HAYEK海克hai ke

Frederick August Hayek

生人1899 ~ 1992年 》93

FYI: aka Frederick August von Hayek. Economist and philosopher. Was awarded the Nobelprize in 1974 for"Economic Science

史实: 经济学者.1974年 嘉奖诺贝尔为了经济. [Nobelprize.org] [See Gunnar Mydal-]

HAYES海斯hai si

Victor "Vic" Hayes

生人1941年 ~ active

FYI: "Father of Wi-Fi" since 1990. ~ today's WLAN. [wireless local area network]

史实: 无线电*无限八路. [see- j.O'Sullivan]

HEARST赫斯特he si te

William Randolph Hearst

生人1863 ~ 1951年 》88

FYI: Politician and newspaper publisher. He invented 'tabloid journalism'. Because of political views, was depicted as the "Scarecrow" in Wizard of Oz by L Frank Baum. The Scarecrow represented the "American farmers" of the twentieth century.(*Q) You furnish the pictures and I'll furnish the war. [bolger-lahr-haley-]

史实: 政治家和报纸出版商.他发明了"小报新闻".由于政治观点, 被L Frank Baum描绘成《绿野仙踪》中的"稻草人".稻草人代表二十世纪的"美国农民".(*q) 你提供图片, 我将提供战争.

HEARST赫斯特he si te

William Randolph Hearst Sr.

生人1863 ~ 1951年 》80

FYI: American businessman, newspaper publisher, and politician known for developing the nation's largest newspaper chain and media company. *Don't be afraid to make a mistake, your readers might like it.

史实: 美国商人,报纸出版商和政治家, 以发展美国最大的报纸连锁和媒体公司而闻名. *不要害怕犯错误, 你的读者可能会喜欢.

HEAVISIDE海维赛德hai wei sai de

Oliver Heaviside

生人1850 ~ 1925年 》75

FYI: Physics, engineering. Patented the "coaxial cable" c.1880

史实: 物理学家, 工程.专利 "同轴电缆".

HEFNER赫夫纳he fu na

Hugh Marston Hefner

生人1926年4月9日 ~ 2017年9月27日 》91

FYI: American business man, Editor-in-Chief PLAYBOY

史实:商业,编辑为了花花公子.

HEIMLICH海姆利杀hai mu li sha

Henry Judah Heimlich

生人1920 ~ 2016年 》96

FYI: medical doctor known for introducing the "Heimlich maneuver" named on his behalf.

史实: 以介绍"海姆利希手法"而闻名的医学博士.

HEINZ海恩茨hai en ci

Henry John Heinz

生人1844年10月11日 ~ 1919年 》74

FYI: German businessman and founder of Heinz tomato ketchup c1876

史实: 希洪将.德国商人，海因茨番茄酱创始人c1876.

HEISENBERG海森布格hai sen bu ge

Werner Karl Heisenberg

生人1901 ~ 1976 》75

FYI: GERMAN physicist who held the equation to the trigger of the A-bomb during WW2 but withheld it from Hitler.

史实: 德国物理学家.他扣压炸弹从希特勒.

HELLER海勒hai li

Joseph Heller

生人1923 ~ 1999年 》76

FYI: Novelist, screenwriter ~ coined: catch-22 c.1961 "Catch-22: a satire."

史实: 小说家，编剧 ~ 创造了:第22条.

HELLYER赫利尔he li er

Paul Theodore Hellyer

生人1923年 ~ active

FYI: Served for the National Defence for Canada. Author of "Money mafia".

史实: 曾为加拿大国防部服务.《金钱黑手党》的作者.

HERSCHEL赫谢尔he xie er

Frederick William Herschel

生人1738 ~ 1822年 》84

FYI: British astronomer, Discovered Uranus in 1781. Discovered Infrared Radiation. First president of the Royal Astronomical Society c1820

史实: 天文学家, 天王星. 皇家天文学会第一任主席C1820

HESIOD赫西奥德ha xi ao de

Hesiod

FYI: c.BC unknown; founder of the farmers almanac

史实: 农历创始人.

HEMINGWAY海明威 hai ming wei

Ernest Miller Hemingway

生人1899年7月21日 ~ 1961 》62

FYI: American novelist, short story writer *awarded the Nobelprize in 1954 for Literature. "Old Man and the Sea:1952 ;The Sun also Rises:1926. *There is no friend as loyal as a book.

史实: 美国小说家,短篇小说作家*于1954年获得诺贝尔文学奖.《老人与海:1952年》*太阳也升起:1926年. * 没有像书一样忠诚的朋友. [Nobelprize.org]

photo by Forest L. Edmonton Highway

HENDAY 亨迪 heng di

Anthony Henday

FYI: British trader for the HBC. In Canada, several places named after him, including the Anthony Henday highway in Edmonton is named in his honor.

史实: 英国HBC交易员.在加拿大.以他的名字命名的几个地方,包括埃德蒙顿的安东尼-亨利高速公路,都是以他的名字命名的.

HENDEE 很低 hen di

George Mallory Hendee

生人1866～1943年 》77

FYI: Founder of the "Indian motorbike".c1901

史实: "印度摩托车" 创始人.

HENDRICK 很都克 hen du ke

E~G~Hendrik

FYI: isolated the Riboflavin molecule in 1926

史实: 维他命 1926年

HENRY 亨利 heng li

Joseph Henry

生人1797～1878年 》81

FYI: Scientist. Invented the "door bell". The [H unit] name in his honor. The first secretary of the Smithsonian.

史实: 科学家.发明了"门铃".以他的名义命名.史密森学会的第一任秘书.

City of Edmonton public archive

HENRY亨利 heng li

William Thomas Henry

生人1871 ~ 1952年 》79

FYI: Real state agent, business man and politician. First served as an Edmonton Alderman then as the mayor from 1914~1917. Henry avenue in Edmonton is named after him.

史实: 真正的国家代理人,商人和政治家.1914年至1917年先后担任埃德蒙顿市议员和市长.埃德蒙顿的亨利大街是以他的名字命名的.

HENRY VIII亨利heng li

Henry Tudor

生人1491年6月28日 ~ 1547年 》56

FYI: As the king, was most notable for being married to six women during his reign. He was an author and composer.

史实: 有六号太太. 他是一位作家和作曲家.

HENSON很森hen sen

James Maury "Jim" Henson

生人1936 ~ 1990年 》54

FYI: Puppeteer and creator of Kermit the frog and Miss Piggy.

*Life's like a movie, write your own ending. Keep believing, keep pretending.

史实: 木偶演员,青蛙克米特和小猪小姐的创造者.*生活就像电影,写下自己的结局. 继续相信,继续假装.

HEPBURN赫本he ben

Audrey Hepburn

生人1907 ~ 2003年 》63

FYI: [a&e] AKA Audrey Kathleen Ruston; Actress, Presidential Medal of Freedom, UNICEF Goodwill Ambassador. Sophie the robot is modeled after Hepburn. *The beauty of a woman is not in a facial mode but the true beauty in a woman is reflected in her soul. It is the caring that she lovingly gives the passion that she shows. The beauty of a woman grows with the passing years.

史实: 女演员,总统自由勋章,联合国儿童基金会亲善大使.机器人索菲是模仿赫本的. * 女人的美丽不是面部表情,而是女人的真正美丽反映在她的灵魂中.她充满爱心地给予了她所表现出的热情.女人的美丽随着岁月的流逝而增长.

HERACLITUS赫拉克利特he la ke li te

Heraclitus

生人535 ~ 475年BC 》60

FYI: Greek philosopher. "The path up and the path down are one and the same."

史实: 希腊哲学家《向上走的路和向下的路是同一条路》

HERBART赫尔巴斯he er ba si

Johann Friedrich Herbart

生人1776 ~ 1841年 》65

FYI: German philosopher and founder of "Pedagogy as an academic discipline."

史实: 德国哲学家和"教育学作为一门学科"的创始人.

HERSHEY赫希he xi

Milton Snavely Hershey

生人1857 ~ 1945年 》88

FYI: American philanthropist. Founder of Hershey's chocolate. (hershey bar 1900, hershey kisses 1907, hershey almonds 1908)

史实: 美国慈善家.好时巧克力的创始人.

HERTZ赫兹he zi

Heinrich Rudolf Hertz

生人1857年2月22日 ~ 1894年 》37

FYI: German physicist researched electromagnetic waves; Hz unit of frequency.

史实: 德国物理学家研究电磁波;频率单位.

HESTON喝斯恩he si en

William Heston

FYI: co-founder of Quaker oats with Henry D. Seymour. Registered the brand c1877. [see -Crowell]

史实: 桂格燕麦与亨利·D·西摩共同创始人.

HESTON喝斯恩he si en

Charlton Heston

生人1923 ~ 2008年 》85

FYI: [a&e] American actor: The Ten Commandments, Ben Herr. Gun activist in America

史实: 美国艺人.十条戒律, 本•赫尔.美国的枪支活动家.

HEWLETT木利特mu li te

Maurice Henry Hewlett

生人1861 ~ 1923年 》62

FYI: Poet and essayist.

史实: 式, 作者.

HEWLETT木利特mu li te

William Redington Hewlett

生人1913 ~ 2001年 》87

FYI: Engineer and inventor and co-founder of Hewlett-Packard.

* There is a time and a place for creativity.

史实: 工程师,发明家,惠普联合创始人 [see D -Packard]*有时间和创造力的地方.

HEYSE海泽hai ze

Paul Johann Ludwig Heyse

生人1830 ~ 1914年 》84

FYI: awarded the Nobel in 1910 for Literature in poetry and prose.

史实: 式, 1910年嘉奖诺贝尔为了文章. [Nobelprize.org]

HICHENS希钦斯xi qin si

Robert Hichens

生人1882 ~ 1940年 》58 》[memorial纪念]

FYI: SS Titanic QM at the Wheel. Command of safety boat # 6

史实: 安全主管为了泰坦尼克号

HICKOK希科克xi ke ke

James Butler "Wild Bill" Hickok

生人1937 ~ 1876年 》39

FYI: He was considered a LEGEND from the Wild West. Professional gambler, scout, spy. Killed during a card game.

史实: 他被认为是来自蛮荒西部的传奇人物.职业赌徒, 童子军, 间谍.在纸牌游戏中被杀.

HICKS希克斯xi ke si

[SIR] John Richard Hicks

生人1904 ~ 1989年 》85

FYI: Renouned economists known for the "welfare theory".

史实: 以"福利理论"闻名的著名经济学家.

HIGGS希格斯xi ge si

Peter Ware Higgs

生人1929年 ~ active

FYI: was awarded the Nobel prize in 2013 for Physics. Also known for the "Higgs mechanism".

史实: 物理学家 .嘉奖2013诺贝尔. [Nobelprize.org]

HIGLEY希格利xi ge li

Dr. Brewster M Higley

FYI: Doctor in Kansas became renown for writing the state song "Home on the Range" c1873.

史实: 堪萨斯医生因写国歌《响家》而声名远扬.

HILBERT希尔伯特xi er bo te

David Hilbert

生人1862 ~ 1943年 》81

FYI: German mathematician. Notable for the "proof theory".

史实: 德国数学家.以"证明理论"著称.

HILL哈乐ha le

Barney Hill

生人1922 ~ 1969年 》47

FYI: American's Barney and wife Betty were common people who had a very uncommon experience in 1961, Sept 19 around 10:30 pm. (The interrupted Journey 1966)

史实: 美国的巴尼和妻子贝蒂是普通人,他们在1961年9月19日晚上10:30左右有着非常不寻常的经历.

HILLARY哈利勒ha li le

Edmund Hillary

生人1919 ~ 2008年 》 89

FYI: Mountaineer and explorer. The first to Climb Mt Everest with T.Norgay.

史实: 登山者和探险家.第一个攀登珠穆朗玛峰的人T.诺盖. [See Tenzing Norgay]

HINCKLEY欣克利xin ke li

Gordon Bitner Hinckley

生人1910 ~ 2008年 》98 》[感念]

FYI: Business man and *15th president of the LDS church 1995-2008.* *Life is meant to be enjoyed, not just endured.*

史实: 十五号耶稣基督后期圣徒教会.*生活是应该享受的, 而不仅仅是忍受.

HINDENBURG兴登堡 xing deng bao

Paul Ludwig Hans Anton von Hindenburg

生人1847 ~ 1934年 》87

FYI: The air ship "LZ- Hindenburg" was named after the Chancellor. 1925~1934 the chancellor was replaced by Hitler c1934

史实: 德国大臣, 年1925-1834兴登堡.

HINES希恩斯 xi en si

Duncan Ludlow Hines

生人1880 ~ 1959年 》79

FYI: restaurant chain and cake brand.

史实: 商业,蛋糕牌子.

HIPPOCRATES希坡卡特司xi po ka te si

Hippocrates

生人460 ~ 370年 BC 》90

FYI: Greece physician The Hippocratic OATH is taken by Doctors in honor of him.

史实: 希腊医生希波克拉底誓言是由医生为他而作的.

HITCHCOCK希区阿克xi qu a ke

[SIR] Alfred Joseph Hitchcock

生人1899 ~ 1980年 》81

FYI: [a&e] Famous American film producer of thriller and suspense shows. *There is no terror in a bang, only in the anticipation of it.*

史实: 美国著名的惊悚片和悬疑片制片人. *爆炸没有恐怖。只有在期待它的时候.

HITCHINGS希钦之xi qin zhi

George Herbert Hitchings

生人1905 ~ 1998年 》93

FYI: scientist and pharmacist. Was awarded the Nobel in 1988 for pharmacology co-award with Black and Elion. [看- James White black, Gertrude belle Elion]

史实: 药剂师 1988年嘉奖诺贝尔. [*Nobelprize.org]

HITLER希特勒xi te le

Adolf Hitler

生人1889年4月20日 ~ 1945年 》56

FYI: Political leader and chancellor of Germany during WW2.

* I use emotion for the many and reserve reason for the few.

史实: 二战期间德国的政治领袖和总理.*我为许多人运用情感，为少数人保留理由.

HODGKIN霍可金huo ke jin

Dorothy Mary Crowfoot Hodgkin

生人1910 ~ 1994年 》84

FYI: is regarded as a pioneer in x-ray crystallography, as well she solved the structure of penicillin. She was also able to advance the knowledge of B12.

史实: 被认为是X射线结晶学的先驱,也解决了青霉素的结构问题.她还能够提高B12的知识. [查看-see Bordan]

HOFFA活法huo fa

James Riddle Jimmy Hoffa

生人1913 ~ 1975年 》62

FYI: Labour union. Founder of the Teamsters.

史实: 工会.团队成员的创始人.

HOFFMAN霍夫曼huo fu man

Jules~A~Hoffman

生人1941年 ~ active

FYI: awarded the Nobel for immunity-medicine in 2011 in Biologist.

史实: 化学家2011年嘉奖诺贝尔. [Nobelprize.org]

HOFMANN霍夫曼huo fu man

Albert Hofmann

生人1906 ~ 2008年 》102

FYI: Swiss scientist who discovered lysergic acid diethylamide (LSD), it was first synthesized on 16 Nov 1938. He was a super-centurion.

史实: 瑞士科学家,发现了麦角酸二乙酰胺（LSD）,1938年11月16日首次合成.他是个超级百夫长.

With permission Alberta government. The garden; Photo by Forest L.

HOLE

Lois Elsa Hole

生人1929 ~ 2005年 》76

FYI: Known as the Queen of Hugs. She was a business woman, academic, author and Canadian politician. From 2000 February 10 she served as the 15th Lieutenant Governor of the Alberta government until her passing.

史实: 被称为拥抱女王.她是一位女商人,学者,作家和加拿大政治家.从2000年2月10日起,她一直担任阿尔伯塔省政府的第15任副省长,直到去世.

HOLL霍尔huo er

George~J~Holl

生人1915 ~ 1975年 》60 》[memorial纪念]

FYI: S.S. Edmund Fitzgerald~ Chief Engineer 10 Nov 1975 memorial

史实: S.S.Edmund Fitzgerald~总工程师.

HOLLIDAY霍利黛huo li dai

John Henry "Doc" Holliday

生人1851 ~ 1887年 》36

FYI: American gambler, gun slinger, DENTIST. OK corral incident

史实: 早美国赌, 枪手, 牙医. [查看~ Earp]

HOLMES霍姆斯 huo mu si

Oliver Wendell Holmes Sr.

生人1809 ~ 1894年 》85

FYI: American physician, poet and polymath. A member of the 5 *Fireside Poets ie: Longfellow, Wittier, Bryant, Lowell, Holmes.

The sound of a kiss is not so loud as that of a cannon, but its echo lasts a great deal longer.

史实: 美国式。。。看式人.5个炉边诗人中的一员. *亲吻的声音不象大跑那样响亮， 但是回声可以持持续更长的时间.

HOMME侯马hou ma

Robert "Bob" Homme

生人1919 ~ 2000年 》81

FYI: The Friendly Giant. Canadian Television personality. Casey and Finnegan were the guests puppets. Order of Canada 1998 Nov 02. *Look up- way up!

史实: 友好的巨人.加拿大电视个性.凯西和芬尼根是客人的木偶.加拿大法令1998年11月2日. *"向上看-向上看".

HOPKINS霍普金斯huo pu jin si

Johns Hopkins

生人1795 ~ 1873年 》78

FYI: Entrepreneur: Johns Hopkins University, Johns Hopkins Hospital. Investor. His first name came from his Grand mothers maiden name.

史实: 企业家:约翰霍普金斯大学,约翰霍普金斯医院.投资者.他的名字来源于他祖母的婚前姓.

HORACE贺瑞斯he rui si

Horace

生人65 ~ 8年 BC

FYI: Aka Quintus Horatius Flaccus. Roman satirist~ Horatian style writing

史实: 罗马讽刺作家~Horatian风格的写作.

HOROWITZ霍洛维茨huo luo wei ci

Vladimir Samoylovich Horowitz

生人1903 ~ 1989年 》86

FYI: Recognized as the greatest pianist of the Twentieth Century.

史实: 公认为二十世纪最伟大的钢琴家.

HOROWITZ霍洛维茨huo luo wei ci

Myer Horowitz

生人1930年 ~ active

FYI: 84 Dec/27. Canadian academic and 9th president of U of A [1979-1989]. Horowitz Theatre Edmonton, Alberta, Canada. *listed on Canadian Who's who 2004. O.C.[1990]

史实: 加拿大学者和美国大学第九任校长[1979-1989].加拿大阿尔伯塔省埃德蒙顿霍洛维茨剧院.*2004年加拿大世界卫生组织.

HOUDIN侯帝恩hou di en

Jean-Eugene Robert Houdin

生人1805 ~ 1871年 》64

FYI: Is considered to be the Father of modern Conjuring.

史实: 被认为是现代变戏法之父. [-Houdini]

HOUDINI侯帝尼hou di ni

Harry Houdini

生人1874 ~ 1926年 》52

FYI: aka Ehrich Weisz, he was a Hungarian escape artist (conjuring). He took his English name from his hero Robert Houdin.

史实: 匈牙利脱险人. 他从他的英雄罗伯特·胡丁那里取了他的英文名. [see- Houdin]

HOUTHAKKER霍撒克huo sa ke

Hendrik Samuel Houthakker

生人1924 ~ 2008年 》83

FYI: American Economist. c1959: The Scope and limits of futures trading.

史实: 美国经济学家.

HOWE哈维ha wei

Elias Howe jr.

生人1819 ~ 1867年 》48

FYI: 1846; c1851 patented the first zipper .

史实: 发明拉链.

HOWARD霍华德huo hua de

Harlan Perry Howard

生人September 8, 1927 – March 3, 2002年 》74

FYI: He was an American songwriter who made many celebrities famous within the gendra of Country Music. Songs such as 'I Fall to Pieces' are now written into the souls of Americans. Ken Burns the director of County Music (PBS) made a great effort to save these relics from the past. *Country Music is Three Chords and the Truth.*

史实: 他是一位美国歌曲作者, 在乡村音乐的风格中使许多名人出名. 现在, 诸如 "我摔成碎片" 之类的歌曲被写入美国人的灵魂.县音乐 (PBS) 的导演肯·伯恩斯 (Ken Burns) 竭尽全力挽救过去的这些文物. *乡村音乐是三个和弦与真理.

HOYLE霍伊尔huo yi er

[SIR] Fred Hoyle

生人1915 ~ 2001年 》86

FYI: British Astronomer rejected the "big bang" in favour of stellar nucleosynthesis. Big Bang was coined by him on 28 March 1949 during a television taping. *When I was young, the old regarded me as an outrageous young fellow, and now that I'm old the young regard me as an outrageous old fellow.

史实: 英国天文. 生道 "大爆炸 "1949年. *当我还年轻的时候, 老人就把我当成是一个令人发指的年轻人, 而现在, 我已经老了, 那个年经人就把我当成了一个令人发指的老家伙.

HOLLERRIED霍利尔德huo li er de

Albert Hollerried

生人1932年 》[memorial纪念]

FYI: mechanic on LZ - Hindenburg

史实: 飞机工程;惨变兴登堡.

HONECKER昂纳克ang na ke

Erich Honecker

生人1912 ~ 1994年 》82

FYI: East German communist politician; tried for treason after German unification. Member of the Third Reich.

**Third Reich refers to "Third Realm or Third Empire"

史实: 东德共产主义政治家;在德国统一后企图叛国.第三帝国的成员.*第三记帝国.

HOOVER胡佛hu fo

William Henry "Boss" Hoover

生人1876 ~ 1932年 》56

FYI: Founded the "Hoover vacuum" company after being introduced to the machine by an inventor. He bought the patent and made history.

史实: 一位发明家将胡佛真空吸尘器引入机器后,成立了胡佛真空吸尘器公司.他买了专利并创造了历史. [查看- Sprangler]

HOOVER胡佛hu fo

John Edgar Hoover

生人1895 ~ 1972年 》77

FYI: FBI director 1935-1972.

史实: 联邦调查局

HOPE霍普huo pu

Bob Hope

生人1903 ~ 2003年 》100

FYI: [a&e] stage Icon and TV comedian. WII troup's entertainer.*I have seen what a laugh can do. It can transform almost unbearable tears into something bearable, even hopeful.

史实: 早艺人, 笑人.威特罗普的艺人.* 我已经知道笑能做什么.它可以将几乎无法忍受的眼泪变成可以忍受甚至希望的东西.

HUBBARD哈怕德ha pai de

Gardener Green Hubbard

生人1822 ~ 1897年 》75

FYI: The founder and first president of the National Geographic Society. Mount Hubbard is named in his honor. Founder of Bell Telephone, AT&T

史实: 慈善家, 建为了国地理.山哈怕德.

HUBBARD哈伯德ha bo de

Lafayette Ronald Hubbard

生人1911 ~ 1986年 》75

FYI: American author and founder of Scientology. Battlefield Earth is his most well known piece.

史实: 美国作家和山达基创始人.

HUBBARD哈伯德ha bo de

Elbert Green Hubbard

生人1856 ~ 1915年 》59

FYI: Died aboard the RMS Lusitania. Renowned American philosopher and author.

史实: 美国作者,哲学.

HUBBLE哈伯ha bo

Edwin Powell Hubble

生人1889年11月20日~ 1953年9月28日 》63

FYI: American astronomer. The Hubble telescope is named in his honor. *Equipped with his five senses, man explores the universe around him and calls the adventure Science.[~ Leavitt]

史实: 美国天文学家.哈勃望远镜是为纪念他而命名的.*配备了五种感官的人探索了周围的宇宙,并称之为冒险科学.

HUCHEL胡扯hu che

Ernst Huchel

生人1937年5月6日 》[memorial纪念]

FYI: senior elevator man on the Hindenburg.

史实: 电机人兴登堡

HUDSON哈德逊ha de xun

Henry Hudson

生人c.1565 ~ 1611年 》47

FYI: English explorer and navigator. Hudson Bay re: Canada.

史实: 英国探险家和航海家.哈德逊湾:加拿大.

HUDSON哈德逊ha de xun

Bruce~I~Hudson

生人1953 ~ 1975年 》22 》[memorial纪念]

FYI: 10 Nov 1975 S.S. Edmund Fitzgerald ~ Deck Hand

史实: 1975年11月10日S.S.Edmund Fitzgerald~甲板手.

HUGGINS赫格恩斯hu ge en si

William Huggins

生人1824 ~ 1910年 》96

FYI: was a pioneer in astronomical spectroscopy.

史实: 是天文学光谱学的先驱. [查看- E.Rutherford, N.Lockyer, G.Hale]

HUGHES户斯hu si

Howard Hughes

生人1905 ~ 1976年 》72

FYI: Hughes Aircraft，Business tycoon.

史实: 休斯飞机公司,商业大亨.

HUGO雨果yu guo

Victor Marie Hugo

生人Feb 26, 1802 - May 22, 1885年 》83

FYI: French poet and novelist of the Romantic period. He wrote "The Hunchback of Notre Dame": ie Quasimodo~the deformed but loving protagonist. RETROSPECT: Quasimodo refers to an 8 day Easter. For the novel it refers to being incomplete [deformed] in nature. *He who opens a school door, closes a prison.

史实: 浪漫主义时期的法国诗人和小说家.他写了 "圣母驼背":即卡西莫多 ~一个畸形但充满爱的主人公. 回顾:卡西莫多指的是8天的复活节.对于小说指的是自然界中的不完整[变形].*打开校门, 关闭监狱的人.

HUMBARD哈明吧达ha ming ba da

Alpha Rex Emmanuel Humbard

生人1919 ~ 2007年　》88

FYI: American tel-evangelist c1960-1980's. He spoke at the funeral of Elvis Presley.

史实: 美国布道.

HUMBOLDT哈伯德ha bo de

Friedrich Wilhelm Heinrich Alexander von Humboldt

生人1769 ~ 1859年　》90

FYI: geographer, naturalist and explorer.

史实: 地理学家,博物学家和探险家.

HUME休谟xiu mo

David Hume

生人1711 ~ 1776年　》65

FYI: Scottish philosopher. * *Beauty in things exists in the mind which contemplates them.*

史实: 苏格兰哲学家. *事物的美存在于思考它们的思想中.

HUNT哈恩特ha en te

Walter Hunt

生人1796 ~ 1859年 》63

FYI: American inventor; c1833 introduced the "lockstich" to make the sewing machine more practical.

史实: 发明"闸为了缝纫机"1833年.

HUNT哈恩特ha en te

Frederick Vinton Hunt

生人February 15, 1905 – April 21, 1972年 》67

FYI: An inventor, scientist and a professor for Harvard University who worked in the field of acoustic engineering. Although the concept of Sonar had been around since WWI, he developed the modern version since WWII. He coined the word *Sonar* as an acronym for (*Sound Navigation Region*).

史实: 一位发明家,科学家和哈佛大学教授,在声学工程领域工作.虽然声纳的概念在第一次世界大战后就已经存在了,但他在第二次世界大战后发展了现代版本.他创造了声纳这个词作为(声音导航区域)的缩写.

HUNTER亨特heng te
Howard William Hunter

生人1907 ~ 1995年 》87

FYI: American Lawyer. 14th President of the Church of Jesus Christ of L.D.S. from 1994 ~ 1995

史实: 律师.四十号:耶稣基督后期圣徒教会.》[感念]

HURWICZ赫维奇he wei qi
Leonid Hurwicz

生人1917 ~ 2008年 》91

FYI: awarded the Nobel Prize in microeconomics c 2007. [Nobelprize.org]

史实: 嘉奖2007 年诺贝尔,薇钱为了.

HURT赫特he te
[SIR] John Vincent Hurt

生人1940年1月22日 ~ 2017年 》77

FYI: [a&e] Renowned British actor.

史实: 英文艺人 [查看-j *Merrick]

HUSBAND哈斯班ha si ban
Richard Douglas "Rick" Husband

生人1957 ~ 2003年 》45 》[memorial纪念]

FYI: NASA: Shuttle Columbia disaster 2003 Feb 1

史实: 美国航天局:哥伦比亚号航天飞机2003年2月1日灾难.

HUSSEIN胡森hu sen
Saddam Hussein Revinathan

生人1937 ~ 2006年 》69

FYI: Iraqi dictator. "Most Wanted List"~America. 2006 Dec 30 he was hanged.

史实: 独裁 '通缉犯名单'.

HUSTED斛斯特hu si te
Marjorie Child Husted

生人1892 ~ 1986年 》94

FYI: aka Betty Crocker; several ladies were Betty Crocker since it's conception. Crocker was the name of the former CEO of the company. The signature belonged to a lady named Lindeberg -[查看-Crocker, Lindeberg]

史实: 贝蒂•克罗克;从怀孕开始,有几个女人就是贝蒂•克罗克.克罗克是公司前首席执行官的名字.签名属于一位名叫林德伯格的女士.

HUTTER赫特he te

Jacob Hutter

生人1500 ~ 1536年 》36

FYI: the founder of the Hutterite movement of the Anabaptist. Burned at the stake. [查看~ammann- simons- hutter:anabaptist]

史实: 再洗礼派的胡特派运动的创始人.在木桩上烧掉了.

HUTTON哈顿ha dun

Edward Francis Hutton

生人1875 ~ 1962年 》87

FYI: "E F Hutton" American Brokerage founder.

史实: 经纪人.E.F.哈顿.

HUXLEY赫胥黎he xu li

Thomas Henry Huxley

生人1825 ~ 1885年 》65

FYI: British scientist and Biologist.

史实: 英国生物学家.

HUXLEY赫胥黎he xu li

Aldous Leonard Huxley

生人1894 ~ 1963年 》69

FYI: author of "Brave New World". Chose to die from LSD injection. *The most valuable of all education is the ability to make yourself do the thing you have to do, when it has to be done, whether you like it or not.

史实: 作者 "勇敢新世纪".*在所有教育中, 最有价值的是使自己能够做自己必须做的事情, 必须完成的事情的能力, 无论是否喜欢.

HUYGENS惠更斯hui geng si

Christiaan Huygens

生人1629 ~ 1695年 》66

FYI: Dutch Mathematician and horologist. Perfected Galileo Pendulum concept. Pendulum Clock c1656

史实: 荷兰数学家和钟表学家.完善了伽利略摆的概念.钟摆时钟C1656.

HYNEK哈尼克ha ni ke

Josef Allen Hynek

生人1910 ~ 1986年 》76

FYI: American astronomer, Ufologist [project blue- book], introduced the "Close Encounter" classifications system.

史实:美国天文学家, 不明飞行物学家[蓝皮书计划],介绍了 "近距离触" 分类系统.

(Pledge 5516)

From Group "H" you can pick one person or up to ten Surnames and write their Surname in Chinese. You may try HORIZONTAL or VERTICAL in the traditional Chinese form.

I

"Everything is temporary."
一切都是暂时的
kate INGERSOLL英格索尔ying ge suo er

IACOCCA 艾科卡 ai ke ka

Lido Anthony "Lee" Iacocca

生人1924 ~ 2019年 》94

FYI: Automotive executive and designer of the 'Mustang'. He would become one of the most noticeable 'pitch man' for the Ford Motor Company and Chrysler with the now famous pitch "If you can find a better car, then buy it!"

史实: "野马" 的汽车执行和设计师.他将成为福特汽车公司和克莱斯勒公司最引人注目的 "推销人", 现在著名的推销 "如果你能找到更好的汽车, 那就买吧! " 他说: "这是一个很好的选择."

IGARASHI 一格认识 yi ge ren shi

Kiyoshi Igarashi

生人1897 ~ 2009年 》112

FYI: 111 years 205 days Japans Supercenturian club

史实: 赵人111岁205日.

IKARASHI 一卡让实 yi ka rang shi

Jokichi Ikarashi

生人1902 ~ 2003年 》111y 178d;

FYI: Japanese Supercenturian

史实:赵世纪人*apetaph.

IMICH 艾米实 ai mi shi

Alexander Imich

生人1903 ~ 2014年 》111y 124d

FYI: Supercenturian

史实: 赵世纪人.

IMOHOF 艾莫侯 ai mo huo (insert jpg 2)

Emilie Imohof

生人1937年 》[memorial纪念]

FYI: hostess LZ- Hindenburg

史实: 空中小姐* 惨变:兴登堡

INGERSOLL英格索尔ying ge suo er

Robert Green Ingersoll

生人1833 ~ 1899年 》65

FYI: American lawyer and orator. Aka "The Great Agnostic."

史实: 律师, 口声人.

IRWIN欧文ou wen

Stephen Robert "Steve" Irwin

生人1962 ~ 2006年 》44

FYI: "the crocodile hunter". Was injured during a filming and died 2006.

史实: "鳄鱼猎人".在拍摄过程中受伤并于2006年去世.

ISHIHARA艾谁哈让ai shei ha ra

Shinobu Ishihara

生人1879 ~ 1963年 》84

FYI: Japanese army surgeon and ophthalmologist who developed the Color Blindness Test for color blindness. The Ishihara Test uses multiple plates [38] where a 'number or squigly line' in color is embedded within an apposing color to test for red-green or 'protanopia or dueteranopia.' First used in 1917 is used by optometrist and is also used for people wanting a professional driving license.

史实: 日本军医和眼科医生, 他开发了色盲测试法。Ishihara测试使用多个板[38], 其中颜色中的 "数字或斜线" 嵌入到相应的颜色中, 以测试红绿色或 "原视性" 或双翅目.第一次使用是在1917年, 由验光师使用, 也用于人们想要专业驾驶执照.

ISHIZAKI伊实奥克yi shi ao ke

Denzo Ishizaki

生人1886 ~ 1999年 》112y 191d

FYI: Supercenturian

史实: 赵世纪人112岁191日.

IVES艾夫斯 ai fu si

Burl Ives

生人1909 ~ 1995年 》86

FYI: [a&e] voice actor and singer "Rudolf the Red Nose Reindeer"

史实: 口声艺人.

IVES艾夫斯 ai fu si

George Frederick Ives

生人1881 ~ 1993年 》111y 146d

FYI: Canadian Supercenturian. Was the last soldier who was to survive the Boer War. [*amazing]

史实: 加拿大超级世纪.是最后一个在布尔战争中幸存的士兵.

From Group "I" you can pick one person or up to ten Surnames and write their Surname in Chinese. You may try HORIZONTAL or VERTICAL in the traditional Chinese form.

J

《仅仅因为它已经出版了，并不意味着它就是福音书》
"Just because it's in print, doesn't mean it's the Gospel."
Michael JACKSON杰克逊jie ke xun

JACKSON杰克逊jie ke xun

Michael Jackson

生人1958 ~ 2009年 》51

FYI: [a&e] American musician and entertainer

史实: 高名歌唱

JACOBSON雅克布森ya ke bu sen

[Dr.] Max Jacobson

生人1900 ~ 年1979 》79

FYI: aka: Miracle Max or Dr. Feelgood, was the personal private Dr. of JFK. As well as many celebrities.

史实: Miracle Max或Feelgood医生是JFK的私人医生.以及许多名人.

JAHAN约翰yue han

Shah Jahan

生人1592 ~ 1666年 》74

FYI: AKA: Shahab-ud-din Muhammad Khrurram; Emperor of India who had the Taj Mahal [crown palace] constructed for his favourite wife Mumtaz Mahal.

史实: 印度皇帝, 为他最爱的妻子穆姆塔兹•马哈尔建造了泰姬陵 (皇宫).

JAMES詹姆斯zhan mu si

"KING" James I

生人1566 ~ 1625年 》33

FYI: *KJV (King James Version- Bible) . *39 books O.T.~27 books N.T. 1604-1611

史实: KJV (国王詹姆斯版本-圣经).*39册O.T.~27册N.T.1604-1611.

JAMES詹姆斯zhan mu si

William James

生人1842 ~ 1910年 》68

FYI: Philosopher and Father of American psychology. * A new idea is first condemned as ridiculous and then dismissed as trivial, until finally, it becomes what everybody knows.

史实: 哲学, 夫子为了美国心里. *一个新的想法首先被指责为荒谬, 当候被认为是琐碎的, 直到最后, 它变成了大家知道东西.

JAMIN朱敏zhu min

Jules Celestin Jamin

生人1818 ~ 1886年 》68

FYI: Physicist created the Jamin interferometer. Name appears with the 72 names on the Eiffel tower..[SW01] 41/72

史实: 新元史上埃菲尔铁塔单名.

Courtesy of Janzen public archives by Forest L.

JANZEN詹森zhan sen

John Janzen

生人1923 ~ 1972年 》?48

FYI: Trained in agriculture, he would later design golf courses all of the world until he became Superintendent of Edmonton's Parks and Recreation Department from 1966-1972, he played a key role in the protection of river valley lands as parks.The John Janzen Nature Centre in Edmonton opened in 1976 is Canada's oldest municipally-operated nature centre.

史实: 他受过农业训练，后来在世界各地设计高尔夫球场，直到1966-1972年成为埃德蒙顿公园和娱乐部门的主管，他在保护河谷土地作为公园方面发挥了关键作用.加拿大最古老的市政自然中心.位于埃德蒙顿的约翰詹森自然中心于1976年开业.

JEFFRIES杰弗里斯jie fu li si

Donald Jeffries

生人1941 ~ 2011年 》70

FYI: History researcher and author of "Survival of the Richest: wealth disparity"

史实: 《最富有者的生存:财富差距》的历史研究者和作者.

JELLINEK杰利尼克jia li ni ke

Emil Jelliek

生人1853 ~ 1918年 》65

FYI: His daughter was Mercedes Adrienne Ramona Manuella Jellinek . The "Mercedes" car is named in her honor. The first Modern car.

史实: 他的女儿是梅赛德斯•阿德里安•拉莫纳•马努埃拉•杰利尼克.这辆"梅赛德斯"车是以她的名字命名的.第一辆现代汽车.

JESUS耶稣ye su

Jesus the CHRIST

生人A.D. 》

FYI: It should be noted that Jesus did not have a family name as we do today.... (Jesus of Nazareth) New Testament. CHRIST was his TITLE which translated from Greek means the "Anointed One". The Christian era * A.D.(Anno Domini) from Latin means "year of the Lord", Human time is reckoned by his birth. 'Jesus the Christ' by Talmage is an excellent read.

史实: 应该注意的是,耶稣没有我们今天这样的姓氏……（拿撒勒人耶稣）新约,基督是他的头衔,从希腊语翻译过来就是"受膏者".拉丁语中的基督教纪元a.d（anno domini）的意思是"主的年",人类的时间是由他的出生来计算的.耶稣基督是一本优秀的读物.

JOSEPHUS约瑟夫斯yue se fu si

Titus Flavisus Josephus

生人37 ~ c.100年

FYI: Historian and author of the Roman-Jewish era

史实: 罗马犹太时代的历史学家和作家.

JAMES詹姆斯jan mu si

Jessy Woodson James

生人1847 ~ 1882年 》35

FYI: American Outlaw. Movies and books are full of the Wild West and this man and his gang.

史实: 美国罪犯.电影和书籍充满了西部的狂野,这个人和他的帮派.

JOAN贞德zhen de

Joan of Arc

生人1413 ~ 1431年 》19

FYI: French heroine and liberator in France. Burned alive for her beliefs in a angelic visitation.

史实: 法国女子-杰为了普通人.死了为了信仰.

JOBS贾伯斯jia bo si

Steve Jobs

生人1955 ~ 2011年 》56

FYI: Comp600uter pioneer and business man. *CEO of Apple, Inc.

*Your time is limited, so don't waste it living someone else's life.

史实: 计算机先驱和商人.苹果公司首席执行官

*您的时间是有限的，所以不要浪费时间过别人的生活.

JOHNSON约翰逊yue han xun

Samuel johnson

生人1709 ~ 1784年 》75

FYI: Writer and Lexiographer

史实: 作家和辞书编纂者.

JONBENET琼贝尼特qiong bei na te

Jonbenet Ramsey

生人1990 ~ 1996年 》6 years old

FYI: Unsolved beauty queen murder

史实: 选美皇后死了.

JONES琼斯qiong si

[Capt] Christopher Jones jr.

生人1570 ~ 1622年 》52

FYI: Captain of the Historic Mayflower of 1620

史实: 1620年梅花航.

JONES琼斯qiong si

James Warren "Jim" Jones

生人1931 ~ 1978年 》47

FYI: Cult religious leader of Peoples Temple- mass murder suicide (918)

史实: 教- 很多人死了918 人.

JOPLIN加普林jia pu lin

Janis Joplin

生人1943年1月19日 ~ 1970年10月4日 》27

FYI: [a&e] American folk singer, song writer. Icon of the 1960's. *On stage I make love to twenty five thousand people; and then I go home alone.*

史实: 美国民歌歌手, 歌曲作者.20世纪60年代的标志.*在舞台上, 我与两万五千人做爱, 然后我一个人回家.

JOYCE乔伊斯qiao yi si

James Augustine Aloysius Joyce

生人1882 ~ 1941年 》59

FYI: Irish novelist. "Ulysses". James Joyce Award in his honour.

史实: 爱尔兰小说 "尤利西斯".

JOUGHIN乔因qiao yin

Charles John Joughin

生人1878 ~ 1956年 》78 》[memorial纪念]

FYI: RMS Titanic chief cook.

史实: 泰坦尼克号首席厨师.

JOULE焦尔jiao er

[Dr.] James Prescott Joule

生人1818 ~ 1889年 》71

FYI: Physicist, mathematician and brewer. The Joule is a derived unit of energy and is named in his honor.

史实: "焦尔 "[Joule] 他名字使用为了气力.

JOUSSELIN焦斯林jiao si lin

Louis Didier Jousselin

生人1776 ~ 1858年 》82

FYI: French engineer. His name is included with the 72 names on the Eiffel tower [SW10] #42/72

史实: 法国工程,新元史上埃菲尔铁塔单名.

JUNG荣格rong ge

Carl Gustav Jung

生人Jul 26, 1875 - Jun 6, 1961 年 》85

FYI: A Swiss psychiatrist and psychoanalyst who founded analytical psychology. Jung's work was influential in the fields of psychiatry, anthropology, archaeology, literature, philosophy, and religious studies. *Show me a sane man and I will cure him for you.

史实: 瑞士精神病学家和精神分析学家, 创立了分析心理学.荣格的作品在精神病学,人类学,考古学,文学,哲学和宗教研究领域具有重要影响.*给我看一个神志清醒的人, 我会帮你治好他的.

JUVENAL焦维那jiao wei na

Juvenal

FYI: [early second century] aka: Decimus Liunus Luvenalis; His writing were "satirical" and abrasive against the authorities of his day. Juvenalian satire.

史实: 他的作品是"讽刺性的", 对当时的权威是粗暴的.尤文的讽刺.

From Group "J" you can pick one person or up to ten Surnames and write their Surname in Chinese. You may try HORIZONTAL or VERTICAL in the traditional Chinese form.

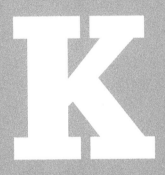

《梦不是你睡觉时看到的东西，而是不让你睡觉的东西》

"Dream is not that which you see while sleeping it is something that does not let you sleep."

A.P.J. Abdul KALAM卡拉姆 ka la mu

KAFKA卡夫卡ka fu ka

Franz Kafka

生人1883 ~1924年 》40

FYI: Czech Jewish novelist, lawyer. "The Metamorphosis","The Trial."

史实: 捷克犹太小说家,律师.

KARAKHAN家拉罕jia la han

Lev Mikhailvich Karakhan

生人1889 ~ 1937年 》48

FYI: Ambassador, executed in Stalin's purge c1937

史实: 代言,1937年死了.

KALAM卡拉姆ka la mu

Avul Pakir Jainulabdeen (A.P.J.) Abdul Kalam

生人1931 ~ 2015年 》83

FYI: Space Scientist and India President (2002-2007)

*Dream is not that which you see while sleeping it is something that does not let you sleep.

史实:太空科学, 2002-2007年总统为了印地啊.*梦不是你睡觉时看到的东西,而是不让你睡觉的东西.

KALMON卡里门ka li men

Allen~G~Kalmon

生人1932 ~ 1975年 》43 》[memorial纪念]

FYI: *SS Edmund Fitzgerald~Lake Superior 10 Nov 1975

史实: 1975年 11月10日S.S. 埃德蒙*菲茨杰拉德 湖高强.

KAMPFE卡吗发ka ma fa

Frederick, Otto and Richard Kampfe

FYI: the brothers designed the safety razor for home use.(c1875 Star razor)

史实: 兄弟全安刀片.

Photo by Forest L.

KAMPRAD卡吗怕若德ka ma pa luo de

Feodor Ingvar Kamprad

生人1926 ~ 2018年 》92

FYI: Business magnate who founded Ikea. Ikea is an acronym for [I]ngvar [K]amprad [E]lmtaryd [A]Gunnard . The last two was the family farm and location.

史实: 创立宜家的商业巨头.宜家是[I]Ngvar [K]Amprad [E]Lmtaryd [A]Gunnard的缩写.最后两个是家庭农场和地点.

KANT坎特kan te

Immanuel Kant

生人1724 ~ 1804年 》80

FYI: Central figure of "modern philosophy".* *Dare to think!*

史实: 现代哲学" 的中心人物. *敢想!

KAPAUN卡波恩ka bo en

[Captain Chaplain] Emil Joseph Kapaun

生人April 20, 1916 ~ May 23, 1951 年 》35

FYI: Served and died in the North Korean war. He was nicknamed 'The Good Thief' as he would find and steal tea, coffee, and medicine for the troops who fought beside him. He was one of twelve priests who died during the Korean war. [special thanks to Dr. 'Deacon' Ian Punnet for sharing on coasttocoastam.com; air date 20July2019]

史实: 在朝鲜战争中服役并去世.他被昵称为 "好贼" ，因为他会找到并偷茶,咖啡和药给在他身边作战的部队.他是在朝鲜战争中去世的十二位神父之一.

KAPITSA卡皮查ka pi cha

Pyotr Kapitsa

生人1894 ~ 1984年 》90

FYI: he was awarded the Nobel in 1978 for low -temperature physics. [Nobelprize.org]

史实: 嘉奖诺贝尔为了物理学家.

KARAGULLA卡让古拉ka ra gu la

Shafica Karagulla

生人1914 ~ 1986年 》72

FYI: A Medical doctor and psychiatrist who took a special interest in psychic perception. After reading the works of Edgar Cayce she began her research and wrote among other works 'Breakthrough to Creativity~ 1940'. She was the aunt of coasttocoastam: George Noory. *There is abundant evidence that many human beings are already expanding the usual five senses into super sensory levels. It is possible that there is already a `mutation in consciousness' taking place.

史实: 对精神知觉有特殊兴趣的医生和精神病学家.在阅读了埃德加·凯斯的作品之后, 她开始了她的研究, 并在其他作品中写作了《到1940年创造力的突破》.她是科斯塔姆的姑妈: 乔治·努里.*有充分的证据表明, 许多人已经将通常的五种感官扩展到超感官水平.可能已经发生了 "意识突变".

KARDASHEV卡达社夫ka da she fu

Nikolai Semenovich Kardashev

生人1932年 ~ Active

FYI: Russian astrophysicist, Doctor of Physical and Mathematical Sciences and creator of the Kardashev classification scheme: c1964

*type one: current level

*type two: harnessing the sun's energy

*type three: harnessing galaxy energy

史实: 俄罗斯天体物理学家,物理和数学科学博士和卡尔达舍夫分类方案的创建者:C1964年: 三个类别文明.类型一; 当前级别, 第二类:利用太阳的能量, 第三类;利用星系能量.

KARINTHY卡林斯ka lin si

Frigyes Karinthy

生人1887 ~ 1938年 》51

FYI: Journalist/playwright. Famous for "six degrees of separation" concept. The idea that all people are six, or fewer, social connections away from each other. As a result, a chain of "a friend of a friend" statements can be made to connect any two people in a maximum of six steps. A, popular phrase which coincides with this concept is 'what a small world' which brings together two people of opposing view are united for a common cause.

史实: 记者/剧作家.以 "六度分离" 概念而闻名.所有人都是六个或更少的人, 彼此之间的社会联系。因此,可以通过一系列 "朋友的朋友" 语句, 以最多6个步骤连接任何两个人.一个与这个概念相提并论的流行短语是 "多小的世界", 它把两个对立的人聚集在一起, 是为了一个共同的事业.

KARMAN卡曼ka man

Theodore von Karman

生人1881～1963年 》81

FYI: Hungarian space engineer. The "Karman-line" ie the division between Earth's atmosphere and Space (100 km above sea level) is named in his honor.

史实:卡曼-经线:世间-空间100公里.

KASEM格森ge sen

Casey Kasem

生人1932～2014年 》82

FYI: AKA Kamel Amin Kasem; Radio personality, Top 40 radio countdown.

史实: 高名广播电台人. 排名前40的收音机倒计时.

KELLOGG凯咯格kai lo ge

Will Keith Kellogg

生人1860～1951年 》91

FYI: Business man and founder of Kellogg cereals Founded 1906

史实: 商业人和先导为了 "凯洛格" 1906年.

KELLER凯乐kai le

Helen Keller

生人1880～1968年 》88

FYI: Deaf and blind author, political activist, and lecturer. She was able to complete her degree with the aid of Anne Sullivan and was highly sought after in speaking circles. "Story of my life." Circa 1903 *I would rather walk with a friend in the dark, than alone in the light.

史实: 聋哑人和盲人作家, 政治活动家和讲师.她能在安妮•沙利文的帮助下完成学位, 并在演讲圈受到高度追捧. "我的生活故事." 大约在1903年. *我宁愿和朋友在黑暗中行走, 也不愿独自在光明中行走.

KELVIN开尔文kai er wen

Lord William Thomson [kelvin]

生人1824～1907年 》83

FYI: aka: William Thomas. Kelvin is now a Thermodynamic temperature scale ~ measured above absolute zero. The name-sake "Kelvin" refers to the river Kelvin.

Kelvin and Lord are "Honorary" bestowed names. [see Celsius, Fahrenheit, Romer, Amonton]

史实: 开尔文现在是一个热力学温标, 在绝对零度以上测量.清酒 "开尔文" 这个名字是指开尔文河.开尔文和洛德是 "荣誉" 称号.

KELLY凯莉kai li

Jackson Deforest Kelly

生人1920 ~ 1999年 》89

FYI: Television, stage and movie Actor~(S/C) "Bones McCoy".

史实: 电视,舞台和电影演员.

KELLY凯利kai li

Grace Patricia Kelly

生人1929 ~ 1982年 》53

FYI: Former actress. She married Prince Rainier in 1956 and became Princess of Monaco.

史实: 艺人 前女演员.1956年她嫁给了兰尼尔王子, 成为摩纳哥公主. [-see Rainier]

KEMMLER凯穆勒kai mu le

William Francis Kemmler

FYI: *First electric chair execution.1890 Aug 06.

史实: *第一次执行电椅.[inset--seeSpitzka]

KENNEDY肯尼迪ken ni di

John Fitzgerald "Jack" Kennedy

生人1917年5月29日 ~ 1963年11月22日 》46

FYI: Often referred to as J. F. K., he served as the 35th US President (1961-1963). The first president to send men to the moon. He preferred to ride in an 'open' car so the people could have an easy view of him. *Forgive your enemies, but never forget their names.

史实: 他经常被称为J.F.K., 曾担任第35任美国总统 (1961-1963).第一位把人送上月球的总统.他更喜欢坐在 "敞篷车" 里, 这样人们就能轻松地看到他.*原谅你的敌人, 但不要忘记他们的名字.

KENNEDY肯尼迪ken ni di

Robert Francis Kennedy

生人1925年11月25日 ~ 1968年6月6日 》43

FYI: American politician, lawyer, author and younger brother to J.F.K.. He authored "The Enemy Within". Advocate for Human Rights and Social injustice. Assassinated June 6, 1968. [see- Sirhan Sirhan]

史实： 美国政治家,律师,作家和J.F.K.的弟弟.他写了《内在的敌人》.提倡人权和社会不公正.1968年6月6日遇刺.

KENNEDY肯尼迪ken ni di

Jonny Kennedy

生人1966 ~ 2003年 》37

FYI: Bio: The Boy Whose Skin fell off; EB~epidermolysis bullosa

史实: 男皮肤剥

KEPLER克普勒ke pu le

Johannes Kepler

生人1571年12月27日 ~ 1630年 》59

FYI: Mathematician and astronomer. "Law's of planetary revolution".

史实: 数学家和天文学 [查看- Melankovich]

KEY可以ke yi

Francis Scott Key

生人1779 ~ 1843年 》64

FYI: American lawyer, author and poet. Wrote the lyrics to "Star-Spangled Banner", originally called "The Defence of Fort McHenry". music by John Stafford Smith [see j.s.SMITH]

史实: 美国律师, 作家和诗人.将歌词写成 "星条旗"，原名 "麦克亨利堡的防御".

KEVORKIAN科沃金 ke wo jin

Jacob "Jack" Kevorkian

生人1928 ~ 2011年 》83

FYI: aka "Dr. Death" was a American pathologist and euthanasia proponent for his assistant death program. Assisted with 133 deaths.

史实: "死亡博士" 是美国病理学家和安乐死的支持者，他的助理死亡计划.协助133人死亡.

KHRUSHCHEV何鲁晓夫he lu xiao fu

Rikita Sergeyevich Khrushchev

生人1894 ~ 1971年 》77

FYI: Soviet secretary-general.

史实: 苏维埃俄国

KHUFU胡夫hu fu

Khnum Khufu

生人2590 ~ 2568年 B.C

FYI: Pharaoh of Egypt

史实: 法老

KILLGALLEN吉尔喝伦ji er he lun

Dorothy Mae Killgallen

生人1913 ~ 1965年 》52

FYI: American Journalist: organized crime journalist and game show participant in "What's My Line" 1950 ~ 1965. Her death is considered a mystery. She was considered the most powerful female voice in America for her era. *I actually turned down an opportunity for a private interview with Adolph Hitler.*

史实: 美国记者: 1950~1965年《我的路线》有组织犯罪记者和游戏节目参加者.她的死被认为是个谜.在她那个时代,她被认为是美国最强大的女性声音.*实际上,我拒绝了一个与阿道夫·希特勒进行私人采访的机会.

KIMBALL金博尔jin bo er

Spencer Wooley Kimball

生人1895 ~ 1985年 》90 》[感念]

FYI: American businessman and 12th President of LDS church.

史实: 商业,十二号耶稣基督后期圣徒教会.

photo by Forest L.

KING金jin

William Lyman Mackenzie King

生人1874 ~ 1950年 》76

FYI: Canadian PM, 12-14-16 pm. image appears on the $50 bill.

史实: 十二, 十四, 十六 加拿大总理.

KING金jin

Martin Luther King

生人Jan 15, 1929 - Apr 4, 1968年 》39

FYI: American Baptist clergyman and civil rights activist 1958 ~ 1968. *Our lives begin to end the day we become silent about things that matter. *In the End, we will remember not the words of our enemies, but the silence of our friends.

史实: 1958~1968年美国浸礼会牧师和民权活动家.*当我们对重要的事情保持沉默的时候，我们的生活就开始结束了.*最后, 我们将不再记得敌人的话, 而是我们朋友的沉默.

KING金jin

Hans Christian King

生人February 15, 1943 ~ January 16, 2019年 》75

FYI: Psychic medium and author 'Guided: Reclaiming the Intuitive Voice of your Soul'. He was a frequent guest on ' Coast to Coast with George Noory.' *Most people don't live their life. They live their reaction to life.

史实: 灵媒和作者 "引导:找回你灵魂的直觉声音".他经常和乔治·努里一起去 "海岸到海岸", 大多数人都过不上他们的生活.他们过着他们对生活的反应.

KIPLING吉卜林ji bu lin

Joseph Rudyard Kipling

生人Dec 30, 1865 - Jan 18, 1936年

FYI: He was an English journalist, short-story writer, poet, and novelist. He was born in India, which inspired much of his work. His most notable work was "The Jungle Book". *I am by nature a dealer in words, and words are the most powerful drug known to humanity.

史实:　他是一位英语记者, 短篇小说家, 诗人和小说家.他出生于印度, 这激发了他的许多工作.他最著名的作品是《丛林书》.*我天生就是言语交易者, 而言语是人类已知的最有力的毒品.

KIRCHHOFF其尔霍夫qi er huo fu

Gustav Robert Kirchhoff

生人1824 ~ 1887年 》63

FYI: German physicist. Coined the term "black body" radiation c.1862. "Kirchhoff's law" named in his honor.

史实:德国物理学家."其尔霍夫法".

KISSINGER基辛格ji xin ge

Henry Alfred Kissinger

生人1923年5月27日 ~ active

FYI: German born American diplomat.

*Corrupt politicians make the other ten percent look bad at.

史实: 德国裔美国外交官. *腐败的政客使其他百分之十的人看上去很糟糕.

Portrait courtesy of Alberta Government

KLEIN克莱因 ke lai yin

Ralph Philip Klein

生人1942 ~ 2013年 》71

FYI: Nicknamed as "King Ralph" because of his long term as 12th Alberta Premier.*O.C.2012

史实: 因长期担任第12任阿尔伯塔省总理而被称为 "拉尔夫国王".

KLINE克莱因ke lai yin

Nathan Schellenberg Kline

生人1916 ~ 1983年 》67

FYI: a leader in antidepressants coined the term "cyborg" [see also - Clynes]

史实: 抗抑郁药的领导者创造了 "电子人" 这个词.

KLOPFER克格普弗ke ge pu fu

Konald Simon Klopfer

生人1902 ~ 1986年 》84

FYI: co founder of Random House-with Bennett Cerf c1925

史实: 先导 "任意家".

KNIEVEL尼维尔ni wei er

Robert Craig "Evel" Knievel

生人1938 ~ 2007年 》69

FYI: professional stuntman with motorbikes.

史实: 提神摩托车特技替身演员.

KNOPF诺夫nuo fu

Adolf Abraham Knopf

FYI: Co founder of Double Day books

史实: 双日图书联合创始人.

KNORR诺尔nuo er

Ludwig Knorr

[memorial纪念]

FYI: chief rigger LZ- Hindenburg disaster

史实: 飞机工程惨变:兴登堡.

KNOTT诺特nuo te

Walter Marvin Knott

生人1889 ~ 1981年 》92

FYI: Founded Knott's Berry Farm and introduced the "Hybred boysenberry"

史实: 成立诺特浆果农场, 引进 "杂交博森浆果". [查看- see R.Boysen]

KNOWLES诺尔斯nuo er si

William Standish Knowles

生人1917 ~ 2012年 》95

FYI: Awarded the Nobel in c2001 for organic chemistry.

史实: 2001年嘉奖诺贝尔为了化学家. [Nobleprize.org]

KNOX诺克斯nuo ke si

John Knox

生人1530 ~ 1572年 》42

FYI: Scottish Theologian and Reformation activist.

史实: 教会.人权斗士.

KOHL科尔ke er

Helmut Josef Michael Kohl

生人1930 ~ 2017年 》87

FYI: German Chancellor (1982-1998)

史实: 曾经德国掌玺大臣.

KOPPEN空盆ko pen

Wladimir Peter Koppen

生人1846 ~ 1940年 》94

FYI: meteorologist, climatologist and botanist. Is known for the "Koppen climate classification".

史实: 气候学*[空盆气候分类]

KORESH科雷斯ke lei si

生人1993年4月19日:

FYI: AKA Vernon Wayne Howell. Religious cult leader of the * Branch Davidian, 'the Waco massacre' April 19,1993

史实: 1933年4有19日.文化冲击.一动死了

KRAFT卡夫ka fu

James Lewis Kraft

生人1874 ~ 1953年 》78

FYI: Canadian-American entrepreneur founder of KRAFT foods. Was the first to patent processed cheese.

史实: 早企业家 ”卡夫 “专利权奶酪.

KRESGE克雷斯吉ke lei si ji

Sebastian Spering Kresge

生人1867 ~ 1966年 》99

FYI: American business man and the founder of Kmart

史实: 商业男, 先导为了K马特.

KROC克罗ke luo

Raymond Albert "Ray" Kroc

生人1902 ~ 1984年 》81

FYI: he purchased the royalties rights to McDonald's from Dick and Mac McDonald's c.1955; 1963 he introduced the fictional "Ronald McDonald" played first by actor Willard Scott to hold the interest of children.[howstuffworks].

史实: 买东西版税从Dick and Mac.

KUBLER~ROSS库布勒•罗斯ku bu le~luo si

Elisabeth Kubler~Ross

生人1926 ~ 2004年 》78

FYI: She was a Swiss-American psychiatrist, a pioneer in near-death studies and the author of the groundbreaking book On Death and Dying, where she first discussed her theory of the five stages of grief, also known as the Kübler-Ross model. The stages are: denial, anger, bargaining, depression and acceptance. *The opinion which other people have of you is their problem, not yours.

史实: 她是一位瑞士裔美国精神病学家, 濒死研究的先驱, 也是一本关于死亡和死亡的开创性著作的作者, 在这本书中, 她首先讨论了她关于悲伤的五个阶段的理论, 也被称为库布勒•罗斯模型.阶段是:否认,愤怒,讨价还价,沮丧和接受.*别人对你的看法是他们的问题, 而不是你的问题.

KUIPER柯伊伯ke yi po

Gerard Peter Kuiper

生人December 7, 1905 ~ December 23, 1973年 》68

FYI: Dutch–American astronomer, planetary scientist, selenographer, author and professor. The Kuiper Belt in the distant part of our galaxy is known as the 'third zone'. Kuiper is regarded as the father of modern planetary science. Carl Sagan was one of his PhD students.

史实: 荷兰-美国天文学家, 行星科学家, 硒测定仪, 作家和教授.我们银河系遥远部分的柯伊伯带被称为 "第三区".柯伊伯被认为是现代行星科学之父.卡尔•萨根是他的博士生之一.

KULIK库里哭ku li ku

Leonid Alekseyevich Kulik

生人1883年11月2日 ~ 1942年4月24日 》59

FYI: Russian meteorologist, noted for his expedition [1927] to investigate the Tungusta event of 1908 June 30. It was the first expedition sponsored by the Soviets. Kulik crater on the moon is named in his honor.

史实: 俄国气象学家, 以考察1908年6月30日的东古斯塔事件而闻名.这是苏联发起的第一次远征.月球上的库利克陨石坑是以他的名字命名的.

KURTZMAN库茨曼 ku ci man

Harvey Kurtzman

生人1924 ~ 1993年 》69

FYI: Cartoonist~Founder of "Mad Magazine". Name recognition of Alfred E. Newman~ Mads mascot. FYI...Neither Kurtzman or Drucker are the depiction of "Newman". * Teenagers are people who act like babies if they're not treated like adults.

史实: 漫画家 ~"疯狂杂志" 的创始人. 动漫 "疯狂杂志", 男生动漫 ;)仅供参考…库尔茨曼和德鲁克都不是 "纽曼" 的写照. *青少年是如果不像成年人那样对待婴儿的人.

From Group "K" you can pick one person or up to ten Surnames and write their Surname in Chinese. You may try HORIZONTAL or VERTICAL in the traditional Chinese form.

L

《生活就是当你忙于制定计划时发生的事情》
"life is what happens when you are busy making other plans."
John LENNON蓝侬lan nong

Sign located in Edmonton; photo by Forest L.

LABATT拉巴它la ba ta

John Kinder Labatt

生人1803～1866年 》63

FYI: Labatt's brewing founded c.1847 -see Molson-Coors

史实: 建1847年烧过啤酒.

St. Albert, Alberta
photo by Forest L.

LACOMBE拉口嘛la ko mo

Father Albert Lacombe

生人c.1827 ~ 1916年 》89

FYI: Serving as a Catholic Priest in Canada. "Man with a heart" was given as a pet name by the Canadian Indians. Two towns bear his namesake. St. Albert is a town in central Alberta and Lacombe is a second town to have his name.

史实: 在加拿大担任天主教牧师."有心脏的人"是加拿大印第安人的昵称.两个城镇与他同名.圣阿尔伯特是阿尔伯塔中部的一个城镇,拉科姆贝是第二个以他的名字命名的城镇.

LAENNEC兰内克lan nei ke

Rene-Theophile-Hyacynthe Laennec

生人1781 ~ 1826年 》45

FYI: A French physician who invented the stethoscope [chest scope]. Original designs were made from hollow wood or paper rolled into a tube. Male doctors would use this method to listen to female patients so as to limit the actually touching of the two during examination and the percussion could be magnified as well using the device.

史实: 发明听诊器[胸腔镜]的法国医生.最初的设计是由中空的木头或卷成管状的纸制成的.男性医生会使用这种方法来倾听女性患者的声音,以限制他们在检查过程中的实际接触,并且可以使用该设备放大打击.

LAGRANGE拉格朗la ge lang

Joseph Louis Lagrange

生人1736 ~ 1813年 》77

FYI: astronomer and analytical engineer. His name is included among the 72 people on the Eiffel tower: [NW06] >43/72

史实: 天文学家.新元史上埃菲尔铁塔单名.

LAKHOVSKY拉卡霍斯可la ka huo si ki

Georges Lakhovsky

生人1869 ~ 1942年 》71

FYI: Engineer, scientist, author and inventor. He published books and articles that claimed and attempted to demonstrate that living cells emit and receive electromagnetic radiations at their own high frequencies, thus DNA has a resonate frequency of 50 GHz and can be returned to health at 54~78 GHz. In 1932 as a bio-electric pioneer he developed the multi-wave oscillator. Modern medicine considers it to be in the category of alternative medicine.

史实：工程师,科学家,作家和发明家.他出版了书籍和文章,声称并试图证明活细胞以自己的高频发射和接收电磁辐射,因此DNA的共振频率为50 GHz, 在54~78 GHz时可以恢复健康.1932年, 作为一个生物电气的先驱,他开发了多波振荡器.现代医学认为它属于替代医学范畴.

LALANDE拉朗德la lang de
Joseph Jerome Le Francois Lalande

生人1732 ~ 1807年 》74

FYI: Astronomer and writer, his name is included among the 72 names on the Eiffel tower; [Eiffel: NW02] 44/72

史实：作者,天文学家.新元史上埃菲尔铁塔单名.

LAMARR拉玛la ma
Hedy Lamarr

生人1914 ~ 2000年 》85

FYI: aka Hedwig Eva Maria Kiesler, *Actress and inventor. Forerunner for Wi-Fi ~WLAN.

史实：艺人, 发明, 早先导无线网路.

LAME拉米la mi
Gabriel Lame

生人1795 ~ 1870年 》75

FYI: mathematician; ie Lame Curves. His name is included among the 72 names on the Eiffel tower: [Eiffel: NE18] 46/72

史实：数.新元史上埃菲尔铁塔单名.

LANDELL兰德里lan de li
Roberto Landell

生人1861 ~ 1928年 》67

FYI: aka Roberto Landell de Moura. First radio broadcast of the human voice June 03 1900

史实：1900年6月3日:第一次点口舌.

LANDSTEINER兰斯特艾阿lan si te ai e

Karl Landsteiner

生人1868～1943年 》75

FYI: Gave evidence that human blood can be divided into groups ie: A, B, AB and O groups. Awarded the Nobel in 1909. 1930 efforts in medicine. [Nobel prize.org]

史实: 1909年诺贝尔为了血型.

LANGEN兰根lan gen

Carl Eugene Langen

FYI: engineer and entrepreneur. Started the first monorail in Wuppertal Germany. As well, first patent for sugar cubes.

史实: 德国发明糖丁. 在德国乌珀塔尔开始了第一条单轨铁路.

LANGLEY狼类lang lei

Samuel Pierpont Langley

生人1834～1906年 》71

FYI: inventor fore-runner to the Wrights air- glider [bolometer]

史实: 发明, 先导为了飞机.

LAPLACE拉普拉斯la pu la si

Pierre Simon Laplace

生人1749～1827年 》78

FYI: Mathematics and statistics (Celestial Mechanics). His name is among the 72 names on the Eiffel tower [Eiffel: NW09] #46/72

史实: 数.新元史上埃菲尔铁塔单名.

LARSEN拉尔森la er sen

Norman Bernard Larsen

FYI: co-creator of WD-40: Water Dispersment- 40 lab trials

史实: 发明WD-40，水机.

LARSON拉尔送la er song

John Augustus Larson

生人1892～1965年 》73

FYI: Developed the first lie detector c1921 [polygraph]

史实: 发明行骗机-测谎.

LAUER劳尔lao er

Jean-Philippe Lauer

生人1902 ~ 2001年 》99

5FYI: Egyptian historian.

史实: 埃及古物学.

Canadian $5 bill and Laurier Park in Edmonton

LAURIER劳里埃lao li ai

[SIR] Henry Charles Wilfrid Laurier

生人1901年11月20日~ 1919年 》77

FYI: He served as the 7th Prime Minister of Canada from 1896~1911. In circa 1900 while the Chinese were immigrating to Canada, he raised their 'head tax' from $100 to 500 per person to inhibit their rapid influx. His image is on the Canadian $5 note since 1972 and an Edmonton park is named in his honor. *Canada is free and freedom is its nationality.

史实: 1896年至1911年任加拿大第七任总理.大约在1900年, 当中国人移民到加拿大时, 他将他们的 "人头税" 从每人100美元提高到500美元, 以抑制他们的快速移民。自1972年起, 他的形象就出现在加拿大5美元纸币上, 为了纪念他, 埃德蒙顿公园被命名为 "埃德蒙顿公园". *加拿大是自由的, 自由是它的国籍.

LAVELLE拉维尔杯la wei er bei

Calixa Lavelle

生人1842 ~ 1891年 》51

FYI: A French Canadian musician and composer is best known for composing the music for 'O Canada' in 1880, which in 1980 became the National Anthem. [see Adolyle-Basille Routier]

史实: 一位法裔加拿大音乐家和作曲家最著名的作品是1880年为 "O Canada" 创作的音乐, 1980年, O Canada成为国家雅典人.

LAVOISIER拉瓦锡la wa xi

Antoine Lavoisier

生人1743 ~ 1794年 》51

FYI: Renouned Chemist who discovered the properties of Oxygen c>1778 and Hydrogen c>1783. Studied under duPont. Named among the 72 people on the Eiffel tower [NW12] 47/72

史实: 化学家.发明:O, H2. 新元史上埃菲尔铁塔单名.

[查看~ see duPont]

LAWRENCE劳伦斯lao lun si

Thomas Edward Lawrence

生人1888 ~ 1935年 》47

FYI: archaeologist and diplomat. The famed "Lawrence of Arabia" is because of his courage. [see-L.Thomas]

史实: 高名劳伦斯*阿拉伯 [阿拉伯的劳伦斯]

LAYTON莱顿lai dun

John Gilbert "Jack" Layton

生人1950 ~ 2011年 》61

FYI: Canadian politician and Leader of the Opposition until his passing: NDP. * *Canada is a great country, one of the hopes of the world.*

史实: 政治家为了加拿大. *加拿大输一个伟大的国家, 是世界的希望之一.

LAYTON莱顿lai dun

Irving Peter Layton

生人1912 ~ 2006年 》94

FYI: aka: Israel Pincu Lazarovich; Romanian born- Canadian poet.

史实: 加拿大式.

LAZARUS拉撒路la sa lu

Emma Lazarus

生人1849 ~ 1887年 》76

FYI: Author of poetry, prose, translator and activist in early America. At the base of the 'Statue of Liberty' is a plaqued ingraved with the words penned by her. *Give me your tired, your poor, Your huddled masses yearning to breathe free, The wretched refuse of your teeming shore. Send these, the homeless, tempest-tossed, to me: I lift my lamp beside the golden door.

史实: 美国早期的诗歌,散文,翻译家和活动家.在"自由女神像"的底部是一个由她写下的字组成的根深蒂固的徽章."把你疲惫的,可怜的,挤在一起渴望自由呼吸的人群, 以及你那汹涌的海岸上可怜的垃圾, 交给我吧.把这些, 无家可归的人, 暴风雪扔给我, 我把灯举到金门旁边.

LEAR乐而le er

John Lear

生人1902 ~ 1978年 》76

FYI: Lear Jet designer and pilot

史实: 发明为了飞机 勒而.

LEARY李尔利 li er li

Timothy Francis Leary

生人1920 ~ 1996年 》75

FYI: Psychologist who experienced with drugs. Richard Nixon referred to him as "The most feared man in American".'turn on, tune in and drop out, think for yourself and question authority".

史实: 有吸毒经验的心理学家.理查德•尼克松称他为"美国最令人畏惧的人", 他说: "打开, 收听, 退出, 为自己着想, 质疑权威.

LEAVITT莱维特lai wei te

Henrietta Swan Leavitt

生人1868 ~ 1921年 》53

FYI: American astronomer who studied "luminosty" of stars which prepared the way for Edward Hubble. She was regarded as the "woman's human computer" in her era.

史实: 天文学家.她学习星星光亮度.

LECHATELIER拉查特利尔la cha te li er

Louis Lechatelier

生人1815 ~ 1873年 》58

FYI: Chemist and industrialist. Louis is noted for producing Aluminum from bauxite. His name is among the 72 on the Eiffel tower [SW05] 48/72

史实: 化学家.新元史上埃菲尔铁塔单名.

LEE李li

Reginald Robinson lee

生人1912年4月15日 》43 》[memorial纪念]

FYI: SS Titanic Crows Nest~ lookout:11:40pm

史实: 惨变:Titanic.

LEE李li

[SIR] Christopher Frank Carandini Lee

生人1922 ~ 2015年 》93

FYI: knighted 2003~drama and charity

史实: 艺人;慈善家.

LEGRAIN勒戈恩le ge en

Georges Legrain

生人1865 ~ 1917年 》52

FYI: Egyptologist of the 19th century. Had discovered over 800 statues.

史实:曾经八百雕像在埃及.

LEGENDRE勒让德le rang de

Adrien-Marie Legendre

生人1752 ~ 1833年 》81

FYI: Mathematician: Legendre polynomials. His name is among the 72 engraved on the Eiffel tower. [NW17] #49/72

史实: 数人.新元史上埃菲尔铁塔单名.

LEHN勒恩le en

Jean-Marie Pierre Lehn

生人1939年 ~ active

FYI: 1987 awarded the Nobel in organic chemistry. Best known for synthesize crown ethers. [查看DJCram, c*j*perdersen,]

史实: 1987年嘉家诺贝尔为了Ether. [Nobelprize.org]

LEIGH丽li

Vivien Leigh

生人1913 ~ 1967年 》57

FYI: aka: Vivien Mary Hartley, Icon of the silver screen such as "Gone with the Wind".

史实: 艺人:"乱世影人"

*1234 courtesy St. Laurent Catholic School

Painting Courtesy of Laurier School

LENNON例侬li nong

John Winston Lennon

生人1940年10月9日 ~ 1980年12月8日 》40

FYI: [a&e] Member of the renowned British musical group called the Beatles. Author, song writer and activist until he was shot and killed. * You either get tired fighting for peace, or you die.

史实: 英国著名音乐团体披头士的成员.作者,歌曲作者和活动家，直到他被枪杀. *你要么为争取和平而疲倦，要么死了. [see Harrison]

LEONOV列昂诺夫lie ang nuo fu

Alexei Arkhipovich Leonov

生人1934年5月30日 ~ 2019年10月11日 》85

FYI: He was a Russian cosmonaut, writer, and artist. On 18 March 1965, he became the first human to conduct a spacewalk, exiting the capsule during the Voskhod 2 mission for 12 minutes and 9 seconds. *If we ever travel far from in the universe to another planet with intelligent life, let's just make patterns in their crops and leave.

史实: 他是俄罗斯宇航员, 作家和艺术家.1965年3月18日, 他成为第一个进行太空行走的人, 在Voskhod 2太空飞行任务中飞行了12分钟9秒. 在他们的庄稼上做图案然后离开.

LE PRINCE勒普兰斯le pu lan si

Louis Aime Augustin le Prince

生人c1841 ~ 1890年 》49

FYI: chemist/film maker "Father of cinema photography"

史实: 先导电影.

LEPSIUS莱普珍斯lai pu zhen si

Karl Richard Lepsius

生人1810 ~ 1884年 》74

FYI: Pioneering Egyptologist, linguist and archaeologist.

史实: 先导埃及, 语言学, 考古.

LESSING辛莱lai xin

Doris May Lessing

生人1919 ~ 2013年 》94

FYI: British novelist and Poet. Awarded the Nobel Prize in Literature~Prose c2007 [Nobelprize.org]

史实: 作者, 式.2007年诺贝尔为了文学.

LEVENE莱文lai wen

Phoebes Aaron Theodore Levene

生人1869 ~ 1940年 》71

FYI: Distinguished between the functions of the DNA and RNA.

史实: 发觉 DNA 和RNA它们不一样.

LEVENSON李文生li wen sheng

Sam Levenson

生人1911 ~ 1970年 》68

FYI: American humorist, television host, journalist.

史实: 电视节目;笑人.

LEVERRIER勒韦尔那la wei er na

Urbain Jean Joseph Leverrier

生人1811 ~ 1877年 》66

FYI: Mathematician who specialized in "celestial mechanics"; Discovered Neptune. His name is among the 72 engraved on the Eiffel tower [NE05] #50/72

史实: 数教.新元史上埃菲尔铁塔单名.

LEVY李维li wei

David~H~Levy

生人1948年 ~ active

FYI: Co-discovery of shoemaker-levy comet. 1994 the comet collided with Jupiter. [-Shoemaker]

史实: Shoemaker*李维 彗星.1994年他筑木星.

LEWIS路易斯lu yi si

Al Lewis

生人1923 ~ 2006年 》83

FYI: [a&e] Was a character actor as the beloved Grandpa of the Munsters television show 1964-66.

史实: 艺人"老伯伯".

LEWIS路易斯lu yi si

Jerry Lewis

生人1926 ~ 2017年 》91

FYI: [a&e] aka Joseph Levitch; actor, comedian. Multiple Dystrophie-Host.

史实: 演员，喜剧演员.多肌营养不良宿主.

LEWIS路易斯lu yi si

Shari Lewis

生人1933 ~ 1998年 》55

FYI: [a&e] Aka Sonia Phyllis Hurwitz; ventriloquist entertainer and puppeteer: Sock puppet~ Lamb chops.

史实: 口技演员和木偶演员Lamb*chops.

LEWIS路易斯lu yi si

Clive Staples Lewis

生人1898 ~ 1963年 》65

FYI: Aka C.S. Lewis. British novelist and writer of the Narnia series.

史实: 作者"纳尼亚".

LEYENDECKER莱恩德克lai en de ke

Joseph Christian Leyendecker

生人1874 ~ 1951年 》77

FYI: Artist :The Saturday Evening Post. Modern Magazine design.

史实: 画皮.星期六晚上报. 现代杂志设计.

LIBERACE利巴日记li ba ri ji

Wladziu Valentino Liberace

生人1919年5月16日 ~ 1987年 》68

FYI: [a&e] Renouned for his piano playing. Regarded as "Mr. Showmanship", as well as his dress code of surprises. *Nakedness makes us democratic, adornment makes us individuals.

史实: 世纪高名艺人钢琴演奏.*赤裸裸使我们民主, 装饰使我们成为一个人.

LIGHTOLLER来托尔lai tuo er

Charles Herbert Lightoller

生人1874 ~ 1952年 》78

FYI:Second Officer board the RMS Titanic. DISTINGUISHED SERVICE CROSS ie; Titanic.

史实: 二副登上了泰坦尼克号.

LILIUS里勤斯 li qin si

Aloysius Lilius

生人c1510 ~ 1576年 》

FYI: Aka Luigi Lilio; Astronomer, chronologist who presented the New age calender proposed to Pope Gergory XIII. 15 October 1582

史实: 天文学家, 提出新纪年历的天文学家 1582年10月15日; 公里.

LISZT李斯特li si te

Franz Liszt

生人1811 ~ 1886年 》75

FYI: composer, conductor, music teacher

史实: 作曲家, 指挥, 音乐院.

LINCOLN林肯lin ken

Abraham Lincoln

生人1809 ~ 1865年 》56

FYI: U.S. president, assassinated in office. *Nearly all men can stand adversity, but if you want to test a man's character, give him power.*

史实: 美国总统死了1865年. *几乎所有男人都可以忍受逆境, 但是如来您想测试一个男人的性格, 请给他力量.

LINDBERGH林丹比各 lin dan bi ge

Charles Augustus Lindbergh

生人1902 ~ 1974年 》72

FYI: author, inventor, explorer and World famous pilot

史实: 作者, 发明人, 探险和飞行员.

LINKLETTER林克莱特 lin ke lai te

Arthur Gordon "Art" Linkletter

生人1912 ~ 2010年 》97

FYI: [a&e] children 's TV personality. "Kids Say The Darndest Things." *Things turn out best for the people who make the best out of the way things turn out.*

史实: 高名主持人; "孩子们说" .*对于娜些从事态发展中获得最大收益的人来说, 事情发展得最好.

LINNAEUS林奈斯lin nai si

Carl Linnaeus

生人1707～1778年 》71

FYI: Father of modern Taxonomy, Scientist. He changed the Celsius scale to read as it is today...(0) freezing point of water. [see Celsius]

史实: 改动一个温度比例尺[Celsius].

LIPTON利普顿 li pu dun

[SIR] Thomas Johnstone Lipton

生人1848～1931年 》83

FYI: Founder of Lipton tea with the tetrahedral bag

史实: 先导茶带子.

LOCKYER了科尔le ke er

[Sir] Joseph Norman Lockyer

生人1836～1920年 》84

FYI: Astronomer who discovered Helium was part of the Suns chemistry. [查看- E.Rutherford, W.Huggins, G.Hale]

史实: 氦上太阳.发现氦的天文学家是太阳化学的一部分.

LOGOSI卢哥斯lu ge si

Bela Logosi

生人1882～1956年 》74

FYI: [a&e] Actor and The Original TV Dracula.

史实: 早高名艺人，第一次"德古拉".

LOGUE罗格 luo ge

Lionel George Logue

生人1880～1953年 》73

FYI: speech and language therapist who successfully treated King George VI stammer. *Elocution~is the study of formal speaking in pronunciation, grammar, style and tone.

史实: 他帮乔治王语言障碍.

LORENZ洛沦兹 luo lun ci

Edward Norton Lorenz

生人1917 ~- 2008年 》90

FYI: mathematician and meteorologist was pioneer of "chaos theory", coined "The Butterfly Effect."

史实: 数老师, 生道 蝴蝶效应 "蝴蝶效应 ".

LORET罗瑞特luo rui te

Victor Clemet Georges Philippe Loret

生人1859 ~ 1946年 》87

FYI: He founded the school of Egyptology at the University of Lyons.

史实: 建校为了埃及古物学.

LORILLARD罗瑞拉德luo rui la de

Griswald Lorillard

生人c1888年

FYI: started the tuxedo fashion for men.

史实: 男衣图案.

LOMAX罗马克斯luo ma ke si

Alan Lomax

生人1915 ~ 2002年 》87

FYI: American Ethnomusicologist.

史实: 美国民族音乐学家.

LOMBARDO隆巴多long ba duo

Guy Lombardo

生人1901 ~ 1977年 》76

FYI: [a&e] aka Gaytano Alberto Guy Lombardo ". Canadian musician who popularized the New year song; Auld Lang Syne~written by Robert Burns.

史实: 国家高名音 "友谊地久天长 ".

LOMONOSUV勒莫弄苏le mo nu su

Mihail Vaslyevich Lomonosuv

生人1711 ~ 1765年 》53

FYI: proposed that Venus had an atmosphere.

史实: 太白星气候

LONG良liang

Huey Pierce Long jr.

生人1893 ~ 1935年 》42

FYI: politician: "every man a king"

史实: 政为了美国.

LONGFELLOW良弗罗 liang fu luo

Henry Wadsworth Longfellow

生人1807 ~ 1882年 》75

FYI: American poet and educator. Was known as one of "The Fireside Poets." Wrote the poem of "Paul Rivere's ride"

*Fireside Poets: Longfellow, William Cullant Bryant, John Greenleaf Whittier, James Russell Lowell, Oliver Wendall Holmes Sr.

史实: 国家式, 老师. 被称为 "炉边诗人" 之一.

LOUD老德lao de

John Jacob Loud

生人1844 ~ 1916年 》72

FYI: designed the ball point pen [查看-Esterbrook]

史实: 发明一个圆珠笔.

LOUIS鲁丝lu si

Antoine Louis

生人1723 ~ 1792年 》69

FYI: French surgeon and physiologist. He designed the prototype to use in the death penalty with Guillotine. [查看- j.i.Guillotine]

史实: 法国医生. 他设计的原型用于死刑断头台.

LOWE洛luo

Harold Godfrey Lowe

生人1882 ~ 1944年 》61 》[memorial纪念]

FYI: Fifth officer RMS Titanic.

史实: 泰坦尼克号记忆.

LOWELL罗威尔 luo wei er

James Russell Lowell

生人1819 ~ 1891年 》72

FYI: American romantic poet, critic, diplomat.

*Fireside Poets: Longfellow, Wittier, Bryant, Lowell, Holmes.

史实: 国家式,评论家, 外交官.

LOVECRAFT吕卡热法特 lv ka re fa te

Howard Philips Lovecraft

生人1890 ~ 1937年 》47

FYI: Twentieth century horror fiction writers. The Alchemist: 1916.

*The oldest and strongest emotion of mankind is fear, and the oldest and strongest kind of fear is fear of the unknown.

史实: 二十世纪恐怖小说作家.炼金术士:1916年.

*人类最古老和最强烈的情感是恐惧, 最古老和最强烈的恐惧是对未知的恐惧.

LOVELL吕花乐lv hua le

James Arthur "Jim" Lovell

生人1928年3月25日 ~ active

FYI: aka James Arthur Lovell Jr: former NASA astronaut [Apollo 13] and retired captain. During the flight of 13 an explosion took place putting all in danger. His famous response is now etched in history, "Houston, we have a problem". (The successful failure).

史实:*太空人在13次飞行中, 发生了爆炸, 使所有人处于危险之中.他那著名的回答现在已刻在历史中:《休斯敦, 我们有问题.》

LUCE卢斯lu si

Henry Robinson Luce

生人1898～1967年 》69

FYI: Founder of TIME magazine.

史实: 先导 "时间报".

LUTHER路德 lu de

Martin Luther

生人1483～1546年 》63

FYI: Reformation protestant leader. Was a main component of the Bible being translated into German.

史实: 教老师, 翻译从德国到英国语.

LUXEMBURG罗森博格 luo sen bo ge

Rosa Luxemburg

生人1871～1919年 》48

FYI: From a Jewish heritage and being denied the normal privileges, She became a philosopher, economist, anti-war vocal force. Member of Spartacus Republic. She would later be executed for her views. Her pseudonym was "Junium", *those who do not move, do not notice their chains!"

史实: 高名哲学从犹太人的传统和被剥夺的正常特权, 她成为一个哲学家, 经济学家, 反战声乐力量.斯巴达克斯共和国成员.她后来会因自己的观点而被处决.

LYELL莱伊尔lai yi er

[SIR] Charles Lyell

生人1797～1875年 》77

FYI: Scottish geologist. Studied earthquakes and volcanoes. He coined the terms: Palaeozoic [ancient life], Mesozoic [age of reptiles] and Cenozoic [new life or current era].

史实: 地质学家, 介绍: 古生代[古生物],中生代[爬行动物时代]和新生代[新生命或现时代].

LYNCH林车 lin che

Edmund Calvert Lynch

生人1885 ~ 1938年 》52

FYI: 1915 Oct 15 became co founder of Merril - Lynch. Stock broker and financier ie: Kmart, JC.Penny etc.

史实: 故事.美林股票经纪人和金融家 .

LYTE莱特 lai te

Eliphalet Oram Lyte

生人1842 ~ 1913年 》71

FYI: American teacher and author and composer of "row row row your boat"

史实:写歌: 划排划船.

From Group "L" you can pick one person or up to ten Surnames and write their Surname in Chinese. You may try HORIZONTAL or VERTICAL in the traditional Chinese form.

M

《我看到人们和事物的优点。对我来说，杯子总是半满的》

"I see the good in people, and in things. To me, the glass is always half full."
Andrew Stuart MCLEAN迈凯鳄恩mai kai e en

*1234 with permission of Roberta MacAdams school.
Courtesy of Catherine MacAdams School

MACADAMS麦克亚当斯mai ke ya dang si

Roberta Catherine MacAdams

生人1818年2月21日 ～ 1959年12月16日 》79

FYI: Serving as a Lt. in the military as a dietitian. She was also elected to parliament [1917-1921] along with Louise McKinney [Famous Five] and was able to pass legislation. Roberta MacAdams school in S. Edmonton honors her name.

史实: 在军队里当中尉当营养师.她还和路易丝•麦金尼（著名的五位）一起当选为议会议员，并通过了立法.埃德蒙顿的罗伯塔•麦克亚当斯学校以她的名字命名.

photo by Forest L.

MACDONALD麦当劳mai dang lao

[SIR] John Alexander MacDonald

生人1815年1月11日 ~ 1891年6月6日 》76

FYI: He was Canada's First PM. As well, he was a controversial figure within Canadian political arena . His image appears on the Canadian $10 bill until Dec 08 2016, [see-Viola Desmond]

史实: 他是加拿大的第一位首相.同时, 他也是加拿大政治舞台上一个有争议的人物.在2016年12月8日之前, 他的形象出现在加拿大10美元的账单上.

MACE马斯ma si

Arthur Cruttenden Mace

生人1874 ~ 1928年 》81

FYI: Egyptologist

史实: 地质学家

Courtesy of Government of Alberta

MACEWAN麦克龙恩mai ke long en

[Dr.] John Walter Grant MacEwan

生人1902年8月12日 ~ 2000年 》97

FYI: Husbandry [agriculture], politician (MLA) also Lieutenant-Governor of Alberta [1966-1974]. Grant MacEwan College named in his honor. Edmonton, Alberta, Canada. O.C.1974. He was the second person to receive a State funeral.

史实: 畜牧业[农业], 政治家（MLA）也是阿尔伯塔省副省长[1966-1974].格兰特·麦克尤恩学院以他的名字命名.加拿大阿尔伯塔省埃德蒙顿市.O.C.1974年.他是第二个参加国葬的人.[G*麦克龙恩学院] [see-Peter Dawson]

MACFARQUHAR麦克法卡尔mai ke fa ka er

Colin Macfarquhar

生人1743 ~ 1793年 》50

FYI: printer and co-founder of Britannica Encyclopedia;1768 ~ Britannica is Latin for British.

史实: 《大英百科全书》的印刷者和联合创始人;1768年至1768年, 大英百科全书是拉丁语.

MACGREGOR马基高ma ji gao

[Dr.] James 'Jim" Grierson MacGregor

生人1905 ~ 1989年 》84

FYI: Educated as a professional engineer he had a love for Alberta and soon began writing of its history and would be the author of 18 books. A History of Alberta - 1972, North-west of sixteen are his most notable. 1973 he was awarded the Order of Canada.

史实: 他受过专业工程师的教育, 热爱阿尔伯塔省, 并很快开始撰写阿尔伯塔省的历史, 成为18本书的作者.阿尔伯塔省的历史-1972年, 16个西北部是他最著名的.1973年, 他被授予加拿大勋章. [*Librarything]

MACH马克ma ke

Ernst Mach

生人1838年2月18日 ~ 1916年 》78

FYI: German physicist. Devised the speed of sound; 1 Mach=1224 km per hr.

史实: 德国高名物理学家, 建速度声.

City of Edmonton public archives

MACKENZIE麦肯齐mai ken qi

Kenneth W. MacKenzie

生人1862年2月3日 ~ 1929年10月9日 》69

FYI: 1899~1901 6th mayor of Edmonton and as Alderman.

史实: 1899~1901年埃德蒙顿市第六任市长兼市议员.

Portrait and bust from the U of A Hospital.

MACKENZIE麦肯齐mai ken qi

Walter Campbell Mackenzie

生人1909年8月17日 ~ 1978年12月15日 》69

FYI: Canadian surgeon and academic. Served as Professor and chairman of the Department of Surgery at the University of Alberta's Faculty of Medicine and was dean from 1959 to 1974. 1974 was a recipient of the Order of Canada.

史实: 加拿大外科医生和学者.曾任阿尔伯塔大学医学院外科教授和主任，1959年至1974年任院长.1974年是加拿大命令的接受者.

Photo by Forest. L

MACPHAIL马凯法ma kai fa

Agnes Campbell Macphail

生人1890 ~ 1954年 》63

FYI: Canadian educator and politician. First female to be elected to Canadian House of Commons [3 times]. *... well I'm no lady, I'm a human being. Her image is also seen on the 2017 [150 edition] Canadian $10 bill.

史实: 加拿大教育家和政治家.第一位当选为加拿大下议院议员的女性（3次）."……好吧，我不是女士，我是人类." 她的形象也出现在2017年（150版）加拿大10美元的账单上.

MACLELLEN麦克茉伦mai ke mo lun

Gordon~F~Maclellen

生人1945 ~ 1975年 》30 》[memorial纪念]

FYI: *SS Edmund Fitzgerald~Lake Superior 10 Nov 1975

史实: S.S. 埃德蒙*菲茨杰拉德 湖高强1975年 11月10日

MACLEOD麦克劳德mai ke lao de
James Farquharson MacLeod

生人1836 ~ 1894年 》58

FYI: Lieutenant-Colonel *North West Mounted Police. Fort Macleod is named in his honor. (Alberta, Canada)

史实: 西北骑警中校.麦克劳德堡以他的名字命名.

MACKENZIE麦肯司mai ken ci
Alexander Mackenzie

生人1822~ 1892年 》70

FYI: 2nd Prime Minister of Canada [1873-1878]

史实: 加拿大第二总理 1873-1878年

MAHLER马勒ma le
Gustav Mahler

生人1860 ~ 1911年 》51

FYI: Austrian composer/classics

史实: 奥地利作曲家/古典作品.

MAILER梅勒mei le
Norman Kingsley Mailer

生人1923 ~ 2007年 》84

FYI: Novelist~journalist. "The White Negro" *Mailer Prize~literary award.

史实: 记者: "白种黑人 ". 白黑人.

MAIMAN梅曼mei man
Theodore Harold "Ted" Maiman

生人1927年11月12日~ 2007年 》80

FYI: "Father of the electron-optic industry." developed the first laser c.1960 May 16, forerunner of the bar-code readers.

史实: 电子光学工业之父〉,《第一台激光器的开发》,1960年5月16日,条形码阅读器的先驱.

MALLROY马尔罗伊ma er luo yi

George Herbert Leigh Mallroy

生人1886 ~ 1924年 》37

FYI: A British mountaineer who took part in three expeditions to Mount Everest. In 1924 he and his partner did not return from the third climb. His body was discovered 1999 May 1 by other climbers. * Why do you want to climb Mt. Everest, Sir? - Because it is there."

史实: 参加过三次探险的英国登山家珠穆朗玛峰.1924年，他和他的合伙人没有从第三次攀登.他的尸体于1999年5月1日被其他人发现.登山者.(问)"-先生，你为什么要攀登珠穆朗玛峰? - 因为它就在那里."

MALUS马鲁斯ma lu si redo

Etienne Louis Malus

生人1775 ~ 1812年 》37

FYI: Engineer and physicist is known for the Malus Law. His name is among the 72 names on the Eiffel tower: [NE07] #51/72

史实: 工程，物里学家.马鲁斯法.新元史上埃菲尔铁塔单名.

MANCINI马西你man xi ni

Enrico Nicola "Henry" Mancini

生人1924 ~ 1994年 》70

FYI: [a&e] Renouned as a musician for Motion picture Scores.

史实: 高名音乐电影.

MANDELA曼德拉man de la

Nelson Rolihlahla Mandela

生人1918年7月18日 ~ 2013年12月5日 》95

FYI: regarded as the "Father of the Nation" in his birth country. His fight against apartheid was his ongoing theme. Honored with the Nobel Peace prize. * When a man is denied the right to live the life he believes in, he has no choice but to become an outlaw. [Nobelprize.org]

史实: 在其出生国被视为"国家之父".他反对种族隔离的斗争一直是他的主题.荣获诺贝尔和平奖. *当一个人被剥夺享有他所信奉的生活的权利时，他别无选择，只能成为违法者.

MANNERS曼尔斯 man er si

Marion Margaret Violet Manners

生人1856 ~ 1937年 》81

FYI: British artist and Noblewoman; sketches ie: CJ Rhodes etc.

史实: 英国艺术家和贵妇人. 矜贵, 美树.

Courtesy of Government of Alberta

MANNING曼宁man ning

Ernest Charles Manning

生人1908 ~ 1996年 》87

FYI: Canadian politician and eighth premier of Alberta Canada [1943-1968]. Beyond politics he was also an announcer on 'Back to the Bible hour' which served Canadian audiences. His son Ernest Preston Manning would also serve in politics and founded the 'Reform Party of Canada'. Manning freeway and the town of Manning Alberta are named after him.

史实: 加拿大政治家和加拿大阿尔伯塔省第八任总理[1943-1968].除了政治,他还是《回到圣经时刻》的播音员,该节目为加拿大观众服务.他的儿子欧内斯特·普雷斯顿·曼宁（Ernest Preston Manning）也将在政界任职, 并创立了 "加拿大改革党" . (Reform Party of Canada). 曼宁高速公路和曼宁阿尔伯塔镇以他的名字命名.

MANSON曼森man sen

Charles Milles Manson

生人1934 ~ 2017年 》83

FYI: aka Charles Milles Maddox; American criminal and cult leader.

史实: 美国罪犯和邪教领袖.

MANZETTI曼色提man se ti

Innocenzo Vincenzo Bartolomeo Luigi Carlo Manzetti

生人1826 ~ 1877年 》51

FYI: forerunner to the telephone. [speaking telegraph]

史实: 曾经电话.

MARCONI马可尼ma ke ni

Guglielmo Marconi

生人1874 ~ 1937年 》63

FYI: Electronic engineer see "Marconi's Law". Historically Tesla and Marconi were competitors.

史实: 电工程 权利要求.

MARIE玛丽ma li

Pierre Marie

生人1853 ~ 1940年 》87

FYI: Neurologist, co-discover (Charcot- Marie- Tooth syndrome).

史实: 神经病医生.

MARIETTE玛丽特ma li te

Francois Auguste Ferdinand Pasha Mariette

生人1821 ~ 1881年 》61

FYI: Egyptologist

史实: 埃及古物学.

MARFAN马凡ma fan

Antoine Bernard-Jean Marfan

生人1858 ~ 1942年 》84

FYI: French pediatrician specializing in deformities of bones.

史实: 孩子医生, 变形.一个被称为 "小花" 的法国修女.特丽莎修女 认为她是一个正直的圣人最好的例子,并把特雷塞 的名字当作自己的名字.

MARTO马头ma tou

Fransico Marto

生人1908 ~ 1919年 》11

FYI: the Fatima story of 1917 May 13 [看-see Lucia Santos]

史实: 花地玛堂区.

MARTO马头ma tou

Jacinta Marto

生人1910 ~ 1920年 》10

FYI: the Fatima story of 1917 May 13 [看-see Lucia Santos]

史实: 花地玛堂区.

MARX马克思ma ke si

Groucho Marx

生人1890 ~ 1977年 》87

FYI: [a&e] aka Julius Henry Marx. Comedian and actor early nineteen century. Host of the radio program "You Bet Your Life."

史实: 喜剧早期电视和无钱电.

MASKEPETOON马斯克普特恩ma si ke pu te en

生人1807 ~ 1869年 》62

FYI: Cree band leader in Western Canada. Was considered a peace keeper of his era. Maskepetoon Wild Life sanctuary (Alberta) named in his honor. [*DBC]

史实: 加拿大西部的Cree乐队领队.被认为是他那个时代的一个和平保护者.马斯凯普顿野生动物保护区 (阿尔伯塔) 以他的名字命名.

MASPERO马斯怕ma si pa

Gaston Camille Charles Maspero

生人1846 ~ 1916年 》70

FYI: Egyptologist

史实: 埃及老师.

MASSEY马赛ma sai

Charles Vincent Massey

生人1887 ~ 1967年 》80

FYI: Canadian lawyer, politician & diplomat. The Right Honourable c. post 1925. *Massey Lectures Series is in his honor (Canada)

史实: 发老师, 政学家, 使馆.*加拿大马赛教程.

MASSEY马赛ma sai

Daniel Massey

生人1798 ~ 1856年 》58

FYI: Former blacksmith and founder of Massey tractors. c1847 [pre- Massey- Ferguson era]

史实: 工程衣机器:1847年到今.

MATTEUCCI马特奇ma te qi

Felice Matteucci

生人1808 ~ 年1887 》81

FYI: combustion engine c.1854 with [*see Eugenio Barsanti]

史实: 工程车.

MATSON马特森ma te sen

Harold "Matt" Matson

FYI: c1945 MATTEL the TOY manufacturer was co-founded by Matson. [see-Elliot Handler]

史实: MATTEL:先导1945年玩具制造商.

MAUNDER马恩德尔ma en de er

Edward Walter Maunder

生人1851年4月12日 ~ 1928年 》77

FYI: British astronomer who discovered that our sun had cycles: Solar Magnetic Cycle~ Maunder effect.

史实: 天文学家:太阳有周的 "Maunder*effect" [马恩德尔影响]

MAYER马尔ma er

Louis Burt Mayer

生人1884 ~ 1957年 》73

FYI: [a&e] Film producer and co-founder of (MGM:metro-goldwyn-mayer)

史实:先导为了电影.

MAXIM马克沁ma ke qin

Hiram Stevens Maxim Sr.

生人1840 ~ 1916年 》76

FYI: Inventor designed: mouse traps, hair curling irons,

史实: 工程:发明

MAXIM马克沁ma ke qin

Hiram Percy Maxim jr.

FYI: son of Hiram Stevens Maxim, founded (ARRL) American Radio Relay League~1914. "Ham radios".

史实: 普通人电台[火腿].

MAXWELL麦克斯韦mai ke si wei

James Clerk Maxwell

生人1831 ~ 1879年 》38

FYI: Light theory (Theory of electromagnetism); pioneer of color photography c1861

史实: 1861年发明光线.

Courtesy Edmonton public archives

MAY梅mei

Charles May

生人1858 ~ 1932年 》73

FYI: 8th mayor of Edmonton 1905~1906. Contractor and politician.

史实: 埃德蒙顿市第八任市长, 1905~1906年.承包商和政治家.

MAYO梅奥mei ao

William Worrall Mayo

生人1819 ~ 1911年 》92

FYI: medical doctor and chemist. The "Mayo Clinic" named in his honor.

史实: 梅奥医生.

MAZES每瑟mai ze

Joseph~W~Mazes

生人1916 ~ 1975年 》59 》[memorial纪念]

FYI: SS*Edmund Fitzgerald~Lake Superior: Special Maintenance Man. 10 Nov 1975

史实: S.S. 埃德蒙*菲茨杰拉德 湖高强1975年 11月10日

MAZZULLO马祖咯ma zu lo

Giuseppe Mazzullo

生人1926 ~ 1961年 》35

FYI: [a&e] Italian stage actor and voice of Topo Gigio. Ed Sullivan Show.

史实: 艺人口声为了.

MCAULIFFE麦考利夫mai kao li fu

Sharon Christa Mcauliffe

生人1986年1月28日 》[memorial纪念] (Q)

FYI: Died on board the Challenger accident~28 Jan 1986~ 73 sec into the flight. All 8 crew members died. *I touch the future. I teach.

史实: 八人死了飞行73秒.跳斩者. *我触及未来.我教书.

MCCAIN麦凯恩mai kai en

John Sidney McCain III

生人1936年8月29日 ~ 2018年 》81

FYI: Former POW during N. Vietnam era, military pilot and American senator. *duty, honor, country!

史实: 越南时代的战俘, 军事飞行员和美国参议员. "责任, 荣誉, 国家!"

MCCAIN麦凯恩mai kai en

Andrew McCain

FYI: Son's Bob, Harrison, Wallace and Andrew carried on the business upon their fathers passing c.1953 McCain frozen foods.

史实: 先导1953年冰品.

MCCANDLESS马卡安德勒ma ka an de le

Christopher Johnson Mccandless

生人1968 ~ 1992年 》24.

FYI: True story, he rejected the wealth and success of his father.

"Into the Wild" directed by -Sean Penn

史实: 事实上, 他拒绝了父亲的财富和成功. "进入野外".

MCCARTHY麦卡易mai ka yi

John~H~McCarthy .

生人1913 ~ 1975年 》62 》[memorial纪念]

FYI: First Mate 10 Nov 1975 *SS Edmund Fitzgerald~Lake Superior 10 Nov 1975 纪念

史实: S.S. 埃德蒙*菲茨杰拉德 湖高强1975年 11月10日.

City of Edmonton public archive

MCCAULEY米卡雷mi ke lei

Matthew McCauley

生人1850年7月11日 ~ 1930年10月25日 》80

FYI: First Mayor of Edmonton c1892-1895. Edmonton was a newly formed town (1892-1904) and belonged to the Northwest Territories prior- 1905 era. [*List of Mayors of Edmonton]

史实: 第一次乡长为了埃德蒙顿 -加拿大.

MCCLINTOCK麦克林托克mai ke lin tuo ke

Barbara McClintock

FYI: Awarded the Nobel prize in 1983 for physiology in medicine. [Nobelprize.org]

史实: 1983年诺贝尔为了生理.

(L)Courtesy of Government of Alberta. Park photo courtesy Forest L.

MCCLUNG麦克勒恩mai ke le en

Nellie Letitia Mcclung

生人1873 ~ 1951年 》78

FYI: Nellie Letitia [nee] Mooney was one of The Famous Five in Canadian history demanding that any woman is to be recognized as a person. She was the first female cabinet member in Alberta. All 5 woman have parks named in their honor located throughout Edmonton near the river. *Never explain, never retract, never apologize. Just get the thing done and let them howl. [see Murphy]

史实: 内莉•莱蒂娅•莫尼是加拿大历史上著名的五位女性之一, 她要求任何一个女人都要被认可为一个人.她是阿尔伯塔省第一位女内阁成员.这5个女人都有以自己的名誉命名的公园, 位于埃德蒙顿河附近.*从不解释, 从不收回, 从不道歉.把事情做好, 让他们嚎叫.

MCCOOL麦卡mai ke

William Cameron "Willy" McCool

生人1961 ~ 2003年 》41 》[memorial纪念]

FYI: NASA: Space Shuttle Columbia; 2003 Feb 1.

史实: NASA: 哥伦比亚天文.

MCCONNELL马卡纳ma ka nei

David Hall McConnell

生人1858 ~ 1937年 》79

FYI: Businessman; 1886 founded AVON.

史实: 先导AVON 1886年.

MCCRAE麦克雷mai ke lei

John McCrae

生人1872年11月30日 ~ 1918年1月28日 》45

FYI: Served as a Lieutenant Colonel and a physician during WW I. He was also an artist and author of "In Flanders Fields". Penned in 1915 May 3. MacCrae was designated as a "Person of National Historic Significance"1946.[wiki] *In Flanders fields the poppies blow Between the crosses, row on row.

史实: 在WWI期间担任中校和医生, 他也是"弗兰德斯领域"的艺术家和作者.在5月3日的 1915.麦克雷被任命为"国家历史意义重大人物" 1946. *在佛兰德斯领域, 罂粟花吹在十 字架之间, 一排排.

MCDONALD麦当劳mai dang lao

Richard James "Dick" and Maurice James "Mac"

FYI: [c.1940] fore runners of today's McDonald's. [-see Crock c.1955]

史实: 曾经麦当劳兄弟.

MCDONNEL麦克唐奈mai ke tang nai

James Smith McDonnell

生人1899 ~ 1980年 》81

FYI: cofounded "Mcdonnel-Douglas" aircraft in partnership with Donald Wills Douglas Sr.

史实: 合作的"麦克唐纳道格拉斯"飞机与唐纳德威尔斯道格拉斯SR合作伙伴关系.

City of Edmonton public archive

MCDOUGALL麦克杜格尔mai ke du ge er

John Alexander McDougall

生人1854 ~ 1928年 》74

FYI: First serving as a Methodist minister along with his father, He was a politician in Canada and an Alderman in Edmonton, then as Mayor of Edmonton. Several places are named in his honor.

史实：他最初和父亲一起担任卫理公会牧师，是加拿大的一名政治家，埃德蒙顿的一名议员，后来成为埃德蒙顿的市长.有好几个地方是以他的名义命名的.

(L) courtesy of the Government of Alberta, Park photo by Forest L.

MCKINNEY 麦金尼 mai jin ni

Louise McKinney

生人1868年6月7日 ~ 1931年 》63

FYI: was one of The Famous Five in Canadian history demanding that any woman is to be recognized as a person. She and Roberta MacAdams were both female cabinet member in Alberta.The Famous Five all have parks located throughout Edmonton near the river. *What, after all, is the purpose of woman's life? The purpose of woman's life is just the same as the purpose of man's life: …

史实: 是加拿大历史上著名的五个要求任何女人都要被承认为一个人的人之一.她和罗伯塔•麦克亚当斯都是阿尔伯塔省的女内阁成员,这五位著名的总统都在埃德蒙顿附近的河边设立了公园. 毕竟,女人生活的目的是什么? 女人生命的目的和男人生命的目的一样……

[see E. Murphy]

MCLEAN 麦克勒安 mai ke le an

Andrew Stuart McLean

生人1948 ~ 2017年 》69

FYI: Voice and Host of "The Vinyl Cafe-CBC". Professor Emeritus of Journalism Ryerson University: Toronto. O.C.2011.*I see the good in people, and in things. To me, the glass is always half full.

史实: 加拿大著名,口声为了 "乙烯基咖啡馆".瑞尔森大学新闻名誉教授: 多伦多.*我看到人们和事物的优点.对我来说,杯子总是半满的.

MCMANUS 麦克马努斯 mai ke ma nu si

Louis Manuel Mcmanus

FYI: Designed the first "Emmy" c1948; a winged lady holding an atom. The name is based on the idea of the "IMMY": image orthicon tube but changed to "Emmy" on behalf of the female figurine.

史实: 设计了第一个 "艾美" C1948;一个带着原子的有翼的女士.这个雕像.

Courtesy of City of Edmonton archives.

MCNAMARA麦克纳马拉mai ke nei ma la
William James McNamara 1913~1914
生人1879 ~ 1947年 》68
FYI: Serving first as an Alderman for Edmonton, was elected mayor 1913~1914.
史实: 第一任埃德蒙顿市议员, 1913~1914年当选市长.

MCSORLEY麦宋雷mai song lei
Earnest~M~McSorley
生人1912年 ~ 1975年11月10日 》63 》[memorial纪念]
FYI: *SS Edmund Fitzgerald: Captain~Lake Superior 10 Nov 1975
史实: S.S. 埃德蒙*菲茨杰拉德 湖高强1975年 11月10日

MCVICKAR麦维卡mai wei ka
Harry~W~McVickar
FYI: Business man and publisher and co founder of "Vogue' c1892.
史实: 商人和出版商, 共同创办的 "时尚 " C1892.

MEAD米德mi de

Margaret Mead

生人1901 ~ 1978年 》71

FYI: Researcher and cultural anthropologist wrote "coming of age".

史实: 研究者和文化人类学家写了《时代的来临》.

MECHANICUS妈看一卡ma kan yi ka

Philo Mechanicus

生人280 ~ 220 年BC 》60

FYI: aka Philo of Byzantium was inventor of the first known GIMBAL, similar to a compass. It is imperative for ships and airplanes. Also and filming while moving.

史实: 研究员和文化人类学家是第一个已知的万向节的发明家, 类似于指南针.船舶和飞机是必不可少的.在拍摄的同时, 还写了《时代的来临》.

MEIGHEN每恨mei hen

[SIR] Arthur Meighen

生人1874 ~ 1960年 》86

FYI: Lawyer and politician c.1926 11th&13 pm of Canada.

史实: 律师和政治家.

MEIR梅厄mei e

Golda Meir

生人1898 ~ 1978年 》80

FYI: Born Goldie Mabovitch in Kiev. She was a teacher in Israel, statesperson, politician and fourth Prime Minister of Israel [1969-1974]; 'The Iron Lady' of Israel. * "You can not shake hands with a clenched fist."

史实: 基辅出生的戈尔迪•马博维奇.她是以色列的教师,政治家,政治家和以色列第四任总理（1969-1974年）;以色列的 "铁娘子".* "你不能握紧拳头握手."

MELVILLE麦尔维尔mai er wei er

Herman Melville

生人1819 ~ 1891年 》72

FYI: American novelist, short story writer and poet. Wrote the novel Moby-Dick-1851

史实: 美国作者, 式:1851年"白鲸".

MERRICK梅里克mei li ke

Joseph Carey Merrick

生人1862 ~ 1890年 》28

FYI: Known as the Elephant Man because of his extreme physical deformities. He could only sleep sitting up, upon his death he was trying to lay down as normal people do which snapped his cervical.

史实: 由于身体畸形而被称为象人.他只能坐着睡觉, 在他死后, 他试图像正常人一样躺下, 折断了他的子宫颈. [查看-Trevis]

》》N.B. at the end of this section, a small poem is included that Merrick used in pamphlets.

MENCKEN门肯men ken

Henry Louis Mencken

生人1880 ~ 1956年 》76

FYI: journalist and scholar of American English.

史实: 记者和大方为了美国英语.

MENDEL门德勒men de le

Gregor Johann Mendel

生人1822 ~ 1884年 》62

FYI: Monk, scientist. Father of modern Genetics. He coined "recessive and dominant".

史实: 僧侣: 生道 "隐形-主宰".

MENDELEEV门捷列夫men jie lie fu

Dmirtri Ivanovich Mendeleev

生人1834 ~ 1907年 》73

FYI: his work provided future changes to the Periodic table c.1869 [-see de Chancourtois]

史实: 他的工作为周期表提供了未来的变化.1869年周期表.

MENDENHALL门登霍尔men deng huo er

Thomas Corwin Mendenhall

生人1841年10月4日 ~ 1924年 》82

FYI: An American physicist and meteorologist who encouraged the U.S.A. to adopt the metric system.

史实: 美国物理学家和气象学家, 鼓励美国采用公制.

MENGELE门格勤men ge qin

Josef Mengele

生人1911 ~ 1979年 》67

FYI: The angel of DEATH within the NAZI party. He designed all the ways to kill the oppressed.

史实: 高名死神为了希特勒.他设计了各种方法来杀死被压迫者.

MENIERE门尼尔mei ni er

Prosper Meniere

生人1799 ~ 1862年 》62

史实: He discovered that the ear disease is caused by a disturbance within the inner ear.

史实: 他发现耳部疾病是由内耳的紊乱引起的.

MENIPPUS门尼普斯men ni psi

Menippus of Gadara

FYI: [3rd BC] Greek writer known for Menippean satire

史实: 作者为了讽刺.

MENZEL们塞里men sai li

Donald Howard Menzel

生人1901 ~ 1976年 》75

FYI: Considered to be one of the first Theoretical physicist in America, He discovered the physical properties of the solar chromosphere thus the chemistry of the stars.
*Menzel's Field Guide: 8 Constellations.

史实: 他被认为是美国最早的理论物理学家之一, 他发现了太阳色球层的物理性质, 从而发现了恒星的化学性质.

MERCER墨赛mo sai

Johnny Herdon Mercer

生人1909 ~ 1976年 》67

FYI: [a&e] American lyrics and songwriter.

史实: 美国作者

MERCURY墨克里mo ke li

Freddie Mercury

生人1946 ~ 1991年 》45

FYI: [a&e] aka Farrokh Bomi Bulsara; "Queen"; lead vocalists. 2001 Rock and Roll HF.

史实: 王后音乐

MERRILL梅里尔mei li er

Charles Edward Merrill

生人1885 ~ 1956年 》70

FYI: Stockbroker, philanthropist. Co partner with Edmund C Lynch

史实: 股票经纪人，慈善家.与Edmund C Lynch合作.

MESSER梅西mei xi

Donald Charles Frederick "Don" Messer

生人1909年5月9日 ~ 1973年 》64

FYI: [a&e] Canadian Icon in Folk music. "The Don Messer's Jubilee".

史实: 高名加拿大音乐.

MESSIER梅西耶mei xi ye

Charles Messier

生人1730年6月26日 ~ 1817年 》88

FYI: French Astronomer who would publish the "nebulae and cluster catalogue". As well, the Messier crater on the moon is named in his honor. [Messier objects]

史实: 法国天文学家出版《星云和星表》同样，月球上的梅西尔陨石坑也是以他的名字命名的.

MICHELANGELO米开朗基罗mai ke lang qi luo~

Michelangelo Buonarroti

生人1475 ~ 1564年 》89

FYI: Renaissance painter >> finger of man touches finger of God.

史实: 文艺复兴时期画家>>人的手指触摸上帝的手指.

MICHELSON米克尔森 mi ke er sen

Albert Abraham Michelson

生人1852 ~ 1931年 》79

FYI: American physicist best known for measuring the speed of light. The first American to receive a Noble Prize c.1907 for his discovery. Light~186 350 miles per second aprox. [Nobelprize.org]

史实：美国物理学家,以测量光速而闻名.1907年,第一个因他的发现而获得诺贝尔奖的美国人.大约每秒186 350英里.

MICHELL米史里mi shi li

John Frederick Carden Michell

生人1933 ~ 2009年 》76

FYI: author, educator, megalith expert.

史实: 作者,教授,巨石大方.

MILANKOVICH马兰空为车ma lan ko wei che

Milutin Milankovich

生人1879 ~ 1958年 》79

FYI: aka Milankovic; Astronomer, climatologist, geophysicist. The "Milakovich cycle" explains the Earth's climate changes. [查看-see wegener]

史实: 天文学家,气象学家,地球物理学家."米拉科维奇周期" 解释了地球的气候变化.

MILL米尔mi er

Henry Mill

生人1683 ~ 1771年 》83

FYI: patented the first typewriter c1714. [see of book.]

史实: 1714年:手打

MILLER 米勤 mi qin

Frederick Edward John Miller

生人1824 ~ 1888年 》63

FYI: Business man and brewer and Founder of Miller beer. c1854

史实: "米勤脾酒"

MILNE米尔恩mi er en

Alan Alexandre Milne

生人1882 ~ 1956年 》74

FYI: Author of "Winnie- the -Pooh". The story book bear was inspired by a London Zoo bear called "Winnipeg". Milne took his idea and made it into a book series for his son, Christopher Robin. The name is also the little boy in the book. *Some people care too much. I think it's called love.*

史实:《小熊维尼》的作者.故事书《熊》的灵感来自伦敦动物园一只
名叫 "温尼伯" 的熊.米尔恩接受了他的想法，并把它编成了他的儿子
克里斯托弗•罗宾的系列丛书.这个名字也是书中的那个小男孩. *有些
人太在乎了.我认为这就是爱.

MINER米尔mi er
Jan Miner
生人1917 ~ 2004年 》86
FYI: [a/e] Actress in commercials such as Madge the manicurist: "Your soaking in it!"
史实: 广告中的女演员, 如美甲师玛奇.

MINSKY闵斯其min si qi
Marvin Lee Minsky
生人1927 ~ 2016年 》88
FYI: MIT Co-founder. Consultant in 2001: Space Roaming.
史实: 麻省理工联合创始人.曾在2001年担任顾问:太空漫游.

Photo by Forest L.~ local info sign

MISENER 米森尔 mi sen er

[Dr.] Geneva Misener

生人1877 ~ 1961年 》84

FYI: The first woman professor at the University of Alberta appointed in 1912 and served within the Department of Classics.

史实: 阿尔伯塔大学第一位女教授于1912年被任命为古典文学系教授.

MITCHELL 米切尔 mi qie er

John Newton Mitchell

生人1913 ~ 1988年 》75

FYI: Attorney General and close friend of Nixon.

史实: 司法部长和尼克松的密友.

City of Edmonton public archives

MITCHELL 米切尔 mi qie er

Frederick John Mitchell

生人1893 ~ 1979年 》86

FYI: An accountant by profession, he served as the 25th mayor of Edmonton; Sept 1959 ~ Oct 1959.

史实: 他是一名专业会计师, 曾任埃德蒙顿市第25任市长;1959年9月至1959年10月.

MITCHELL米切尔mi qie er

W~O~Mitchell

生人1914 ~ 1998年 》84

FYI: aka William Ormand Mitchell was a Writer and broad castor. "who has seen the Wind"- 1947. O.C.

史实: 转播《谁见过风》1947年

MITCHELL米切尔mi qie er

Dr. William~A~"Bill" Mitchell

生人1911 ~ 2004年 》93

FYI: creator of Tang, Pop rocks, jell-o, powdered egg whites.

史实: 先导为了"蛋清粉."

MOCKFORD莫克福特mo ke fu te

Frederick Stanley Mockford

生人1897 ~ 1962年 》65

FYI: Senior radio officer invented the distress call "Mayday"c.1923. It was the English translation of French "m'dair" (venez m'dair) ~ "come and help me"

史实: "Mayday" 来帮我!

MOHOROVICHICH莫霍罗维奇mo huo luo wei qi

[Dr.] Andrija Mohorovichich

生人1857 ~ 1936年 》79

FYI: geologist & seismologist. The father of modern geology.

史实: 地址学家， 地震学.

MOLSON莫尔森mo er sen

John Molson

生人1763 ~ 1836年 》73

FYI: founder of Molson brewery c.1786

史实: 1786年 "米勤脾酒".

MOMMSEN莫姆森mo mu sen

Theodre Mommsen

生人1817 ~ 1903年 》86

FYI: Was awarded the Nobel for literature c1902. "A history of Rome" [Nobelprize.org]

史实: 1902年 Nobel为了文艺.

[MONA] LISA蒙娜丽莎meng na li sha

Lisa Antonio Maria Del Giocondo [nee Gherardini]

生人1479 ~ 1542年 》63

FYI: [a&e] "Mona" is a combination of the French words "ma Donna"... meaning "My lady". [see leonardo* De* Vinci]

史实: "Mona"是法语单词"Ma Donna"的组合…意思是"我的夫人".

MONGE忙mang

Gaspard Monge

生人1746 ~ 1818年 》72

FYI: Mathematician: Father of descriptive geometry. His name is engraved on the Eiffel tower. [SE18] 52/72

史实: 数老师.新元史上埃菲尔铁塔单名.

MONROE梦露meng lou

Marilyn Monroe

生人1926 ~ 1962年 》36

FYI: [a&e] aka Norma Jeane Mortenson; actress, model and singer and sex symbol of the 50's.

史实: 演员,模特和歌手以及50年代的性象征.

MONSANTO孟山都meng shan du

Emmanuel Mendes de Monsanto

生人1808 ~ 1868年 》60

FYI: Was a sugar merchant and financier. His daughter Olga would marry J.F. Queeny and finance the saccharin Monsanto Empire. [see Queeny][*Geni]

史实: 是个糖商和金融家.他的女儿奥尔加将与J.F.奎尼结婚,并资助糖精孟山都帝国.

MONSON曼森man sen

Thomas Spencer Monson

生人1927 ~ 2018年 》90

FYI: WW2 veteran. Church leader and author. He worked in the publication industry and with Deseret News Press. 2008 he was called to serve as the President of the L.D.S. until his passing.* *May we ever choose the harder right instead of the easier wrong.*

史实: 主持为了耶稣基督后期圣徒教会. *愿我们选择更难的对而不是更容易的错误.

MONTAIGNE蒙田meng tian

Michel Eyquem de Montaigne

生人1533 年02月28日~ 1592年 》59

FYI: Is considered one of the most influential writers of the French Renaissance.*Friendship is the highest degree of perfection in society.

史实:被认为是法国文艺复兴时期最有影响力的作家之一.*友谊是社会上最高水平的完善.

MONTALBAN蒙塔尔里meng ta er li

Ricardo Gonzalo Pedro Montalban

生人1920 ~ 2009年 》88

FYI: [a&e] aka: Ricardo Gonzalo Pedro Montalban y Merino. Hollywood Icon; Fantasy Island and Star Trek Franchise.

史实: 好莱坞偶像;梦幻岛和星际迷航系列.

MONTESSORI蒙台梭利meng tai suo li

[DR.] Maria Tecla Artemisia Montessori

生人1870 ~ 1952年 》82

FYI: Educator, AMS (American Montessori Society)

史实: 高名老师美国蒙台梭利协会.

MONTGOMERY蒙哥马利meng ge ma li

Lucy Maud Montgomery

生人1874 ~ 1942年 》67

FYI: poet and prolific writer: "Anne of Green Gables". * *In this world you've just got to hope for the best and prepare for the worst and take whatever God sends.*

史实: 作者《清秀佳人》.* 在这个世界上, 您只是希望拥有最好的, 为最坏的事情做准备, 并接受上帝所差的一切.

MOODY魔蒂mo di

James Paul moody
生人Titanic 1912 》[memorial纪念]
FYI: sixth officer RMS Titanic.
史实: 第六军官泰坦尼克号.

MOODY魔蒂mo di

Dwight Lyman Moody
生人1837 ~ 1899年 》62
FYI: Evangelist: Moody Church.
史实: 魔蒂教.

MORGAN摩尔根mo er gen

John Pierpont "JP" Morgan Sr.
生人1837 ~ 1913年 》 76
FYI: Entrepreneur Banker. (80M dod~1913)
史实: 创业者银行.

MORGAN摩根mo gen

Frank Morgan
生人1890 ~ 1949年 》59
FYI: [a&e] actor and Wizard in Wizard of Oz; Represented the manipulative politician in any era.
史实: 艺人,《绿野仙踪》中的演员和巫师;代表任何时代操纵欲强
的政治家.

MORGAN摩根mo gen

Edward Paddock Morgan
生人1910 年6月23日~ 1993年1月27日 》83
FYI: An American journalist and writer who reported for newspapers, radio, and television media services. *A book is the only place in which you can examine a fragile thought without breaking it, or explore an explosive idea without fear it will go off in your face. It is one of the few havens remaining where a man's mind can get both provocation and privacy.

史实: 一位美国记者和作家报纸, 广播和电视媒体服务.*一本书是
只有在这里您可以检查脆弱的思想而无需打破它, 或探索一个爆炸性想法, 而不必担心它会
在你的脸.它是男人心中剩下的少数避风港之一
可以同时获得挑衅和隐私.

MORGENTALER摩根泰勤mo gen tai qin
Dr. Henekh "Henry" Morgentaler
生人1923 ~ 2013年 》90
FYI: Dr. and Pro-choice advocate
史实: 特意选择支持选择倡导者.

MORIN默认mo ren
Arthur Jules Morin
生人1795 ~ 1880年 》85
FYI: Physicist. Invented the dynamometer. His name is engraved on the Eiffel tower.
[SE12] 53/72
史实: 物理学家.新元史上埃菲尔铁塔单名.

MORISON莫日森mo re sen
Stanley Morison
生人1889 ~ 1967年 》78
FYI: Typographer
史实: 印刷业

MORLACCHI莫拉持mo la chi
Giuseppina Morlacchi
生人1846 ~ 1886年 》40
FYI: [a&e] She introduced the "cancan" dance to the New West of c1900
史实: 她介绍 "cancan"舞1900年

MORRIS莫里斯mo li si
Phillip Morris
生人1835 ~ 1873年 》38
FYI: tobacconist founded in 1854: Marlboro- Virginia slims etc
史实: 烟草商.

MORRIS莫里斯mo li si

Second Lieutenant Lionel Bertram Frank Morris

生人1897 ~ 1916年9月17日 》19

FYI: Of the war heroes and casualties of WWI, Morris was shot down and killed by the German Ace nick named 'The Red Baron'. It was the Baron's first air kill. Morris flew for the 'Royal Flying corps.

史实: 在第一次世界大战的英雄和伤亡中, 莫里斯被一位名叫 "红男爵" 的德国王牌尼克击毙.这是男爵的第一次空袭.莫里斯参加了皇家飞行队的飞行.

MORSE莫尔斯mo er si

Samuel Finley Breese Morse

生人1791 ~ 1872年 》81

FYI: Painter and inventor of 'The Morse Code' with the assistance of Leonard Gale. It was based on the theory of Electromagnetism. The first words were "What hath God wrought" was voiced on 1844 may 24.

史实: 在伦纳德•盖尔的帮助下创作了《摩尔斯电码》.它是以电磁学理论为基础的.1844年5月24日, 第一个词是 "上帝所做的".

MOSER莫斯尔mo si er

Robert Moser

生人1937年5月6日 ~ 》[memorial纪念]

FYI: LZ- Hindenburg mechanic

史实: 车工程, 兴登堡.

MOTT模特mo te

John Raleigh Mott

生人1865 ~ 1955年 》90

FYI: Awarded the Nobel in 1946 for Peace Movement. [Nobelprize.org]

史实: 嘉奖诺贝尔1946 为了平安.

MOUTON穆通mu tong

Gabriel Mouton

生人1618 ~ 1694年 》76

FYI: French scientist and early pioneer of the metric system

史实: 法国 教授.先导公制.

MOUNTBATTEN蒙巴顿meng ba dun

[Lord] Louis Mountbatten

生人1900～1979年 》79

FYI: Royalty and WW2 veteran.

史实: 皇室成员和二战老兵.

MOWAT莫厄特mo e te

Farley Migill Mowat

生人1921～2014年 》92

FYI: Canadian environmentalist. Author "never cry wolf". 1981 O.C. * *Without a function, we cease to be. So, I will write till I die.*

史实: 加拿大环境保护主义者.作者 "永不哭泣的狼".1981年. *没有功能, 我们就不再是.所以, 我会写直到我死.

MOZART莫扎特mo za te

Wolfgang Amadeus Mozart

生人1756～1791年 》35

FYI: [a&e] aka Johannes Chrysostmus Wolfgangus Theophilus Mozart. Composer of the classical era. Symphonic, chamber, operatic and choral. * *When I am traveling in a carriage, or walking after a good meal, or during the night when I cannot sleep; it is on such occasions that ideas flow best and most abundantly.*

史实: 古典时期的作曲家.交响乐,室内乐,歌剧和合唱. * 当我在马车上旅行, 跟后顿饭后散步时或夜间无法入睡时;正是在这种情况下, 思想才是最好, 最丰富的.

MURDOCK默多克mo duo ke

William Mcmaster Murdoch

生人1873～ 年1912 》39 》[memorial~纪念]

FYI: First Officer Titanic

史实: 泰坦尼克号大副.

Statue courtesy of Forest L.;(r) courtesy of Alberta Government

MURPHY墨菲mo fei

Emily Gowan Murphy

生人1868～1933年 》65

FYI: Canadian Woman's rights activist, jurist, author. Woman are "persons" legislation. [c 1917]. "The Famous Five"- memorial. This statue is located in Emily Murphy park in Edmonton. All 5 ladies have a park near the river of central Edmonton. She is the only lady with a statute in Edmonton. * Whenever I don't know whether to fight or not, I fight.

史实: 加拿大妇女权利活动家, 法学家, 作家。女人是 "人" 的立法.[公元1917年]. "著名的五个" -纪念馆。这座雕像位于埃德蒙顿的艾米丽墨菲公园.所有5位女士都在埃德蒙顿市中心附近有一个公园.她是埃德蒙顿唯一有法律规定的女人. * 无论何时我不知道是否战斗，我都会战斗.

MURROW穆罗mu luo

Edward Roscoe Murrow

生人1908～1965年 》57

FYI:aka Egbert Roscoe Murrow. Broadcast journalist.

史实: 广播记者.

MUYBRIDGE迈布里奇mai bu li qi

Eadweard James Muybridge

生人1830 ~ 1904年 》74

FYI: aka Edward James Muggeridge; Early motion picture and inventor of the "zoopraxoscope" movie projector. c.1879. First film of Yosemite Valley.

史实: 早期的电影和"动物镜"电影放映机的发明者.C.1879.

MYRDAL缪尔达尔miao er da er

Gunner Myrdal

生人1898 ~ 1987年 》89

FYI: aka Karl Gunnar Myrdal had a law and economic degree. Was awarded the Nobel with F. A. Hayek for Economics in 1974.

史实: 嘉奖诺贝尔为了经济学家. [Nobelprize.org]

MYRDAL缪尔达尔miao er da er

Alva Myrdal

生人1902 ~ 1986年 》84

FYI: Wife of Karl Myrdal. Was awarded the Nobel in 1982 for arms control and disarmament.

史实: 嘉奖诺贝尔为了裁军. [Nobelprize.org]

************** In memory of Joseph Merrick *************

Tis true my form is something odd,

的确，我的状态有些奇怪.

But blaming me is blaming God;

但是责备我是责备上帝

Could I create myself anew

我可以重新创造自己吗?

I would not fail in pleasing you.

我不会让你失望的.

If I could reach from pole to pole

如果我能从一极到达另一极

Or grasp the ocean with a span,

或者用跨度把握大海

I would be measured by the soul;

我会用灵魂来衡量

The mind's the standard of the man

心智是人的标准

~ adapted from "False Greatness" by Isaac Watts

From Group "M" you can pick one person or up to ten Surnames and write their Surname in Chinese. You may try HORIZONTAL or VERTICAL in the traditional Chinese form.

《对人类最大的利益》

~

"For the greatest benefit to Mankind"
Alfred NOBEL诺贝尔nuo bei er

NAMBU南部nan bu

Yoichiro Nambu

生人1921 ~ 2015年 》94

FYI: Was awarded the Nobel in 2008 for Particle Physics.

史实: 2008 嘉将诺贝尔为了质点物理学家. [Nobelprize.org]

NAPOLEON拿破仑na po lun

Napoleon Bonaparte

生人1769 ~ 1821年 》52

FYI: French Emperor and military genius.

史实: 法国皇帝还有军事天才.

NASH纳什na shen

John Forbes Nash jr.

生人1928 ~ 2015年 》87

FYI: Mathematical genius, was awarded the Nobel Peace Prize in Mathematics. (a beautiful mind-2001)

史实: 数老师.嘉奖诺贝尔为了数

NAVIER纳维尔na wei er

Claude Louis Naiver

生人1785 ~ 1836年 》51

FYI: Engineer and Founder of Structural Analysis. His name is engraved among the 72 names on the Eiffel tower [NW16] 54/72

史实: 工程.嘉奖诺贝尔为了解析几何.新元史上埃菲尔铁塔单名.

NAVILLE那威勒na wei le

Henry Edourd Naville

生人1844 ~ 1926年 》82

FYI: Swiss Archeologist, Egyptologist and bible scholar

史实: 瑞士考古学家,埃及学家,圣经学者.

NESTLE内斯特来nei si te lai

Heinrich [Henri] nestle'

生人1814 ~ 1890年 》76

FYI:He was a confectioner of drinks. [雀巢que chao] is the original meaning for "nest".

史实: 先导巧克力.帕子[雀巢que chao]

NEVILLE那威勒na wei le

Eric Neville

生人1939 ~ 2015年 》76

FYI: CFRN TV personality: PopKorn Play House With host "Klondike Eric" 1960 and 1970's. Edmonton, Alberta, Canada. * Captain Kirk basically set his phaser on destruct and blew Popcorn play house off the air.

史实: CFRN电视个性: '波普科恩游乐场'与东道主 "克朗代克埃里克" 1960年和1970年的 埃德蒙顿, 阿尔伯塔,加拿大. * 柯克船长基本上将他的相位器设置为破坏和自爆爆米花播 放空中的房子.

NEWBERRY牛吧日niu ba ri

Percy Edward Newberry

生人1869 ~ 1949年 》80

FYI: Egyptologist and author

史实: 作者, 埃及学家.

NEWCOMB扭康niu kang (insert jpg 2312)

Simon Newcomb

生人1835 ~ 1909年 》74

FYI: Astronomer and applied mathematics.

*[Newcomb's Table of the Sun/ ephemiades]

史实: 天文学家和应用数学.*纽康的太阳桌

NEWTON牛顿niu dun

[SIR] Isaac Newton

生人1642 ~ 1727年 》85

FYI: British mathematician, physicist, theologian.

史实: 英国数学家, 物理学家, 神学家.

NIELSEN尼尔森ni er sen

Leslie William Nielsen

生人1926 ~ 2010年 》84

FYI: [a&e] Canadian Actor, comedian and producer. Canadian and Hollywood walk of fame. "King of Spoofs"; O.C.

史实: 加拿大艺人，喜剧演员和制片人.

NIGHTINGALE南丁格尔nan ding gei er

Florence Nightingale

生人1820年5月12日 ~ 1910年 》90

FYI: The founder of modern nursing. "Nightingale school for nurses c.1860". aka "Lady with the lamp".

史实: 建为了近代护理学. '带灯的女士'.

NICHOLAS尼克拉斯ni ke la si

SAINT Nicholas

生人270 ~ 343年 A.D. 》73

FYI: 4 th century Saint. Nicholas of Myra was translated from the Dutch "Sinterklass" or Santa Claus. Translated as "圣诞老人"~sheng dan lao ren.... into English is "holy birth old person". Then lovingly changed it to "Old man Christmas".

史实: 神尼可拉斯，"圣诞快乐"圣诞老人.

NICHOLAS尼克拉斯ni ke la si

Nicholas II

生人1868 ~ 1918年 》50

FYI: Aka: Nicholas Romanov and TSAR of Russia, he, his wife and 5 children were assassinated together on 16 July 1918.

史实: 1918年7月16日; 尼可拉斯和家, 大家死了.

NIELSEN内里森nei li sen

Arthur Charles Nielsen Sr.

生人1897 ~ 1980年 》83

FYI: American business man and Marketing analysis. Nielsen Ratings Report.

史实: 美国商业人与市场分析.尼尔森评级报告.

NIETZSCHE尼采ni cai

Friedrich Wilhelm Nietzsche

生人1844 ~ 1900年 》56

FYI: German philosopher whom is quoted the most by the academic world. *The doer alone learneth.

史实: 德国哲学家, 学术界引用最多.*行动者独自学习.

NIMOY尼魔一ni mo yi

Leonard Simon Nimoy [memorial]

生人1931 ~ 2015年 》84

FYI: [a&e] American actor, author, photographer. Known to millions as "Spock".

史实: 美国演员,作家,摄影师.被数百万人称为"斯波克".

NIXON尼克森ni ke sen

Richard Milhous Nixon

生人1913 ~ 1994年 》81

FYI: US President (1969-74) *1971 took America off of the Gold standard.

史实: 美国总统（1969-74）*1971年使美国脱离金本位制.

NOBEL诺贝尔nuo bei er

Alfred Bernhard Nobel

生人1833 ~ 1896年 》63

Founder of the Nobel Peace Prize. "For the greatest benefit to Mankind". Scientist, linguist and inventor of dynamite. See top quote.

史实: 1895年建 诺贝尔平安."为了人类最大的利益".科学家,语言学家和炸药发明者.

NORGAY诺给nuo gei

Tenzing Norgay

生人1914年5月29日 ~ 1986年 》72

FYI: AKA Namgyal Wangdi. 1953-may-29 mt Everest. Mountain guide with Sir Edmund Hillary. It should be noted that in Tibet, all citizens are given the first name of 'Tenzing'. Listed among the top 100 influential people of the twentieth century.

史实: 爬山和游导.1953年5月29日怕-MT Everest. 应该注意的是, 在西藏, 所有的公民都被冠以"Tenzing"的名字.被列为20世纪最具影响力的100人之一.

NOSTRADAMUS诺查丹玛斯nuo cha dan ma si

Michel de Nostradamus

生人1503 ~ 1566年 》62

FYI: Notable seer and doctor. " Les Prohetes"

史实: 医生和先见者.

Photo by Forest L.

NOTLEY那特雷na te lei

Walter Grant Notley

生人1939年1月19日 ~ 1984年10月19日 》45

FYI: Served as the leader of the Alberta New Democratic Party until his death in a plane crash c.1984. His daughter Rachel also followed in her fathers footsteps and serves as the Leader of the NDP since 2014 and the Premier of Alberta from 2015-2019. This bust is located near Edmonton city center over looking the river valley.

史实: 在1984年左右死于飞机失事之前, 他一直是阿尔伯塔新民主党的领导人.他的女儿雷切尔也追随父亲的脚步, 自2014年起担任国家民主党领袖, 2015-2019年担任阿尔伯塔省总理.这座半身像位于埃德蒙顿市中心附近, 俯视着河谷.

From Group "N" you can pick one person or up to ten Surnames and write their Surname in Chinese. You may try HORIZONTAL or VERTICAL in the traditional Chinese form.

"No man should escape our universities without knowing how little he knows!"
《任何人都不应该在不知道自己知道多少的情况下逃离我们的大学》
Robert J. OPPENHEIMER奥本海默ao bin hai mo

OBANHEIN欧版还那o ban hai na

William~J~Obanhein

生人1924 ~ 1994年 》72

FYI: officer~posed for N. Rockwell paintings; "Policeman with Boy." Saturday Evening Post collection.

史实: 警官~为N·罗克韦尔的画摆姿势; "警察和男孩." 星期六晚间集邮.

O'BRIEN噢比任o bi ren

Eugene~W~O'Brien

生人1925 ~ 1975年 》50 》[memorial纪念]

FYI: Wheelsman: 10 Nov 1975 *SS Edmund Fitzgerald

史实: 1975年 11月10日S.S. 埃德蒙*菲茨杰拉德 湖高强

OCKHAM奥卡姆ao ka mu

William of Ockham [Occam]

生人1287 ~ 1347年 》60

FYI: *Occam's razor: He established the methodological principle of logic and physics.*the "razor" is a metaphor...used to dissect ideas. Ockham was his home village.

史实: 奥卡姆.他建立了逻辑和物理的方法论原理. "剃刀" 是一个比喻……用来解剖思想.奥卡姆是他的家乡.

O'CONNELL奥康内尔ao kang nei er

Daniel O'Connell

生人1775 ~ 1847年 》72

FYI: Irish liberator.

史实: 爱尔兰释放

OEMING奥命ao ming

Albert Frederick Hans Oeming

生人1925 ~ 2014年 》88

FYI:*Boxer and zoologist, philanthropist, . Founder of Al Oeming's Game Farm in Alberta Canada. Co-founder "Stampede Wrestling"

史实: 拳击手和动物学家, 慈善家.阿尔伯塔加拿大奥明游戏农场的创始人.联合创始人 "竞技场摔跤". [see Stu Hart.]

OHM欧姆ou mu

Gorge Simon Ohm

生人1789 ~ 1854年 》65

FYI: Ohm's law of electricity.

史实: 欧姆定律.

OISTRAKH奥伊斯特拉赫ao yi si te la he

David Fyodorrovich Oistrakh

生人1908 -~ 1974年 》66

FYI: classical musician and renouned violinist of the twentieth century. [BBC radio]

史实: 古典音乐家和二十世纪著名小提琴家.

O'LEARY奥利里ao li li

Brian Todd O'Leary

生人1940 ~ 2011年 》71

FYI: He was an American scientist, author, and former NASA astronaut. He was a part of a group of scientist-astronauts chosen with the intention of training for the Apollo Applications Program. *The truth will set you free, but first it will piss you off!

史实:他是美国科学家、作家和前美国宇航局宇航员.他是一组科学家宇航员中的一员, 他们被选中是为了训练阿波罗应用程序. *真理会让你自由, 但首先它会让你生气!

photo by Forest L. via Ukrainian Village ~ Olesdow (l) settlers (r)

OLESKOW奥莱斯科ao lai si ke

Josef Oleskow

生人1860 ~ 1903年 》43

FYI: aka Dr. Joseph Oleskiw; Ukrainian professor of agronomy who promoted Ukrainian immigration to the Canadian prairies. His efforts helped encourage the initial wave of settlers from 1896~1897. He selected seventeen families which would resettle and become the Ukrainian Canadian community in the Edmonton area. The Historic site of "The Ukrainian Village" East of Edmonton honors his name with with a bust. Oleskiw Park in Edmonton is named in his honor.

史实: 乌克兰农学教授，他推动乌克兰移民到加拿大大草原.他的努力有助于鼓励1896年至1897年初的移民潮。他选择了17个家庭，这些家庭将在埃德蒙顿地区重新定居并成为乌克兰-加拿大社区.埃德蒙顿以东的"乌克兰村庄"的历史遗迹以半身像来纪念他的名字.埃德蒙顿的奥尔斯基公园以他的名字命名.

O'NEILL欧尼尔ou ni er

Eugene Gladstone O'Neill

生人1888 ~ 1953年 》65

FYI: American playwright

史实: 美国剧作家.

OORT奥尔特ao er te

Jan Hendrik Oort

生人1900 ~ 1992年 》92

FYI: Dutch astronomer. New York times~"one of the century's foremost explorers of the universe". Oort cloud named in his honor.

史实: 天文学家:奥尔特云.荷兰天文学家.《纽约时报》~ "本世纪最重要的宇宙探险家之一".奥尔特•克劳德以他的名字命名.

OPPENHEIMER奥本海默ao bin hai mo

Julius Robert Oppenheimer

生人1904 ~ 1967年 》63

FYI: Academic, physicist. He head of the Los Alamos Laboratory and is among those who are credited with being the "father of the atomic bomb" for their role in the Manhattan Project. *Now I am become Death, the destroyer of worlds.

史实： 学术,物理学家.他是洛斯阿拉莫斯实验室的负责人,也是那些因在曼哈顿项目中的作用而被誉为"原子弹之父"的人之一.*现在我变成了死亡,世界的毁灭者.[-see Serber- Tibbets- Sweeny]

ORBISON奥比森ao bi sen
Roy Kelton Orbison
生人1936 ~ 1988年 》52
FYI: [a&e] An American Icon in the music industry in the mid twentieth century. He had a distinct look as well as a distinct voice and was nicknamed "the Caruso of Rock".
史实: 二十世纪中叶美国音乐界的标志.他有着独特的外表和独特的声音,被昵称为"岩石的卡鲁索". [~ see Harrison-Petty]

ORWELL奥威尔ao wei er
George Orwell [pseudonym]
生人1903 ~ 1950年 》47
FYI: aka Eric Arthur Blair; British novelist, essayist, journalist, critic who coined the word "doublethink". *To see what is in front of one's
Nose requires a constant struggle.
史实: 英国小说家,散文家,记者,评论家, 发明了"双重思想".*看看自己面前有什么鼻子需要不断地挣扎.

OSMOND奥斯曼ao si man
Humphry Fortescue Osmond
生人1917 ~ 2004年 》86
FYI: English psychiatrist who coined the term "Pyschedelic" from the medicinal use of hallucinogenic drugs.
史实: 英国精神病医生,从迷幻药的医学用途中创造了术语"药师药".

O'SULLIVAN欧苏勒文ou su le wen
John o'Sullivan
FYI: Electrical engineer, credited for developing Wi-Fi and LAN from Radio Astronomy.
[查看-see Hayes]
史实: 电工程从射电天文学发展出Wi-Fi和LAN.

OSWALD奥斯瓦尔德ao si wa er de (insert jpg 1246)

Lee Harvey Oswald

生人1939 ~ 1963年 》24

FYI: c.1963 the assassination of J.F.K . Collectively, multiple witnesses disagree with the single shooter theory. Many witnesses claim 8 shots.

史实: 1963年, J.F.K.被暗杀.总的来说, 多个证人不同意单枪手理论.许多目击者声称有8枪.

OTTOKAR噢托卡尔ou te ka er

King Premysl Ottokar II of Bohemia

生人1233 ~ 1278年 》45

FYI: Founded the town of Budejovice and [Budweiser] brewery c.1265

史实: 他建Budweiser 啤酒厂.

OVERTON奥尔特恩ao er te en

Joseph~P~Overton

生人1960 ~ 2003年 》43

FYI: Known for the "Overton Window". a conception for the ideal range for think tank protocol of public policy.

史实: 高名为了 "奥尔特恩窗户" 专业在公方针.

OWEN欧文ou wen

Gary Owens

生人1934 ~ 2015年 》81

FYI: aka Gary Bernard Altman was a Voice actor and comedian. He was the baritone announcer for Laugh-in.

史实: 口声为了电影.

From Group "O" you can pick one person or up to ten Surnames and write their Surname in Chinese. You may try HORIZONTAL or VERTICAL in the traditional Chinese form.

P

拼尽全力，哪拍烦事缠身

Always make a total effort, even when the odds are against you!

Arnold PALMER帕尔姆pa er mu

PACKARD帕卡德pa ke de

David Packard

生人1912 ~ 1996年 》83

FYI: Electrical engineer and co founder of Hewlett-Packard HP [1939] .[see-Hewlett]

史实: 惠普电气工程师兼联合创始人.

PALMER帕尔姆pa er mu

Arnold Daniel Palmer

生人1929 ~ 2016年 》87

FYI:[S] *World Golf Hall of Fame. [see-Nicklaus]. *Always make a total effort, even when the odds are against you!

史实: 高名高球. * 拼尽全力, 哪拍烦事缠身

PALEY帕利pa li

William Samuel Paley

生人1901 ~ 1990年 》89

FYI: He acquired the Columbia Phonographic Broadcasting System and founded the Columbia Broadcasting System (CBS) and developed it into a multi-channel empire. Author of "as it happened."

史实: 建 哥伦比亚广播公司. (CBS)

PANNES怕那斯pa na su

John Pannes

生人1937年5月6日 》[memorial纪念]

FYI: Hindenburg Passenger,

史实: 乘客 惨变:兴登堡.

PANNES怕那斯pa na su

Emma Pannes

生人1937年5月6日 》[memorial纪念]

FYI: Hindenburg Passenger

史实: 乘客惨变:兴登堡.

PAUL保罗bao luo

Saul (Hebrew) Paul (Latin)

FYI: Saul of Tarsus a Roman citizen. Acts 9:4-5. Galatians 1:16.

史实: 神经:使徒行传 9:4-5

PARKER帕卡pa ke

Robert Leroy Parker

生人1866 ~ 1908年 》42

FYI: aka Butch Cassidy; was a U.S. train robber and bank robber, and the leader of a gang of criminal outlaws known as the "Wild Bunch". *Harry Alonzo Longabaugh* was his partner known as the "Sundance Kid" and both died in a shoot out [1908~11~7] by local police in a South American town.

史实: 是一个美国火车劫匪和银行劫匪，以及一个被称为"野帮"的犯罪团伙的头目.哈里•阿朗佐•朗加堡是他的搭档，被称为"圣丹斯小子"，两人都死于南美洲一个小镇当地警察的枪战中.

PARKER帕卡pa ke

Bonnie Elizabeth Parker

生人1910 ~ 1934年 》24

FYI: Bonnie and Clyde. Early Twentieth Century crime.

史实: 邦妮和克莱德.二十世纪初的犯罪.

PARKINSON帕金森pa jin sen

James Parkinson

生人1755 ~ 1824年 》69

FYI: Parkinson's disease "Essay on the Shaking Body: c1817" WPD: April 11.

史实: 《帕金森氏病》振体论文: C1817 [see-J*M*Charcott]

PARKS帕克斯pa ke si

Rosa Louise McCauley Parks

生人Feb 4, 1913 - Oct 24, 2005年 》92

FYI: American activist in the civil rights movement best known for her pivotal role in the Montgomery bus boycott, as she refused to give up her seat to a Caucasian man on a bus. The United States Congress has called her "the first lady of civil rights" and "the mother of the freedom movement. *I have learned over the years that when one's mind is made up, this diminishes fear; knowing what must be done does away with fear.

史实: 美国民权运动积极分子以在蒙哥马利抵制蒙哥马利的举足轻重的角色而闻名, 因为她拒绝将座位交给白人在公共汽车上. 美国国会称她为"民权第一夫人"和"自由运动之母." *多年来我了解到, 只要下定决心, 这就会减少恐惧; 知道必须做些什么就能消除带着恐惧.

Courtesy of Government of Alberta; Parlby Park courtesy Forest L.

PARLBY 帕尔比 pa er bi

Mary Irene Parlby

生人 1868 ~ 1965年 》97

FYI: aka Mary Irene [nee] Marryat was one of The Famous Five in Canadian history demanding that any woman is to be recognized as a person. She was the first female cabinet member in Alberta. The Famous Five also included: Henrietta Edwards, Nellie McClung, Louise McKinney and Emily Murphy. Each lady has a park named in their honor all are located near the river in Edmonton. *If politics mean … then it mostly assuredly is a woman's job as much as it is a man's job.

史实: 是加拿大历史上著名的五个要求任何女人都要被承认为一个人的人之一. 她是阿尔伯塔省第一位女内阁成员. 著名的五位成员还包括:亨利埃塔爱德华兹,内莉麦克隆,路易丝麦金尼和艾米丽墨菲. 每一位女士都有一个以自己的名字命名的公园, 都位于埃德蒙顿的河边.*如果政治意味着……那么, 它基本上是一个女人的工作, 就像男人的工作一样.

Edmonton Public Archives

PARSONS帕森斯pa sen si

Sidney Parsons

生人1893 ~ 1955年 》62

FYI: Canadian politician and former mayor [1950-1951] of Edmonton Alberta Canada. Parsons road is located in South Edmonton.

史实: 加拿大政治家,加拿大阿尔伯塔省埃德蒙顿市前市长 (1950-1951年).帕森斯路位于埃德蒙顿南部.

PASCAL帕斯卡尔pa si ka er

Blaise Pascal

生人1623 ~ 1662年 》39

FYI: French mathematician invented the adding machine.

史实: 法国人发明加机

PASSY帕斯pa si

Paul Edouard Passy

生人1859 ~ 1940年 》101

FYI: A French linguist and founder of the International Phonetic Association [IPA] c1886

史实: 法国语言学家:1886年IPA

PASTEUR巴斯德ba si de

Louis Pasteur

生人1822 ~ 1895年 》73

FYI: French chemist and biologist. Discovered the vaccines for anthrax and rabies. "pasteurization' the process is named in his honor.

史实: 法国化学家和生物学家.发现了炭疽和狂犬病的疫苗."巴氏杀菌"这个过程是以他的名字命名的.

Display at Edmonton International airport.
*photo by Forest L.

PATRICIA帕特里夏pa te li xia

Princes Patricia of Connaught

生人1886 ~ 19774年 》88

FYI: was born into royalty and was the granddaughter of Queen Victoria. Her name sake is attached to the Canadian Infantry and the brigade is called the 'Princess Patricia's light infantry Brigade' in Edmonton.

史实: 出生于皇室,是维多利亚女王的孙女.她的名字清酒附属于加拿大步兵队,该旅被称为"公主帕特丽夏轻步兵旅".

PATTERSON怕特森pa te sen

Roger Patterson

生人1933 ~ 1972年 》39

FYI: "Patty" was filmed during an outing by Roger Patterson and Robert "Bob" Gimlin on 1967 Oct 20 [frame 352]; Patty is regarded as a member of the Sasquatch or Big foot family.

史实: 1967年10月20日 大鞋 [352]帕蒂被认为是大脚野人或大脚野人的一员.

PATTON巴顿ba dun

George Smith Patton jr.

生人1885 ~ 1945年 》60

FYI: was a senior American officer of General's during WWII

史实: 将军为了美国.

PAVAROTTI帕瓦罗蒂pa wa luo di

Luciano Pavarotti

生人1935 ~ 2007年 》82

FYI: [a&e] Luciano was a world renouned opera tenor with the THREE TENORS.

史实: 卢西亚诺是世界著名的三大男高音歌剧男高音.

PAVLOV巴甫洛夫ba fu luo fu

Ivan Petrovich Pavlov

生人1849 ~ 1936年 》87

FYI: Expertise in physiology of digestion c.1904 [Nobelprize.org]

史实: 1904年诺贝尔 为了生理.

PEABODY皮博迪pi bo di

George Foster Peabody

生人1852 ~ 1938年 》86

FYI: American banker and philanthropist; "Peabody award" for radio and communications. 1940 the first award in Radio broadcasting was issued. c1948 Television was included.

史实: 美国银行家和慈善家;无线电和通讯 "皮博迪奖" .1940年,无线电广播第一个奖项颁发.包括C1948电视.

PEALE皮勒pi le

Norman Vincent Peale

生人1898 ~ 1993年 》95

FYI: Pastor and author. "The Power of Positive Thinking".[1952] Nixon and Trump were members of his congregation. [see-j.c.Penny]

史实: 教, 作者:"积极思考的力量".[1952年]

PEARSON拍尔森pai er sen

Lester Bowels "Mike" Pearson

生人Apr 23, 1897 ~ Dec 27, 1972 年 》75

FYI: Canadian scholar, lawyer, diplomat, 14th pm of Canada. O.C.

史实: 加拿大学者, 律师, 曾经PM 十四号.

PEARSON拍尔森pai er sen

Capt Robert Pearson

FYI: Capt Pearson of Air Canada was forced to do an emergency landing of Flight 143~ 1983 July 23. Gimli Glider photo

史实: 1983年7月23日 飞机杰;安全掣.

PECKOL佩卡尔pe ka er

Karl~A~Peckol

生人1955 ~ 1975年 》20 》[memorial纪念]

FYI: *SS Edmund Fitzgerald~ 10 Nov 1975.

史实: 1975年11月10日*SS Edmund Fitzgerald"

PEDERSEN皮德森pi de sen

Charles~J~Pedersen

生人1904 ~ 1989年 》85

FYI: 1987 awarded the Nobel in organic chemistry. Best known for synthesis crown ethers.

史实: 1987年获得诺贝尔有机化学奖.最著名的合成冠醚.

[查看- DJCram,JMLehn][Nobelprize.org]

PELLER佩勒pei le
Clara Peller

生人1902 ~ 1987年 》85

Spokesperson for Wendy's commercials "Wheres the Beef?

史实: 代言人.

PELOUZE陪楼斯pe lou si
Theophile Jules Pelouze

生人1807 ~ 1867年 》60

FYI: CHEMIST. His name is included among the 72 listed on the Eiffel tower [NE16] *55/72

史实: 化学家.新元史上埃菲尔铁塔单名.

PEMBERTON彭仏顿peng ba dun
John Styth Pemberton

生人1832 ~ 1888年 》56

FYI: American pharmacist and chemist; *invented Coke~Cola c.1886 [see-f.m. Robinson]

史实: 美国人先导为了'可口可乐'.

Photo from cereal box by Forest L.

PENN佩恩pie en

William Penn

生人1744 ~ 1788年 》44

FYI: He was a Quaker in the early era. His image was first used for the branding of Quaker oats. As well, was the founder of the State of Pennsylvania. "Sylvania" translates into wooded land. Penn wrote the book "No Cross, No Crown".

史实: 早Quaker, 先导宾夕法尼亚 . 作者 "没有十字架就没有王冠"

"没有磨难~没有王冠".

PENNEY盆尼pen ni

James Cash Penney

生人1875 ~ 1971年 》96

FYI: J.C.Penney was a businessman and entrepreneur who founded J.C. Penney in 1902. He was also a business tutor to Sam Walton.

史实: 商业人. 导师为了S.沃尔顿. [看see- n.v.PEALE, s.Walton]

PENFIELD彭菲尔德peng fei er de

Dr. Wilder Graves Penfield

生人1881 ~ 1976年 》95

FYI: neurosurgeon who was heralded as "The Greatest Living Canadian".c1950

史实: 1950年最好加拿大人.

PERDONNET彭董那peng do na

Jean Albert Auguste Perdonnet

生人1801 ~ 1867年 》66

FYI: Railroad engineer. Is among the 72 names on the Eiffel tower. [NE05] # 56~72

史实: 火车工程.新元史上埃菲尔铁塔单名.

PERKINS帕金斯pa jin si

Marlin Perkins

生人1905 ~ 1985年 》81

FYI: Zoologist. Host of the " Wild Kingdom".

史实: 动物学.主持 "野味".

PEROT佩罗pei luo

Henry Ross Perot

生人1830~ 2019年 》89

FYI: American billionaire business magnate, philanthropist and presidential candidate for 1992 and 1996. * *The activist is not the person who says the river is dirty. The activist is the person who cleans up the river.*

史实: 美国亿万富翁,商界大亨,慈善家,1992年和1996年总统候选人.(q) 活动家并不是说河流很脏的人.活动家是清理河流的人.

PERRIER培里耳pei li er

Francois Perrier

FYI: Geographer and mathematician. Among the 72 Listed on the Eiffel tower. [SW17] 57/72

史实: 数人, 地理学家.新元史上埃菲尔铁塔单名.

PERRY佩里pei li

Antoinette "Tony" Perry

生人1888 ~ 1946年 》58

FYI: TONY AWARD is named in her honor in theatre. She co-founded the American Theatre wing.

史实: 上场人. 尊重他名.

PETIET皮特pi te

Julius Petiet

生人1813 ~ 1871年 》58

FYI: ENGINEER ; he was honored to teach at Ecole Centrale Paris. Is listed among the 72 names on the Eiffel tower. [NE01] #58 ~72

史实: 工程;新元史上埃菲尔铁塔单名.

PETRIE佩特里pei te li

[SIR] William Mathew Flinders Petrie

生人1853 ~ 1942年 》89

FYI: Egyptologist who first discovered the "merneptah stele" * he developed the system of "dating" of relics.

史实: 埃及学家;仿古.他开发了文物 "年代测定" 系统.

PETTY彭特pe te
Tom Earl Petty
生人1950年10月20日 ~ 2017年 》66
FYI: writer and musician.
史实: 作者和音乐.

PICASSO皮卡送pi ka so
Pablo Picasso
生人1881 ~ 1973年 》91
FYI: painter, sculptor.
史实: 画家,雕刻家.

PILLSBURY拍斯布瑞pai si bu rui
Charles Alfred Pillsbury
生人1842年12月3日 ~ 1899年
FYI: American flour industrialist who built the Pillsbury doe name.
史实: 美国人商人.

PIRRIE皮尔日pi er re
Lord Williams James Pirrie
生人1847 ~ 1924年 》77
FYI: Ship builder and designer of TITANIC [查看-see T.Andrews] 史实: 泰坦尼克号的
造船和设计师.

PITMAN皮特曼pi te man
[SIR] Issac Pitman
生人1813 ~ 1897年 》84
FYI: instituted the Pitman Shorthand system in 1837. [see- jrGREGG]
史实: 1837年 先导为了简称写.

PHILIP斐里伯fei li bo
(Prince) Philip [Mountbatten]
生人1921年6月10日 ~ active

FYI: aka Mountbatten-Windsor. Husband to Queen Elizabeth II. All of royal heritage are addressed by their Noble First name only. * *I am the only man in the country not allowed to give his name to his children.*

史实: 王子;老公为了王后.所有皇家遗产中只有他们高贵的名字. *

我是该国唯一不允许给自己的孩子起名字的人.

PHILLIPS斐里伯fei li bo

John George "Jack" Phillips

生人1887 ~ 1912年 》25 》[memorial纪念]

FYI: Titanic 1912 Senior Wireless Telegraph operator.

史实: 泰坦尼克号1912年高级无线电报操作员.

PHILLIPS斐里伯fei li bo

Henry Frank Phillips

生人1889 ~ 1958年 》69

FYI: Phillips head screwdriver named after him after refining the patent from JP thompson.

史实: 菲利普斯螺丝起子的名字是以他改进了JP汤普森的专利后的名字命名的.

PHUC复克fu ke

Phan Thi Kim Phuc

生人1963年 ~ active

FYI: 1972 June 08, age 9 'little girl just after Cambodia bombing'.

史实: 1972年6月8日，9岁的"柬埔寨爆炸后的小女孩".

Used with permission

PICARD皮卡德pi ka de

Joseph Henri Picard

生人1857 ~ 1934年 》77

FYI: A French Canadian business man and alderman in Edmonton. A full french K-12 school ~ Ecole J.H. Picard School In Edmonton is named in his honor.

史实: 　埃德蒙顿的法裔加拿大人和议员.埃德蒙顿的一所完整的法国K-12学校~Ecole J.H.Picard学校以他的名字命名.

PLANCK普兰克pu lan ke

Max Karl Ernst Ludwig Planck

生人1858 ~ 1947年 》89

FYI: Father of Quantum Theories. Nobel: 1918 for physics in energy quanta.

史实: 量子理论之父. 1918年, 诺贝尔为了量子论.

PLATO柏拉图bo la tu

Plato

生人423 ~ 347 B.C.年 》76

FYI: Greek philosopher and writer. Considered to be the most quoted of the Greek's.
* *Wise men talk because they have something to say; fools, because they have to say something.*

史实: 作者, 希腊文.被认为是希腊语中引用最多的. * 智者之所以说话,是因为他们有话要说.傻瓜,因为他们不得不说些什么.

PLUTARCH普鲁塔克pu lu ta ke

Lucius Mestrius Plutarchus

生人Circa 46 ~ 120年 》 74

FYI: Roman-Greek biographer and essayist. [IEP]

史实: 希腊文散文.

PLUMMER怕路马如pa lu ma er

Henry Stanly Plummer

生人1874 ~ 1936年 》62

FYI: Medical doctor and inventor. Co-founder MAYO CLINIC.

史实: 医学博士和发明家.联合创始人梅奥诊所.

POE坡po
Edgar Allen Poe

生人1809 ~ 1849年 》40

FYI: American writer, editor, literary critic.

史实: 美国作家,编辑,文学评论家.

POINSOT坡恩斯特po en si te
Louis Poinsot

生人1777 ~ 1859年 》82

FYI: French mathematician, geometric mechanics. Listed among the 72 names on the Eiffel tower. [SE09] #59/72

史实: 法国数.新元史上埃菲尔铁塔单名.

POISSON泊松po song
Simeon Denis Poisson

生人1781 ~ 1840年 》59

FYI: French mathematician and physicist. Listed among the 72 names on the Eiffel tower. [SE17] #60/72

史实: 法国数. 新元史上埃菲尔铁塔单名.

POLO 波罗bo luo
Marco Polo

生人1254 ~ 1324年 B.C. 》70

FYI: Italian merchant, explorer and writer, *Silk Road to China. "you would not believe half of what I have seen".(Q)

史实: 高名中国旅游 '丝绸之路'."你不会相信我看到的一半".

POLONCEAU坡降素po jiang su
Camille Polonceau

生人1813 ~ 1859年 》46

FYI: Railway engineer who introduced the Polonceau Truss: considered "one of the most successful roof designs of the Twentieth century. His name is among the 72 engraved on the Eiffel tower [NE09] #61~72

史实: 火车工程. 新元史上埃菲尔铁塔单名.

POLLOCK波拉克bo la ke

Paul Jackson Pollock

生人1912 ~ 1956年 》44

FYI: American painter who developed a style called "drop painting".

史实: 美国画家, 发展了一种称为"滴涂"的风格.

POMPEY庞培pang pei

Gnaeus Pompeius Magnus

生人67 ~ 35年 BC 》28

史实: aka: Sextus Pompeius Magnus Pius; Italian politician. City named in his honor. City destroyed by the eruption of Vesuvius c 79

史实: 意大利政治家.以他的名字命名的城市.被维苏威火山爆发摧毁的城市.

PONCELET庞塞勒pang sai le

Jean Victor Poncelet

生人1788 ~ 1867年 》79

FYI: Renouned for Projective Geometer. He is listed with the 72 names on the Eiffel tower [NW04] #62~72

史实: 射影几何.新元史上埃菲尔铁塔单名.

PONTIAC庞体克 pang ti ke [zhang]

[chief] Pontiac

生人1720 ~ 1769年 》49

FYI: aka: Obwandiyag was one of the early Indian ban leaders of early America who fought against the British as well as the French. *They came with a Bible and their religion stole our land, crushed our spirit … and now tell us we should be thankful to the 'Lord' for being saved.

史实: 奥万迪亚格 (Obwandiyag) 是美国早期反对印度和法国的早期印度禁令领导人之一.*他们带着圣经, 他们的宗教信仰偷走了我们的土地, 粉碎了我们的精神……现在告诉我们, 我们应该感谢"主"的得救.[查看- J.Stanley]

PONZI庞兹pang zi

Charles Ponzi

生人1882 ~ 1949年 》66

FYI: aka: Carlo Pietro Giovanni Guglielmo Tebaldo Ponzi. Italian born~ American swindler and con artist. Pyramid Scheme or Ponzi. scam.

史实: 意大利出生的美国骗子和骗子.金字塔计划或庞氏骗局.

POPPER怕彭pa peng

Karl Popper

生人1902 ~ 1994年 》92

FYI: SIR Karl Raimund Popper. British philosopher of Science.

史实: 英国科学哲学家.

PEROT佩罗pei luo

Henry Ross Perot

生人1930 ~ 2019年 》89

FYI: Billionaire businessman in the information technology industry. He ran twice in the Presidential races of America. *The activist is not the person who says the river is dirty. The activist is the person who cleans up the river.

史实: 信息技术行业的亿万富翁商人.他曾两次参加美国总统竞选.活动家并不是说河流很脏的人.活动家是清理河流的人.

POST坡斯特po si te

Charles William "C.W" Post

生人1854年10月26日 ~ 1914年

FYI: Cereal manufacturer.

史实: 谷物制造商.

POUND怕安pa an

Ezra Weston Loomis Pound

生人1885 ~ 1972年 》87

FYI: American expatriate poet. *Ripostes-1912 [25 poems], the Cantos-c.1917 [120 sec]

史实: 美国人, 式在监禁.

POVICH坡维奇po wei qi

John~J~Povich

生人1916 ~ 1975年 》59 》[memorial纪念]

FYI: Wheels man ;*10 Nov 1975 SS Edmund Fitzgerald

史实: 纪念: 1975年 11月10日S.S. 埃德蒙*菲茨杰拉德 湖高强

PRATT普拉特pu la te

James~A~Pratt

生人1931 ~ 1975年 》44 》[memorial纪念]

FYI: S.S.Edmund Fitzgerald: Second Mate. Lake Superior 10 Nov 1975.

纪念~史实: S.S. 埃德蒙*菲茨杰拉德 湖高强1975年 11月10日

PRESLEY普雷斯利pu lei si li

Elvis Aaron Presley

生人1935 ~ 1977年 》44

FYI: [a&e] Television movies and Music Icon of the twentieth century. *love me tender~can't help falling in love~are you lonesome tonight. * *Truth is like the sun. You can shut it out for a time, but it ain't goin' away.*

史实: 二十世纪的电视电影和音乐偶像.*温柔地爱我~情不自禁地坠入爱河~你今晚寂寞吗? * 真相就像太阳.您可以将其关闭一段时间, 但不会消失.

PRICE普赖斯pu lai si

[Pte] George Lawrence Price

生人1892年12月25日 ~ 1918年11月11日 》24

FYI: [256265 - private in the Canadian infantry] is regarded as the final soldier to die in WWI minutes before the war was officially to end.

史实: 加拿大步兵中的私人士兵被视为二战结束前几分钟的最后一名士兵.

PRICE普赖斯pu lai si

Weston Andrew Valleau Price

生人1870 ~ 1948年 》77

FYI: Dentist who founded the National Dental Association. He did research on nutrition and dental health.

史实: 呀生先导 他成立国家呀肯协会. 他研究为了营养与口腔健康.

PRICE普瑞斯pu rui si

Vincent Price

生人1911 ~ 1993年 》82

FYI:[a&e] Hollywood Icon of humor/horror actor. * *It's as much fun to scare as to be scared.*

史实: 笑和恐怖片人. * 收到惊吓与受到惊吓一样有趣.

PRITZKER普里茨克pu li ci ke

Jay Arthur Pritzker

1922年 ~ 1999年 》76

FYI: American entrepreneur and founder of "PRITZKER prize" c1979 for architecture.

史实: "普里茨克 将" 为了结构.

PROCTER普罗克特pu luo ke te

William Procter

生人1801 ~ 1884年 》83

FYI: Candle maker and Industrialist. Proctor & Gamble founded c. 1837 [see-J.Gamble]

史实: 蜡烛制造商和实业家.宝洁公司成立于1837年.

PROTAGORAS普罗塔哥拉pu luo ta ge la

Protagoras

生人490 ~ 420年B.C. 》70

FYI: Greek Philosopher tutored by Plato.

史实: 柏拉图辅导的希腊哲学家.

PRUDHOMME普露多姆pu luo duo mu

Sully Prudhomme

生人1839 ~ 1907年 》68

FYI: AKA; Rene Francois Armand Prudhomme. First to receive Nobel in Literature c1901 for poetry. [Nobelprize.org]

史实: 1901年;第一次诺贝尔为了式.

PRUSS普鲁斯pu lu si

Max Pruss

生人c1937年 》[memorial纪念]

FYI: (cpt) of the Hindenburg

史实: 队长为了飞机惨变;兴登堡.

PTOLEMAEUS 托勒密tuo le mi

Claudius Ptolemaic

生人90 ~ 168年 》78

FYI: Greek Astronomer.

史实: 希腊文天学家.

PUGIN普跟pu gen

Augustus Welby Northmore Pugin

生人1812 ~ 1852年 》40

FYI: Architect and designer of the Tower of London, principal the Bell Tower which houses the Big Ben. [查看sir Benjiman Hall.]

史实: 伦敦塔的建筑师和设计师, 大本钟所在的钟楼的负责人.

PULITZER 普利策将pu li ce jiang

Joseph Pulitzer

生人1917 ~ 2000年 》83

FYI: Journalism pioneer award. Was publisher of "New York World". The first Pulitzer Prize was presented in 1917. Journalism, photography, literature, history, poetry, music and drama are the award categories.

史实: 新闻先锋奖.是《纽约世界》的出版商.第一个普利策奖是在1917年颁发的.新闻,摄影,文学,历史,诗歌,音乐和戏剧是获奖类别.

PYE拍pai

[Lord] Henry James Pye

生人1744 ~ 1833年 》69

FYI: Renouned British poet

史实: 高名英国诗人.

PYTHAGORAS 比大的拉斯 bi da ge la si

Pythagoras

生人570 ~ 495B.C.年 》

FYI: invented the Pythagorean theorem of triangles.

史实: 发明了毕达哥拉斯三角形定理.

From Group "P" you can pick one person or up to ten Surnames and write their Surname in Chinese. You may try HORIZONTAL or VERTICAL in the traditional Chinese form.

Without the sense of security which property gives, the land would still be uncultivated.
《如果没有财产所赋予的安全感，土地仍然是未开垦的》
Francois QUESNAY奎尼kui ni

QUARANTELLI夸兰特理kua lan te li

Enrico "Henry"~L~Quarantelli

生人1924 ~ 2017年 》93

FYI: Sociologist and author of Handbook of Disaster Relief.

史实: 社会学家,《救灾手册》的作者.

QUASIMODO夸斯莫懂kua si mo dong

Salvatore Quasimodo

生人1901 ~ 1968年 》67

FYI: Writer of poetry. Awarded the Nobel in 1959 for literature [Nobelprize.org]

史实: 诺贝尔为了式.

QUEENY夸尼kua ni

John Francis Queeny

生人1859 ~ 1933年 》74

FYI: founder of Monsanto Pharma Industries. circa1901. The name Monsanto is borrowed from his wife's Spanish family.

史实: 他是马伞头 孟山都这个名字是从他妻子的西班牙家庭借来的.

QUESNAY亏你qui ni

Francois Quesnay

生人1694 ~ 1774年 》80

FYI: known as the "Confucius of Europe", published The Economic Table c.1755).

史实: 被称为 "欧洲的孔子",出版了经济表c.1755.

QUIBELL球不里qui bu li

James Edward Quibell

生人1867 ~ 1935年 》68

FYI: Egyptologist

史实: 埃及学家.

From Group "Q" you can pick one person or up to five Surnames and write their Surname in Chinese. You may try HORIZONTAL or VERTICAL in the traditional Chinese form.

R

Even if your on the right track, you'll get run over if you just sit there.
即使你走的路是对的，如果停滞不前，也会被车压死
Will ROGERS罗杰斯luo jie si

RAFFERTY如法题ru fa ti

Robert~C~Rafferty

生人1913 ~ 1975年 》62 》[memorial纪念]

FYI: Stuart / cook; *SS Edmund Fitzgerald; 10 Nov 1975

史实: S.S. 埃德蒙*菲茨杰拉德 湖高强1975年 11月10日

RAINER雷纳lei na\

Prince Rainer (III)

生人1923 ~ 2005年 》82

FYI: AKA Rainer Louis Henri Maxence Bertrand Grimaldi Prince of Monaco. Ruled over Monaco for 56 years [see graceKelly]

史实: 王子 雷纳 君Monaco 为了56时间

RAMON拉蒙la meng

llan Ramon

生人1954 ~ 2003年 》48

FYI: AKA Llan Wolferman. Llan means 'tree' in Hebrew. First Israeli Astronaut in the NASA space program: Payload [sp:]. Because of the 90 minutes between sunrises, he commented by saying "Jerusalem we have a problem". Space Shuttle Columbia Disaster: 2003 Feb 01. [-see Memorial Wall~纪念]

史实: 太空人.Columbia 2003年2月1日《耶路撒冷我们有问题》

REED若德ru de

Alan Reed

生人1907 ~ 1977年 》70

FYI: [a&e] AKA: Herbert Theodore Bergman. Reed was an actor and voice actor best known for his voice of "Fred Flinstones". [see Hanna-Barbera.]

史实: 高名电影口声 [查看H-B]

RANDALL兰德尔lan de er

[SIR] John Turton Randall

生人1905 ~ 1984年 》79

FYI: Physicist and Biophysicist. Pioneer of the structure of the DNA. Developed the key component of the microwave oven (cavity magnetron). Shared Nobel Prize c.1962: Physiology of Medicine. [see- Crick,Watson]

史实: 物理学家.研制了微波炉的关键部件 先导"空腔磁控管 ".

RASKIN拉斯金la si jin

Jef Raskin

生人1943 ~ 2005年 》62

FYI: Human-computer interface expert who introduced the Mac computer idea for Apple c.1970's.

史实: 先导电脑机.

RASPUTIN拉斯普京la si pu jing

Grigori Yefimovich Rasputin

生人1869 ~ 1916年 》47

FYI:*Russian mystic "holy man" befriended by Tsar Nicholas II. Chief councillor for the Tsar and claimed to see the future and revered for his healing abilities.

史实: 俄罗斯神秘主义.

RAY雷lei

James Earl Ray

生人1928 ~ 1998年 》70

FYI: Alleged killer of American Civil Rights leader Martin Luther King. Was on the FBI Most Wanted list.

史实: 据称是美国民权领袖马丁·路德·金的凶手.在联邦调查局通缉名单上.

RAVENSCROFT莱文新克格福特lai wen xin ke ge fu te

Thurl Arthur Ravenscroft

生人1914 ~ 2005年 》91

FYI: [a&e] Actor and voice of Tony the Tiger..."Good? They're grreatt!" He was also the lead singer for "How the Grinch Stole Christmas c1966. [Thurls Bio]

史实: 演员和老虎托尼的声音…… "好吗? 他们是格兰特! 他也是"圣诞怪杰如何偷了圣诞 C1966" 的主唱.

REAGAN雷根lei gen

Ronald Wilson Reagan

生人1911 ~ 2004年 》93

FYI: Actor and 40th US president [81-89], Governor of California [67-75]. His policies were dubbed "Reaganomics". His famous speech "Mr. Gorbachev, tear down this wall" to Mikhail Gorbachev brought about change to the world. Circa 1970 June 12

史实: 美国高名电影人, 美国总统.《戈尔巴乔夫先生, 拆掉这堵墙》1970年6月12日

REDENBACHER热嗯把卡re en ba ke

Orville Clarence Redenbacher

生人1907 ~ 1995年 》88

FYI: Received a degree in Agronomy. With C. Bowman, they developed a popcorn strain called "Redbow" (O.R. popcorn). *I want to make it clear that I am real.

史实: 获得农学学位.与鲍曼合作, 他们开发了一种爆米花品种, 叫做 "红弓" （O.R.爆米花）.引述为 "我想澄清我是真实的".

REE热义re yi

Paul Ludwig Carl Henirich Ree

生人1849 ~ 1901年 》52

FYI: German author and Philosophizer. *I have to philosophize. When I run out of material, perhaps it is better that I die.

史实: 德国作者, 哲学《我必须进行哲学思考.当我用完了材料, 也许我死了更好》

REGNAULT雷格诺特lei ge luo te

Henri Victor Regnault

生人1810 ~ 1878年 》68

FYI: Chemist and was known for thermodynamics. Listed among the names on the Eiffel tower [SE03] 63/ 72 . Crater Regnault on the moon is named in his honor.

史实: 化学家:热力学.新元史上埃菲尔铁塔单名.

REID若达ruo da

William Ronald "Bill" Reid jr.

生人1920 ~ 1998年 》78

FYI: A Canadian artist and sculptor. A sample of his work is shown on the reverse of the Canadian 20.00 bill. "The Spirit of Haida Gwaii"

史实: 加拿大雕像他的样本工作显示在加拿大20.00法案的背面.

Painting courtesy St. Laurent Catholic School

RIEL瑞尔rui er

Louis David Riel

生人1844年10月22日 ~ 1885年10月16日 》41

FYI: Canadian politician in early Canada and founder of the province of Manitoba, Canada. He was at odds with the then politicians and hanged.

史实: 加拿大早期的政治家和加拿大马尼托巴省的创始人.他与当时的政治家意见不一致, 被处以绞刑.

REINER蕊纳尔rui na er

Markus Reiner

生人1886 ~ 1976年 》90

FYI: an Israeli scientist who is known for his work on rheology (rate of flow). [see-e.c.bingham]

史实: 以研究流变学而闻名的以色列科学家.

REIS雷斯lei si

Johann Philipp Reis

生人1834 ~ 1874年 》40

FYI: German scientist and inventor. 1861 Had developed the Reis telephone or "make or break" phone. He had wrote the paper "On the radiation of electricity" c1859. His idea for the phone came from studying the inner ear [tympanic membrane- malleus-incus]. Forerunner to the telephone that Bell succeeded at.[wiki]

史实: 曾经为了电话Bell.他写了一篇论文 "关于电的辐射" c1859.他发明手机的想法来自于对内耳的研究.贝尔成功打电话的先行者.

REISACHER雷萨车尔lei sa che er
Alois Reisacher
生人1937年5月3日 》[memorial纪念]
FYI: mechanic on board the LZ- HINDENBURG.
史实: 车工程兴登堡.

REISNER瑞斯那尔rui si na er
George Andrew Reisner
生人1867 ~ 1942年 》75
FYI: Egyptologist. Among his accomplishments he found the tomb of Hetepheres I, mother of Khufu.
史实: 埃及学家.

REMINGTON热命特恩re ming te en
Eliphalet Remington
生人1816 ~ 1896年 》80
FYI: Manufacturer of guns
史实:制作枪.

RENTSCHLER伦斯勤lun si le
Frederick Brant Rentschler
生人1887 ~ 1956年 》69
FYI: Aircraft engineer who partnered with Pratt-Whitney machine tool corp and founded "Pratt-Whitney"c1925.
史实: 飞机工程师, 与普惠机床公司合作, 创建了 "普惠" C1925.

REVEEN若分ruo fen
生人1935 ~ 2013年 》78
Peter James Reveen

FYI: illusionist and stage hypnotist. "The Superconscious World" 1987; 2007 won the DRAGON award: Drama, Romance, Artistry, Glamour, Originality and Necromancy.

史实: 魔术师和舞台催眠师.1987年;2007年获 "超自然世界" 金龙奖:戏剧,浪漫,艺术,魅力,独创性和巫术.

REVERE日文ri wen

Paul Revere

生人1734 ~ 1818年 》84

FYI: American silversmith, industrialist. American Revolutionist; April 18~19 1775~"Midnight Horse Ride". [see-H.W.Longfellow]

史实: 美国银匠, 工业家.美国革命家;1775年4月18日至19日.

RHODES罗得斯luo de si

Cecil John Rhodes

生人1853 ~ 1902年 》48

FYI: British mining magnate. The Rhodes scholarship in his honor was to encourage Leadership.

史实: 商家, 矿业, 政界 *罗兹学者,

RICCI里基li qi

Matteo Ricci

生人1552 ~ 1620年 》68

FYI: Was one of many Jesuit Priests who was proficient in mathematics and cartography, would journey to China to learn its language and its history and share it in his Portuguese language. He records that the use of the word 'Mandarin' or mandarim in Portuguese [mandare in Latin] is translated as being 'Councillor or Minister' hence government official or scholar. In recent centuries the term 'Mandarin", soon came to be known as the common speech of the officials, and now regarded as the 'speech of the people'. Within main land China, they refer to their language today as 'pu tong hua' [普通话] or common speech.

史实: 他是众多精通数学和制图的耶稣会神父之一, 他将前往中国学习其语言和历史, 并用葡萄牙语与人分享。他记录说, 在葡萄牙语中使用 "普通话" 或 "曼达里语" （拉丁语为 "曼达里语" ）被翻译为 "议员或部长", 因此是政府官员或学者.近几个世纪, "普通话" 一词很快就被称为官员们的共同语言, 现在被认为是 "人民的语言".在中国大陆的主要地区, 他们今天称他们的语言为 "普通话" 或 "普通语言".

RICHTER里克特li ke te

Charles Francis Richter

生人1900～1985年 》85

FYI: Seismologist invented the scale to measure earths physical inside movement.[c. 1935] [see Beno Gutenberg]

史实: 地震学家发明了地秤来测量地球的物理内部运动. 1935.

RIDE莱德lai de

Sally Kristen Ride

生人1951～2012年 》61 》[memorial纪念]

FYI: Physicist. First American woman in space. Space Shuttle Challenger STS-7

史实: 物理学家.Challenger 7号

RIEFENSTAHL里芬施塔尔li fen shi ta er

Helene Bertha Amalie "Leni" Riefenstahl

生人1902～2003年 》101

FYI: German film producer, director, writer.

史实: 她是德国创造电影.

RIGGS里格斯lei ge si

Robert "Bobby" Larimore Riggs

生人1918～1995年 》77

FYI: Tennis Champion who competed with Billie Jean King "battle of the sexes"1973. International Tennis Hall of Fame c1967.

史实: 网球.他竞争反对Billie*Jean*King 1973年. 他引入网球名人堂年1967.

RILKE里尔克li er ke

Rainer Maria Rilke

生人1875～1926年 》51

FYI: AKA: Rene Karl Wilhelm Johann Josef Maria Rilke. Poet & novelist. 'The Book of Hours'

史实: 作者 '书时间'.

RIPLEY里普利li pu li

Robert Leroy Ripley

生人1890 ~ 1949年 》59

FYI: American cartoonist and entrepreneur. Known for "Ripley's believe it or not". Book and TV program. *Their is nothing more stranger than Man.

史实: 美国人查看 ～ 找出 ～ 发现. "他们并不比男人更奇怪."

RIPPA热怕re pa

Paul~M~Rippa

生人1953 ~ 1975年 》22 》[memorial纪念]

FYI: *SS Edmund Fitzgerald~Lake Superior 10 Nov 1975

史实: S.S. 埃德蒙*菲茨杰拉德 湖高强1975年 11月10日

RITTER利特li te

Johann Wilhelm Ritter

生人1776 ~ 1810年 》34

FYI: German chemist and physicist. Discovered ultraviolet radiation [cool radiation]

史实: 德国化学家和物理学家.发现的紫外线辐射[冷辐射]

RIVERS里弗斯li fu si

Joan Rivers

生人1933 ~ 2014年 》81

FYI: [a&e] AKA Joan Alexandra Molinsky. Icon among female comedian.

史实: 美国笑人, 好莱坞令人.

ROBERTS罗伯茨luo bo ci

Oral Roberts

生人1918 ~ 2009年 》91

FYI: AKA Granville Oral Roberts. American Methodist- Pentecostal Televangelist.

史实: 美国教卫理公会-五旬节派电视福音传道者.

ROBERVAL罗贝万勒luo bei wan le

Gilles Personne de Roberval

生人1602 ~ 1675年 》73

FYI: Mathematician. Coined: trochoid.~wheel.

史实: 发明水伦.

ROBINSON罗宾森luo bin sen

Frank Mason Robinson

FYI: Was a marketing specialist who combined the names from Coco leaves and kola nuts to read Coca-cola c1885. His choice of lettering was from "Spencerian script".[查看- see j.s.Pemberton, P.R. Spencer]

史实: 是一位营销专家，他将可可叶和可乐果的名字结合起来阅读了可口可乐C1885.

ROBSON罗本森luo ben sen (insert jpg 0716)

John Robson

生人1824 ~ 1892年 》68

FYI: Canadian journalist and politician. Served as the 8th premier of British Columbia. Mount Robson is named in his honor.

史实: 加拿大记者和政治家.曾任英属哥伦比亚省第八任总理.罗布森山以他的名字命名.

ROCKEFELLER 洛克菲勒luo ke fei le

John Davison "JD" Rockefeller Sr.

生人1839 ~ 1937年 》97

FYI: Oil barren, He founded Standard oil [j.r.] son.

史实: 建 标准由.

ROCKEFELLER洛克菲勒luo ke fei le

John Davison Rockefeller jr.

生人1874 ~ 1960年 》86

FYI: Financier and philanthropist son of J.D.

史实: 金融家和慈善家.

ROCKEFELLER洛克菲勒luo ke fei le

David Rockefeller

生人1915 ~ 2017年 》101

FYI: Grandson of J.D.; Banker. TOD~3.3Billion

史实: J.D.的孙子;银行家.

ROCKNE罗克luo ke

Knute Kenneth Rockne

生人Mar 4, 1888 - Mar 31, 1931年 》43

FYI: Was a Norwegian-American football player and coach at the University of Notre Dame. Rockne is regarded as one of the greatest coaches in college football history. He designed the football of today and added the air valve to keep it inflated. *Win or lose, do it fairly.

史实: 是圣母大学的挪威裔美国足球运动员和教练.洛克（Rockne）被认为是大学橄榄球史上最伟大的教练之一.他设计了今天的足球,并增加了空气阀以保持其充气. *输赢,公平地做.

ROCKWELL洛克威尔luo ke wei er

Norman Perceval Rockwell

生人1894 ~ 1978年 》84

FYI: painter and newspaper illustrator ~ he could see the world as no other person could.

史实: 画家和报纸插图画家~他能像其他人一样看到世界.

RODBELL罗德贝尔luo de bei er

Martin Rodbell

生人1925 ~ 1998年 》73

FYI: Awarded the Nobel in 1994 for biochemistry, co-discoverer of "G-proteins." [Nobelprize.org]

史实: 1994年诺贝尔为了G-Proteins [蛋白质]

RODDENBERRY罗顿巴里luo dun ba li

Gene Roddenberry

生人1921 ~ 1991年 》70

FYI: [a&e] AKA: Eugene Wesley Roddenberry. Freelance writer, screen writer and producer and creator of STAR TREK. * It isn't all over; everything has not been invented; the human adventure is just beginning.

史实: 自由撰稿人,银幕作家和星际迷航的制片人和创造者.

* 还没有结束; 一切还没有被发明; 人类的冒险才刚刚开始.

ROEBUCK罗巴克luo ba ke

Alvah Curtis Roebuck

生人1864 ~ 1948年 》84

FYI: c1891 became co-founder of Sears Roebuck [see- r.w.SEARS] [*Sears archives.]

史实: 商业先导.

ROEDER罗德luo de

Gunther Roeder

生人1881 ~ 1966年 》75

FYI: Egyptologist

史实: 埃及古物学者.

ROGERS罗杰斯luo jie si

Fred Mcfeely Rogers

生人1928年3月20日 ~ 2003年3月27日 》74

FYI: Mr. Rogers Neighbourhood was a children's program that he was host of from 1928-2003. He is regarded as an "American Treasure".*If you could only sense how important you are to the lives of those you meet, how important you can be to the people you may never even dream of. There is something of yourself that you leave at every meeting with another person.

史实: 罗杰斯先生的邻居是一个儿童节目, 他是1928-2003年主办.他被视为 "美国宝藏".*如果您仅能感觉到自己对遇到的人的生活有多么重要, 那么对于您甚至从未梦想过的人们来说, 您有多么重要.在与另一个人的每次会面中, 您都会离开自己.

ROGERS罗杰斯luo jie si

Will Rogers

生人1879 ~ 1935年 》56

FYI:[a&e] aka: William Penn Adair "Will" Rogers; TV personality. American cowboy, humorist, newspaper columnist. *Even if your on the right track, you'll get run over if you just sit there.

史实: 电视个性.美国牛仔, 幽默作家, 报纸专栏作家. *即使你走的路是对的, 如果停滞不前, 也会被车压死.

ROGET荣格特ro ge te

Peter Mark Roget

生人1779 ~ 1869年 》90

FYI: Author of Roget's Thesaurus c.1852. British physician and lexicographer.

史实: 作者;荣格特类书词典.

ROGGEVEEN罗赫芬luo he fen

Jacob Roggeveen

生人1659 ~ 1729年 》69

FYI: Dutch explorer who found the Island with large humanoid statutes. The Island was named Easter Island due to the timing of finding the Island. c1722

史实: 荷兰探险家, 发现这个岛上有大量的人形法规.由于找到复活节岛的时间, 这个岛被命名为复活节岛.C1722

ROLLS罗尔斯luo er si

Charles Stewart Rolls

生人1877 ~ 1910年 》32

FYI: co-founder of Rolls-Royce c1906.[see- h.ROYCE]

史实: 先导罗尔斯商业.

ROMER罗马尔luo ma er

Ole Christensen Romer

生人1644 ~ 1710年 》66

FYI: he developed the speed of light theory and forerunner of the temp scale. [see-查看 Amonton, Celsius, Fahrenheit, Kelvin]

史实: 他先导光原理和温比例.

RONTGEN荣跟rong gen

Wilhelm Conrad Rontgen

生人1845 ~ 1923年 》78

FYI: Mechanical engineer and physicist. Was awarded the Nobel Prize for Physics c1901. Inventor of the x-ray. Element 111 or "Roentgenium" is named in his honor. [see- h.Ruhmkorff] [Nobelprize.org]

史实: 机器工程:1901年诺贝尔:发明-X光. "伦琴" 是以他的名字命名的.

RONNEBERG若那博戈ruo na bo ge

Joachim Holmboe Ronneberg

生人1919年8月30日 ~ 2018年 10月 21日

FYI: WWII, he led a team of demolition experts against the German

史实: 二次天战;蘸德国他和事同拆迁.

ROONEY如尼ru ni

Andrew Aiken "Andy" Rooney

生人1919 ~ 2011年 》92

FYI: American radio and TV personality: 60 minutes commentator. Always spoke of common satires of day to day life. *We're all proud of making little mistakes. It gives us the feeling we don't make any big ones.

史实: 美国广播电视个性:60分钟评论员.总是谈论日常生活中常见的讽刺.*我们都为犯小错误而自豪.这让我们觉得我们没有做什么大的.

ROOSEVELT罗斯福luo si fu

Franklin Delano Roosevelt Sr.

生人1882 ~ 1945年 》63

FYI: AKA: FDR [32] US President. Following the Japanese incident of Sunday, December 7th, 1941, he is quoted as "a date which will live in infamy". The People's President.

史实: FDR[32] 美国总统.1941年12月7日, 日本事变之后, 他被引述为 "一个将以恶名为生的日子".人民主席.

ROPER罗佰尔luo bai er

Elmer Earnest Roper

生人1893 ~ 1994年 》101

FYI: Supercenturian, former mayor of Edmonton [1959-1963]. Roper road named in his honor in Edmonton, Alberta, Canada.

史实: 一百年,曾经市长为了埃德蒙顿加拿大.罗佰尔路*埃德蒙顿.

RORSCHACH罗夏luo xia

Hermann Rorschach

生人1884年11月8日 ~ 1922年 》37

FYI: Swiss psychoanalyst who developed the "ink blot" test or "Rorschach Test" for personality, psychotic and neurological disorders.*wiki

史实: 瑞士精神分析学家, 他开发了人格,精神和神经障碍的 "墨迹测试" 或 "罗夏测试".

ROSE罗索luo suo

Hilly Rose

生人1926～2017年 》91

FYI: [a&e] Radio Hall of Fame. radio legend and author. *"But that's not what I called about."* [*C2C]

史实: 广播名人堂.电台传奇和作者."但这不是我所说的."

ROTHBARD罗斯巴德luo si ba de

Murray Newton Rothbard

生人1926～1995年 》69

FYI: Economist and author "what has the government done with our money."

史实: 经济学家作者 "政府用我们的钱做了什么?".

ROTHMAN罗斯曼luo si man

Louis Rothman

生人1869～1926年 》57

FYI: Founded Rothman brand cigarettes in 1890. c1902 rented a small shop in "Pall Mall" and named his cigarettes after the mall in England. He rolled all by hand.

史实: 先导罗斯曼和生道Pall*Mall 1902年.以英国购物中心的名字命名他的香烟.他用手打滚.

ROTBLAT罗特布拉特luo te bu la te

Joseph Rotblat

生人1908～2005年 》97

FYI: awarded the Nobel Prize for the diminishing nuclear arms c.1995. *Genesis of Eden. [*Nobelprize.org]

史实: 1995年嘉奖诺贝尔为了得主.

Photo by Forest L.

ROUE鲁伊lu yi

Williams James Roue

生人1879 ~ 1970年 》90

FYI: Designed the Canadian bluenose schooner. The same boat can now be seen on the reverse of the Canadian dime.

史实: 设计了加拿大蓝鼻帆船.同样的船现在可以在加拿大硬币背面看到.

ROUS劳斯lao si

Francis Peyton Rous

生人1879 ~ 1972年 》91

FYI: awarded the Nobel Prize for discovering tumor-inducing virus c1966. [*Nobelprize.org]

史实: 1966年嘉奖诺贝尔为了切除.

ROUTHIER鲁蒂埃lu di ai

Adolphe-Basile Routhier

生人1839 ~ 1920年 》61

FYI: Canadian judge, author and lyrist. In 1880 he was commissioned to pen the lyrics for the Canadian anthem. The original version was in French. It would later be translated into an English version by R. S. Weirs . The version will be seen in miscellaneous. [see Weirs].

史实: 加拿大法官,作家和作词人.1880年，他受命为加拿大国歌作词.原版是法语的.随后由R.S.Weirs翻译成英文版本.该版本将出现在Miscellaneous中.

ROWAND荣瓦恩德ro wa en de

John Rowand

生人1787 ~ 1854年 》67

FYI:Fur Trader for the Hudson Bay Company in early Canada and Independent merchant at Fort Edmonton c1823. [Rowand see jg_Macgregor]

史实: 加拿大早期哈德逊湾公司的皮草贸易商　商业埃德蒙顿1823年.

ROWE罗luo

William Leonard Rowe

生人1931 ~ 2015年 》84

FYI: Philosophy of Religion, "The Friendly Atheist".

史实: 哲学宗教 "友善无神论者".

ROYCE罗伊斯luo yi si

Frederick Henry Royce

FYI: co-founder of Rolls-Royce c1906.

史实: 先导为了罗伊斯.

RUBY如比ru bi

Jack Leon Ruby

FYI: aka; Jacob Leonard Rubenstein. Night club owner and organized crime. Fatally shot Oswald while in police custody; 1963 Nov 24.

史实: 夜总会老板和有组织犯罪.在警方拘留期间致命地射杀了奥斯瓦尔德　1963年11月24日　死了Oswald

RUDKIN如德肯ru de ken

Margaret Rudkin

生人1897 ~ 1967年 》70

FYI: Founder of Pepperidge Farms.

史实: 美国人建佩珀里奇衣.

RUHMKORFF如马口发ru ma kou fa

Heinrich Daniel Ruhmkorff

FYI: His name sake-John Rowand developed a high energy coil now used for cathoid tubes in x-ray's. [查/see- w.c.RONTGEN]

史实: 发明 "阴极管" 为了X光的.

RUMI如迷ru mi

Mawlana Jala ad-din Muhammad Rumi

生人1207 ~ 1273年 》66

FYI: Poet, Persian philosopher, theologian. * *Inside you there's an artist you don't know about. He's not interested in how things look different in moonlight.*

史实: 诗文,哲学家,神学家. * 在你里面, 有一个你不认识的艺术家.他对月光下的事物看起来并不感兴趣.

Photo by Forest L.

RUNDLE如恩德勒ru en de le

Robert Terrill Rundle (Reverend)

生人1811 ~ 1885年 》74

FYI: Is considered one of the first missionaries in Western Canada c1840. Mt Rundle and Rundle park in Edmonton are in honor of his services. [*dictionary Canadian biography]

史实: 被认为是加拿大西部最早的传教士之一.伦德尔山和伦德尔公园在埃德蒙顿是为了纪念他的服务.

RUSHMORE拉什莫尔la shi mo er

Charles~E~Rushmore

生人1857 ~ 1931年 》91

FYI: American business man and attorney after whom Mt. Rushmore is named. *Washington-Jefferson-Roosevelt-Lincoln [查看-see Borglum]

史实: 美国商业, 律师, 山拉什莫尔[mt Rushmore]*华盛顿杰斐逊·罗斯福·林肯.

RUSKA鲁斯卡lu si ka

Ernst Ruska

生人1906 ~ 1988年 》66

FYI: aka Ernst August Friedrich Ruska. Awarded the Nobel in1986 for physics; electron optics [*Nobelprize.org]

史实: 1986 年嘉奖诺贝尔在物理为了电子眼睛.

L) Public photo in front of his old home, R) courtesy of Albert government gallery.

RUTHERFORD卢瑟福lu se fu

Alexander Cameron Rutherford

生人1857 ~ 1941年 》84

FYI: Canadian lawyer and politician. First Alberta premier c.1905

史实: 政治家.1905年艾伯特第一次总理.

RUTHERFORD卢瑟福lu se fu (insert jpg 5653)

Ernest Rutherford

生人1871 ~ 1937年 》66

FYI: known as the Atom man, is regarded as the second Newton among his peers.
Award the Nobel in chemistry in 1908. First discovery; elements continue to change.
Second discovery: the model of the atom. Third discovery: splitting of the atom.

[看- wHIGGINS, nLOCKYER, gHale] [Nobelprize.org]

史实: 高名为了原子武器人. *华盛顿杰斐逊第一次发现;元素继续变化。第二个发现:原子模
型.第三个发现:原子分裂.

RYLE莱尔lai er

[SIR] Martin Ryle

生人1918 ~ 1984年 》92

FYI: British Radio Astronomer. Awarded the Nobel prize for Physics for the radio telescope c1974. This Nobel prize was co-shared by Antony Hewish but the work had been personally performed by Jocelyn Bell Burnell. [see-j.b.BURNELL] [Nobelprize.org]

史实: 英国收音机天文.1974年嘉奖诺贝尔为了射电.

From Group "R" you can pick one person or up to ten Surnames and write their Surname in Chinese. You may try HORIZONTAL or VERTICAL in the traditional Chinese form.

S

One glance at a book and you hear the voice of another person, perhaps someone dead for 1000 years. To read is to voyage through time.

《当你看一本书的时侯，你可以听到这个人内心的声音，也许这个人已经去世了几千年.阅读就是在时间的长河里遨游航行.》

Carl SAGAN 萨根sa gan

SABIN萨宾sa bin

Albert Bruce Sabin

生人1906 ~ 1993年 》87

FYI: Polish American researcher. Sabin's (OPV) "oral polio vaccine" was stronger and more effective then the Salk vaccine. [cha-see- Salk]

史实: 波兰裔美国研究员.沙宾的 "口服脊髓灰质炎疫苗" 比沙尔克疫苗更强,更有效.

SADAT萨达特sa da te

Anwar Sadat

生人1918 ~ 1981年 》62

FYI: aka Muhammad Anwar El-Sadat; 3rd president of Egypt. Assassinated 1981 October 6.

史实: 三个总统埃及.

SAFER塞弗sai fei

Morley Safer

生人1931 ~ 2016年 》84

FYI: Broadcast journalist and reporter. "60 Minutes".

史实: 转播记者60分钟.

SAGAN萨根sa gan

[Dr.] Carl Edward Sagan

生人1934 ~ 1996年 》62

FYI: Professor of astrophysics, author, TV producer, planetary scientist, educator, skeptic. This was Carl Sagan. *Cosmos ~1980, Contact ~1985. *Pioneer Plaque and Voyager recording. "billions upon billions" is now known as a Sagan Unit.

**One glance at a book and you hear the voice of another person, perhaps someone dead for 1000 years. To read is to voyage through time.

史实: 天体物理学教授,作家,电视制片人,行星科学家,教育家,怀疑论者.这是卡尔·萨根.*Cosmos~1980年, 联系~1985年.*先锋牌和旅行者记录. "几十亿对几十亿" 现在被称为萨根单位.

《当你看一本书的时侯,你可以听到这个人内心的声音,也许这个人已经去世了几千年.阅读就是在时间的长河里遨游航行.》

SALK索尔克suo er ke

[Dr.] Jonas Edward Salk

生人1914 ~ 1995年 》81

FYI: American researcher and virologist. Developed the polio vaccine-c.1955. "can you patent the sun?"[see-Sabin]

史实: 小儿麻痹疫苗.

SAMSON萨马伞sa ma san

William "Will" Samson jr.

生人1933 ~ 1987年 》54

FYI: [a&e] Native American painter, actor, and rodeo performer.

史实: 美国土著画家,演员和竞技表演演员.

SANDBURG伞布戈san bu ge

Carl August Sandburg

生人1878 ~ 1967年 》89

FYI: Swedish- American poet, writer and editor. Regarded as "a major figure in American literature." L*B* Johnson quoted: "He was America."

史实: 作者,式,编辑. 约翰逊引用了他的话:"他是美国人."

SANDERS伞得日斯san dei ri si

Harland David Sanders

生人1890 ~ 1980年 》90

FYI: aka; Colonel Harland David Sanders. c1952 opened the first store in Utah. He was named an "honorary" Colonel by his local community for KFC. "It's finger licking good".

史实: 1952年建.他被当地社区任命为肯德基荣誉上校."手指舔得很好."

SANTOS桑托新sang tuo xin

Lucia de Jesus dos Santos

生人1907 ~ 2005年 》98

FYI: The Fatima story: Lucia was the oldest of the 3 witnesses. [see Marto: Fransico and Jacinto] last photo taken was 1957. [*immaculateheart.com]

史实: 法蒂玛.

SAUVAGE萨威戈sa wei ge

Francois Clement Sauvage

生人1814 ~ 1872年 》58

FYI: French geologist and mining engineer; Is among the 72 listed Eiffel tower. [NE15] >64/72 names.

史实: 地质学家, 新元史上埃菲尔铁塔单名.

SAUVY索维suo wei

Alfred Sauvy

生人1898 ~ 1990年 》92

FYI: Demographer, anthropologist and historian of the French economy. He coined the term Third World (used during the cold war) as it refers to the economic conditions of the world compared to the Capitalist [first: America, Canada, Japan, South Korea, Western European], Communist bloc [second: Soviet Union, China, Cuba], and all others [third or developing] countries.

史实: 人口学家,人类学家和法国经济历史学家.他创造了术语"第三世界"(冷战期间使用), 因为它指的是与资本主义国家(第一:美国,加拿大,日本,韩国,西欧),共产主义集团(第二:苏联,中国,古巴)以及所有其他[第三或发展中]国家相比的世界经济状况.是的.

SAXE萨克斯sai ke si

John Godfrey Saxe

生人June 2, 1816 – March 31, 1887年 》71

FYI: An American poet who learned about the Indian metaphor of 'The Blind Men and the Elephant" which teaches how people interpret life from different perspectives. The parable can be found in Buddhism, Hinduism and Jainism. *Laws, like sausages, cease to inspire respect in proportion as we know how they are made.

史实: 一位美国诗人,他学习了印度的"盲人和大象"的比喻,它教人们如何从不同的角度解读生活.这个比喻可以在佛教,印度教和耆那教中找到.*法律,像香肠一样,不再像我们知道的那样,按比例激发人们的尊重.

SCHAWBE施瓦布shi wa bu

Les Schawbe

生人1917 ~ 2007年 》80

FYI: Founder and owner of "Les Schawbe" c.1952 an automotive (tires) industry.

史实: 先导》施瓦布 施瓦布, 汽车 (轮胎)工业.

SCHEEF希义发xi yi fa

Willi Scheef

生人1937年5月6日 》[memorial纪念]

FYI: mechanic LZ-129 Hindenburg

史实: 车工程兴登堡.

SCHELLING希耶恩xi ye en

Thomas Crombie Schelling

生人1921 ~ 2016年 》95

FYI: awarded the Nobel in 2005 for the Economic Science for Game Theory *
[Nobelprize.org]

史实: 2005年嘉奖诺贝尔为了博弈理论.

SCHENCK希恩克xi en ke

Nicholas Michael Schenck

生人1881 ~ 1969年 》88

FYI: Film Exec~MGM.(Metro-Goldwyn-Mayer)

史实: 电影老板.

SCHINDLER辛德勤xin de le

Oscar Schindler

生人1908 ~ 1974年 》66

FYI: German industrialist who rescued 1200 Jews during WWII. 1982 Israel
Government stated "Righteous Among the Nations." "Schindler's list"-1993-Spielberg.
*Jewish Virtual Library.

史实: 德国工业家, 二战期间救出了1200名犹太人.1982年, 以色列政府称 "国家中的正义"
, "辛德勒名单" ——1993年斯皮尔伯格.*犹太虚拟图书馆.

SCHLAMBERG淑兰贝格shu lan bei ge

Phillip Schlamberg

生人1945年8月14日》19

FYI:[Second Lt] *The last recorded pilot to be shot down over Japan. "The Last Fighter
pilot: Don Brown"

史实: 最后飞机下. "最后一名战斗机飞行员:唐•布朗"

SCHLAPP施拉普shi la pu

Ernst Schlapp

生人1937年5月6日 》[memorial纪念]

FYI: electrician LZ-129 Hindenburg

史实: 电工程兴登堡.

SCHMIDT史密特shi mi te (insert jpg 5.2)

Bernhardt Woldemar Schmidt

生人1879 ~ 1935年 》56

FYI: German optician. In 1930 he introduced the Schmidt Telescope. He would adapt it to fit with a Cassegrain type mirror.

史实: 德国眼镜商.1930年, 他引进了施密特望远镜.他会调整它以适应卡塞格伦式的镜子.[查- cassegrain]

SCHMIDT史密特shi mi te

Klaus Schmidt

生人1953 ~ 2014年 》61

FYI: Archeologist discovered Gobekli Tepe "belly hill" in Turkish: S.E. Turkey 1996 *oldest temple known~ c.9600-7300 BC

史实: 地质学家,发现 *已知最古老的寺庙~ [肚子小丘]

SCHNEIDER施耐德shi nai de

Eugene Schneider

FYI: aka: Joseph Eugene Schneider; INDUSTRIALIST, his name appears on the Eiffel tower.[SW04] *65/72

史实: 工程人 新元史上埃菲尔铁塔单名.

SCHNITGER希尼特格xi ni te ge

Heinrich Schnitger

生人1925 ~ 1964年 》39

FYI: patented the eppendorf piston stroke micro-pipette

史实: 造 micro-pipette为了药.

SCHOPENHAUER施盆哈尔shi pen ha er

Arthur Schopenhauer

生人1788 ~ 1860年 》72

FYI: German philosopher. He is best known for his 1818 work 'The World as Will and Representation'. He was among the first thinkers in Western philosophy to share and affirm significant tenets of Eastern philosophy. *Every truth passes through three stages before it is recognized. In the first it is ridiculed, in the second it is opposed, in the third it is regarded as self evident.

史实: 德国哲学家.他最著名的作品是1818年的《世界如意志和代表》.他是西方哲学中最早分享和肯定东方哲学重要原则的思想家之一.

*一切真理都经过三个阶段.首先,它是被嘲笑的.第二,它遭到强烈反对.第三,它被认为是不言而喻的.

SCHOLL施乐shi le

William Mathias Scholl

生人1882 ~ 1968年 》85

FYI: Podiatrists and founder of Dr. Scholl's [Foot care products] *In Chinese these two symbols [爽健] replace the name SCHOLL: 爽健shuang jian means "to feel well".

史实: 商业鞋医生, 建施乐医生.

SCHREIBMULLER施若布姆勒shi ru bu mu le

Josef Schreibmuller

生人1937年5月6日 》[memorial纪念]

FYI: Chief mechanic; LZ 129 Hindenburg

史实: 高飞机工程;兴登堡.

SCHUELLER书拉尔shu la er

Eugene Paul Louis Schueller

生人1881 ~ 1957年 》76

FYI: French Biomedical researcher and founder of L oreal c1909. Oreale was a hair color formula he had made. *Slogan: "because I'm worth it" was the first of several such slogans.(*)L oreal history.

史实: 法国科研, 先导L'oreal.

SCHULTZ徐拉特思xu la te si

Charles Monroe Schultz

生人1922 ~ 2000年 》82

FYI: nick named "Sparky" was an American cartoonist of Peanuts comic strip c1950. Charlie Brown, Lucy, Linus, Snoopy. Apollo 10 was named "Charlie Brown" and the Lunar module was "Snoopy". 1962: National Cartoonist Association award. * *Just remember, once you're over the hill you begin to pick up speed.*

史实: 尼克叫 "斯帕克", 是一位美国漫画家的花生漫画C1950.查理•布朗,露西,莱纳斯,史努比.阿波罗10号被命名为 "查理•布朗", 登月舱被命名为 "史努比".1962年:国家漫画家协会奖. [Peanuts] *

只要奇住, 一旦您越过山坡, 您就会开始加快速度.

SCHUMACHER徐吗克xu ma ke

Ferdinand Schumacher

生人1822 ~ 1908年 》86

FYI: American entrepreneur, referred to as The Oatmeal King. A member of Quaker Oats company.

史实: 美国人企业家*麦王.

SCHUSTER书斯特shu si te

Max Lincoln Schuster

生人1897 ~ 1970年 》33

FYI: Paperback market and publisher.

Simon and Schuster publishing c1921.[see r.l.SIMON] (*)S&S

史实: 平装书市场和出版商. 西蒙和舒斯特出版c1921.

SCHWABE舒瓦邑shu wa ba

Gustave Christian Schwabe

生人1813 ~ 1897年 》84

FYI: German financier; funded the White Star Line~Titanic series. (*)The Man

史实: 德国商业银行.

SCHWEITZER施韦策shi wei ce

Albert Schweitzer

FYI: He was a theologian, organist, writer, humanitarian, philosopher, and physician. 1952 received the Nobel Peace Prize for his philosophy of "Reverence for Life".

Eventually all things fall into place. Until then, laugh at the confusion, live for the moments, and know EVERYTHING HAPPENS FOR A REASON.

史实: 他是一位神学家,风琴家,作家,人道主义者,哲学家和医生.1952年诺贝尔和平奖,因其"崇尚生命"的哲学而获得.*最终所有的事情都会发生.在那之前,嘲笑困惑,活在当下,知道一切发生的原因.

SCOTT司各特si ge te

Leon Scott

生人1817 ~ 1879年 》62

FYI: aka: Eduard-Leon Scott. Printer and inventor. His "phone-autograph" the first prototype to record sound waves on vinyl. Precursor to the phonograph. c.1854.

史实: 打印机和发明家.他的"电话签名"是第一个在乙烯基上录制声波的原型.留声机的前身.

SEARS西尔斯xi er si

Richard Warren Sears

生人1863月12月7日 ~ 1914年 》 50

FYI: 1891 founded Sears Roebuck with Alva Curtis Roebuck

史实: 1891年建 希尔斯[Sears]

Photo by Forest L. ~ 福瑞斯特

SECORD赛克德sai ke de

Laura Secord

生人1775 ~ 1868年 》93

FYI: Laura Secord [nee] Ingersoll. Laura Secord Chocolate company was named in honor of her Canadian bravery of the War of 1812 against the Americans. In 2012, 200 years since the war her image was minted on the .25 cent coin to remember bravery.

史实: 劳拉·塞克德巧克力公司是为了纪念她在1812年加拿大对美国战争中的勇敢.2012年, 在战争爆发200年后, 为了她的勇敢, 她的形象被刻在了0.25美分的硬币上.

SEEGER西格xi ge

Peter Seeger

生人1919 ~ 2014年 》94

FYI:[a&e] American Folk Singer. *Peter, Paul and Mary.*"Where Have All The Flowers Gone?"

史实: 美国民谣歌手.*彼得,保罗和玛丽."所有的花都去哪儿了?"

SEGUIN萨古恩sa gu en

Marc Sequin

生人1786 ~ 1875年 》89

FYI: French engineer; developed the first suspension bridge. Is named among the 72 names on the Eiffel tower.

[NW01] #66/72 insert

史实: 工程.发明吊桥.新元史上埃菲尔铁塔单名.

SEIFERT塞弗尔特sai fu er te

Jaroslav Seifert

生人1901 ~ 1986年 》85

FYI: Awarded the Noble prize in 1984 for Poetry/Literature. [*Noble prize.org]

史实: 1984年嘉奖诺贝尔为了式.

SELWYN赛尔温sa er wen

Archibald Selwyn

生人1877 ~ 1959年 》82

FYI: Broadway and stage, co-founders of "Goldwyn"~MGM.

史实: 百老汇和舞台联合创始人.建 MGM

SENECA 塞内加 sai ni jia

Lucius Annaeus Seneca

生人 4B.C. ~ 65 A.D. 年 》69

FYI: Roman Stoic philosopher, statesman, dramatist. He was a major philosophical figure of the Roman Imperial Period.*As long as you live, keep learning how to live.*

史实: 罗马斯多葛哲学家, 政治家, 剧作家.他是罗马帝国时期一位重要的哲学人物. *只要你活着, 就要不断学习如何生活.

SERBER 塞佰尔 sa bai er

Robert Serber

生人 1909 ~ 1997 年 》86

FYI: American physicist of the Manhattan Project who named the bombs ie: Little boy [Hiroshima], Fat Man [Nagasaki]. -see Tibbets.

史实: 曼哈顿计划的美国物理学家,他把炸弹命名为:小男孩（广岛）,胖男人（长崎）.

SERTURNER 塞尔恶纳 sai er e na

Friedrich Serturner

FYI: aka: Friedrich Wilhelm Adam Serturner; the first to isolate morphine from opium. The Greek god of dreams "Morpheus". c1815 began wide spread use.

史实: 第一个从鸦片中分离出吗啡的人.希腊梦之神 "墨菲斯".C1815开始广泛使用.

SEUSS 苏斯 su si

Theodore "Ted" Seuss Geisel

生人 1904 ~ 1991 年 》87

FYI: aka Doctor Seuss was a German born author and cartoon illustrator. Many of his works turned into films. *1957~ The Cat in the Hat, 1960~ Green Eggs and Ham. *Don't cry because it's over. Smile because it happened.*

史实: 苏斯医生是一位出生于德国的作家和卡通插画家.他的许多作品都变成了电影. *不要哭了, 因为结束了.微笑, 因为发生了.

SEYMOUR 塞墨尔 sai mo er

Henry Seymour

FYI: co-founded Quaker Oats with William D Heston c1877

[查 -Crowell]

史实: 先导贵格会教徒麦.

SHACKLETON萨克里顿sa ke li dun

Ernest Shackleton

生人1874 ~ 1922年 》48

FYI: was an explorer of the Poles. His "endurance" story c1914-1916 tells of a "Third Man factor" who is now considered from the Angelic realm to save them from death. -see[查看- John Geiger]~third man factor.

史实: [三个男]是一个波兰探险家.他的"耐力"故事C1914-1916讲述了一个"第三人因素", 他现在被认为是从天使界拯救他们免于死亡.

SHAKESPEAR莎士比亚sha shi bi ya

William Shakespear

生人1564 ~ 1616年 》 52

FYI: Poet, writer and one of the worlds most well known playwright and actor. * *The soul's joy lies in doing.*

史实: 诗人,作家和世界上最著名的剧作家和演员之一. * 灵魂的喜悦在于做事.

SHAMBAUGH霞马巴xia ma ba

Jessie Field Shambaugh

生人1881 ~ 1971年 》90

FYI: aka: Celestia Josephine "Jessie" Field Shambaugh. She is considered the MOTHER of 4H: head- hand- hearts- health. She designed the 4H Clover emblem. 4H is a North American youth program [查看-see Hall-Graham]

史实: 她被认为是4H的母亲:头部-手-心脏-健康.她设计了4H三叶草徽章.4H是北美青年计划.

SHANNON杀那按sha na an

Claude Elwood Shannon

生人1916 ~ 2001年 》95

FYI: Mathematician, electrical engineer and cryptographer. Known as "The Father of Information Theory". (A Mathematical Theory of Communication:1948)

史实: 数, 电工程, 夫子为了广告.

SHAPLEY莎普利sha pu li

Harlow Shapely

生人1885 ~ 1972年 》67

FYI: Astronomer.* coined the phrase "habitable zone"in 1953. The first scientist to measure the MILKY WAY galaxy with approximate 400 Billion suns. Shapley and Hubble had a professional working relationship. At one point he considered Hubble's work to be "junk science" until one day he received evidence on the contrary. *Here is the letter that destroyed my universe!"

史实: 天文学家.1953年, 天文学家创造了"宜居地带"这个短语.第一位用约400亿个太阳来测量MILKY WAY星系的科学家.沙普利和哈勃有着专业的工作关系.一次, 他认为哈勃的工作是"垃圾科学", 直到有一天, 他收到相反的证据"这是摧毁我的宇宙的信! "

SHAPLEY莎普利sha pu li
Floyd Stowell Shapely
生人1923 ~ 2016年 》93
FYI: American mathematician. Awarded the Nobel Prize in 2012 for Economic sciences for market design. [*Nobelprize.org]
史实: 数人.2012面嘉奖诺贝尔为了经济活动.

SHARIF沙里夫sha li fu
Omar Sharif
生人1932年 ~ Active
FYI: [a&e] aka Michel Dimitry Chalhoub. Icon Egyptian actor; fluent in Arabic, French, English, Spanish, Greek and Italian. *Lawrence of Arabia, Dr. Zhivago most noted films.(*wiki-BaiDu)
史实: 电影.多种语音 ~ 六个语.

SHAW肖xiao
George Bernard Shaw
生人1856 ~ 1950年
FYI: He was an Irish playwright, critic, polemicist and political activist. *We don't stop playing because we grow old, we grow old because we stop playing.
史实: 他是爱尔兰剧作家,评论家,辩论家和政治活动家.*我们不会因为变老而停止比赛,我们会因为停止比赛而变老.

SHELLEY事利shi li
Mary Wollstonecraft Shelley
生人1759 ~ 1797年

FYI: English novelist, short story writer essayist. While still in her teens she is best known for writing Frankenstein . *My education was neglected, yet I was passionately fond of reading.

史实: 她十几岁时就以写《科学怪人》而闻名.*我的教育被忽略了,但我仍然非常喜欢阅读.

SHERMAN杀而曼sha er man

Nate Harold Sherman

生人1898 ~ 1980年 》 82

FYI: He started MIDAS [Muffler Installation Dealers Association Service] circa1956.

史实: 他大约在1956年创立了midas[消声器安装经销商协会服务].

SHOEMAKER舒梅克shu mei ke

Eugene Merle Shoemaker

生人1928 ~ 1997年 》 69

FYI: geologist and astronomer. Comet Levy-Shoemaker... the comet hit Jupiter on July 1994. His "ashes buried on the Moon". [查看see Levy]

史实: 地质学家和天文学家.利维•肖梅克彗星…这颗彗星于1994年7月撞击木星.他的 "灰烬埋在月球上".

SHOEN舒恩shu en

Leonard Samuel "Sam" Shoen

生人1916年2月29日 ~ 1999年

FYI: American entrepreneur and founder of U-hual.

史实: 美国企业家和铀氢氧化物的创始人.

SHOLES斯科尔斯si ke er si

Latham Christopher Scholes

生人1819 ~ 1890年 》71

FYI: Newspaper editor and Inventor of the QWERTY board[1868]. Is based on the "mechanical" version, the layout kept frequently combined letters physically apart, which limited the number of collisions between type bars. Later the patent was sold to P. Remington and refined. All QWERTY boards are based on the Latin-script alphabet. 《 insert [~s.w.SOULE, c.Glidden] (*)Y.D, E.B.

史实: 发明为了QWERTY 电脑基于 "机械" 版本,布局经常将组合字母物理分开,从而限制了类型条之间的冲突数量.后来,专利被卖给P.Remington并加以改进.所有的QWERTY板都基于拉丁字母表.

SICARD斯克德si ke de

Jean-Athanase Sicard

生人1872 ~ 1929年 》57

FYI: French neurologist and radiologist. Was instrumental in developing dyes for radiology diagnosis. Collet-Sicard syndrome named in his honor.

史实: 放射学.发明颜料为了X光.

SILVA杀尔法sha er fa

Jose Silva

生人1914 ~ 1999年 》85

FYI: Parapsychologist is regarded as the pioneer in Mind-I/Q therapy.

史实:心里IQ:精神学.

SILVER丝勒威si le wei

Dr. Spencer Ferguson Silver

FYI: Chemist* co-invented the glue for "post-it-note" c.1968. Arthur Fry adjusted the composition to make it more adhesive.

史实: 化学家发明*邮政汇票粘合剂.

SIMON斯曼si man

Theodore Simon

生人1872 ~ 1961年 》89

FYI: French Psychologist who helped develop the Binet-Simon Intelligence scale. [看-see alfred*binet]

史实:法国精神冰雪;Binet*Simon:智慧等第.

SIMON斯曼si man

Richard Leo Simon

生人1899 ~ 1960年 》61

FYI: Simon and Schuster publishing. "Fads and Trends". [see- m.Schuster]

史实: S*S 出版*时尚事事.

SIMON斯曼si man

Marvin Neil Simon

生人1927年7月4日~ 2018年 》91

FYI: American playwright, screen writer and author.

史实: 美国剧作家,银幕作家和作家.

SIMONS斯曼丝si man zi

Menno Simons

生人1496 ~ 1561年 》65

FYI: a member of the Anabaptist group. Founded the Mennonite religion. [查看~ Ammann- Simons- Hutter: anabaptist]

史实: 建门诺派信徒宗教.

SIMMONS斯曼丝si man zi

John~D~Simmons

生人1975年11月10日 》62 [memorial~纪念]

FYI:*SS Edmund Fitzgerald~Lake Superior

史实: S.S. 埃德蒙*菲茨杰拉德 湖高强1975年 11月10日纪念.

SINCLAIR辛克莱xin ke lai

Upton Beall Sinclair jr.

生人1878 ~ 1968年 》90

FYI: American writer who won the Pulitzer prize for Fiction c1943. Because of his influence, the "Code of Ethics"c1923 was formed in journalism. His book "the Jungle" c1905 was an eye opener for all reading about the meat industry.

史实: 美国作者.在他的影响下,"道德准则" C1923在新闻界形成.

SINCLAIR辛克莱 xin ke lai

Allan Gordon Sinclair

生人1900 ~ 1984年 》83

FYI: Canadian reporter, Front Page challenge panellist. *Will the real Gordon Sinclair please stand up!"c1966. O.C. c.1979.

史实: 加拿大新闻学. *真正的戈登•辛克莱能站起来吗? "

photo by Forest L. 福瑞斯特

SINGER 丝纳格 si ni ge

Isaac Merrit Singer

生人1811 ~ 1875年 》61

FYI: Founder Singer Sewing as the first high speed sewing machines based on the *Thomas Saint* primary idea. He added a foot peddle power system with belt attached. It was the next step in today's evaluation of technology. His design made them all portable.

史实: 方正辛格缝纫机作为第一台高速缝纫机的基础上,圣托马斯的初衷. 他增加了一个连着皮带的脚踏动力系统.这是今天技术评估的下一步. 他的设计使它们都便于携带.

SITCHIN 思陈 si chen

Zecharia Sitchin

生人1920 ~ 2010年 》90

FYI: Russian-American author and frequent guest on coasttocoast AM. He proposed an explanation for our human origins involving ancient astronauts.

史实: 俄裔美国作家和经常到访的客人.他提出了一个关于古代宇航员的人类起源的解释.

SITTING BULL 坐牛 zuo niu

生人1831 ~ 1890年 》59

FYI: Hunkpapa Lakota leader. Led the resistance against the American forces of his time. [zuo~sitting, niu~ bull]. [看-see Buffalo Bill, j.McLaughlin]

史实: 领导了他那个时代对美国军队的抵抗.

SKEAT斯克特si ke te

Walter William Skeat

生人1835 ~ 1912年 》77

FYI: British philologist who helped develop the English grammar system in his era. [~ H. SWEET]

史实: 帮助他那个时代发展英语语法系统的英国语言学家.

SKELTON斯卡里特嗯si ka li te en

Red Skelton

生人1913 ~ 1997年 》84

FYI:[a&e] aka; Richard Bernard "Red" Skelton. Early stage, radio, actor and singer.

史实: 早期,电台,演员和歌手.

SMITH史密斯shi mi si

Robert Weston Smith

生人1938 ~ 1995年 》57

FYI: [a&e] AKA; Wolfman Jack- The Legend; Icon in radio for North America. Known for his deep BASS voice and humour.

史实: 传说;北美电台的图标.他以低沉的低音和幽默著称.

SMITH史密斯shi mi si

[Captain] John Edward Smith

生人1850 ~ 1912年4月15日 [memorial~纪念]

FYI:1912 April 15: British merchant naval officer and Captain of the RMS Titanic. He was known as an Icon of "stiff upper lip" of spirit and discipline.

史实: 英国商船军官和皇家海军泰坦尼克号船长.他被称为精神和纪律的"硬上唇"的象征.

SMITH史密斯shi mi si

Joseph Smith jr.

生人1805 ~ 1844年 》39

FYI: Founder of the Church of Jesus Christ of Latter-day Saints. Was martyred for his beliefs of a "living Christ" hence "The First Vision". Translated the *Book of Mormon*.

史实: 建为了耶稣基督后期圣徒教会 *翻译了摩门教的书.

Statue on the Alberta Legislature grounds.
Photo by Forest L.福瑞斯特

SMITH史密斯shi mi si

John Alexander Smith

生人1820 ~ 1914年 》94

FYI: *AKA ~ Lord Strathcona was the last man to put a spike of the National Canadian Railway 1885 NOV 07; Criagellachie B.C.

史实: 1885年11月7日*历史终于他置于末国立加拿大铁.

SMITH史密斯shi mi si

John Stafford Smith

生人1750 ~ 1836年 》86

FYI: British composer and musicologist, best known for writing the music for the American Patriotic song of "Star-Spangled Banner". [~F.S.KEY]

史实: 英国作曲家和音乐学家,以为美国爱国歌曲创作音乐而闻名.*[星撒旗子]

SMITHIES史密义丝shi mi yi si

Oliver Smithies

生人1928 ~ 2017年 》89

FYI: Awarded the Nobel for modifying cancerous geno's in genetics c 2007. [*Nobelprize.org]

史实: 2007年嘉奖诺贝尔为了基因组.

SMITHSON史姆森shi mu sen

James Smithson

生人1765 ~ 1829年 》64

FYI: British Scientist and mineralogist who requested that his estate become the Smithsonian Institution devoted to: The Arts, humanities and Sciences in America.

史实: 英国人矿物学*美国史密森学会. [院:文理*人道]

SNELLIUS斯内利厄斯si nei li e si

Willebrord Snellius

FYI: AKA Willebrord Snel van Royen. Best known for developing the Quadrant of Snellius for measuring the circumference of the earth while at sea. The Lunar crater *Snellius* bears his named after him.

史实:　最著名的是开发斯内留斯象限仪测量地球在海上的周长.斯内留斯环形山以他的名字命名.

SNOW斯诺si nuo

Edgar Parks Snow

生人1905 ~ 1972年 》77

FYI: American journalist who wrote many articles about Communism in China. Became personal friends with and interviewed Mao Ze Dong. Author of "Red Star over China". *"*Do not suppose, first of all, that Mao Tse-tung could be the "saviour" of China. Nonsense. There will never be one "saviour" of China. Yet undeniably you feel a certain force of destiny in him.*"

史实: 美国记者,写了许多关于中国共产主义的文章.与毛泽东成为私人朋友,并采访了他.《中国红星》的作者.*首先,不要认为毛泽东可以成为中国的 "救世主".胡说.中国永远不会有一个 "救世主".但不可否认,你在他身上感受到了某种命运的力量."

SOCRATES苏格拉底su ge la di

生人469 ~ 399年B.C. 》70

FYI: Classical Greek philosopher and Founder of Western Philosophy. * *Let him that would move the world, first move himself.*

史实: 古典希腊哲学家和西方哲学的创始人. * 让他感动世界, 先感动自己.

SOUBIROUS苏比鲁su bi lu

生人Jan 7, 1844 ~ Apr 16, 1879年 》35

Bernadette Soubirous

FYI: Known historically as Saint Bernadette of Lourdes. She was the soul recipient of 'The Marian Apparitions' from 11 Feb to 16 July 1858, during her era she was persecuted heavily by authorities for sharing her visions. The town of Lourdes is now a pilgrimage site. The book and movie "The Song of Bernadette' 1943 is based on the true story of her life. *I'm happier with my crucifix on my bed of pain than a queen on her throne.

史实: 历史上她被称为卢尔德的圣伯纳黛特.1858年2月11日至7月16日,她是"玛丽安幽灵"的灵魂接受者,在她的时代,她因分享自己的幻象而受到当局的严重迫害.卢尔德现在是一个朝圣地点。这本书和电影"1943年伯纳黛特之歌"是根据她的真实生活故事改编的.*在痛苦的床上钉十字架,我比坐在王位上的女王更快乐.

SPARTACUS斯巴达克si ba da ke

生人111 ~ 71年 B.C.

FYI: Was a Thracian Gladiator and accomplished military leader, but enslaved at the end of his life.

史实: 古角斗士和军人.

SPENCER斯宾塞si bin sa

Herbert Spencer

生人April 27, 1820 ~ December 8, 1903年 》83

FYI: Was a British philosopher and sociologist who was intellectually active during the Victorian period. Prior to Darwin, he was first to coin 'Survival of the Fittest'. *A jury is composed of twelve men of average ignorance.

史实: 是一位英国哲学家和社会学家,在维多利亚时期非常活跃.在达尔文之前,他是第一个提出"适者生存"的人.*陪审团由十二个一般无知的人组成.

SPENCER斯宾塞si bin sa

Platt Rogers Spencer

platt rogers spencer

FYI: Developed a penmanship known as "Spencerian" that was popular and was used for the Coca-Cola design.

史实: 他文章是叫"斯宾塞式的"*用为了可口可乐.

[查看- f.m.Robinson]

SPENGLER斯盆格勒si pen ge le

William~J~Spengler

生人1975年11月10日 》59 [memorial~纪念]

FYI:*SS Edmund Fitzgerald~Lake Superior

史实: S.S. 埃德蒙*菲茨杰拉德 湖高强1975年 11月10日.

SPITZKA丝皮特兹卡si pi te zi ka

Edward Charles Spitzka

生人1852 ~ 1914年 》62

FYI: Was an alienist, neurologist, anatomist; was at the first American electrocution. [查看-see kemmler]

史实: 神经学*解剖*目睹第一次电刑.

SPOCK斯帕克si pa ke

Benjamin Mclane Spock

生人1903 ~ 1998年 》85

FYI: American pediatrician known for [Baby and Child Care:1946]. *You know more than you think you do.

史实: 美国医生*小儿科. "你知道的比你想象的要多".

SPRANGLER斯潘格勒si pan ge le

James Murray Sprangler

生人1848 ~ 1915年 》72

FYI: was the inventor of the early models of the vacuum cleaner and sold his patent to Hoover. [查看~ w.HOOVER]

史实: 发明为了真空泵机曾经胡佛真空.

STALIN斯大林si da lin

Joseph Vissarionovich Stalin

生人1878 ~ 1953年 》74

FYI: Soviet dictator who instituted the "Great Purge":1934-1939. Ideologically a Marxist-Leninism. *"the death of a comrade is a tragedy, the death of millions is a statistic."

史实: 苏共*原苏联《同志之死是悲剧,百万之死是统计数字》

STANFORD斯坦福德si tan fu de

Amasa Leland Stanford

生人1824 ~ 1893年 》69

FYI: American tycoon, industrialist and politician. In 1885
Stanford University was founded in memorial of the passing of his only son.

史实: 斯坦福德大学*商业企业家*记忆他儿子.

STANLEY斯坦雷si tan lei

John Mix Stanley

生人1814 ~ 1872年 》58

FYI: renouned painter of the New western frontier. Painted many prominent leaders.
[看~ see Pontiac]

史实: 画家*世界高名人.

This coin commemorates 125 years of the STANLEY CUP. Photo by Forest L. ~ 福瑞斯特

STANLEY斯坦雷si tan lei

Frederick Arthur Stanley

生人1841 ~ 1908年 》67

FYI: AKA: Lord Stanley, the Stanley Cup is named in his honor. As well, he is one of
the first inductees into the Canadian Hall of Fame.

史实: '斯坦利杯' *冰球将为了加拿大.

Photo by Forest L. ~ 福瑞斯特

STANLEY斯坦雷si tan lei
George Francis Gillman Stanley
生人1907 ~ 2002年 》95
FYI: Canadian historian, author and teacher and designer of the Canadian flag c1965. Order of Canada c1976. * After hundreds of proposals, the selection rested on three designs. Then it was decided that the chief design would have 3 maple leaves gripped as one 'stem', it would be RED on a White background, with Red boarders.
史实: 加拿大历史学家,加拿大国旗C1965的作者,教师和设计师.加拿大法令C1976.*经过上百次的提议,最终选择了三种设计方案.然后决定主要设计将3片枫叶夹在一起作为一个"茎",它将是白色背景上的红色,带有红色的木板.

STAPP斯塔普si ta pu
[Col] John Paul Stapp
生人1910 ~ 1999年 》89
FYI: U.S. Air Force officer, surgeon, physician and biophysicist and pioneer in acceleration and deceleration on humans in a pre space program called 'Project Manhigh'. Became known as 'the fastest man on earth.' Stapp's law in his honor.
史实: 美国空军军官,外科医生,医生和生物物理学家,在一个名为"曼高计划"的太空前项目中率先对人类进行加速和减速.被誉为"世界上最快的人".斯塔普的定律是为了纪念他.

STEELE斯第尔si di er
[Sir] Richard Steele
生人1672 ~ 1729年 57
FYI: Irish writer and politician.*Reading is to the mind what exercise is to the body.
史实: 爱尔兰作家和政治家. * "读书对头脑来说就像运动对身体一样."

STERN斯特恩si te en

Itzhak Stern

生人1901 ~ 1969年 》68

FYI: He was the accountant for Oscar Schindler and personally typed the name list of "Schindlers list" to save Jews from the Nazis (Schindlerjuden~"Schindler's Jews")

史实: 他是奥斯卡•辛德勒的会计, 亲自打了 "辛德勒名单" 的名单, 以拯救犹太人脱离纳粹.

STEVENSON斯蒂文森si di wen sen

Robert Louis Balfour Stevenson

生人1850 ~ 1894年 》44

FYI: Scottish writer, short stories, poems. "Treasure Island, Jekyll and Hyde."

史实: 作者,式*[宝岛] 金银岛.

STINCHFIELD斯坦菲尔德si tan fei er de

Augustus~W~Stinchfield

生人1842 ~ 1917年 》75

FYI: American physician and co-founder of "the Mayo Clinic".[see-Mayo]

史实: 美国医生 *梅奥诊所.

courtesy of St. Laurent School

St. LAURENT圣劳伦特sheng lao lun te

Louis Stephen St. Laurent

生人1882 ~ 1973年 》91

FYI: lawyer and politician. Served in the 12th term of Canada as Prime Minister [1948-57] His signature on his autograph in this Edmonton Catholic school is signed as Saint Laurent.

史实: 律师和政治家.在加拿大第12任总理期间（1948-57年），他在埃德蒙顿天主教学校签名的签名是圣洛朗.

STOCKLE斯特快乐si te ke le

Alfred Stockle

生人1937年5月6日 [memorial~纪念]

FYI: engine mechanic; LZ- Hindenburg

史实: 飞机工程, 兴拖布.

STOKER斯特克尔si te ko er

Abraham "Bram" Stoker

生人1847 ~ 1912年 》65

FYI: writer and author, "Dracula... *we learn from failure, not from success! [*goodreads]

史实: 写, 作者."德古拉…我们从失败中学习, 而不是从成功中学习! "

STOKES斯特克斯si te ke si

Alexander Alec Rawson Stokes

生人1919 ~ 2003年 》84

FYI: Published works on the structure of the DNA. [see-post Cricks,Watson]

史实: [DNA] 写上去氧核糖酸.

STOLLERY斯特克斯si te ke si

[Dr.] Robert Stollery

生人1924 ~ 2007年 》82

FYI: Former president of Poole Construction,was the driving force behind Edmonton's Stollery Children's Hospital, and numerous other charitable organizations.

史实:　普尔建设公司的前总裁是埃德蒙顿新托勒里儿重医院和许多其他慈善组织的幕后推手.

STRAUSS斯特劳斯si te lao si

David Friedrich Strauss

生人1808 ~ 1874年 》66

FYI: German liberal Protestant Theologian. He wrote about the "Historical Jesus"

史实: 写, 作者 [历史*耶稣]

STRAUSS斯特劳斯si te lao si

Levi Strauss

生人1829 ~ 1902年 》73

FYI: Levis jeans and Co-inventor with Jacob Davis.

史实: 发明-先导*裤子[牛仔裤]

STRAVINSKY斯特拉文斯奇si te la wen si qi

Igor Fyodorovich Stravinsky

生人1882 ~ 1971年 》89

FYI: Russian born composer and conductor.

*The Firebird (1910) *The Right of Spring (1913)

史实: 俄语作曲者指挥.

STRONG强qiang

Henry Alva Strong

生人1838 ~ 1919年 》81

FYI: co-founder of Kodak film c.1888 [see-g.Eastman]

*qiang is literal not phonetic.

史实: Eastman和他建 Kodak照片机.

STRUGHOLD斯特格宏si te ge hour

Herbutes Strughold

生人1898 ~ 1986年 》88

FYI: He was a Physiologist "Father of space medicine" he coined the phrase "habital zone ~ goldylock zone" (circa 1953.)

史实: 他生道 [居住区-Goldylock区]住所. [*P.Science]

STRUTT斯特拉特si te la te

John William Strutt

生人1842 ~ 1919年 》88

FYI: aka. Lord Rayleigh. Was awarded the Nobel in 1904 for discovering argon. Rayleigh waves explains the color of the blue sky. [*Nobel-peace.org]

史实: 嘉奖诺贝尔为了瑞利波解释了蓝天的颜色.

STURM施图姆shi tu mu

Jacque Charles Francois Sturm

生人1803 ~ 1855年 》52

FYI: Mathematician. Known for Sturm Theorem: speed of sound under water. His name appears on the Eiffel tower. [SW18] #67/72

史实: 施图姆理论*新元史上埃菲尔铁塔单名.

SUESS休斯xiu si

Eduard Suess

生人1831 ~ 1914年 》82

FYI: geologist who was renouned for the "Gondwana Super Continent theory" prior to the Great Tetonic Land Division. Coined the phrase "Biosphere". [看-see Vernadsky]

史实: 地质学家, 因 "冈瓦纳超级大陆理论" 而闻名于大提顿大陆划分之前.创造了 "生物圈" 这个词.

SULLIVAN萨丽芬sa li fen

Anne Sullivan

生人1866 ~ 1936年 》70

FYI: AKA: Johanna Mansfield Sullivan Macy; She was Keller's teacher. A successful case story of "the blind leading the blind", as both ladies were blind from a young age, but battled their way through a seeing world. Both went to University and obtained their degree. *Education in the light of present-day knowledge and need calls for some spirited and creative innovations both in the substance and the purpose of current pedagogy.

史实: 海伦凯勒老师, 一个成功的例子是 "盲人带领盲人", 因为两位女士从小就双目失明, 但在一个视觉世界中挣扎.两人都上了大学并获得了学位. * 根据当前的知识和需求进行教育, 需要在当前教育学的实质和目的上进行一些精神和创造性的创新.

SULLIVAN萨利芬sa li fen

Edward Vincent "Ed" Sullivan

生人1902 ~ 1974年 》72

FYI:[a&e] American Icon television personality

史实: 高名艺人, 广播.

SWANN斯万si wan

Ingo Douglas Swann

生人1933 ~ 2013年 》80

FYI: developed the remote viewing program.

史实: 开发了远程查看程序.

SWEENY肌肉萎缩ji ruo wei suo

Charles~W~Sweeny

生人1919 ~ 2004年 》84

FYI: He flew the "Bockscar" that carried the "Fat Man" to Nagasaki 1945 Aug 09. Fat man was not a reference to Churchill but was picked from a movie of the same era. [-see Tibbets- Oppinheimer- Serber]

史实: 他有飞机到日本*[胖人] 原子弹.

SWEET斯威特si wei te

Henry Sweet

生人1845 ~ 1912年 》67

FYI: English philologist, phonetician and grammarian. His work is considered the forerunner to the IPA system. c1877: A Handbook of Phonetics. "the man who taught Europe Phonetics". [see- j.r.GREGG]*wiki

史实: 英国句型*先导为了[IPA]体系*1877年刊物.

SWIFT萨沃特sa wo te

Jonathan Swift

生人1667 ~ 1745年 》78

FYI: Satirist, essayist, poet and clerk. author of [Gulliver Travels:1726]. He at times chose to use pseudonym of Lemuel*Gulliver.

史实: 式,写,作者 [格列佛游记: 1726]

SYNCELLUS斯尼厕鲁斯si ni ce lu si

George Syncellus

生人c810年 A.D.

FYI: The Monk was known mostly as an historian of his era. The Surname mentioned is in regards to his abode, in this case "Syncellus" literally means CELL MATE.

史实： 僧人，作者，哲学.提到的姓氏是关于他的住所，在这种情况下，"合子"字面意思是细胞伴侣.

SZPILMAN什皮尔曼shen pi er man

Wladyslaw Szpilman

生人1911 ~ 2000年 》88

FYI: Polish pianist and classical composer. His life is shared in 2002 "The Pianist", as he struggled to survive during the holocaust.

史实： 波兰钢琴家和古典作曲家.2002年,当他在大屠杀中挣扎求生时,"钢琴家"分享了他的生命.

From Group "S" you can pick one person or up to ten Surnames and write their Surname in Chinese. You may try HORIZONTAL or VERTICAL in the traditional Chinese form.

Tkindness is the language which the deaf can hear and the blind can see.
《善意的语音, 聋人可以听见盲人可以看见》
Mark TWAIN吐温tu wen

TAIT泰坦tai tan

Peter Guthrie Tait

生人1831 ~ 1901年 》72

FYI: Scottish mathematical physicist. Author "Treatise on Natural Philosophy".

史实: 物理学家, 作者[自然哲学论] 自然主义

TATE泰特tai te

[SIR] Henry Tate

生人1819 ~ 1899年 》80

FYI: Sugar merchant and philanthropist

史实: 糖商人, 慈善家.

TAYLOR泰勒tai le

Dame Elizabeth Rosmond "Liz" Taylor

生人1932 ~ 2011年 》79

FYI:[a&e]; Hollywood Icon.

史实: 好莱坞炬.

TAYLOR泰勒tai le

John Taylor

FYI: 3rd president of LDS church.

史实: 曾经三个总统耶稣基督后期圣徒教会

TAYLOR泰勒tai le

Jane Taylor

生人1783 ~ 1824年 》37

FYI: Poet and author of "Twinkle, twinkle, little Star"

史实: 式, 作者 "闪烁闪烁小星"

TALMAGE塔尔梅奇ta er mei qi

James Edward Talmage

生人1862 ~ 1933年 》70

FYI: English chemist and geologist. Latter-Day Saint Apostle, Christian author: Jesus the Christ.

史实: 地质学家,教作者 [耶稣一个基督].使徒为了耶稣基督后期圣徒教会.

TANDY潭底tan di

Charles David Tandy

生人1918～1978年 》60

FYI: Tandy corp. and co-founder of Radio Shack.

史实: 先导为了美国商业无线电棚屋.

TANNER谈尔tan er

Jerald Dee Tanner

生人1938～2006年 》68

FYI: American researcher on modern religion. Publisher of periodicals. *"Times and Season."

史实: 美国研究机构.[时节*季节]太无时报*季节.

TCHAIKOWSKY柴可夫斯基chai ke fu si ji

Pyotr llyich Tchaikovsky

生人1840～1893年 》53

FYI: Russian composer. First composer in Carnegie Hall c.1891

史实: 俄罗斯艺人. 1891年第一次在.卡内基丁.

TEILHARD泰亚尔tai ya er

Pierre Teilhard

生人c1881～1955年 》74

FYI: AKA: Pierre Teilhard de Chardin; French idealist philosopher and Jesuit Priest. His free time was spent in Paleontology.* co-partner of Peking man.

史实: 哲学和教.学生为了古生物学家》北京人.

TEMPLE特魔怕te mo pa

Shirley Temple

生人1928～2014年 》85

FYI:[a&e] aka: Shirley *Temple *Black. She was and Icon Child star in early Hollywood and ambassador to Ghana as an adult.

史实: 哈里瓦孩子星然后加纳形象大使.

painting courtesy of Saint Laurent school.

TERESA特蕾莎te lei sha
MOTHER Teresa [pseudonym]
生人1910年6月26日 ~ 1997年9月5日 》87
FYI: aka: Agnus Gonxha Bojaxhiu was a Catholic nun from Calcutta. She adopted the name "Theresa" from Theresa of Lisieux, a French nun. But chose to use the Spanish spelling of 'Teresa'. She was awarded the *Nobel Peace Prize c1979; Medal of Freedom from USA c1985 . *if you judge people, you have no time to love them." [see Therese] [*Nobelprize.org]
史实: 是加尔各答的天主教修女.她从法国修女丽苏的特蕾莎那里取名为"特蕾莎".但选择使用西班牙语拼写的"teresa".她被授予*诺贝尔和平奖C1979;美国自由勋章C1985."如果你评判别人,你就没有时间去爱他们."

TERESHKOVA特若丝口瓦te ruo si kou wa
Valentino Vladimirovna Tereshkova
生人1937年 ~ active
FYI:c.1963 first woman in space (vostok-6)
史实: 1963年第一次女在天空.

TERRELL特雷尔te lei er

Nancy Terrell

FYI:"Miss Nancy"or Nancy Clandenin Terrell was the first ROMPER room hostess.
"Magic mirror", Romper room Prayer, "pop goes the weasel"song. c.1953-1994

史实: 1953年到1994*第一次女罗布*房间复员.

TESLA特斯拉te si la

Nikola Tesla

生人1856年7月10日 ~ 1943年 》87

FYI: physicist, inventor and electrical engineer. The Father of A.C. As well, is considered
the inventor of the radio.

*If you want to find the secrets of the Universe, think in terms of energy, frequency
and vibration."

史实: 高名发明,电工程,物理学家.夫子为了电波

*如果你想找到宇宙的秘密,想想能量,频率和振动.

THANT丹dan

U Thant

生人1909 ~ 1974年 》65

FYI: Burmese diplomat. United Nations University and lectures series.

史实: 外交, 联合国大学讲演.

THATCHER撒切尔sa qie er

[Baroness] Margaret Hilda Thatcher

生人1925 ~ 2013年 》88

FYI: British conservative pm 1979-1990. The British gave her the name of "The Iron
Lady". Same as Indira Ghandi of India.

史实: 曾经英国总统.

THERESE特蕾莎te lei sha

[St] Theresa of Lisieux

生人1873 ~ 1897年 》24

FYI: b. Marie~Francoise~Therese Martin; The French nun known as "The Little
Flower". The name is a reflection of Matt 6:29. In 1888 at 15 years she became a nun,

at 24 she died from tuberculosis. In 1997, the church declares her a 'Doctor of the Church'. She was Mother Teresa's guiding inspiration of a righteous saint and wanted to follow in her foot steps and adopted the name "Therese" and used the Spanish translation of Teresa to avoid confusion. 'The Story of a Soul'~1898 explains 'The Little Flower' in detail. *When one loves, one does not calculate. [see M-Teresa]

史实：被称为"小花"的法国修女.1888年，15岁的她成为了一名修女，24岁的她死于肺结核.1997年，教会宣布她为"教会医生".她是特蕾莎修女的指导灵感，是一位正义的圣人，她想跟随她的脚步，采用"特蕾莎"这个名字，并用西班牙语翻译特蕾莎以避免混淆."灵魂的故事"~1898年.*当一个人爱的时候，他不会计算.

THENARD特纳德te na de
Louis Jacque Thenard
生人1777 ~ 1857年 》80
FYI: Chemist. Was considered an above average Chemist of his era. His name is among the 72 listed on the Eiffel tower. [SE15] #68/72
史实: 高名化学家.新元史上埃菲尔铁塔单名2007

THOMAS托马斯tuo ma si
Rex David Thomas
生人1932 ~ 2002年 》69
FYI: Business man and philanthropist who was the founder of Wendy's c1969. As a young man, he worked for Col. Harland Sanders. Wendy was the nick-name of his red haired daughter.
史实: 美国商业,企业家[温迪]

THOMAS托马斯tuo ma si
Mark~A~Thomas
生人1954 ~ 1975年 》21 》1975年11月10日纪念
FYI: *SS Edmund Fitzgerald~Lake Superior
史实: S.S. 埃德蒙*菲茨杰拉德 湖高强1975年 11月10日

THOMAS托马斯tuo ma si
Lowell Jackson Thomas
生人1892 ~ 1981年 》89

FYI: writer and broadcaster. Best known for publicizing "T.E. Lawrence".
[see-T.E.Lawrence]
史实: 写, 广播.以宣传 "T.E.劳伦斯" 而闻名.

THOMSON汤姆森tang mu sen
Roy Herbert Thomson
生人1894～1976年 》82
FYI: Canadian newspaper proprietor who who later join with Reuters. He owned the Times and The Sunday Times.
史实: 加拿大报系商业.他拥有《泰晤士报》和《星期日泰晤士报.》

THOMPSON汤普森tang pu sen
David Thompson
生人1770～1857年 》87
FYI: Canadian fur trader, surveyor and map-maker for Hudson Bay Company. "The Greatest Land geographer who ever lived" [j.b.Tyrell]
史实: 早加拿大先导.[大卫汤普森高路]

THOMPSON汤普森tang pu sen
[SIR] John Sparrow David Thompson
生人1845～1894年 》49
FYI: Canadian lawyer, judge, politician and 4th pm of Canada. *He was the driving force behind the Criminal Code of Canada.
史实: 律师,政治家,第四个首相为了加拿大.写犯罪密码

THORVALDSSON托瓦德宋tuo wa de son
Erik Thorvaldsson
生人950～1003年 AD 》53
FYI: "Erik the Red" as he was better known was a Norse explorer that founded Greenland.
史实: "埃里克红" 探索和先导为了格陵兰

TIBBITS特比特丝te bi te si
Paul Warfield Tibbits jr.
生人1915～2007年 》92

FYI: United States air force and pilot of the "Enola Gay" that dropped "Little Boy" on Hiroshima~1945. "Enola Gay" was named after his mother. [-see SERBER-Sweeny]

史实: 1945年飞机人为了 [伊诺拉*盖伊]以他母亲的名字命名. 小子原子弹.

TIFFANY蒂芙尼di fu ni

Louis Comfort Tiffany

生人1848 ~ 1933年 》85

FYI: American artist and designer of stained glass. Church window mosaics, lamps, gates etc.

史实: 美国款式璃为了教的.

TOLKIEN托尔金传duo er jin zhuan

John Ronald Reuel Tolkien [(j.r.r.) Tolkien]

生人1892 ~ 1973年 》81

FYI: British writer, poet, University professor. Best known for "the Hobbit, Lord of the Rings." Was ranked sixth among the "Top 50 British writers since 1945." Was close friends with C.R. Lewis.

史实: 高名英国作者,式.大学授衔.[指环王]

TOLSTOY托尔斯泰tuo er si tai

Lev "Leo" Nikolayevitch Tolstoy

生人1828 ~ 1910年 》82

FYI: Russian writer, philosopher. He is best know for "War and Peace", but his writing range repitoire was very extensive.

* Everyone thinks of changing the world, but no one thinks of changing himself.

史实: 俄罗斯作者,哲学.[战争*和平] *每个人都想改变世界,但没有人想改变自己.

TOMLINSON汤林送tang lin song

Ray Tomlinson

生人1942 ~ 2016年 》74

FYI: Pioneer computer programmer who implemented the first email "because it seemed like a nice idea". He chose the "@" symbol to tell which user was at the computer. The first emails were for the Defense Agencies before being introduced to the public. 2012 was inducted in the Internet Hall of Fame.[Thoughtco.]

史实: 首创的计算机程序员,他实现了第一封电子邮件 "因为这似乎是一个好主意".他选择 "@" 符号来告诉计算机上的用户是谁.第一封电子邮件是在向公众介绍之前发给国防部的.

TORRICELLI托里折利tuo li zhe li

Evangelista Torricelli

生人1608 ~ 1647年 》39

FYI: physicist and mathematician invented the barometer.The "torr" is a unit of pressure within vacuum. As well, a lunar crater is named after him.

史实: 数老师,物理学家,发明一个晴雨表.

TOOTH图斯tu si

Howard Henry Tooth

生人1856 ~ 1925年 》60

FYI: British Neurologist co-discovery of Charcott- Marie- Tooth disease. His speciality was Cranial nerves. 史实: 1815-1925年; 英国人神经学家合著发现CMT疾病.他专业是脑神经.

TRANSTROMER传斯特马尔chuan si te ma er

Thomas transformer

生人1931 ~ 2015年 》84

FYI: AKA: Thomas Gosta Transtromer; Swedish poet, psychologist and translator. He received the Nobel in 2011 for Literature in the field of Poetry. Is considered one of the most influential poets of Scandinavia. [Nobleprize.org]

史实: 瑞典诗人,心理学家和翻译家.他在2011年获得了诗歌领域的诺贝尔文学奖.被认为是斯堪的纳维亚最有影响力的诗人之一.

TRESCA特雷斯卡te lei si ka

Henry Edouard Tresca

生人1814 ~ 1885年 》74

FYI: French mechanical engineer; Father of the field of Plasticity. Eiffel considered him to be the 3rd most important person. Listed on the Eiffel Tower. [NE03] 69/72

史实: 法国工程.新元史上埃菲尔铁塔单名.

TRIGER特格尔te ge er

Jacques Triger

生人1801 ~ 1867年 》61

FYI: Geologist who invented the Triger Process. He is mentioned on the Eiffel tower. [SW15] 70/72

史实: 法国地质学家,发明.新元史上埃菲尔铁塔单名.

TROUT特劳特te lao te

John Francis "Jack" Trout

生人1935 ~ 2017年 》83

FYI: founder of advertising agency and Marketing Warfare Theory. He joined with Al Ries in a consulting firm and authored a book together. (The location).

史实: 先导广告商业 .[位置]

TRUDEAU特如都te ru du

Joseph Philippe Yves Pierre Elliot Trudeau

生人1919年10月18日 - 2000年

FYI: Lawyer and statesman; 15th pm of Canada [74-79]. Introduced Official Languages Act (1969). "Just watch me" became his cutting words against foes. Order of Canada. His son Justin is 23rd PM.

史实: 律师,十五首相为了加拿大[74-79顷].介绍两个语仿真."只管看着我"成了他反对敌人的尖刻话语.

TRUMP特良普te liang pu

Frederick Trump

生人1869 ~ 1918年 》49

FYI: German American businessman and developer. Grandfather of President Donald Trump.

史实: 德国商业人.开发商.祖父为了特朗普.

TUPPER图普尔tu pu er

[SIR] Charles Tupper

生人1821 ~ 1894年

FYI: member of Canadian father of Confederation. Former Pm of Canada

史实: 曾经首相为了加拿大.

TUPPER图普尔tu pu er

Earl Silas Tupper

生人1907 ~ 1983年 》76

FYI: Chemist, business man, inventor and founder of Tupperware c1938.

史实: 化学家,商业人,发明.先导*特百惠1938年

TURGENEV屠格涅夫tu ge nie fu

Ivan Sergevich Turgenev

生人1818 ～ 1883年 》65

FYI: Russian novelist, poet, playwright and translator.
His greatest work is "Fathers and Sons"[1862].

史实: 俄罗斯式,翻译.他最伟大的作品是.《父子》

TURING图玲tu ling

Alan Mathison Turing

生人1912 ～ 1954年 》41

FYI: computer scientist, logician and cryptoanalyst . He was extremely important in breaking codes needed to end WWII. (Turing award)

史实: 电脑科学家.他在破译结束二战所需的密码方面极为重要.* 每年 "图玲嘉奖"

TURNURE图女儿tu nv er

Arthur Baldwin Turnure

FYI: He was an American business man who was co founder of "Vogue" c1892. It was to target the Upper Class of America

史实: 美国商业先导VOGUE:1982年.它的目标是美国的上层阶级.

TUSSAUDS杜莎夫人du suo fu ren

"Madam" Marie Tussauds

生人1761年12月1日 ～ 1850年 》88

FYI: Madam Tussauds brought the magic of "wax" creation to the world. From the worst criminal to the latest movie star within London. *"The Cavern of the Great Thief's, The Chamber of Horrors"are her great legacy.

史实: 高名专家在蜡像馆.*"大盗的洞穴，恐怖的房间"是她的伟大遗产.

TUTANKHAMEN图坦卡门tu tan ka men

生人1332 ～ 1323年B.C. 》

FYI: came to power at about age 9 as Pharaoh. Is known by the pet name of King Tut. Although powerful and respected, he had to deal with several health issues which shortened his life. [*NGeographic].

史实: 高名历史人*九岁是王将. 尽管他很有权势,也很受尊重,但他不得不处理好几个健康问题,这些问题缩短了他的生命.

TUTHILL杜斯尔du si er

William Burnet Tuthill

生人1855 ~ 1929年 》74

FYI: Architect of CARNEGIE HALL.

史实：设计者为了卡内基丁.

TWAIN吐温tu wen

Mark Twain [pseudonym]

生人1835 ~ 1910年 》75

FYI: AKA: Samuel Langhorne Clemens . American writer, humorist, entrepreneurial, lecturer. His works include "Adventures of Huckleberry Finn". He had a long time friendship with Nikola Tesla. His pen name came from his youth on the river boats, as the pilot would call out "mark twain" referring to "two fathoms" ...safe for boat travel. He claimed it as his pen name. *Kindness is the language which the deaf can hear and the blind can see.

史实：美国作家, 幽默作家, 企业家, 讲师。他的作品包括《哈克贝利费恩历险记》.他和尼古拉·特斯拉有着长期的友谊。他的笔名来源 于他年轻时在河上的船上,飞行员会叫他"马克吐温", 意思是 "两个英寻" …可以安全的乘船旅行.他声称这是他的笔名. * 善意的语音, 聋人可以听见盲人可以看见

TYNDALE廷代尔ting dai er

William Tyndale

生人1494 ~ 1563年 》69

FYI: The first to translate the New testament into English... "the Tyndale Bible". 1563 Oct 6, he was first strangled to death and then burnt. His last words were "Lord, open the King of England's eye's!"

史实：神经翻译到英语."上帝,打开英格兰国王的眼睛! "

TYRRELL带勒尔dai le er

Joseph Burr Tyrrell

生人1858 ~ 1957年 》99

FYI: A geologist who discovered the Albertosaurus in southern Alberta Canada c.1884. Royal Tyrrell museum in his honor.

史实：加拿大地学家,查出第一次[艾伯特恐龙]

From Group "T" you can pick one person or up to ten Surnames and write their Surname in Chinese. You may try HORIZONTAL or VERTICAL in the traditional Chinese form.

Beliefs are what divide people. Doubts unite them

《信念使人分裂。怀疑他们团结起来》

Sir peter USTINOV尤斯季诺夫long si ji nuo fu

UDALL尤德尔you de er

Morris King Udall

生人1922 ~ 1988年 》66

FYI: American Politician and pro basket ball player.

史实: 美国政治家.

ULAM乌兰wu lan

Stanislavsky Marcin Ulam

生人1909 ~ 1984年 》75

FYI: Participated in the Manhattan Project and fostered the Nuclear Pulse Propulsion program.

史实: 参与曼哈顿项目,推动核脉冲推进计划.

UMEKI于米卡yu mi ka

Miyoshi Umeki

生人1929 ~ 2007年 》78

FYI: Japan-American singer actress. Was the first Asian woman to win an academy award in America.

史实: 日本裔美国女歌手.是第一位在美国获得奥斯卡奖的亚洲女性.

UNDERHILL昂德希尔ang de xi er

Frank Hawkins Underhill

生人1889 ~ 1971年 》82

FYI: Canadian journalist, essayist, historian. Massey Lectures Series: The image of Confederation 1963. 1967 Order of Canada. [*Brittanica, wiki:]

史实: 加拿大新闻学, 历史.马赛教程.

UNDERWOOD昂德沃德ang de wo de

Micheal Underwood

生人1736 ~ 1820年 》64

FYI: physician and surgeon, was first to recognize the child health issues of poliomyelitis [gray marrow inflammation]. [查看- see Salk, Sabin]

史实: 医生.孩子们和[小儿麻痹症]

UNDSET优斯特you si te

Sigrid Unset

生人1882 ~ 1949年 》87

FYI: She was an author of novels, short stories and essays of life in 15 century Norway. Awarded the Nobel in 1928 for literature. [Nobelprize.org]

史实: 作者小说.十五世纪诺威.1928年嘉奖诺贝尔为了文学.

UREY尤雷you lei

Harold Clayton Urey

生人1893 ~ 1981年 》87

FYI: American physical chemist who was awarded the Nobel in 1934 for the discovery "deuterium". Was classmates with C.Sagan. [*nobelprize.org]

史实: 1934年嘉奖诺贝尔为了*氚

USERKAF鸟瑟卡夫niao se ka fu

Userkafa

生人c.2494 ~ 2487年BC

FYI: First Pharaoh of Egypt.

史实: 埃及第一次法老.

USTINOV优斯特诺夫you si ti nuo fu

[SIR] Peter Alexander Ustinov

生人1921年4月16日 ~ 2004年3月28日 》85

FYI: British actor, diplomat, radio and TV personality. Knighted in 1990. Was proficient in speaking English, French, Spanish, Italian, German, Russian, Turkish and modern Greek. * *Since we are destined to live out our lives in the prison of our minds, it is our duty to furnish it well.*

史实:英国演员,外交官,广播电视明星.他懂和说八个语. * 由于我们注定要在我们的牢狱中过着我们的生活, 因此, 有责任做好它.

UT湖特hu te

Huynh Cong "Nick" UT

FYI: photographer journalism~1973 Photo of the Year."The Terror of War"~P.T.K Phuc. The photo would send a new message back to America and stop the war. [看- see-Phuc]

史实: 他感奋我的世界什么时候照片*馥:1973年.

UTZON鸟松niao song

Jorn Utzon

生人1918 ~ 2008年 》90

FYI: Danish Architect. *Pritzker prize ~ "Sydney Opera House"

史实: 结构*悉尼歌剧院.

From Group "U" you can pick one person or up to ten Surnames and write their Surname in Chinese. You may try HORIZONTAL or VERTICAL in the traditional Chinese form.

"When you reach your highest goal,
choose a new one!"
《当你达到你的最高目标时，选择一个新的》

N. B Within the German culture, the inclusion of "von" with a surname would suggest that the previous Surname and higher-ranking surname could be joined together to guarantee power and financial security. In this list of Surnames, von Hindenburg is a perfect example as he was born Paul von Beneckendorff. The spoken name ie: Beneckendorff vs Hindenberg depended on the dignitaries to whom they spent time with. Commoner vs royalty.

*在德国文化中，"von"加上一个姓氏意味着可以将以前的姓氏和更高级别的姓氏结合在一起，以保证权力和财政安全。在这个姓氏列表中，冯欣登堡是一个完美的例子，因为他出生的保罗冯贝内肯多夫。这个名字叫贝内肯多夫和兴登堡，这取决于他们与谁共度时光的显要人物。平民vs皇室。

VAALER瓦勒wa le

Cohan Vaaler

生人1866～1910年 》46

FYI: Norwegian inventor circa 1899 submitted the paper clip patent. Many have submitted similar patents.

史实: 1899年发明回形针.

VAIHINGER韦星格wei xing ge

Hans Vaihinger

生人1852～1933年 》81

FYI: German Philosopher and student of "Kant". The philosophy of "As if" is one of his famous writings. The philosophy of how mortal man views our existence.

史实: 德国哲学家.他写 "如果".凡人如何看待我们存在的哲学.

VALENTINE瓦林特恩 wa lin te en

生人A.D.226年 ~ [14 Feb- 269]

FYI: The first "greeting card" is in memory of Saint Valentine. This priest was imprisoned, tortured and martyr for marrying soldiers to ladies in secret to avoid service in war. (lovers festival is known as 情人节qing ren jie 14 Feb) In China it is actually 7 month 7day.

史实: 他发明第一次情人节卡.这位牧师因秘密将士兵嫁给妇女以逃避战时服役而被监禁,折磨和殉道.

VAN ALLEN范艾伦fan ai lun

James Alfred van Allen

生人1914 ~ 2006年 》91

FYI: American scientist who discovered two bands of intense radiation that surround the earth. [Van Allen Radiation Belt-1958][*AAS]

史实: 美国科学家,发现了环绕地球的两条强辐射带.

VAN ANDEL范安得fan an de

Jay van Andel

生人1924 ~ 2004年 》80

FYI: Business man, entrepreneur and philanthropist and co-founder of Amway. "Amway" is short for the American Way".

史实: 美国商业,企业家,慈善家."安利" 意思美国性命.

[看- see r.DEVOS]

VAN BRUNT范布伦特fan bu lun te

James~K~Van Brunt

FYI: N. Rockwell's model for several paintings. N.Rockwell used several people, but used Van Brunt the most

史实: 罗克韦尔的几幅画模型.罗克韦尔雇佣了好几个人,但最雇佣的是范布伦特. [*Sat E-post]

VANDERBUILT范达比拉特fan da bi la te

Cornelius Vanderbilt

生人1794 ~ 1877年 》83

FYI: American business magnate in railroads and shipping. In his era was to be the richest man in America.

史实: 美国商业》火车开站.

van GOGH梵高fan gao

Vincent Willem van Gogh

生人1853 ~ 1890年 》38

FYI:Renouned painter of landscapes, still lifes, portraits. He created well over 2000 paintings at his peak.

史实: 著名的风景画家,静物画家,肖像画家.他在巅峰时期创作了2000多幅油画.

VANIER瓦尼尔wa ni er

Jean Vanier

生人1928 ~ May 7, 2019 年 》91

FYI: Canadian philosopher, theologian and humanitarian. Massey Lecture Series-1998: Becoming Human.

Order of Canada-1986.

史实: 哲学,神学家.1998年马赛教程.

Van't HOFF瓦恩特哈法wa en te ha fa

Jacobus Henricus Van't Hoff

生人1852 ~ 1911年 》59

FYI: van't Hoff received the Nobel Prize in chemistry c1901 for unlocking the mystery of osmosis in plants and animals. [*Nobelprize.org]

史实: 1901年嘉奖诺贝尔为了化学家,渗透压.

VARLEY瓦尔雷wa er lei

Cromwell Fleetwood "C.F." Varley

生人1828 ~ 1883年 》55

FYI: English engineer for early Telegraphs, fore runner to the telephone.

史实: 电工程,电报机,曾经电话.

Vega威戈wei ge

Joseph de la Vega

生人1650 ~ 1692年 》42

FYI: Merchant, poet and philanthropist in 17th century Amsterdam. He published "Confusion of confusions- 1688" an introduction to the Stock-exchange market. *the first rule in speculation is: never advise anyone to buy or sell.

史实: 1688年,介绍交易所 *投机的第一条规则是:不要建议任何人买卖.

VEIL韦伊wei yi

Simone Annie Liline Veil

生人1927 ~ 2017年 》90

FYI: French lawyer and politician.

史实: 律师, 政治家.

VELIKOVSKY威卡菲斯克wei ka fei si ke

Immanuel Velikovsky

生人1895 ~ 1979年 》84

FYI: Author, psychologist. Futurist, Worlds in collision1950

史实: 作者,心理学家.未来主义者,碰撞中的世界 ．

VERNADSKY维尔捇茨琪wei er nei ci qi

Vladimir Ivanovich Vernadsky

生人1863 ~ 1945年 》82

FYI: Soviet mineralogist and geochemist. Noted for his concept of "The Biosphere-1926".

史实: 矿物学.1926年:生物圈. [看-see Suess]

VESPUCCI维斯普哥wei si pu ge

Amerigo Vespucci

生人1454 ~ 1512年 》57

FYI: Italian explorer and navigator. "America" is named in his honor. "Americas" or Americus is the Latin form.

史实: 年寿1454-1512; 意大利勘探员和领航者."美国 "因他的荣耀而被命的."美洲 "或者 " 美洲 " 是拉丁语的形式. [看-see m.Waldseemuller]

VICAT维卡wei ka

Louis Vicat

生人1786 ~ 1861年 》75

FYI: Engineer who developed a needle for measuring cement hardness. His name is among the 72 listed on the Eiffel tower.[SE06] 71/72

史实: 工程, 发明器为了水泥.新元史上埃菲尔铁塔单名.

VICKREY维克瑞wei ke rui

William Vickrey

生人1914 ~ 1996年 》82

FYI: Received the Nobel in 1996 Economics of Information. [Nobleprize.org]

史实: 1996年嘉奖诺贝尔为了经济学者.

courtesy John Walter Museum. Photo by Forest L. ~ 福瑞斯特

VICTORIA维多利亚wei duo li ya

[Queen] Alexandrina Victoria Hannover

生人May 24, 1819 ~ Jan 22, 1901年 》81

FYI: aka Queen Victoria. House of Hannover. Historically known as 'The Victorian Era' her rein was 1819~1901 which lasted 63 years 9 months. She ascended the throne on 1837 June 20 at the age of 18 years old and chose to be called 'Victoria' over her dislike of Alexandrina. She was to be referred to as the "Mother of Confederation". Victoria Day celebrated in Canada is the last Monday of May in memory of her birthday. The early versions of the King James bible is written in 'Victorian English style' to keep the legacy of old English alive. The Victorian Cross is given out for bravery in war time. *We are not interested in the possibilities of defeat; they do not exist. [in part Encyclopedia Britannica]*

史实: 汉诺威之家.历史上被称为"维多利亚时代"的雷因是1819年至1901年,持续了63年9个月.1837年6月20日,18岁的她登上了王位,由于不喜欢亚历山大,她选择了被称为"维多利亚".她被称为"邦联之母".加拿大庆祝维多利亚节是5月的最后一个星期一,以纪念她的生日.早期版本的詹姆斯国王圣经是用"维多利亚式英语风格"写的,以保持古英语的遗产.在战争时期,维多利亚十字勋章是为勇敢而颁发的.*我们对失败的可能性不感兴趣;它们不存在.

VITRUVIAS维特鲁威wei te lu wei

Marcus Vitruvias Pollio

生人c80年 ~ 15年 B.C. 》65

FYI: Roman author, architect, civil engineer and military engineer. He is the renaissance depiction by Da Vinci as "Vitruvia man"

史实: 作者,结构,工程,军工程.他是"维特鲁威男".

VIVALDI维瓦尔第wei wan er di

Antonio Lucio Vivaldi

生人1678 ~ 1741年 》63

FYI: Italian Baroque composer.

史实: 意大利巴洛克作曲家.

VOLPE威乐普wei le pu

Nicholas~A~Volpe

生人1911 ~ 1992年 》81

FYI: painter of various artist

史实: 画 为了普通人.

VOLTA伏特fu te

Alessandro Giuseppe Antonio Anastasio Volta

生人1745 ~ 1827年 》82

FYI: Italian physicist and chemist. He developed the voltage meter. He also discovered Methane.

史实: 物理学家发明伏特测试器.

VOLTAIRE伏尔泰fu er tai

生人1694 ~ 1778年 》84

FYI: AKA Francois-Marie Arouet. Enlightenment writer and philosopher.1718 he took on the [pseudonym] Voltaire. * Common sense is not so common.

史实: 者学, 写. 写启发.1718年, 他接任伏尔泰(化名). *常识不是那么普遍.

von BEHRING马贝林ma bei lin

Emil von Behring

生人1854 ~ 1917年 》53

FYI: c1901 he received the Nobel in physiology for medicine, for discovery of serum to fight against diphtheria. [*Nobelprize.org]

史实: 1901年嘉奖诺贝尔为了药.

von BRAUN沃内布芳恩wo nei bu fang en

Wernher Magnus Maxmilian Freiherr von Braun

生人1912 ~ 1977年 》65

FYI: Rocket engineer. Working along NASA he helped America put men on the moon.

史实: 火箭工程师.他与美国宇航局合作，帮助美国将人类送上月球.

Von DANIKEN冯丹尼肯feng dan ni ken

Erich Anton Paul von Daniken

生人1932 ~ Active

FYI: Author and researcher. "chariots of the gods"[1968], co-founder of SETI.

史实: 作者,研究."神的战车".

Von FEUERBACH费尔巴哈fei er ba ha

Ludwig Andeas von Feuerbach

生人1804 ~ 1872年 》68

FYI: German philosopher & anthropologist. "The essence of Christianity"

史实: 德国哲学家和人类学家."基督教的本质".

von FRISCH马弗利士ma fu li shi

Karl Ritter von Frisch

生人1886 ~ 1982年 》96

FYI: Austrian ethologist who received the Nobel in physiology circa 1973 for research on the Honey Bee ie; the "Waggle dance." [*Nobelprize.org]

史实: 密封研究.1973年嘉奖诺贝尔为了研究.

von GOETHE玩哥德wan ge de

Johann Wolfgang von Goethe

生人1749 ~ 1832年 》83

FYI: German writer and statesman. * *We do not have to visit a madhouse to find disordered minds; our planet is the mental institution of the universe.*

史实: 写, 政治家. * 我们不必去疯人院去寻找混乱的头脑.我们的星球是宇宙的精神机构.

von HELMHOLZ赫姆霍尔兹he mu huo er zi

Hermann Ludwig Ferdinand von Helmholz

生人1821 ~ 1894年 》73

FYI: German physician and physicists. Invented the "opthalmoscope" which allows Dr.s to examine inside the eye.

史实: 德国医生和物理学家.发明了"眼底镜",让医生可以检查眼睛内部.

von HINDENBURG冯兴登堡feng xing deng bao

Paul Ludwig Hans Anton von Hindenburg

生人1847 ~ 1934年 》87

FYI: AKA; Paul von Beneckendorff [c1799]. General field marshal of Germany. 1933 he handed over chancellorship to Hitler. The Hindenburg air ship named in his honor. [*see chapter heading].

史实: 德国元帅1934年.1933年,他把总理职位移交给了希特勒.兴登堡航空母舰以他的名字命名.

von RICHTOFEN冯里希特霍芬feng li xi te huo feng

Manfred Albrecht Freiherr von Richthofen

生人1892年5月2日~ 1918年4月12日 》36

FYI: German Air Force Ace.The RED BARON of WWI had 80 reported combat victories. He was the most feared of all German pilots to be in a *"dog fight"* against. All fighter planes of that era had three rows of wings on top of each other (Triplane) and powered by a rotary 110 hp. Von Richtofen had his plane painted red with a black cross on the top wing. Movies and songs have been made about the "Red Baron".

史实: 德国空军王牌.第一次世界大战的红色男爵有80次报告战斗胜利.他是所有德国飞行员中最害怕与之"斗狗"的人.那个时代的所有战斗机都有三排机翼（三翼），由110马力的旋转翼驱动.冯·里奇托芬把他的飞机漆成红色,在机翼的顶部画了一个黑色的十字.电影和歌曲都是关于"红男爵"的.

von TRAPP冯特拉普feng te la pu

Georg Ludwig Ritter von Trapp

生人1880 ~ 1947年　》67

FYI: Naval Officer from Austri-Hungary. The Sound of Music (1965) movie is based on his life. In the movie "Christopher Plummer" played Von Trapp, Bill Lee provided the 'voice over'.

史实: 奥匈帝国海军军官.音乐之声（1965）电影是以他的生活为基础的.

VONNEGUT冯内古特feng nei gu te

Kurt Vonnegut

生人1922 ~ 2007年　》84

FYI: Writer : player piano (1952).

史实: 作者, 写很多文章.

von ZEPPELIN齐柏林qi po lin

Ferdinand Adolf Heinrich August Graf von Zeppelin

生人1838 ~ 1917年　》79

FYI: German General and the manufacturer of Airships such as the Zeppelin and Hindenburg

史实: 企业家飞机.

VYSE沃义瑟wo yi se

Richard William Howard Vyse

生人1746 ~ 1825年　》78

FYI: Anthropologist and Egyptologist.

史实: 地质学家, 埃及学家.

From Group "V" you can pick one person or up to ten Surnames and write their Surname in Chinese. You may try HORIZONTAL or VERTICAL in the traditional Chinese form.

W

《想象一个这样的世界:地球上任何一个人都可以自由的获得人类全部知识的总和》
"Imagine a world in which every single person on the planet is given free access to the sum all human knowledge."
Jimmy Donald WALES威尔士wei er shi

WADATI沃达蒂wo da di

Kiyoo Wadati

生人1902 ~ 1995年 》93

FYI: is in charge monitoring earthquakes Central Meteorological Observatory of Japan: Seimologist. [-see Richter].

史实: 负责日本中央气象台地震监测:地震学家.

WADE威德wei de

[SIR] Thomas Francis Wade

生人1818 ~ 1895年 》76

FYI: Sinologist-linguist, political adviser: Chinese Romanization into English [.c1867]

史实: 拼音乔从英国语到汉语.

WADDINGTON沃丁顿wo ding dun

Miriam Waddington

生人1917 ~ 2004年 》87

FYI: aka E.B. Merritt; Canadian poet, short story writer, translator. Her poem was on the back of the $100 Canadian bill. Then replaced by Medical Innovations.

史实: 加拿大诗人,短篇小说作家,翻译.她的诗在加拿大100美元钞票的背面.然后被医学创新所取代.

WALD沃尔德wo er de

George David Wald

生人1906 ~ 1997年 》91

FYI: American scientist who studied pigments in the eye. Received the Nobel in 1967 for physiology. *Massey Lectures Series 1970: Therefor Choose Life.

史实: 学习眼色素.1967年嘉奖诺贝尔为了生理.马赛教程.

WALDSEEMULLER瓦尔德赛马wa er de sai ma

Martin Waldseemuller

生人c1470 ~ 1520年 》50

FYI: *world maps, the first to write "America" in honor of Amerigo [See-a.vespucci]

史实: 他写美国上他图荣誉他朋友.

WALES威尔士wei er shi

Jimmy Donald Wales

生人1966 ~ active

FYI: American Internet entrepreneur and founder of Wikipedia; wiki is Hawaiian for "quick". From Bomis> Nupedia (2000-2003) > Wikipedia(present)* *Imagine a world in which every single person on the planet is given free access to the sum all human knowledge.*

史实: 网吧企业家,先导为了维基百科.* 想象一个这样的世界:地球上任何一个人都可以自由的获得人类全部知识的总和.

WALLACE华勒斯hua li si

Alfred Russel Wallace

生人8 January 1823 ~ 7 November 1913年 》90

FYI: an explorer, collector, naturalist, geographer, anthropologist and political commentator. Most famously, he had the revolutionary idea of evolution by natural selection entirely independently of Charles Darwin. 1904 'Mans place in the Universe' explored new concepts including higher and lower vibrations of mans immortal soul. *Truth is born into this world only with pangs and tribulations, and every fresh truth is received unwillingly..*

史实: 探险家,收藏家,博物学家,地理学家,人类学家和政治评论家.最著名的是,他有完全独立于达尔文的自然选择进化的革命性思想.1904年,他出版了《人类在宇宙中的地位》一书,探讨了包括人类不朽灵魂的高振动和低振动在内的新概念.*真理在这个世界上诞生,只有痛苦和磨难,每一个新的真理都是不情愿地接受的.

WALLACE华勒斯hua li si

William Roy Dewitt Wallace

生人1889 ~ 1981年 》92

FYI: American Magazine Publisher and founder of Readers Digest. First issue c. 1922

史实: 1922年新闻学*读文摘.

WALLACE华勒斯hua li si

Myron Leon "Mike" Wallace

生人1918 ~ 2012年 》94

FYI: journalist, reporter and Television announcer 60 Minutes.

史实: 新闻,广播为了.[六十分钟]

WALSCH沃尔什wa er shi

Neale Donald Walsch

生人1943 ~ active

FYI: American author, actor, screen writer and speaker. "Conversations with God"1995 [series].

史实: 作者, 艺人, 演说者..1995年交谈圣帝.

courtesy of John Walter Museum ~ Ferry from N Edmonton to S Edmonton, Portrait, family portrait.

WALTER瓦特尔wa te er

John Walter

生人1849 ~ 1920 年 》71

FYI: He was a business man who migrated to Canada from Scotland. He established a ferry business crossing the North Saskatchewan river near the Edmonton trading post. The current 'Walterdale bridge' and John Walter Museum (three log buildings) is located near the river in Edmonton. He is regarded as one of the first Millionaires in Edmonton.

史实: 他是从苏格兰移民到加拿大的商人.他在埃德蒙顿贸易站附近的萨斯喀彻温河北岸建立了一家渡船公司.目前的"沃尔特代尔大桥"和约翰沃尔特博物馆(三栋原木建筑)位于埃德蒙顿河附近.他被认为是埃德蒙顿最早的百万富翁之一.

WALTON瓦拉田wa la tian

Ralph~G~Walton

生人1975年11月10日 》58 [memorial- 纪念]

FYI: *SS Edmund Fitzgerald~Lake Superior 10 Nov 1975

史实: S.S. 埃德蒙*菲茨杰拉德 湖高强1975年11月10日.

WALTON瓦拉田wa la tian

Samuel Moore Walton

生人1918 ~ 1992年 》70

FYI: American business man and entrepreneur who started Walmart. "Made in America"

史实: 美国商业,企业家*沃尔玛.

WILSON威尔森wei er sen

Bill Wilson

FYI: William Griffith Wilson; Co-founder of Alcoholic Anonymous (AA). For the duration of the group sir names were not used to keep everyone at an Anonymous mental level.

史实:酒精匿名组织(AA)联合创始人.在整个实验组中,sir的名字并不是用来让每个人保持匿名的精神状态.

WAPNER沃普讷尔wo pu na er

Joseph Albert Wapner

生人1919 ~ 2017年 》98

FYI:TV personality in judiciary setting. 1981: People's Court.

史实: 广播律师.

WARD沃德wo de

Barbara Mary Ward

生人1914 ~ 1981年 》67

FYI: British economist; Massey Lectures series c.1961 "The Rich Nations and the Poor Nations."

史实:1961年:马赛马赛教程.

WARE维尔wei er

Lancelot Lionel Ware

生人1915 ~ 2000年 》85

FYI: Barrister and biochemist. Co-founder of Mensa [1946]. Mensa is Latin for "round table" of information.

史实: 律师和生物化学家.门萨联合创始人[1946].门萨语是拉丁语, 意思是 "圆桌会议". [看- r.Berrill]

WARREN沃伦wo lun

Earl Warren

生人1891 ~ 1974年 》83

FYI: American jurist and politician. The "Warren Commission" is named in his honor.

史实: 美国法学家和政治家."沃伦委员会" 是以他的名誉命名的.

WARNER华纳兄弟hua na

Harry Morris & Hirsch Moses Warner

FYI: WARNER BROS studios.circa~1923. Xiong di [兄弟] "brothers" was the first studio to introduce "talkies" moving away from the Silent Film Era.

史实: 1923年华纳兄弟.电影.

WASHINGTON华盛顿hua sheng dun

George Washington

生人1732 ~ 1799年 》67

FYI: Founding Fathers of the United States. *First U.S. president. "Father of the country"

史实: 建美国 "国家之父" .

WATERHOUSE华特哈斯hua te ha si

Thomas Greaves Waterhouse

生人1811 ~ 1885年 》74

FYI: Businessman, philanthropist.

史实: 商业, 慈善家.

WATERHOUSE华特哈斯hua te ha si

Edwin Waterhouse

生人1841 ~ 1917年 》76

FYI: Price- Waterhouse-Cooper is a joint venture of three British accountants which became world wide.

史实: 三个人, 英国会计.

WATSON沃特森wo te sen

James Watson

生人1928 ~ living

FYI: Genetics DNA co-discover 1953.*if your the most intelligent person in the room, your in the wrong room!"

史实: 1953年先导DNA.*如果你是房间里最聪明的人, 你就错了房间!

WATSON沃特森wo te sen

Thomas John Watson

生人1874 ~ 1956年 》 82

FYI: American business man, philanthropist. The founder of IBM. Ranked in the top 100 most influential people of the twentieth Century. 1943: "I think there is a world market for maybe 5 computers."

史实: IBM 先导.《我认为世界上有5台电脑的市场》

WATT瓦特wa te

James Watt

生人1736 ~ 1819年 》83

FYI: Scottish engineer, the (W) symbol for a unit of power is named in his honor. Inventor of the steam engineer.

史实: 电工程.(W) 是他名字为了电.

WATTS瓦特斯wa te si

Isaac Watts

生人1674 ~ 1748年 》74

FYI: Hymn writer, theologian, logician.

史实: 赞美诗作家, 神学家, 逻辑学家.

WAYNE微那wei na

John Wayne [pseudonym]

生人1907 ~ 1979年 》82

FYI: AKA: Marion Robert Morrison. He was an American Icon of cowboys and war movies. His stage name is credited to a discussion between Raoul Walsh and Winfield Shehan who adopted this new name for Morrison from the legendary ("mad" Anthony Wayne.) His nickname "duke" came from his childhood dog.

史实: 高名,美国人电影.他的绰号 "公爵" 来自他童年的狗.

WEBSTER韦伯斯特wei bo si te

Noah Webster

生人1758 ~ 1843年 》84

FYI: American Lexicographer. Standardizing written English. *Webster dictionary 1806 named in his honor.

*Established the Copyright Act of 1831

史实: 1806年:韦伯斯特词典. 1831年:权利要求.

WEBSTER韦伯斯特尔wei bo si te er

John Webster

生人1943 ~ 2017年 》74

FYI: Cleveland radio icon.

史实: 克利夫兰 广播.

WEIDENREICH威顿若出wei dun ruo chu

Franz Weidenreich

生人1873 ~ 1948年 》75

FYI: Anthropologist. re- Peking Man.

史实: 人类学.北京人.

WEGENER韦格拁wei ge ne

Alfred Lothar Wegener

生人1880 ~ 1930年 》50

FYI: German geophysicist and meteorologist. Proposed the THEORY of "continental drift" in 1912

史实: 地质学家,1912年:大陆漂移.

WEIRS韦尔斯wei er si

Robert Stanley Weirs

生人1856 ~ 1926年 》70

FYI: Judge, poet and lyricist. Penned the English version of The Canadian Athem 'O Canada'. See miscellaneous. [Routhier].

史实: 法官,诗人和抒情诗人.写了加拿大雅典语 "O Canada" 的英文版.见杂项.

WEISER威斯尔wei si er

Johann Conrad Weiser jr.

生人1696 ~ 1760年

FYI: Interpreter and translator for the Mohawks c.1712

史实:c1712年 口译员为了"莫哈克"人人.

WEISS威斯wei si

David~E~Weiss

生人1975年11月10日 ~ 》22 》[memorial纪念]

FYI: 22; *SS Edmund Fitzgerald~Lake Superior

史实: S.S. 埃德蒙*菲茨杰拉德 湖高强1975年11月10日.

WEISSENBERG威森布格wei sen bu ge

Karl Weissenberg

生人1893 ~ 1976年 》84

FYI: Austrian physicist notable for work with rheology.

史实: 物理学家高名为了流变学.

WELDON韦尔登wei er deng

[Sir] Anthony Weldon

生人1583 ~ 1648年 》65

FYI: 17th Century courtier and politician

史实: 17世纪的朝臣和政治家.

WELK威尔克wei er ke

Lawrence Welk

生人1903 ~ 1992年 》89

FYI: "The Lawrence Welk Show". Legend of the Big Band Era. *Dreams do come true, even for someone who couldn't speak English and never had a music lesson or much of an education.

史实: "劳伦斯威尔克秀".大乐队时代的传奇. * 梦想成真, 甚至于那些不会说英语, 从未听过音乐课或没有接受过很多教室的人.

WELLS威尔斯wei er si

Herbert George "H.G." Wells

生人1866 ~ 1946年 》79

FYI: writer, author, "Father of Science Fiction"; War of the World's.

史实: 传奇人物, 作者.夫子为了科学幻想:战之间世界.

WELLES威尔斯wei er si

George Orson Welles

生人1915 ~ 1985年 》70

FYI: [a&e] voice actor (War of the World's)1938, actor (Citizen Kane)1941

史实: 口声艺人:战之间世界[1938], [1941] 普通Kane

WERFEL韦费尔wei fei er

Franz Viktor Werfel

生人10 September 1890 – 26 August 1945年 》55

FYI: Novelist, playwright and poet. After leaving Germany during WWII, he traveled to France where he learned of the story of Saint Bernadette Soubirous of Lourde and wrote a novel of the same name concerning her life. The book [1941] would be followed by a movie "The Song of Bernadette'1943. [~ Soubirous]

史实: 小说家,剧作家和诗人.二战期间离开德国后,他前往法国,在那里他了解了路德的圣伯纳黛特·苏比罗斯的故事,并写了一部同名小说,讲述了她的生活.这本书(1941年)后面是一部电影《伯纳黛特之歌》.

WESSON味素wei su
Daniel Baird Wesson
生人1825 ~ 1906年 》81
FYI: co-founder of Smith&Wesson fire arms~c1854.
史实: 1854年建史密斯威森大枪.

WEST威斯特wei si te
John Anthony West
生人1932 ~ 2018年 》96
FYI: American author, lecturer and guide.
史实: 美国人作者演讲.

WEST威斯特wei si te
Adam West
生人1928 ~ 1917年 》88
FYI: Adam West Anderson. Actor and original Batman.
史实: 高名艺人; Batman

WESLEY维斯雷wei si lei
John Wesley
生人1703 ~ 1791年 》88
FYI: English cleric and theologian. He began the Methodist movement.
史实: 英国神学家.建卫理公会教徒教会.

WESTINGHOUSE威斯汀豪斯wei si ting hao si
George Westinghouse jr.
生人1846 ~1914年 》67
FYI: Inventor, entrepreneur. In 1869 April 13 he designed and patented the railway '*air brake*' to improve the stopping distance. From the nineteen twenties the same design would be applied to large trucks and city buses.

史实: 发明家、企业家.1869年4月13日, 他设计并申请了铁路 "空气制动器" 专利, 以提高停车距离.从二十世纪二十年代起, 同样的设计将应用于大型卡车和城市公共汽车.

WHEELER惠勒hui le
John Archibald Wheeler
生人1911 ~ 2008年 》97
FYI: Theoretical physicist. Coined ""*Wormhole*" : "quatum foam", neutron moderator, it from bit and Black-Hole".
史实: 物理学家.生道 "冲动".

WHITE怀特huai te
Edward Higgins White
生人1930 ~ 1967年 》37 》[memorial纪念]
FYI: First Astronaut to walk in space. Died during pre-launch of Apollo 1 fire. [January 27.1967] [see-Grissom, Chafee]
史实: 第一次天文做.1967年死了.

WHITEHEAD怀特黑德huai te hei de
Robert Whitehead
生人1823 ~ 1905年 》82
FYI: English engineer who perfected the underwater torpedo for military purposes.
史实: 英国军工程;水下鱼雷.

WHITTIER维特尔wei te er
John Greenleaf Whittier
生人1807 ~ 1892年 》85
FYI: American Quaker and anti-slavery advocate Author of "Snow Bound". [-see Fireside poets: Bryant- Holmes- Longfellow- Lowell- Whittier.]
史实: 美国贵格会教徒和反奴隶制倡导者,著有《雪界》.

WIENER维纳wei na
Norbert Wiener
生人1894 ~ 1964年 》69
FYI: Mathematician, philosopher.（控制论）
史实: 数,哲学.

WILBRAND威巴德wei ba de

Julius Bernhard Friedrich Adolf Wilbrand

生人1839 ~ 1906年 》67

FYI: German chemist who developed TNT c1863 [tri-nitro-toluene]

史实:德国化学家.梯恩梯.

WILDE王尔德wang er de

Oscar Fingal O'flaheritie Wills Wilde

生人1854 ~ 1900年 》46

FYI: Irish writer, playwright and novelist.*An Ideal Husband and The Ballad of Reading Gaol was his best noted works.

史实: 爱尔兰作家,剧作家和小说家.理想的丈夫和朗诵高尔的民谣是他最著名的作品.

WILDE王尔德wang er de

Henry Tingle Wilde jr.

生人1872 ~ 1912年 》[memorial纪念]

FYI: Titanic chief officer. RMS Titanic

史实: 将航.

WILDE王尔德wang er de

Stuart Wilde

生人1946 ~ 2013年 》67

FYI: Lecturer, teacher, humorist, essayist . Metaphysical teacher.

史实: 老师, 讲演:形而上学.

WILHELM威廉wei lian

Blaine~H~Wilhelm

生人1975年 11月11日~ 》52 [纪念]

FYI: *SS Edmund Fitzgerald~Lake Superior 10 Nov 1975

史实: S.S. 埃德蒙*菲茨杰拉德 湖高强1975年 11月10日

WILKINS威尔金斯wei er jin si

Maurice Hugh Frederick Wilkins

生人1916 ~ 2004年 》87

FYI: pioneer research into DNA.

史实: 查研究:DNA [~see Crick, Watson]

WILLIAMS威廉姆斯wei lian mu si

Ted Williams

生人1918 ~ 2002年 》63

FYI: [S] aka Theodore Samuel Williams; .344 batting average, 521 home runs. Hall of Fame baseball. First to be CRYONICALLY frozen.

史实: 高名在高球.第一次人" 低温地".

WILLIAMS威廉姆斯wei lian mu si

Robin Mclaurin Williams

生人1951 ~ 2014年 》63

FYI: World famous comedian and actor.

史实: 高名艺人，电影.

WILLIAMS威廉姆斯wei lian mu si

Howard Andrew Williams

生人1927 ~ 2012年 》85

FYI: [a&e] The Andy Williams show. Icon singer of 'Moon river' song.

史实: 游艺:月河歌.

WILLIAMS威廉斯wei lian mu si

[SIR] George Williams

生人1821 ~ 1905年 》84

FYI: British philanthropist and founder of YMCA *1894 [Young Mens Christen Association] was Knighted by Queen Victoria.

史实: 英国慈善家,基督教青年会（YMCA）创始人1894年（青年男子基督联合会）被维多利亚女王授予爵士称号.

WILLS威廉斯wei lian si

Lucy Wills

生人1888 ~ 1964年 》76

FYI: British Hematologist who discovered Folic acid in 1933

史实: 1933年查看叶酸.

City of Edmonton public archives

WILSON威尔逊wei er xun

Herbert Charles Wilson

生人1859 ~ 1909年 》50

FYI: Canadian politician and physician. He served as Mayor for what was known as the 'Town of Edmonton' prior to it becoming a city. Wilson Industrial park in Edmonton bears his name.

史实: 加拿大政治家和医生.在埃德蒙顿成为一座城市之前, 他曾担任该市的市长.埃德蒙顿的威尔逊工业园以他的名字命名.

WILSON威尔逊wei er xun

Samuel Wilson

生人1766 ~ 1854年 》87

FYI: *Mascot Poster for Uncle Sam c1918 ** the Goatee was only an advertisement feature. His real job was a meat packer for the civil war troupes. The packaged meat was always stamped U.S: United States, however the troupes referred to him as "Uncle Sam" and the phrase stuck.

史实: 1918年吉祥物为了[叔叔Sam].

WILSON威尔逊wei er xun

Herbert Rees Wilson

生人1929 ~ 2008年 》79

FYI: Forerunner of the X-ray diffraction of cell nuclei along with DNA studies. insert

史实: 细胞核X射线衍射的先驱:DNA [看-see Crick, Watson]

WILSON威尔逊wei er xun

Louis Binito Wilson

FYI: Pathologist. He set the standard for Laboratory procedures within the Mayo clinic c1905-1937

史实: 病理学为了梅奥临床条例.

WILSON威尔逊wei er xun

Benjamin Davis Wilson

生人1811 ~ 1878年 》67

FYI: Statesman~politician. 2nd mayor Los Angeles. Mount Wilson~California named in his honor and Wilson observatory.

史实: 政治家. 山威尔逊,威尔逊天文台.

WINCHESTER温切斯特wen qie si te

Oliver Fischer Winchester

生人1810 ~ 1880年 》70

FYI: Winchester repeating rifle.

史实: 温切斯特枪.

WINCHELL温彻尔wen che er

Walter Winchell

生人1897 ~ 1972年 》75

FYI: Considered to be the First Gossip Columnist in America.

史实:高名刘兰蜚语报.

WINFIELD问飞德wen fei de

Darrell Hugh Winfield

生人1929 ~ 2015年 》94

FYI: He worked professionally in the rodeo circuit until he was spotted by an Ad agency to represent the image of a Real Man smoking a cigarette. Marlboro Man. *Circa 68-89

史实: 他在竞技表演圈里工作很专业, 直到广告公司发现他是一个真正的男人抽烟的形象.万宝路人.

WINSPEAR温斯皮尔wen si pi er

Dr. Francis G. Winspear

生人1903 ~ 1997年 》94

FYI: An accountant by training, then renouned philanthropist, educator and entrepreneur. The Winspear Music consortium in Edmonton is named in his honor. Alberta Order of excellence and Order of Canada.

史实: 一个会计通过培训, 然后放弃慈善家,教育家和企业家.阿尔伯塔卓越秩序与加拿大秩序.

WISE惠恩hui en

Brownie Wise

生人1913 ~ 1992年 》79

FYI: [aka Brownie Mae Humphrey] American saleswoman (tupperware parties) who developed the first "Party Plan" concept.

史实: 美国女商业为了特百惠 .

WITTIG维蒂希wei di xi

Georg Wittig

生人1897 ~ 1987年 》90

FYI: received the Nobel for organic chemistry

史实: 嘉奖诺贝尔为了化学家. [* Nobelprize.org]

WOLF沃尔夫wo er fu

Ricardo Wolf

生人1887 ~ 1981年 》94

FYI: inventor & philanthropist. The Wolf prize consists of: agriculture, chemistry, mathematics, medicine, physics and the Arts.

史实: 发明, 慈善家."沃尔夫奖":数,农,化,药,物理,艺术.

WOLFF沃尔夫wo er fu

Gustav William Wolff

FYI: partnership with Harland ship building. Titanic.

史实: 与哈兰造船公司合作.泰坦尼克号.

WOLSEY沃斯雷wo si lei

Thomas Wolsey

FYI: royal chaplain to Henry v111. c.1473;

史实: 教会.

Photo by Forest L. ~ 福瑞斯特

WOODLAND伍德兰wu de lan

Norman Joseph Woodland

生人1921 ~ 2012年 》93

FYI: From his youth learning Morse code he would later use the same idea toward inventing the bar code. The idea came to him as he played with sand in a sand box c.1948/49. 'instead of dots and dashes, I can have thick and thin bars.' With Bernard Silver results came in to use c.1974 in Florida.[National Inventor Hall of Fame]. [*usatoday]

史实: 从他年轻时学习莫尔斯电码开始, 他后来也会用同样的想法来发明条形码.1948/49年, 当他在沙盒里玩沙子的时候, 他想到了这个主意。"代替点和破折号, 我可以有粗细的棒子." 伯纳德•西尔弗的研究结果在1974年的佛罗里达州开始使用.

WOODRUFF伍掉夫wu diao fu

Wilford Woodruff

生人1807 ~ 1898年 》96

FYI: 4th president LDS church, politician, farmer.

史实: 曾经教会:耶稣基督后期圣徒教会;四号

WOOLF沃尔夫wo er fu

Adeline Virginia Woolf

生人1882 ~ 1941年 》59

FYI: British writer. Jacobs room, Between the Acts, The Years.

史实: 英国作家.雅各布房间,在幕与年之间.

WOOLWORTH伍尔沃斯wu er wo si

Frank Winfield Woolworth

生人1852 ~ 1919年 》66

FYI: Entrepreneur and founder of F.W.Woolworth [five and dime concept]

史实: 慈善家.先导伍尔沃斯商业.

WRIGHT莱特lai te

Wilbur and Orval

FYI: inventors of the fixed wing heavier then air airplane 1903 Dec 17. They began with gliders and bicycles until they understood enough about aerodynamics. Wilbur was in the pilots seat.

史实: 1903年12月17日固定翼重于空气的飞机的发明者.他们从滑翔机和自行车开始,直到对空气动力学有足够的了解.威尔伯坐在飞行员的座位上.

WRIGLEY威格里wei ge li

William *L* Wrigley jr.

生人1861年9月7日~ 1932年

FYI: Entrepreneur, Confectionery magnate "Wrigley gum". Wrigley Spearmint and Juicy fruit debut c.1893

史实: 1862年,口香糖.

WURTZ武尔茨wu er ci (insert jpg 1558)

Charles Adophe Wurst

生人1817～1884年 》67

FYI: Chemist, [wurtz reaction]. His name is among the 72 on the Eiffel tower [NE03]
*72/72

史实: 化学家."武尔茨反应".新元史上埃菲尔铁塔单名.

From Group "W" you can pick one person or up to ten Surnames and write their Surname in Chinese. You may try HORIZONTAL or VERTICAL in the traditional Chinese form.

The man who stands for nothing will fall for anything.
《什么都不代表的人，什么也不会相信》
Malcolm X习shi

*[in most cases in Chinese. The "X" has a "she" pronunciation. Otherwise, the name is LITERAL in translation.]

*[在大多数情况下是中文."x"有"she"的发音.否则,名称在翻译中为文字.]

X习xi

Malcolm x [Malcolm Little]

生人1925 ~ 1965年 》39

FYI: Muslim minister. Human Rights Activist "Little" was the name white slave masters imposed upon my paternal forebears." He felt "X" would be a better alternative than the name Little.

史实: 穆斯林教会.人权

Xandre萨德若san de ruo

Vcentealei Xandre

生人1898 ~1984年 》86

FYI:A Spanish poet. Received the Nobel for literature in 1977 "for creative writing". [*Nobelprize.org]

史实: 1977年嘉奖诺宝尔为了文学.

XENIKAS泽纳基斯ze ne ji si

Iannis Xenakis

生人1922 ~ 2001年 》81

FYI: Greek-French composer and music theorist.

史实: 希腊-法国作曲家和音乐理论家.

XENOPHANES色诺芬尼se nuo fen ni

生人570 ~ 470年 BC 》100

FYI: A traveling poet and sage.

史实: 式夫子.

From Group "X" you can pick one person or up to ten Surnames and write their Surname in Chinese. You may try HORIZONTAL or VERTICAL in the traditional Chinese form.

《忘记我们的烦恼是明智的，
他们总是新的来取代他们》
"It is wise for us to forget our troubles, their
are always new ones to replace them.
Brigham YOUNG亚嗯ya en

YALE耶鲁ye lu

Elihu Yale

生人1649 ~ 1721年 》72

FYI: British merchant and slave trader. Yale University is named in his honor.

史实: 英国商业.耶鲁大学.

YAMAGUCHI亚玛古吃ya ma gu chi

Tsutumo Yamaguchi

生人1917 ~ 2010年 》93

FYI: First known person to survive both atomic bombs in Japan. Fat man~Hiroshima 1945 Aug 06, Little boy~Nagasaki 1945 Aug 09. *"I could have died on either of those days! Everything that follows is a bonus."

史实: 第一次人生存多原子弹; 1945年8月6日Hiroshima, 8月9日Nagasaki.* "那两天我都可能死! 接下来的一切都是奖金."

YAMASAKI雅马萨奇ya ma sa qi

Minoru Yamasaki

生人1912 ~ 1977年 》65

FYI: American architect: Designed the World Trade Center.

史实: 美国结构*世界贸易中心.

YASGUR亚斯古尔ya si ge er

Max B. Yasgur

生人December 15, 1919 – February 9, 1973年 》53

FYI: He was an unknown struggling dairy farmer until he met with *Michel Lang* and agreed to let his land be used for the Woodstock music and art movement held between August 15 and August 18, 1969. *That's what this country is all about and I am not going to let you throw them out of our town just because you don't like their dress or their hair or the way they live or what they believe. This is America and their going to have their festival. If we join them, we can turn those adversities that are the problems of America into a hope for a brighter and more peaceful future.

史实: 他是一个默默无闻的苦苦挣扎的奶农,直到他遇到了米歇尔朗,并同意让他的土地用于1969年8月15日至8月18日之间举行的伍德斯托克音乐和艺术运动.*这就是这个国家的一切,我不会因为你不喜欢他们的衣服,头发,生活方式或信仰而让你把他们赶出我们的城市.这是美国，他们要去参加他们的节日.如果我们加入他们，我们就可以把美国面临的困难变成一个更光明,更和平的未来的希望.

YEATS叶丝ye si
William Butler Yeats
生人1865 ~ 1939年 》74
FYI: 19th century poet, some consider him to be the Greatest poet of the century.
史实: 19世纪的诗人,有人认为他是本世纪最伟大的诗人.

YELCHIN龙金long jin
Anton Yelchin [memorial]
生人1989 ~ 2016年 》27
FYI: Russian born actor best know for his Star Trek portrayal of Chekov. Trekky fans will miss him in future movies.
史实: 俄罗斯出生的演员,以其对契科夫的《星际迷航》的刻画而闻名.崔基的影迷们在未来的电影中会想念他.

YELTSIN叶利茨ye li ci
Boris Nikolayevich Yeltsin
生人1931年2月1日~ 2007年 》76
FYI: President of Russian 1991-1999
史实: 俄罗斯总统.

YERKES耶基斯ye ji si
Charles Tyson Yerkes
生人1837 ~ 1905年 》68
FYI: American financier: Chicago transit system. Yerkes observatory.
史实: 建地铁为了芝加哥.耶基斯查看星.

YOGI优琪you qi
Maharashi Mahesh Yogi
生人1918 ~ 2008年 》90
FYI:Transcendental Meditation Master. He was known among the celebrities such as the Beetles.
史实: 艺人参禅夫子.

YOUDE尤德you de

[Sir] Edward Youde

生人1924 ~ 1986年 》62

FYI: Diplomat to Hong Kong and China mainland and Sinologist.

史实: 香港政治家.汉学家.

YOUNG亚恒ya heng

Brigham Young

生人1801 ~ 1877年 》76

FYI: American pioneer and LDS leader who succeeded Joseph Smith.

史实: 美国商业.耶稣基督后期圣徒教会;二号将

YOUNG亚恒ya heng

Thomas Young

生人1773 ~ 1829年 》56

FYI: English physician and physicist. He established the wave theory of light. As well, his interest in Egyptology led to his translating of the Rosetta Stone of three languages.

史实: 医生，物理学家。光波长。翻译为了罗塞塔石碑

YOUNG亚恒ya heng

John Watts Young

生人1930 ~ 2018年 》88

FYI: American Astronaut, test pilot, aeronautical engineer. *9th person to walk on the Moon.

史实: 太空人,飞机人.九号人做上月.

From Group "Y" you can pick one person or up to ten Surnames and write their Surname in Chinese. You may try HORIZONTAL or VERTICAL in the traditional Chinese form.

Z

《抱最大的希望，做最坏的打算，从结果中学习》

"Expect the best. Prepare for the worst. Capitalize on what comes."
Hilary Hinton "zig" ZIGLER齐格勒qi ge le

ZAMORA塞莫拉sai mo la

Lonnie Zamora

FYI: Peace Officer and UFO close encounter, 1964 April 24, Friday 5:50 pm. Socorro, New Mexico

史实: 警察看幽浮.新墨西哥州索科罗1964年.

ZEMANEK赛曼克sai man ke

Heinz Zemanek

生人1920 ~ 2014年 》94

FYI: Austrian computer pioneer. Nicknamed "Mailufterl" - German for "May Breeze." for creating Wirlwind a computer at MIt.

史实: 电脑程序员为了MIT.

ZLOTOWITZ做罗特威兹zuo luo te wei zi

Meir Zlotowitz

生人1943 ~ 2017年 》75

FYI: Orthodox Jewish rabbi who authored ArtScrolls.

史实: 正教犹太拉比.作者 "ArtScrolls" [文艺作品]

ZACKRY咋可如zu ke ru

James Zackry

生人1881 ~ 1993年 》111years 211days

FYI: A member of the SuperCentenarian family. 111years 211days *List of verified oldest people. Wikipedia

史实: 上一百年.*已验证的最年长者列表.维基百科.

ZANGWILL翠威尔cui wei er

Israel Zangwill

FYI: British author. He was known as "the Dickens of the Ghetto". "The Melting Pot - 1908" also expresses his thoughts of different cultures living together in one country.

史实: 英国人作者. "狄更斯为了贫民区"

ZANUCK赞奥克zan ao ke

Darryl Francis Zanuck

生人1902 ~ 1979年 》77

FYI: Film producer from the silent era to the sound era.

史实: 电影从安静到声时代.

ZAPRUDER萨普德尔sa pu de er

Abraham Zapruder

生人1905 ~ 1970年 》65

FYI: JFK assassination witness who took the motion picture [486fr] of the historic moment 1963 November 22:12:30 [see marie muchmore* Oville nix]

史实: 看JFK死了, 他拍摄历史.

ZATOPEK扎托皮克za tuo po ke

Emil Zatopek

生人1922 ~ 2000年 》78

FYI: known as the "marathon man", set new records during the '40's". He introduced the concept of "interval training" as well as "hypo-ventilation training".

史实: 马拉松人.介绍间歇训练.

ZAYTSEV柴瑟夫chai se fu

Vasily Grigoryevich Zaytsev

生人1915 ~ 1991年 》76

FYI: WWII Soviet sniper. He had over 300 kills on his record during war time with the Germans. The movie (Enemy at the Gates 2001) *Patiently await the moment for one, and only one, well-aimed shot. [*RT]

史实: 二次大战狙击手.人人300死了. *请耐心等待片刻, 只有一张, 对准目标.

ZDANKSY丹斯其dan si qi

Otto Karl Josef Zdansky

生人1894 ~ 1988年 》94

FYI: Austrian Paleontologist *co-discovery of Peking Man c.1921

史实: 1921年古代北京人.

ZELLER泽勒 ze le

Walter Phillip Zeller

生人1890 ~ 1957年 》67

FYI: Founded the Zellers thrift stores for Canadians.
史实: 先导泽勒可见商业.

ZEUNER泽那尔ze ne er

Gustav Anton Zeuner

生人1828 ~ 1907年 》89

FYI: German physicist and mineralogists

史实: 德国物理学家.

ZIEGFELD兹格法里德zi ge fa li de

Florenz Edward Ziegfeld jr.

生人1867 ~ 1932年 》65

FYI:"the glorify of the American Girl"~Producer and Impresio! "The Art of Show business".

史实: 漂亮女艺人.

ZIGLER齐格勒qi ge le

Hilary Hinton "Zig" Zigler

生人1926 ~ 2012年 》86

FYI: Author, motivational speaker. [See You at The Top-1975].*You can have everything in life you want, if you help enough people get what they want.

史实: 作者,激励 "如果你帮助足够多的人得到他们想要的, 你可以拥有生活中你想要的一切."

ZIMMER吉穆耳 ji mu er

Heinrich Robert Zimmer

生人1890 ~ 1943年 》63

FYI: He was a German INDOLOGIST and historian of Asian Arts (East Indian).

史实: 他是德国印支学家和亚洲艺术历史学家.

ZIMMERMANN齐默尔曼qi mo er man

Philip~R~Zimmermann

FYI: pretty good privacy (program) "Internet Hall of Fame" [*p_ZIMMERMANN]

史实: 专业为了电脑网吧.

ZIPPE兹怕zi pa

Franz Xaver Maximilian Zippe

生人1791 ~ 1863年 》72

FYI: Natural philosopher, scientist and mineralogist.

史实; 哲学, 矿物学.

ZIRKEL齐克尔qi ke er

Ferdinand Zirkel

生人1838 ~ 1912年 》74

FYI: German geologist and mineralogists.

史实: 矿物学, 地质学家.

ZOLA左拉zuo la

Emile Edourd Charles Antoine Zola

生人1840 ~ 1902年 》62

FYI: French naturalist, novelist and journalist. *nominated for the Nobel prize in literature c1901 and 1902.

史实: 作者,新闻学.1901年诺贝尔在文学.

ZUCKMAYER租克梅珥zu ke mei er

Carl Zuckmayer

生人1896 ~ 1977年 》81

FYI: German playwright. Goethe prize c1952

史实: 德国戏剧家.

ZWEIG茨威格ci wei ge

Stefan Zweig

生人1881 ~ 1942年 》61

FYI: Austrian novelist, playwright, journalist and biographer.

史实: 奥地利小说家,剧作家,记者和传记作家.

From Group "Z" you can pick one person or up to ten Surnames and write their Surname in Chinese. You may try HORIZONTAL or VERTICAL in the traditional Chinese form.

* coming soon ~ 365 Voices From the Past is an in depth look at the quotes of many individuals from this book as well as additional people that I have researched. Feel free to contact me with your favourite historic person of interest.

Study everything, at all times, everywhere
无论何时何地，都有学习一切
朱熹zhu xi 1130~1200时

NOTABLE CHINESE

Common Chinese names along with their Meanings

常见的中文名称及其含义

In Asia, they do not follow a basic English Alphabet with their names. To list them here would require using them in a pin yin Romanization setting. The FAMILY name takes all priority over the "title" or given names. Some are given only one casual name, while yet others are given 2 side by side. In rare cases, they might have 3 or more casual names. Tom, Dick and Jane have no special meanings in English, but the same is not true with Chinese. A boy or a girl can have the same casual name as it does not have a "gender" to qualify it. Often, a person will have their casual name doubled, it is to "reinforce" the first!

The names of people and places listed are random in nature with the small exception of prominent leaders and places. The English alphabet used here is only a general guideline and NOT the rule as many surnames are the same in China hence do not connect one particular family to another.

在亚洲，他们的名字不遵循基本的英文字母表.要在这里列出它们，需要在拼音罗马化设置中使用它们.姓氏优先于"头衔"或名字.有些只给了一个非正式的名字，而另一些则给了两个并列的名字.在极少数情况下，他们可能有3个或更多的非正式名字.汤姆，迪克和简在英语中没有特殊的意思，但汉语中的意思却不一样。一个男孩或女孩可以有相同的非正式的名字，因为它没有一个"性别"来符合它。经常，一个人会把自己的随便名字翻倍，这是"强化"第一！所列的人名和地名在性质上是随机的，主要领导和地名除外.这里使用的英文字母只是一个通用的准则，而不是规则，因为在中国，许多姓氏都是相同的，因此不会将一个特定的家庭连接到另一个家庭.

介绍到写汉字

~

intro to writing Chinese characters

MOST COMMON FAMILY NAMES ARE GROUPED IN TO 10.

*王*周*邓*孔*孙*李*杨*吴*张*毛

However, it is possible to read hundreds of separate Sir names without duplication. 但是，可以不重复地读取数百个单独的SIR名称.

As a former teacher working in Chinese schools an average list would show 50 names without very little repeats. The combination of casual names can be in the thousands and often reflect nature in all of its variety as well as verbs and adjectives.

作为一名在中国学校工作的前教师，一份平均的名单上会列出50个名字，而不会重复太多.非正式名字的组合可以是几千个，经常反映各种各样的性质，以及动词和形容词.

* just a sample of student given names.
叶 ye[leaf], 健康 jian kang[healthy],
晓 xiao[early dawn] 雨 yue[rain], 梦 meng [dream], 德 de[Honorable]

》》》》》》》》名表 - name list 》》》》》》》》》》》》》》》》
Listed in Romanization format for easy searching [查看]
以罗马格式列出，便于搜索

1 High tone
2 Rising
3 Falling then rising
4 falling

曹操

cao cao

生人155～220年

The legend of 曹操 in China is held mainly by the Older generations.

He was a famous statesman in his time, poet and calligrapher.
In "Romance of the Three Kingdoms", he is the villain.

*It's not the size that counts in an army, but skill. It's not prowess that counts in a General, but finesse.

曹cao2; surname, refers to class or grade as well

操cao4; means to grasp or hold, to manage

》》》》》》》》》》》》》》》》》》》》》》》 practice portion 《《《《《《《《《《《《《《《《《《《《《《《

曹					
操					

刘备

Liu Bei

生人161～223年

Jining China Photo by Forest L. ～ 福瑞斯特

Liu Bei is a renouned historic figure who fought against Cao Cao [曹操]
In the story of The Three Kingdoms of early South China during the warring years. He established the Shu Han Dynasty. The movie "Red Ciff" is based on this historical venture.

* All men have their appointed time; that's something no horse can change.

刘liu2; surname
备bei4; to prepare*get ready*to provide

》》》》》》》》》》》》》》》》》》》》》》》》 practice portion 《《《《《《《《《《《《《《《《《《《《《《《《《

刘					
备					

李白
Li Bai

生人701~ 762年

Renouned Tang Dynasty poet.
李li3; surname*plum
白bai3; white*snowy*pure*bright*clear*to write wrong character*to explain*venacular

In a universe animated by the interaction of yin (female) and yang (male) energies, the moon was literally yin visible. Indeed, it was the very germ or source of yin, and the sun was its yang counterpart.

》》》》》》》》》》》》》》》》》》》》》》》》》》 practice portion 《《《《《《《《《《《《《《《《《《《《《《《《《《

李					
白					

蔡元培

Cai Yuanpei

生人1868 ~ 1940年

Liberal educationalist. President of Beijing University from 1917-19.

蔡cai4; Tortoise
元yuan2; Surname，money，first
培pei2; to cultivate

》》》》》》》》》》》》》》》》》》》》》》》》   practice portion   《《《《《《《《《《《《《《《《《《《《《《《

蔡					
元					
培					

曹雪芹

Cao Xueqin

生人1715～1764年

*Accepted author of Dream of Red Mansions.

Yin-yang is a sort of force,' said Xiang-yun. 'It's the force in things that gives them their distinctive forms. For example, the sky is Yang and the earth is Yin; water is Yin and fire is Yang; the sun is Yang and the moon is Yin.

曹cao2; surname*refers to class or grade as well
雪xue3; surname*snow*to wipe away
芹qin2; celery

》》》》》》》》》》》》》》》》》》》》》》》》 practice portion 《《《《《《《《《《《《《《《《《《《《《《《《

曹					
雪					
芹					

毛泽东
Mao Zedong
生人1893 ~ 1976年

Photo by Forest L. ~ 福瑞斯特 ~ Statue in Orange Park

Chinese communist leader. Two foreigner men played a prominent role in 毛 life. Journalist Edgar Snow (American) who wrote "Red Star over China". The other was the physician Norman Bethune (Canadian), who died from an infection while treating soldiers.

Both are mentioned in "福瑞斯特". His image appears on all paper bills in China. The smallest coin (currency) is a "jiao" 角。The sound is phonetic and is borrowed from his surname.

A revolution is not a dinner party, or writing an essay, or painting a picture, or doing embroidery; it cannot be so refined, so leisurely and gentle, so temperate, kind, courteous, restrained and magnanimous. A revolution is an insurrection, an act of violence by which one class overthrows another.

毛mao2; surname*hair*feather*wool*devalue》》》1/10 元 = 角jiao
泽ze2; pool*pond*lustre*damp*moist
东dong1; surname*East*landlord

》》》》》》》》》》》》》》》》》》》》》》》 practice portion 《《《《《《《《《《《《《《《《《《《《《《《《

毛					
泽					
东					

周恩来
Zhou EnLai

生人1898 ~ 1976年

He was a Chinese communist leader and Prime Minister from 1949~ 1976年.
*All diplomacy is a continuation of war by other means.

周zhou1; surname**to circle*weekly*lap*cycle*complete
恩en1; favor*grace*kindness
来lai2; to come*to arrive*to come round*ever since*next

》》》》》》》》》》》》》》》》》》》》》》》　practice portion　《《《《《《《《《《《《《《《《《《《《《《《《

周					
恩					
来					

程砚秋

Cheng Yanqiu

生人1904～1958年

Famous Beijing opera singer and actor.

程cheng2; surname*rule*order*formula*sequence
眼yan3; eye
球qiu2; ball

》》》》》》》》》》》》》》》》》》》》》》》》》 practice portion 《《《《《《《《《《《《《《《《《《《《《《《《

程					
眼					
球					

邓丽君

Deng LiJun

生人1953～1995年

Also known as Teresa Teng from Taiwan. She was a well known singer in the Asian markets until her early unexpected death.

邓deng4; common surname
丽li4; beautiful
君jun;1 monarchy*lord*ruler

》》》》》》》》》》》》》》》》》》》》》》》》》 practice portion 《《《《《《《《《《《《《《《《《《《《《《《《《

邓					
丽					
君					

吴承恩

Wu Chengen

生人1500～1582年

Renouned as a novelist, his works all loved by all who read the books or see the Television version or "Journey to the West" and is one of four classical novels of Chinese literature. Featuring; the Monk, golden monkey, pig man and

吴wu2; surname*South-East Chinese provinces.
承cheng2; to bear*to carry*to hold*to take charge*owing*to receive.
恩en1; favor*grace*kindness.

》》》》》》》》》》》》》》》》》》》》》》》 practice portion   《《《《《《《《《《《《《《《《《《《《《《《《《

吴				
承				
恩				

邓小平

Deng XiaoPing

生人1904 ~ 1997年

Chinese communist leader for 1978-1990. Creator of "socialism with characteristics".

*Keep a cool head and maintain a low profile. Never take the lead - but aim to do something big.

邓deng4; common surname.
小xiao3; small*tiny*few*young
平ping2; flat*level*equal*calm*peaceful

〉〉〉〉〉〉〉〉〉〉〉〉〉〉〉〉〉〉〉〉〉〉〉 practice portion 《《《《《《《《《《《《《《《《《《《《《《《

					邓
					小
					平

韩彦直

Han YanZhi

生人1131~?

Song dynasty botanist, author of classifications of orange trees

韩han2; surname*one of the Seven Hero States.
彦yan4; surname*color*face*countenance
直zhi2; straight*frank*straightforward*vertical

》》》》》》》》》》》》》》》》》》》》》》》   practice portion   《《《《《《《《《《《《《《《《《《《《《《《

韩					
彦					
直					

慧能

Hui Neng

生人636～713年 BC

Taught and practiced Buddhism

*Look within!... The secret is inside you.

慧hui4; surname*intelligent
能neng2; surname*be able to*ability*

〉〉〉〉〉〉〉〉〉〉〉〉〉〉〉〉〉〉〉〉〉〉〉〉〉　practice portion　《《《《《《《《《《《《《《《《《《《《《《《

慧					
能					

韩信

Han Xin

生人196年BC ~ ?

First general of first Han emperor Liu Bang. Also made kites famous for Weifang, the city of kites in Shandong province.

韩han2; sir name, one of seven warring states
信xin4; letter

》》》》》》》》》》》》》》》》》》》》》》》》》 practice portion 《《《《《《《《《《《《《《《《《《《《《《《《《

韩					
信					

霍元甲

Huo YuanJia

生人1868～1910年

One of many renown marshal arts specialists. Often used on movie sets as an extra or to train actors.

霍huo4; surname*suddenly

元yuan2; surname*Chinese currency*primary*first

甲jia3; first of the ten heavenly stems*nail(toe)

》》》》》》》》》》》》》》》》》》》》》》》 practice portion 《《《《《《《《《《《《《《《《《《《《《《《

霍					
元					
甲					

孔夫子
Kong Fuzi

生人551~ 479年 BC

*Born as 孔丘 kong qiu. His more well known Latin name of Confucius which is spoken in modern English today. Therefore the Fuzi (夫子) is his title respectfully known as "Grand Master"!

The great teacher and philosopher of old China. His writings are taught in all schools in China and the same with his statue persona.
His birth name was Kong [丘]: Qiu means mound or hilly.

Life is really simple, but men insist on making it complicated.

Photo of Confucius with Forest L. ~ 福瑞斯特

孔kong3; ~ surname
夫fu1; grand
子zi3; master

Prior to the birth of the Peoples Republic of China, all writing was Lateral and [Right to Left] in direction.

》》》》》》》》》》》》》》》》》》》》》》》》 practice portion 《《《《《《《《《《《《《《《《《《《《《《《《《《

					孔
					夫
					子

周有光
Zhou Youguang
生人1906～2017年

Influential writer as well as the founder of the pinyin style of writing for foreigners to read and speak Chinese. He lived to be over 110 years.

In 1958 Pin Yin was officially adopted by the Chinese government.

周zhou1; surname*to circle*weekly*lap*cycle*complete
有you3; have*there is*to exist*to be
光guang1; light*ray*bright*

》》》》》》》》》》》》》》》》》》》》》》》》   practice portion   《《《《《《《《《《《《《《《《《《《《《《《

周					
有					
光					

雷锋

Lei Feng

生人1940 ~ 1962年

Since the days of Mao Zedong, Lei Fang has been used as the military model of excellency. The middle schools and the common person see his poster all over China. Bus stops, air terminals, malls.

雷lei3; surname*thunder*terrific
锋feng1; point of spear*edge of a tool*vanguard

》》》》》》》》》》》》》》》》》》》》》》》》》 practice portion 《《《《《《《《《《《《《《《《《《《《《《《《《

雷					
锋					

李青运
Li Qingyun

生人1677～1933年》+250 year

Once reached the age of 100, the government would issue a congratulatory certification every 50 years thereafter until he died at 250 years of age.

李li3; surname*plum
青qing1; green/blue*youth*young
运yuan2; to move*to transport*to use*to apply*fortune*luck*fate

》》》》》》》》》》》》》》》》》》》》》》》》 practice portion 《《《《《《《《《《《《《《《《《《《《《《《《《

					李
					青
					运

*please note that this rendition is in simplified Chinese and not in the ancient way as seen on the internet. ** Left to right was the original form.

李小龙

Li XiaoLong

生人1940 ~ 1973年

Bruce Lee, a martial art expert was born in America but grew up in Hong Kong. He was both an actor as well as a martial arts teacher. He is listed among the 100 most influential people of the 20 century by Time magazine. With his American wife he had two children until his death.

李li3; surname*plum
小xiao3; small*tiny*few*young
龙long2; dragon

》》》》》》》》》》》》》》》》》》》》》》》》 practice portion 《《《《《《《《《《《《《《《《《《《《《《《《

李					
小					
龙					

鲁班

Lu Ban

生人507～444年 BC

Legendary master craftsman. Referred to as the Father of Chinese carpentry

鲁lu3; surname*crass*stupid*rude

班ban1; surname*team*class*squad*work shift*ranking

》》》》》》》》》》》》》》》》》》》》》》》》 practice portion 《《《《《《《《《《《《《《《《《《《《《《《

鲁					
班					

孟子
Mencius [Mengzi]
生人372～289年BC

Historically he was a contemporary of Confucius. Both were teachers of the same philosophies. Both lived near or in the town of QuFu in South Shandong province. Both are given a positive vote by the Chinese in general. 子 and 夫子 refer to their status as teachers. The Latin form of Mengzi is "Mencius".

孟meng4; surname*first month of a season*eldest brother
子zi3; son*child*seed*egg***can refer to a teacher.

》》》》》》》》》》》》》》》》》》》》》》》》　practice　portion　《《《《《《《《《《《《《《《《《《《《《《《《

孟					
子					

梅兰芳

Mei Lanfang

生人1894 ~ 1961年

Considered to be the greatest of all Beijing Opera, singer and dancers and teachers.

梅mei2; Surname*plum flower
兰lan2; surname*orchid*Lanzhou city
芳fang1; fragrant

》》》》》》》》》》》》》》》》》》》》》》》   practice portion   《《《《《《《《《《《《《《《《《《《《《《《

梅					
兰					
芳					

钱学森

Qian Xue Sen

生人1911 ~ 2009年

A scientist and aeronautical engineer. He moved from China to America with his wife to continue his scientific studies. They both returned to China where he tested the Atomic bomb on Chinese soil.

钱qian2; surname*coin*money
学xue2; to learn*to study*science*ology
森sen1; forest

》》》》》》》》》》》》》》》》》》》》》》 practice portion 《《《《《《《《《《《《《《《《《《《《《《《

钱					
学					
森					

詹天佑

Zhan Tianyou

生人1861～1919年

Chinese railroad engineer and forerunner of today's high-speed rail.

詹zhan1; surname*excellent*verbose

天tian1; day*sky*heaven

佑you4; to assist*to protect

》》》》》》》》》》》》》》》》》》》》》》》》》   practice portion   《《《《《《《《《《《《《《《《《《《《《《《《

詹					
天					
佑					

Genghis Khan

生人1162 ~ 1227年 [pseudonym]

Was born as 'Tiemujin' and was given the Royal rank name of Ghenghis Khan meaning Supreme ruler of an Empire [khagnate].

Chinggis is regarded as a more accurate phonetic rendering of Ghenghis. He was not of Chinese descent although he is mentioned in Chinese lore. From Mongolian translated into Chinese, his name means 'blacksmith'

铁 tie3; steel
木 mu4; wood
真 zhen1; real, genuine.

》》》》》》》》》》》》》》》》》》》》》》》 practice portion 《《《《《《《《《《《《《《《《《《《《《《《

铁					
木					
真					

* A partial collection of Chinese currency. Collected from 2010~2018. In all cases 中国人民银行 ~ zhong guo ren min bi yin hang ~ China peoples bank.

Top, two minority men. Bottom, the chrysanthemum and the national emblem.Considered [rare]. The four small stars represent: the workers, peasants, petty bourgeoisie and the national bourgeoisie four classes.

2 jiao coin is considered RARE by Chinese authorities as of 2019.

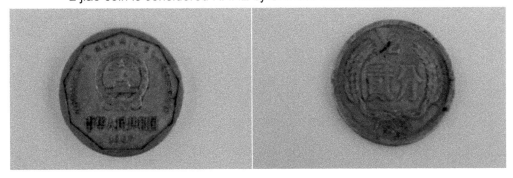

5 jiao note; the ladies wear the traditional dress of minority people.
This note is considered VERY RARE as of 2019.

5 jiao coin with the Orchid blossom.

The Great Wall on the old one yuan.

Top; the current Chinese one yuan with Mao and Bottom; Xihu
lake in the southeastern Chinese Hangzhou.
Courtesy Forest L. 福瑞斯特

The flower on its face is a chrysanthemum and appears on the face of all bills and coins.

Taishan mountain in Eastern Shandong province.

The author with daughter [Rebecca] and two new friends climbing Taishan in 2018.

The scenic Three Gorges of Hebei province.

Lijiang river in South China on the Chinese 20 yuan.

The Potala Palace in Lhasa on the Chinese 50 yuan.

The Great Hall of the People is seen on the back of the Chinese 100.

HISTORICAL MOMENTS

1929 October 18

~Now that we are Persons~

The Canadian Famous Five

Murphy*McKinney*Edwards*Parbly*McClung

墨菲 麦金尼 爱德华兹 帕利 麦克隆

*used with permission Albert Legislature archives.

Mayors of Edmonton ~ Alberta ~ Canada
1892 ~ 1988

*photo included; n/a

1* Matthew McCauley麦考利mai ke li 1892~1895

2* Herbert Charles Wilson威尔逊wei er sun 1895~1896

3* Cornelius Gallagher加拉赫jia li her 1896~1896

4* John Alexander MCDOUGALL麦克杜格尔mai ke du ge er 1896~1897, 1907~1908

5* William Somerville EDMISTON埃德米斯顿ai de mi si dun 1897~1899

6* Kenneth W. MacKenzie麦肯齐mai ken qi 1899~1901

7* William Short肖特xiao te 1901~1904; 1912~1913

8* Charles May梅理mai li 1905~1906

9* William Antrobus Griesbach格里斯巴赫ge li si ba her 1906~1907

10* Robert Lee李li 1908~1910

11* George S. Armstrong阿姆斯特朗a mu si te liang 1910~1912

12* William J. McNamara麦克纳马拉mai ke nei ma la 1913~1914

13* William Thomas Henry亨利heng li 1914~1917

14* Harry Marshall Erskine Evans埃文斯ai wen si 1917~1918

15* Joseph Clark克拉克ke li ke 1918~1920; 1934~1937

16* David Milwyn Duggan达根da gen 1920~1923

17* Kenny Blatchford布拉奇福德bu li ke fu de 1923~1926

18* Ambrose Bury伯里bo li 1926~1929

19* James McCrie Douglas道格拉斯da ke li si 1929~1931

20* Dan Knott诺特nuo te 1932~1934

21* John Wesley Fry弗莱fei lai 1937~1945

22* Harry Dean Ainlay安利an li 1945~1949

23* Sidney Parson帕森pa sen 1949~1951

24* William HAWRELAK霍若拉克huo ru la ke 1951~1959

25* Frederick John Mitchell米切尔mi qie er 1959~1959

27* Elmer Earnest Roper罗珀luo po 1959~1963

27* Vincent Dantzer丹泽dan ze 1965~1968

28n/a Ivor Dent 德恩特de en te1968~1974

29 x2* Terry Cavanagh卡瓦纳ka wen na 1975~1977

31* Lawrence Decore装饰zhuang xi 1983~1988

Courtesy Ukrainian Village~ photo by Forest L. [L: foot peddle powdered]

~缝纫机年表~
The Sewing Machine Chronology

c1755; Charles Frederick WEISENTHAL维森塔尔wei sen ta er

c1790; Thomas SAINT 圣sheng

c1833; Walter HUNT哈恩特ha en te

c1846; Elias HOWE jr. 哈维ha wei

c1856; Issac Merritt SINGER 森哥尔sen ge er

c1892; Barthelemy THIMONNIER蒂莫尼珥di mo ni er

The pioneers of the first practical typewriter with the qwerty board.
Circa 1714~1800's

Courtesy of Ukrainian Village~photo by Forest L.
Henry MILL密尔mi er
生人1683–1771年 patented the first typewriter in 1714

The qwerty team
Carlos GLIDDIN格莱丁ge lai ding
生人November 8, 1834 – March 11, 1877年

Latham Christopher SHOLES斯科尔斯si ke er si
生人Feb 14, 1819 - Feb 17, 1890年

Samuel Willard SOULE灵魂ling hun (soul)
生人Jan 25, 1830 ~ Jul 12, 1875年

The Peking Man ~北京猿人
~ The Team ~
680, 000 ~ 780,000 years
周口店

Here is primitive man, now all we have to do is find him .
这是原始人，现在我们要做的就是找到他. -Andersson.

* Wikipedia states that 4 teeth from the original dig now are at the Paleontological Museum of Uppsala University. All other remains are unknown at this time.

ANDERSSON 安德森an de sen
Johan Gunnar Andersson >1960(86); *Archaeologist. **co-discovery of Peking man c.1921-26.

BLACK 布莱克bu lai ke
Davidson Black >1934; (步達生）*Paleonanthropologist. * Homo erectus pekinensis; [see Andersson/zdansky.]

BOHLIN 博林bo lin
Anders Birger Bohlin 1898-1990;
*Swedish Palaeontologist. ** c1950 Homo erectus confirmed.

GRANGER 格兰杰ge lan jie
Walter W Granger ; 1921 began the "initial" excavation of zhoukoudian.

TEILHARD 泰亚尔tai ya er
Pierre Teilhard c1881~1955 ; Paleontology.-q
* co-partner of peking man (peirre teilard de Chardin).

WEIDENREICH魏登赖希wei deng lai xi
Franz Weidenreich 1873-1948(75); Anthropologist.
* succeeded D. Black re- Peking Man. **"Weidenreich Theory of Human Evolution"

ZDANKSY 丹斯其dan si qi
Otto Karl Josef Zdansky >1988; **Austrian Paleontologist **co-discovery of Peking Man c.1921-26

photographed at the U of A: Walter MacKenzie centre and seen on the 100 Canadian note.

DOUBLE HELIX Model

"if your the most intelligent person in the room, your in the wrong room!"
如果你是房间里最聪明的人，那你就错了房间
James WATSON沃特森wo te sen

CONTRIBUTIONS OF

ASTBURY 阿斯特伯里a si te bo li
William Thompson Astbury; discovered the Alpha helix, pioneer to the DNA 51 moment.

AVERY 埃弗里ai fu li
Oswald Theodore Avery;
molecular biologist, forerunner to the DNA photo 51 slide

BRAGG 布拉格bu la ga
Sir William Lawrence Bragg; Bragg's Law of X-ray refraction, for runner to the DNA photo 51 slide.

CRICK卡尔可ka er ke
Francis Crick; DNA co-discover 1953

CHARGOFF 贾格夫jia ge fu
Erwin Chargoff; Established the 2 rules of the DNA structure, for runner of the DNA photo 51 slide.

DONOHUE 德那乎de na hu
Jerry Donohue; Hydrogen bonding theory. Pionneer to discovering DNA.

FRANKLIN 富兰克林fu lan ke lin
Rosalind Elsie Franklin; X-ray crystallographer of DNA

GOSLING高斯林gao si lin
Raymond G. Gosling; x-ray diffraction of photo 51. Understudy of Franklin.

GRIFFITH 格里菲恩ge li fei en
Frederick Griffith >1941; Pioneer of observing cells transforming into a new strain ie;
DNA replication circa 1928.

LEVENE 莱文lai wen
Phoebus Aaron Theodore Levene: Distinguished between the functions of the DNA
and RNA.

RANDELL 兰德尔lan de er
John Turton Randell SIR >1984(79); Pioneer of the structure of the DNA.

STOKES 斯特克斯si te ke si
Alexander Alec Rawson stokes; Published works on the structure of the DNA.

WATSON 沃特森wo te sen
1928- ; James Watson ;Genetics DNA co-discover 1953."if your the most intelligent
person in the room, your in the wrong room!"

WILKINS 威尔金斯wei er jin si
Maurice Hugh Frederick Wilkins; pioneer research into DNA. Circa 1948-51.

WILSON 威尔逊wei er xun
Herbert Reese Wilson >2008(79); X-ray diffraction of cell nuclei along with DNA
studies.

Hindenburg Disaster

1937 May 6

Crew men~16

BIALAS比亚拉斯bi ya li si; rudi ~engine mechanic

DIMMLER 迪马尔di ma er; wilhelm~ engineering officer

EICHELMANN艾歇尔曼ai ge er man; franz~ radio operator

FLACKUS弗拉克斯 fa la ke si; fritz~ cook's assistant

HOLLERRIED霍勒里德huo le li de; albert~ mechanic

HUCHEL赫谢尔he xie er ;ernst~ senior elevatorman

IMOHOF 伊莫夫yi mo fu; emilie ~hostess

KNORR 诺尔nuo er;ludwig ~ chief rigger

MOSER莫瑟mo se ;robert ~mechanic

MULLER 米勒mo le; richard assistant chef

REISACHER赖萨赫lai sai se; alois mechanic

SCHEEF 谢夫xie fu; willi mechanic

SCHLAPP施拉普shi la pu ;ernst electrician

SCHREIBMULLER施莱布勒shi lai bu le ;josef ~chief mechanic

SCHULZE舒尔茨shu er ci ;max bar~ stewart

STOCKLE 斯特啊克勒si te a ke le;alfred ~engine mechanic

HAGAMAN哈嘎曼ha ga man ;allen orlando civilian linesman.

Passengers ~10~

ANDERS 安得尔an de er; ernst rudolf

BINCK 宾克bin ke; birger

DOLAN 得兰de lan; burtis john

DOUGLAS道格拉斯dao ge la si ;edward

DOEHNER 多纳 duo nei; hermann

ERDMANN尔德曼er de man; fritz

FEIBUSCH费布士fei bu shi; moritz

PANNES 潘斯pan si; john

PANNES潘斯pan si; emma

REIHOLD赖后德rei ho de; otto

CHALLENGER ACCIDENT

1986 Jan 28

"I touch the future. I teach."

我触及未来.我教书.

Christa MCAULIFFE麦考利夫mai kao li fu

JARVIS 贾维斯jia wei si

MCAULIFFE 麦考利夫mai kao li fu

RESNIK 雷斯尼克lei si ni ke

SCOBEE 科比ke bi

MCNAIR 麦克奈尔mai ke nai er

SMITH 史密斯shi mi si

ONISUKA 奥尼斯卡ao ni si ka

~ Space Shuttle Columbia ~
2003 February 1~ Memorial Wall

ANDERSON 安德森an de sen

BROWN 布朗bu lang

CHAWLA乔拉qiao la

CLARK 克拉克ke la ke

HUSBAND 哈斯班ha si ban

MCCOOL麦卡mai ke

RAMON 拉蒙la meng

TITANIC NOTABLE PEOPLE......
1912 April 15

"The Titanic had gone. The 'unsinkable' ship - but it had gone down to simple."

泰坦尼克号已经离开了.那艘 "不沉" 的船——但是它已经变得简单了.

-Henry Allingham

ANDREWS 安德鲁斯an de lu si: thomas andrews jr;

~Chief builder of the TITANIC

BELL贝尔bei er: joseph g. bell;
*Chief Engineer aboard the Titanic.

BOXHALL 巴斯赫ba si he: joseph groves boxhall >1967;
*Fourth officer Titanic.

BRIDE 比日德bi ri de: harold sydney bride;
*Junior Wireless operator.

FLEET福利特fu li te: frederick fleet; Titanic "look out" seamen.
*First to spot the Iceberg. (希舰队: fleet ie: ships.)

HARTLEY 贺特力he te li: wallace henry hartley:
~Bandleader on the RMS Titanic.

HICHENS 希琴斯xi qin si: robert hichens~
*Titanic QM at the Wheel.

JOUGHIN 乔因qiao yin: charles john joughin~
*RMS Titanic chief cook.

LIGHTOLLER 莱托勒lai tuo le: charles herbert lightolloer~
*Second Officer board the RMS Titanic. DISTINGUISHED SERVICE CROSS

MURDOCK 默多克mo duo ke: william mcmaster murdock~
*First Officer Titanic.

PHILLIPS 斐里伯斯fei li bo si: john george "jack" phillips~
*Senior Wireless operator

PIRRE 皮埃尔pi ai er: Lord williams james pirre~
*TITANIC designer and ship builder

SCHWABE 施瓦布shi wa bu: gustave christian schwabe; german financier.
~Funded the White Star Line~Titanic series.

WILDE 瓦尔德wa er de: henry tingle wilde jr.; Ships Chief officer.

*Edmund Fitzgerald ~ 10 Nov 1975

NAMED IN HONOR OF ITS PRESIDENT AND CHAIRMAN

ARMAGOST 呵马朵斯特a ma ga si te: micheal e 37岁

BEETCHER 比初bi chu: frederick j 56岁

BENTSEN本森ben sen; thomas d 23岁

BINDON 宾丹bin dan; edward f 47岁

BORGESON 布格森bu ge sen; thomas d 41岁

CHAMPEAU 莎普sha pu; oliver j 41岁

CHURCH 主尔区zhu er qu; nolan s 55岁

CUNDY 困迪kun di; ransom e 53岁

EDWARDS 艾德沃德斯ai de wo de si; thomas e 50岁

HASKELL哈斯科拉ha si ke le; russel g 40岁

HOLL 哈勒ha le; george j 60岁

HUDSON 亨利heng li: bruce l 22岁

KALMON 卡里门ka li men: allen g 43岁

MACLELLEN 麦克茉伦mai ke mo lun: gordon f 30岁

MAZES 马泽ma ze; joseph w 59岁

MCCARTHY麦卡锡mai ka yi; John h 62岁

MCSORLEY麦克索利 mai ke suo li; earnest m 63岁

O'BRIEN 奥勃良ao bo liang; eugene w 50岁

PECKOL 佩科尔pei ke er; karl a 20岁

POVICH波维奇pei wei ke; john j 59岁

PRATT 普拉特pu la te: james a 44岁

RAFFERTY拉菲蒂la fei di; robert c 62岁

RIPPA 里帕 li pai; paul m 22岁

SIMMONS 斯曼斯si man si; john d 62岁

SPENGLER 斯宾格勒si bin ge le; willam j 59 岁

THOMAS 托马斯tuo ma si: mark a thomas; 21岁

WEISS 维斯wei si; david e 22岁

WILHELM 维廉wei lian; blaine h 52岁

The Wreck of the Edmund Fitzgerald.歌
~Gordon Lightfoot ~

Church of Jesus Christ of Latter-day Saints
~ leadership since 1830 ~

SMITH 史密斯shi mi si: joseph jr. :1830 ~ 1844 time in office: 14 years

YOUNG 亚恒ya heng: brigham >1847 ~ 1877: 30 years

TAYLOR 泰勒tai le: john >1880 ~ 1887: 7 years

WOODRUFF 半圆威尔 ban yuan wei er: wilson >1889 ~ 1898: 9 years

SNOW 斯诺si nuo: lorenso > 1898 ~ 1901: 3 years

SMITH 史密斯shi mi si: joseph f > 1901 ~ 1918:17 years

GRANT 格兰特ge lan te: heber j > 1918 ~ 1945: 27 years

SMITH 史密斯shi mi si: george albert > 1945 ~ 1951:6 years

MCKAY 迈凯伊mai kai yi: david o > 1951 ~ 1970: 19 years

SMITH 史密斯shi mi si: joseph fielding >1970 ~ 1972: 2 years

LEE 李li: harold b > 1972 ~ 1973: 1years

KIMBALL 金博尔jin bo er: spencer w. > 1973 ~ 1985: 12 years

BENSON 本森bin sen: ezra taft > 1985 ~ 1994: 8 years

HUNTER 亨特heng te: howard w >1994 ~ 1995: 9 months

HINCKLEY 欣克利xin ke li: gordon b > 1995 ~ 2008: 13 years

MONSON 曼森men sen: thomas s - 2008 ~ 2018: 10 years

In memory of …..Star Trek

Majel Barret 巴雷特ba lei te

James Doohan 杜汉du han

Deforest Kelly 卡里ka li

Gene Roddenberry 罗顿巴黎luo dun ba ri

Leonard Nimoy 尼魔ni mo

Anton Yelchin 龙金long qin

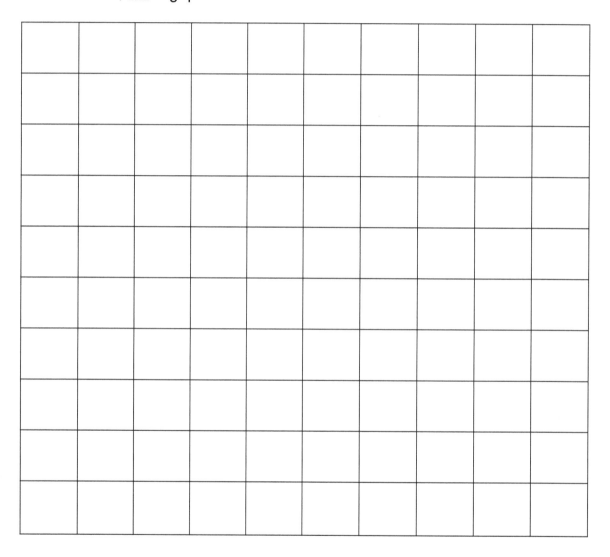

FYI: THE BOOK OF NAMES
~ 700 ~

Within China, most people choose their own English name or a name that they fancy. From my students of 8 years teaching and from a dating site I am a member of ... the ladies have chosen the following names. Occasionally they will pick a Man's name for fun. Their are rare times when a Phonetic name has a really nice sound and is included, so, see if you can spot it! A blue * is a lady I actually met for dating purposes ~ still single! French is also chosen by some. Only a few names are selected by Thai ladies as the collection comes from the same website. I have screen saved all of the ladies with their names to verify. For protection purposes the photo is not included. Please enjoy!

在中国，大多数人选择自己的英文名字或自己喜欢的名字。从我8年教书的学生和一个约会网站上，我是……女士们选择了以下名字。偶尔他们会为了好玩而选择一个男人的名字。他们是罕见的时候，当一个语音名称有一个非常好的声音，并包括，所以，看看你能发现它! 蓝色*是我为了约会而认识的一位女士~还是单身! 有些人也会选择法语。只有少数几个名字是由泰国妇女选择，因为收集来自同一个网站。我已经把所有的女士和她们的名字存了下来核实。出于保护目的，不包括照片。请欣赏!

>Aanline-Abbg-Ace-Acelin-Aesa-Afra-Ahha-Ahong-Ai-Aili-Ailis-Ait-Akali-Aki-Akuti-Alan-Aletta-Alician-Allc-Aimmee-Am-Amne-Amiee-Ambep-Anady-Anda-Andy-Anemne-Annababy-Angelababy-Angel_boby-ANGELA BaBe-Angle-Annaxuan-Anndy-Anny-Aly-Aodaly-Aom-Aomei-Aommy-Aourora-Apple-Apple   Green-April-Apricot-Arche-Arena-Ashah-Astrid-Audra-Aurora-Ausa-Autumn-Avocodo-Avon-Ayla-Ayva-Azura

>Babe-Baby-Babiysh-Baisy-Banpan-Banana-Baorui-Barbie-Bathshua-Beauty-Bee-BeeBee-Beenie-Begonia-Believe-Bell-Ben-Beryl-Beua-Bibi-Birdy-Birdie-Boa-

Boliva-BonnieRu-Bonnin-Bow-Boss-Brandy-Branna-Brian-Brisa-Blueberry-Bubles-Bunny-Burlen

>Cacheral-Calleigh-Cake-Cami-Camy--Candece-Candy-Canna-Caro-Carry-Cartoon-Cat-Catherin-Cathyjo-Ceasar-Cecly-Ceraly-Chacha-Change-Charcy-Charmer-Chao-Chaumet--Cheese-Cher-Cherish-Cherry-Charcy-Chesely-Chicca-Chisa-Chole-Cima-coey-Cora-Chorry-Chriss-Cician--Cicy-Cidy-Ciman-Cizi-Cloud-Cloudy-Coffee-Colo-Comie-Constane-Cooky-Cookies-Cornie-Crace Tan-Crace-Canna-Crazy-Crazybaby-Crazy Mama-Creamy-Curing-Cyheria-

>Da-Daisy-Daizy-Dale-Danny-Dara-Darcy-Dawn-Day-Debin-Dennis-Denny-Deep-Dextrad-Dita-Diamond-Dior-Dodo-Dories-Dorren-Douy-Dream-Dreamy

>Earn-Easy-Eavan-Echo-Eiffel-Eleven-Elf-Elodie-Emerald-En-Eniko-Eoris-Eri-Erinuse-Esse-Ether-Ewa-Every-Evol-Evony

>Fairy-Fawn-Fancy-Fang-Faug-Feier-Fend-Fendy-Fern-Fifi-Fig-Filly-Fine-Fion-Fiona-Flavia-Flavor-Flower-Folli-Fruit-Fountain-Frances-Freya-Frorida-Funny-

>Gaby-Gae-Garbo-Gemmeni-Gen/Gen-Genia-Gentle-Gill-Ginnirfer-Good-Gotgi-Grane-Grannysmith-Grape-Green-Greentea-Griselda-Groot-Gustave-

>Haby-Hac-Halar-Halping-Hamew-Hanes-Happy-Harley-Hattie-Hayle-Hedda-Hedi-Herina--Hobby-Honey-HoneyJ-Hulda-Humour-Honeysuckle wjsxq15964

>iane-ice-ice snow-icey-ina-itali-isla-iulala-imme-

>Jacca-Jaclina-Jacy-Jady-Jany-Jaunty-Jay-Jelly-Jemmy-Jenniefer-*Jerreffe-Jessica--Jessica_baby-Jesszca-Jewel-Jigsaw-Jinger-Jipin-Juhua-Juice-July-Jully-Justina-June-Junnier-Jmey-Joe-Jolly-Joye-Jojo-Johnny-Jora-Jotti-Joss-Journey-Junly-Jow-Jvonne

>**K**aly-Kally-Kaith-Kaka-Kama-Karida-Karice-Kassia-Kathna-Keke-Kelesy-kell-Ker-Ketty-Keypat-Kevy-Kexi-Kexy-Kilwi--Kirin-Kitar-Kitty-kitten-Kiwi-Kiy-KK-Kntle-Koey-Koko-Komi-Kors

>**L**-Laca-Ladda-Lainey-Lamu--Landing-Lane-Latte-Lavender-Leaf-Leaves-Leehom-Lemon-Lenny-Leon-Letha-Lofar-Licy-Life-Line-Lign-Lilac-Lius-Livia-Liy-Lips-Liss-Lisy-Lizie-Lo-Lohus-Lona-Long-Lris-Lrma-Lotus-Louis-Love-Lovely-Luby-Lucca-Lucia-Lucifer-Luck-Lucyka-Lucky-Lucky dan-Lukee-Luoffe-Luss-Lychee-Lyven

>**M**ag-Maira-Maimei-Makaha-Mali-Manday-Man-Manic-Many-Manny-Maper-Marhaba-Marrie-Marry-Mars--Mashi-Mata-Masia-May-Mcy-Medn-Medina941 Meim-Meris-Mermaid-Meroy-Mikaa-Mijjor-Mint-Milk-Milky-Miaomiao-Miffy-Miss-Misszoe-Melody-Memory-Meow-MeowMeow-Merlin-Messy-Mi-Mikaa-Mickey-Mimosa-Mint-Minhzhi*-Minnow-Mmei-Mochi-MoMo-Mon-Moly-Mondy-Monny-Moncy-Moon-Moonlight-Morning-Morry-Muffin-Muses-MyMy-

>**N**accy-namie-Negara-Nary-New-Nglina-Nice-Niko-Nikitta-Nissa-Niver-Nono-Nooby-Noodee-Noon

>**O**cean-Odile-Ofelia-Olia-Olina-Olve-OMee-Omi-On-Orange-Orchard-Orly-Ou-

>**P**ag-Paganini-Pancake-Pancy-Pandora-Papa-Paris-Party-Peach-Pear-Pearl-Pen-Penny-Pepper-Peony-Petal-Phenix-Phocbe-Pigpig-Pie-Pink-Pinky-Piper-Pita-Pitaya-Ploy-Pooky-Pony-Poper-poppice-Poppy-Porn-Prince-Puff-Pupu-Pure-Purity-Psyche-

>**Q**baby-Qill-Qiu'e-Qamar-Quen-Queen-Queena-Queenie-Queeny-Quenna-

>**R**abbit-Racehle-Rache-Rae-Rain-Rainbow-Rainer-Ran-Ran_Ran-Randy-Rasberry-Red-Regina-Regine-Rian-Rinalee-Rine-Riva-River-Robin-Roles-Rose_Darling-Rosy-Ruiz-Ruru

>**S**abella-Saffi-Sail-Salome-Sami-Sandny-Sanny--Sandwich-Schnee-Sea-Seeelip-Sel-Sency-Secina-Serlley*--Seven-Shadow-Shally-Sharen-Sharow-Shary-Shasha-Sher-Shirlay-Shing-Shiny-Sidly-Sigrid-Siki-Silk-Silver-Sin-Sinda-Sindy-Sior-Sisee-Sisnon-Sky-Skye-Slim-Slinna-Smile-Snake-Snidel-Snow-Snowy-Soal-Sookie-Sora-Soso-Souffle-Soyeon-Special-Spears-Spring-Star-Starfruit-Starry-Strawberry-Stephy-Styong-Suan-Subo-Sucy-Sun-Sundy-Sunflower-Sunnie-Sunny-Sunshine-Sura-Suvain-Swallow-Sweetie-SweetAngel-

>**T**ammy-Tangerine-Taurus-Teddy-Teemo-Teemy-Tenny-Teri-Tin-Tine-Tip-Tobey-Tom-Trace-TracyQ-Tragady-Tree-Truda-Tulip-Tum-Tuna-Twickle-

>**U**na-Uranus

>**W**anting-Wanni-warmmy-Wasabi-Water-Waterlily-Wayne-Welkin-Wina-Windy-Wing-Winter-Weddy-Wennie-Winnie-Wonderful-

>**V**awa-Vear-Venas-Venus-Viana-View-Vigny-Vikkcy-Vin-Vina-Vnion-Violet-Virtue-Vit-Vitamine-Vivi-Voile-Vna*Vouer-

>**X**avil-Xinm-Xj-

>**Y**achne-Yabo-Yalih-Yatti-Year-Yeen-Yike-Yily-Yinhfen-YMD-Yocy-Yoo-Yoki-Yoky-Yona-Younger-Yovela-Yooy-Yoyo-Yukin-Yummy-Yuonne-

>**Z**oya-Zve-

Traditional Foreign names

The Chinese people who elect to chose a traditional name get the name usually from the movies or books that they have read in school. The same names can be found also within the collection in this book.

COGNITIVE LEARNING EXCERCISES

Learning takes place in 4 ways: hearing followed by spoken, followed by reading then finally writing. The cognitive mind is forced to grow as you learn to read than write. This book intentionally gives you many opportunities. Enjoy!

学习的方式有四种:听,说,读,写.当你学会读书而不是写字时,认知思维就会被迫成长.这本书故意给你很多机会.享受!

Hearing听力	Spoken口语
reading阅读	writing写作

The LEARNING curve: The speed by which we learn something new to us. The boxes provided are designed to give you practice. One to three is simply an introduction, where as the remaining in most cases helps to 'cement' the idea in your mind. You will be building new dendrite cells in your brain... they are memory cells. Writing is the most difficult faze of learning as it involves physical application of your thinking processes. Once conquered you will have a feeling of extreme elation. "得意洋洋"

学习曲线:我们学习新事物的速度.提供的盒子旨在让您练习.一到四只是一个简单的介绍,在大多数情况下,五到十有助于"巩固"你的想法.你将在你的大脑中建立新的树突细胞…它们是记忆细胞.写作是最困难的学习方式,因为它涉及到你思维过程的物理应用.一旦被征服,你会有一种极度兴奋的感觉.

~John George Diefenbaker~

*He who does not know the past can never understand the
present, and he certainly can do nothing for the future.*
不了解过去的人永远不会了解见在，他当然不能为未来做任何事情。

ALDRIN奥尔德林ao er de lin

Buzz Aldrin

*My first inclination is to be a bit skeptical about the claims that human-produced
carbon dioxide is the direct contributor to global warming.*
我的第一个倾向是对人为产生的二氧化碳是导致全球变暖的直接原因的说法有些怀疑.

~

*We need the next generation to be motivated and to push technological boundaries,
to seek out new innovations.*
我们需要激励下一代并突破技术界限，以寻求新的创新

奥					
尔					
德					
林					

ALLINGHAM阿玲哈姆a ling ha mu

Henry William Allingham

"The Titanic had gone. The 'unsinkable' ship - but it had gone down to simple."
泰坦尼克号已经离开了.那艘"不沉"的船——但是它已经得
简单了.

~

Cigarettes, whisky and wild women...give longevity!

《香烟、威士忌和野女人……长寿!》

阿					
玲					
哈					
姆					

AMUNDSEN啊曼森a man sen

Roald Engelbregt Agravning Amundsen

Adventure is just bad planning..

冒险只是不好的计划.

啊					
曼					
森					

ANDERSEN安德森an de sen

Hans Christian Andersen

Where words fail, music speaks.

如果说不出话来, 音乐就会说话.

~

Life itself is the most wonderful fairy tale.

人生本身就是最美妙的童话.

~

Every man's life is a fairy tale written by God's fingers.

每个人的生活都是用上帝的手指写的童话.

~

Just living is not enough... one must have sunshine, freedom, and a little flower.

仅仅生活还不够... 必须有阳光，自由和有一朵小花.

~

Being born in a duck yard does not matter, if only you are hatched from a swan's egg.

如果只是从天鹅卵孵化出来的话，出生在鸭场就没关

~

Most of the people who will walk after me will be children, so make the beat keep time with short steps.

跟在我后面的大多数人都是孩子，所以要使节拍保持时间短.

ANDERSEN安德森an de sen

安					
德					
森					

ANDERSSON安德森an de sen

Johan Gunnar Andersson

Here is primitive man, now all we have to do is find him.

这里是原始人，现在我们要做的就是找到他

安					
德					
森					

ANGELOU安杰鲁an jie lu

Maya Angelou

I've learned that people will forget what you said, people will forget what you did, but people will never forget how you made them feel.

我了解到人们会忘记你说的话，人们会忘记你的所作所为，但是人们永远不会忘记你如何表达自己的感受.

~

If you don't like something, change it. If you can't change it, change your attitude.

如果您不喜欢某些东西，请进行更改.如果您无法更改，请更改您的态度.

安					
杰					
鲁					

ARAFAT啊拉法特a la fa te

Yasser Arafat

Peace, for us, is an asset and in our interest. It is an absolute human asset that allows an individual to freely develop his individuality unbound by any regional, religious, or ethnic fetters.

对我们而言，和平是一项资产，符合我们的利益.这是一项绝对的人力资产，可以使个人自由地发展自己的个性，不受任何区域，宗教或种族束缚的束缚.

啊					
拉					
法					
特					

ARMSTRONG阿姆斯特朗a mu si te lang

Neil Alden Armstrong

That is one small step for a man, one giant leap for mankind!

《这是人类的一小步，人类的一大步！》

阿					
姆					
斯					
特					
朗					

ASHEVAK阿舍瓦克a she wa ke

Kenojuak Ashevak

There is no word for art. We say it is to transfer something from the real to the unreal. I am an owl, and I am a happy owl. I like to make people happy and everything happy. I am the light of happiness and I am a dancing owl.

艺术是没有字的.我们说这是将某些东西从真实转移到虚幻.我是猫头鹰，也是快乐的猫头鹰.我喜欢让人们开心，让一切都开心.我是幸福之光，我是跳舞的猫头鹰.

阿					
舍					
瓦					
克					

ASIMOV啊斯嘛a si ma

Isaac Asimov

Education isn't something you finish.

教育不是你完成的事情

~

Any book worth banning is a book worth reading.

任何值得禁止的书都是值得阅读的书.

~

Writing, to me, is simply thinking through my fingers.

对我来说, 写作只是用手指思考.

~

Self - education is, I firmly believe, the only king of education there is.

我坚信, 自我教育是唯一的, 教育之王.

ASIMOV啊斯嘛a si ma

啊				
斯				
嘛				

ATTENBOROUGH爱登堡ai deng bao

[SIR] Richard Samuel Attenborough

I passionately believe in heroes, but I think the world has changed its criteria in determining who it describes as a hero.

我充满激情地相信英雄, 但我认为世界已经改变了确定英雄人物德标准.

爱				
登				
堡				

BACH巴赫ba he

Johann Sebastian Bach

"I play the notes as they are written, but it is God who makes the music."
我按字面上的音符演奏，但这是上帝创造的音乐.

巴					
赫					

BACON培根pei gen

[SIR] Francis Bacon

In order for the light to shine so brightly, the darkness must be present.
为了使光线如此明亮地发光，必须在黑暗.

培					
根					

BAUDRILLARD鲍德里亚bao de li ya

Jean Baudrillard

We live in a world where there is more and more information, and less and less meaning.
我们生活在一个信息越多. 含义越来越少的世界.

~

The only thing worse than being bored is being boring.
唯一比无聊更糟糕是无聊。

鲍					
德					

里					
亚					

BEETHOVEN贝多芬bei duo fen

Ludwig Van Beethoven

Music is the one incorporeal entrance into the higher world of knowledge which comprehends mankind but which mankind cannot comprehend.

音乐是进入人类的高等知识世界的唯一入口.人类无发理解.

贝					
多					
芬					

BEGIN贝京bei jing

Menachem Begin

Peace is the beauty of life. It is sunshine. It is the smile of a child, the love of a mother, the joy of a father, the togetherness of a family. It is the advancement of man, the victory of a just cause, the triumph of truth.

和平是生命之美.是阳光.它是孩子的微笑,母亲的爱,父亲的喜悦,家庭的团聚.这是人的进步,正义事业的胜利,真理的胜利.

贝					
京					

BELL贝尔bei er

Alexander Graham Bell

Before anything else, preparation is the key to success.
除此之外, 准备是成功的关键.

贝					
尔					

BELL贝尔bei er

Arthur William Bell III

The greatest question of all is whether our experience on this planet is "it" or whether there is something else. Things in the supernatural realm give support, strangely perhaps, to the things we take on faith.最大的问题是我们在这个星球上的经历是 "它" 还是其他什么东西.奇怪的是, 超自然领域的事物可能会支持我们所信仰的事物.

贝					
尔					

BENSON本森bin sen

Ezra Taft Benson

If you really want to receive joy and happiness, then serve others with all your heart. Lift their burden, and your own burden will be lighter.
如果您真的想获得快乐和幸福, 那就全心全意为他人服务.减轻他们的负担, 您自己的负担就会减轻.

本				
森				

BERKELEY柏克莱bai ke lai

George Berkeley

Truth is the cry of all, but the game of few.

真理是所有人的呐喊, 但很少有人参与.

柏					
克					
莱					

BERLE比丽bi li

Milton Berle

If opportunity doesn't knock, build a door.

如果机会没有敲门, 那就盖一扇门.

~

Laughter is an instant vacation.

笑声是一个瞬间的假期

比					
丽					

BERRA贝拉bei la

Lawrence Peter "Yogi" Berra

90 percent of baseball is mental; the other half is physical.

90%的棒球是精神上的, 另一半是身体上的.

贝					
拉					

BERRILL贝尔里bei er li

Roland Berrill

All good thoughts should be shared around the table!

所有好的想法都应该在桌子周围分享!

贝					
尔					
里					

BERTON布特bu te

Pierre Frances de Marigny Berton

I only write books about dead people. They can't sue..

我只写有关死者的书.他们不能起诉.

布					
特					

BIRD比尔德bi er de

Mary Brave Bird

The thing to keep in mind is that laws are framed by those who happen to be in power and for the purpose of keeping them in power.

要牢记的是,法律是由那些掌权的人制定的. 目的是使其保持执政的目的.

比					
尔					
德					

BISMARCK俾斯麦bi si mai

Otto Eduard Leopold von Bismarck

Politics is the art of the possible.

政治是可能的艺术.

俾					
斯					
麦					

BLANC布朗克bu lang ke

Melvin Jerome "Mel" Blanc

That's All Folks!

全是这样的人

布				
朗				
克				

BONO博弄bo nong

Salvortore Philip Sonny Bono

Don't cling to fame. You're just borrowing it. It's like money. You're going to die, and somebody else is going to get it.

不要固守名气.您只是在借钱.就像钱.你会死的, 其他人会死的.

博				
弄				

BRADBURY 吧如大步以 ba ru da bu yi
Ray Douglas Bradbury

You can't try to do things; you simply must do them.
您无法尝试做事; 您只需要做.

~

Everything is generated through your own will power.
一切都是通过自己的意志力产生的.

If you hide your ignorance, no one will hit you and you'll never learn.
如果您隐藏自己的无知, 没有人会打您, 您将永远学不会.

There are worse crimes then burning books. One of them is not reading them.
有比焚书更为恶劣的犯罪, 其中之一就是不读书.

You don't have to burn books to destroy a culture. Just get people to stop reading them.
您无需烧毁书籍即可破坏一种文化.只是让人们停止阅读它们.

Remember, with writing, what you're looking for is just one person to come up and tell you, 'I love you for what you do.
记住, 写作的时候, 你只需要一个人站出来告诉你, '我爱你, 因为你所做的一切.

A book has got smell. A new book smells great. An old book smells even better. An old book smells like ancient Egypt.
一本书有气味.一本新书闻起来很香.一本旧书闻起来更好.一本老书闻起来像古埃及.

We are cups, constantly and quietly being filled. The trick is, knowing how to tip ourselves over and let the beautiful stuff out.
我们是杯子, 不断地安静地充满.诀窍是, 知道如何给自己打翻, 让美丽的东西散发出来.

Collecting facts is important. Knowledge is important. But if you don't have an imagination to use the knowledge, civilization is nowhere.收集事实很重要.知识很重要.但是, 如果您没有想象力来使用这些知识, 那么文明就无处可寻.

I know you've heard it a thousand times before. But it's true – hard work pays off. If you want to be good, you have to practice, practice, practice. If you don't love something, then don't do it.

我知道您已经听过一千遍了.但这是真的－辛勤工作会带来回报.如果你想成为一个好人,就必须练习,练习,练习.如果您不爱某事,那就不要做.

BRADBURY吧如大步以ba ru da bu yi

吧					
如					
大					
步					
以					

BRAHMS勃拉姆斯bo la mu si

Johannes Brahms

If there is anyone here who I have not insulted, I beg his pardon.

如果这里有我没有侮辱过的人,请原谅.

勃					
拉					
姆					
斯					

BRYNNER比任热 bi ren re

Yuliy Borissovich Brynner

When I am dead and buried, on my tombstone I would like to have it written, 'I have arrived.' Because when you feel that you have arrived, you are dead.

当我死后被埋葬时, 我想在墓碑上写下 "我已经到了". 因为当您感觉到自己已经抵达时, 您已经死了.

比					
任					
热					

BURNS步任斯 bu ren si

George Burns

Too bad that all the people who know how to run the country are busy driving taxicabs and cutting hair.

可惜的是, 所有知道如何管理这个国家的人都忙着开出出租和剪头发.

步					
任					
斯					

CARLIN卡林 ka lin

George Denis Patrick Carlin

Don't just teach your children to read … teach them to question what they read. Teach them to question everything!

不要只是教你的孩子阅读···教他们质疑他们所读的内容.教他们质疑一切!

I think its the duty of the comedian to find out where the line is drawn and cross it deliberately .

我认为喜剧演员的职责是找出画线的地方, 然后故意穿过它.

卡					
林					

CARNEGIE卡内基ka nei ji

Dale Breckenridge Carnegie

Talk to someone about themselves and they'll listen for hours.

与某人谈论他们自己, 他们会听几个小时.

卡					
内					
基					

CASH卡实ka shi

Johnny Cash

Well, you wonder why I always dress in black, Why you never see bright colors on my back, And why does my appearance seem to have a somber tone. Well, there's a reason for the things that I have on. I wear the black for the poor and the beaten down, Livin' in the hopeless, hungry side of town, I wear it for the prisoner who has long paid for his crime.

好吧, 你想知道为什么我总是穿黑色衣服, 为什么你永远看不到我的背上明亮的色彩, 为什么我的外表看起来有些阴沉.好吧, 我拥有这些东西是有原因的.我为穷人和被殴打的人穿黑色的衣服, 在小镇绝望, 饥饿的一面生活, 为长期为他的罪行付出代价的囚犯戴上黑色的衣服.

卡					
实					

CASSIDY卡西迪ka xi di

Theodore Crawford "Ted" Cassidy

"You rang?"

《你打电话?》

卡					
西					
迪					

CASSIN卡心ka xin

Rene Cassin

All human beings are born free and equal in dignity and rights.

人人生而自由，在尊严和权利上一律平等.

卡					
心					

CASTRO卡斯特罗ka si te luo

Fidel Alejandro Castro Ruz

Victory has thousands father but failure always find itself an orphan.

胜利有成千上万的父亲，但失败总是使自己成为孤儿.

卡					
斯					
特					
罗					

CHANEL 香奈儿 xiang nai er

Gabrielle Bonheur "Coco" Chanel

I don't do fashion, I AM fashion.

我不做时尚, 我是时尚.

My life didn't please me, so I created my life.

我的生活不讨我喜欢, 所以我创造了我的生活.

Fashion fades, only style remains the same.

时尚褪色只有风格保持不变.

To achieve great things, we must first dream.

实现维大的事情, 我们必须首先梦想.

A girl should be two things: classy and fabulous.

一个女孩应该有两点: 优雅和漂亮.

Elegance comes from being as beautiful inside as outside.

优雅来自内外都一样美丽.

In order to be irreplaceable, one must always be different.

为了不可替代, 一个人必须始终保持不同.

I don't care what you think about me. I don't think about you at all.

我不在乎你对我的看法。 我根本不考虑你。

Don't spend time beating on a wall, hoping to transform it into a door.

不要花时间在墙上敲打，希望将其变成一扇门.

The best things in life are free. The second best things are very, very expensive.
生活中最好的东西都是免费的.第二好的东西非常非常昂贵.

You can be gorgeous at thirty, charmimg at forty, and irresistible for the rest of your life.
三十岁时年可以变得美丽， 四十岁时可以变得迷人，并且在您余生中都无法抗拒.

"Where should one use perfume?" a young woman asked. "Wherever one wants to be kissed."
一位年经女子问道：”应该在哪利使用使用香水？“ 任何想要被亲吻的地方.

Innovation! One cannot be forever innovating. I want to create classics.
革新! 一个不可能永远创新.我想创造经典.

There is no time for cut-and-dried monotony. There is time for work. And time for love. That leaves no other time.
没有时间进行单调的干燥.有时间上班.和爱的时间.这没有别的时间了.

Fashion is not something that exists in dresses only. Fashion is in the sky, in the street, fashion has to do with ideas, the way we live, what is happening.
时尚可不仅仅存在于穿着的衣服.时尚在天空中, 在大街上, 时尚与想法, 我们的生活方式以及正在发生的事情有关.

CHANEL香奈儿xiang nai er

香				
奈				
儿				

CHAPLIN卓别林zhuo bie lin
Charles Spencer Chaplin
Simplicity is not a simple thing.
简单不是一件容易的事.

In the end, everything is a gag.

最后，一动都是堵嘴.

A day without laughter is a day wasted.

没有欢笑的一天是没有意义的

Imagination means nothing without doing.

想象力没有做就没有任何意义.

I am at peace with God. My conflict is with Man.

我与上帝和平.我与人的冲突.

You have to believe in yourself. That's the secret.

您必须相信自己.那是秘密.

You'll never find rainbows, If you're looking down…

您将永远找不到彩虹，如果您低头 …

You'll find that life is still worthwhile, if you just smile.

如果您只是微笑，您会发现生活仍然值得.

I will not join any club who will take me as a member.

我不会加入任何会成为我会员的俱乐部.

Time is the best author. It always writes the perfect ending.

时间是最好的作者.它总是写出完美的结局.

You are only as good as the woman you are standing beside.

你和站在旁边的女人一样好.

I have found that great ideas come when you have a great desire to have them.

我发见，当您渴望拥有一个伟大的想法时，他们就会来.

I do not need drugs to be a genius, do not take a genius to be human, but I need your smile to be happy.

我不需要毒品成为天才，不需要天才成为人类，但是我需要你的微笑才能快乐。

Life is a play that does not allow testing. So, sing, cry, dance, laugh and live intensely, before the curtain closes and the piece ends with no applause.

生活是不允许测试的戏剧. 因此, 唱歌, 哭泣, 跳舞, 大笑和生活激烈, 在帷幕关闭之前, 这首歌没有掌声结束.

CHAPLIN 卓别林 zhuo bie lin

卓				
别				
林				

CHAUCER 乔叟 qiao sou

Geoffrey Chaucer

Nothing Ventured, Nothing Gained.

不入虎穴, 焉得虎子.

乔				
叟				

CHRISTIE 克里斯蒂 ke li si di

Agatha Christie

I have sometimes been wildly, despairingly, acutely miserable,
racked with sorrow, but through it all I still know quite certainly that
just to be alive is a grand thing.

我有时候经历了狂绝望, 极度悲惨, 悲痛欲绝, 但通过这一切, 我仍
然很清楚地知道, 活着是一件大事.

克				
里				

斯					
蒂					

CHURCHILL丘吉尔qiu ji er

[SIR] Winston Leonard Spencer-Churchill

Never, never, never give up.

绝对绝对绝对不要放弃

~

The farther back you can look, the farther forward you are likely to see.

您可以向后看得越远，就越有有可能看到越远.

~

Let us brace ourselves to our duties and so bear ourselves that, if the British Empire and its Commonwealth last for a thousand years, men will still say 'This was their finest hour'."

让我们振作起来履行我们的职责，并承担起自己的责任，这样，如果大英帝国及其英联邦持续一千年，人们仍然会说'这是他们最美好的时刻'."

CHURCHILL丘吉尔qiu ji er

丘					
吉					
尔					

CLARK克拉克ke la ke

Arthur Charles Clark

A well-stocked mind is safe from boredom.

储备充足的头脑可以避免无聊.

The future is not to be forecast, but created.

未来不是可以预测的，而是可以创造的.

If children have interests, then education happens.
如果孩子有兴趣，就会进行教育.

~

In all the universe there is nothing more precious than mind.
在所有宇宙中, 没有什么比心灵更珍贵了.

Any sufficiently advanced technology is indistinguishable from magic.
任何足够先进的技术都无法与魔术区分开.

~

I'm sure the universe is full of intelligent life. It's just been too intelligent to come here.
我确信宇宙充满了智慧的生活.来这里太聪明了.

~The limits of the possible can only be defined by going beyond them into the impossible.
可能性的极限只能通过超越不可能的极限来定义.

Two possibilities exist: Either we are alone in the Universe or we are not. Both are equally terrifying.
存在两种可能性：要么我们独自一人在宇宙中, 要么我们不是.两者同样令人恐惧.

I want to be remembered most as a writer - one who entertained readers, and, hopefully, stretched their imagination as well.
做为一位作家, 我最想被人记住吸引者的人们, 并希望也能扩大他们的想象力.

~

When you finally understand the universe, it will not only be stranger than you imagine, it will be stranger than you can imagine.
当您最终了解了宇宙时,它不仅会比您想象的要陌生, 而且会比您想象的要陌生.

~

New ideas pass through three periods: 1) It can't be done. 2) It probably can be done, but it's not worth doing. 3) I knew it was a good idea all along!
新想法经历了三个阶段：1）无法做到.2）也许可以做到, 但是不值得这样做.3）我一直都知道这是个好主意!

~

Sometimes when I'm in a bookstore or library, I am overwhelmed by all the things that I do not know. Then I am seized by a powerful desire to read all the books, one by one.

有时, 当我在书店或图书馆里时, 我不知所措的一切使我不知所措.然后, 我被一种渴望阅读所有书籍的强烈愿望所吸引.

~

Perhaps, as some wit remarked, the best proof that there is Intelligent Life in Outer Space is the fact it hasn't come here. Well, it can't hide forever - one day we will overhear it.

也许, 正如一些机智人士所说, 外太空中存在智能生命的最好证明就是它还没有出现.好吧, 它不可能永远隐藏-有一天我们会偷听它.

People go through four stages before any revolutionary development: 1. It's nonsense, don't waste my time. 2. It's interesting, but not important. 3. I always said it was a good idea. 4. I thought of it first.

人们在经历任何革命性发展之前都经历了四个阶段：1.这是胡扯, 不要浪费我的时间. 2.这很有趣, 但并不重要. 3.我总是说这是个好主意.4.我首先想到了.

CLARK克拉克ke la ke

克					
拉					
克					

COHEN科恩ke en

Leonard Norman Cohen

There is a crack in everything.That's how the light gets in.

一切都有裂缝. 这就是光线的进入方式.

科					
恩					

COLEMAN科尔曼ke er man

Patrick Vincent Coleman

Hold up the train. Ammunition ship afire in harbour making for Pier 6 and will explode. Guess this will be my last message. Good-bye boys.

停下火车.弹药船在港口起火, 驶向6号码头, 将爆炸.我想这是我最后的留言了.再见, 孩子们.

科					
尔					
曼					

CONFUCIUS孔夫子kong fu zi

You can not open a book without learning something.

没有学习你就不能打开一本书.

Life is really simple, but men insist on making it complicated.

生活真的很简单, 但是人们坚持要让生活变得复杂.

It does not matter how slowly you go, as long as you do not stop.

只有走不停, 走多慢都没关系.

Choose a job you love, and you will never have to work a day in your life!

选择一份自己喜欢工作您将一生都不必工作一天.

Learning without thought is labor lost; thought without learning is perilous.

没有思想的学习会浪费劳动力.没有学习的思想是危险的.

By three methods we may learn wisdom; first by reflection, which is noblest; second, by imitation, which is easiest; and third by experience, which is the bitterest.

我们可以通过三种方法来学习智慧.首先是反思, 这是最崇高的; 其次, 通过模仿, 这是最简单的; 第三是经验, 这是最痛苦的.

CONFUCIUS孔夫子kong fu zi

孔					
夫					
子					

COSELL口测kou ce

Howard William Cosell

This is Howard Cosell telling it like it is.
这是霍话德*科赛你说的那样.

After all, is football a game or a religion?
毕竟, 足球是一扬比赛还是一种宗教?

What's right isn't always popular. What's popular isn't always right.
正确的方法并开总是受欢迎.流行并不总是正确的.

Stand for something. Don't quest for popularity at the expense of morality and ethics and honesty.
代表某事. 不要以道德, 道德和诚实为代价来寻求受欢迎.

Then there is a still higher type of courage - the courage to brave pain, to live with it, to never let others know of it and to still find joy in life; to wake up in the morning with an enthusiasm for the day ahead.
然后, 还有一种更大的勇气:勇敢地忍受痛苦, 与痛苦相处, 从不让别人知道它并仍然在生活中找到快乐的勇气.早晨充满热情地为前一天醒来.

COSELL口测kou ce

口					
测					

COUSTEAU哭思头ku si tou

Jacque-Yves Cousteau

The sea is the universal sewer.

大还是通用的下道.

哭					
思					
头					

CRICK卡尔可ka er ke

Francis Crick

I had discovered the gossip test—what you are really interested in is what you gossip about.

我发现了八卦测试-您真正感兴趣的是您八卦.

卡					
尔					
可					

CRONKITE克朗凯特ka lang kai te

Walter Leland Cronkite Jr.

... and that's the way it is!

就是这样!

卡					
朗					

凯					
特					

DANGERFIELD丹戈菲尔德dan ge fei er de

Roger Dangerfield

I get no respect!.

我没有宗师!

丹					
戈					
菲					
尔					
德					

DARWIN达尔文da er wen

Charles Robert Darwin

A man who dares to waste one hour of time has not discovered the value of life.

一个敢于浪费一个小时时间的人并没有发现生命的价值.

达					
尔					
文					

Da VINCI达芬奇da fen qi

Leonardo Da VINCI

Learning never exhausts the mind.

学习永远不会耗尽思想.

Time stays long enough for those who use it.

时间对于使用它的人来活足够长.

~

The noblest pleasure is the joy of understanding.

最崇高的荣幸就是理解的喜悦.

~

The painter has the Universe in his mind and hands.

画家的思想和双手都拥有宇宙.

~

One can have no smaller or greater mastery than mastery of oneself.

一个人对自己的掌握不会比它更大或更精通.

~

Study without desire spoils the memory, and it retains nothing that it takes in.

没有欲望的学习破坏了记忆. 它没有保留任何东西.

~

Painting is poetry that is seen rather than felt, and poetry is painting that is felt rather than seen.

绘画是看得见而不是感觉的诗歌，而诗歌是看得见而不是感觉的绘画.

Da VINCI达芬奇da fen qi

达				
芬				
奇				

DEAN得能dei neng

James Dean

Live fast, die young, leave a good looking corpse.

活得快， 早逝，留下一个好看的尸体.

Dream as if you'll live forever. Live as if you'll die today.

梦想，就像你将永远活着.生活就好像你今天要死.

Dance as if no one's watching. Love as if it's all you know.

好像没人在看一样跳舞.爱，就好像你所知道的一样.

I think the prime reason for existence, for living in this world is discovery.

我认为生话在这个世界上的根本原因是发现.

Am I in love? Absolutely. I'm in love with ancient philosophers, foreign painters, classic authors, and musicians who have died long ago.

我恋爱了吗? 绝对.我爱上了早逝的古代哲学家, 外国画家, 古典作家和音乐.

DEAN得能dei neng

得					
能					

DESCARTES笛卡特di ka er

Rene Descartes

I think, therefore I am.

我想，因此我就是.

~

Conquer yourself rather than the world。

征服自己而不是世界

~

It is not enough to have a good mind, the main thing is to use it well.

拥有足够的头脑还不够，主要是要善用它.

~

The reading of all good books is like conversation with the finest men of past centuries.
读所有书就象与过去几个世纪的最优秀人物交谈.

DESCARTES笛卡特di ka er

笛					
卡					
特					

DIANA戴安娜dai an na

Princess Diana

Carry out a random act of kindness, with no expectation of reward, safe in the knowledge that one day someone might do the same for you.

在知道某人天可能会为您做同样的事情的情况下。请放心递进一次不带回报的随意的善举.

DIANA戴安娜dai an na

戴					
安					
娜					

DICKINSON

Emily Elizabeth Dickinson

Forever is composed of nows.

永远是由当下组成的.

Dickinson 狄金森di jin sen

狄					
金					
森					

DIEFENBAKER迪芬贝克di fen ba ka

John George Diefenbaker

He who does not know the past can never understand the present, and he certainly can do nothing for the future.

不了解过去的人永远不会了解现在，他当然能未来做任何事情.

~

I am a Canadian, free to speak without fear, free to worship in my own way, free to stand for what I think right, free to oppose what I believe wrong, or free to choose those who shall govern my country. This heritage of freedom I pledge to uphold for myself and all mankind.

我是加拿大人，可以自由发言而无所畏惧，可以自由地以自己的方式崇拜，可以自由地代表我认为正确的事物，可以自由地反对我认为错误的事物，或者可以自由选择将统治我国的人.我保证为自己和全人类维护这种自由的遗产.

~

The Liberals are the flying saucers of politics. No one can make head nor tail of them and they never are seen twice in the same place.

自由主义者是政治的飞碟.没有人能制造它们的头和尾，在同一个地方它们从来没有两次被看见过.

DIEFENBAKER迪芬贝克di fen ba ka

迪					
芬					

贝					
克					

DILLER迪乐di le

Phyllis Ada Driver Diller

A smile is a curve that sets everything straight.

微笑是一条曲线, 可以使所有事物变得笔直.

迪					
乐					

DISNEY迪斯尼di si ni

Walt Elias Disney

Growing old is mandatory, but growing up is optional.

变老是必须的, 但成长是可以选择的.

~

If you can dream it, you can do it. Always remember this whole thing was started by a mouse.

如果您可以梦想, 那么您可以做到.永远记住这整个过程是由鼠标启动的.

~

We keep moving forward, opening new doors, and doing new things, because we're curious and curiosity keeps leading us down new paths.

我们不断前进, 打开新的门, 做新的事情, 因为我们很好奇, 好奇心使我们走上新的道路.

DISNEY迪斯尼di si ni

迪					
斯					

尼					

DOSTOEVSKY陀思妥耶夫斯基tuo si tuo ye fu si ji

Fyodor Mikhailovich Dostoevsky

Nov 11, 1821 - Feb 09, 1881

The soul is healed by being with children.

与孩子在一起可以治愈灵魂.

The secret of man's being is not only to live but to have something to live for.

人存在的秘密不仅在于生活, 还在于为生活而话.

陀					
思					
妥					
耶					
夫					
斯					
基					

DOUGLAS杜格拉斯du ge la si

Thomas Clement "Tommy" Douglas

I don't mind being a symbol but I don't want to become a monument.

There are monuments all over the Parliament Buildings and I've

seen what the pigeons do to them.

我不介意成为象征, 但我不想成

为纪念碑.国会大厦上遍布着纪念碑, 我已经看到了鸽子对它们的作

用.

杜					
格					
拉					
斯					

DOYLE道尔dao er

Arthur Conan Doyle

When you have eliminated the impossible, whatever remains, however improbable, must be the truth.

当您消除了不可能的事情之后，无论多么不可能的事情，剩下的都是事实.

道					
尔					

DUDEK杜德克du de ke

Louis Dudek

A critic at best is a waiter at the great table of literature.

评论家充其量不过是文学大舞台上的诗应生.

杜					
德					
克					

DURAS都拉斯du la si

Marguerite Duras [pseudonym]

A Man and a Woman, Say What You Like, They're Different.

一个男人和一个女人，说你喜欢的，他们是不同的

~

Compared with your past beautiful outlooking, I love your nowaday tortured face more.

与你过去美丽的外表相比，我更爱你现在扭曲的脸.

都					
拉					
斯					

EDISON爱迪生ai di sheng

Thomas Alva Edison

Our greatest weakness lies in giving up. The most certain way to succeed is always to try just one more time.

我们最大的弱点在于放弃.成功的最确定的方法是总是再尝试一次.

爱					
迪					
生					

EDWARDS爱德华兹ai de hua zi

Henrietta Muir Edwards

This decision marks the abolition of sex in politics… We sought to establish the personal individuality of woman.

这一决定标志着政治上废除了性······我们试图建立女性的个人个性.

爱					
德					
华					
兹					

EINSTEIN爱因斯坦ai yin si tan

Albert Einstein

The more I learn, the more I realize how much I don't know.
我学的越多，就越意识到自己不知道的东西有多少.

~

Anyone who has never made a mistake has never tried anything new.
从未犯错的人从未尝试过任何斯事物.

The only reason for time is so that everything doesn't happen at once.
时间的唯一原因是确保一动都不会立即发生.

Life is like riding a bicycle. To keep your balance, you must keep moving.
生活就像骑自行车.为了保持平衡，您必须继续前进.

Wisdom is not a product of schooling, but of the life-long attempt to acquire it.
知道不是学校教育的产物，而是终身学习的产物.

Insanity: doing the same thing over and over again and expecting different results.
精神错乱：一遍又一遍地做同样的事情，期望得到不同的结果.

Education is what remains after one has gotten what one has learned in school.
教育是人们在学校到的东西之后剩下的东西.

The human mind is not capable of grasping the Universe. We are like a little child entering a huge library. ...
人类的思维无法掌握宇宙.我们就像一个小孩进入一个巨大的图书馆. ...

I fear the day that technology will surpass our human interaction. The world will have a generation of idiots.

我担心科技将超越人类互动的那一天.世界将有一代白痴.

There are only two ways to live your life. One is as though nothing is a miracle. The other is as though everything is a miracle.

生活只有两种方式. 一个好像没有什么是奇迹. 另一个好像一切都是奇迹.

EINSTEIN爱因斯坦ai yin si tan

爱					
因					
斯					
坦					

EISENHOWER艾森豪威尔ai sen hao wei er

Dwight David Eisenhower

Plans are nothing; planning is everything.

计划无济于事;规划就是一切.

Never waste a minute thinking about people you don't like.

不要浪费时间思考喜欢的人.

What counts is not necessarily the size of the dog in the fight - it's the size of the fight in the dog.

重要的不一定是战斗中狗的大小—它是犬中战斗的大小.

艾					
森					

豪					
威					
尔					

EMERSON爱默生ai mo sheng

Ralph Waldo Emerson

Every artist was first an amateur.

每个艺术家最初都是业余爱好者.

~

Win as if your used to it, lose as if you enjoyed it for a change.

胜利就好像您习惯了, 失败就好像您喜欢改变一样.

~

Write it on your heart that every day is the best day in your year.

请记住, 每天都是一年中最美好的一天.

~

For every minute you are angry you lose sixty seconds of happiness.

每生气一分钟, 就会失去六十秒的幸福.

~

I cannot remember the books I've read any more than the meals I have eaten, even so, they have made me.

除了吃过的饭吃, 我已经不清我读过的书了, 即使如此, 它们也使我受益匪浅.

EMERSON爱默生ai mo sheng

爱					
默					
生					

EURIPIDES欧里比得斯ou li bi de si

Euripides

Question everything. Learn something. Answer nothing.

质疑一切.学点东西.什么都不要回答

欧					
里					
比					
得					
斯					

FERBER菲伯fei bo

Edna Ferber

Christmas isn't a season. It's a feeling.

圣诞节不是一个季节.这是一种感觉.

~

It's terrible to realize you don't learn how to live until you're ready to die, and then it's too late.

很难意识到, 在你准备好死亡之前, 你不会学会如何生活, 然后就太晚了.

~

Life can't defeat a writer who is in love with writing, for life itself is a writer's lover until death.

生活不能打败一个热爱写作的作家, 因为生活本身就是一个作家的情人, 直到死.

FERBER菲伯fei bo

菲					

伯					

FERMI费米fei mi

Enrico Fermi

Where is everybody?

《哪里大家》

费					
米					

FLEMING弗莱明fu lai ming

[SIR] Alexander Fleming

Nature makes penicillin; I just found it.

大自然制造青霉素;我刚刚找到了.

~

One sometimes finds what one is not looking for.

有时候,人们会找到不想要的东西.

~

For the birth of something new, there has to be a happening.

对于新事物的诞生,必须要发生.

~

The unprepared mind cannot see the outstretched hand of opportunity.

措手不及的头脑看不到机遇.

~

It is the lone worker who makes the first advance in a subject; the details may be worked out by a team, but the prime idea is due to enterprise, thought, and perception of an individual.

在一个学科上取得进步的是孤独的工人.细节可以由团队制定,但主要想法是由于个人的进取心,思想和感知.

~

For the birth of something new, there has to be a happening. Newton saw an apple fall; James Watt watched a kettle boil; Roentgen fogged some photographic plates. And these people knew enough to translate ordinary happenings into something new.

对于新事物的诞生，必须要发生.牛顿看见苹果掉了下来.詹姆斯•沃特（James Watt）看着水壶烧开.伦琴给一些照相底片弄雾了.这些人足够了解，可以将平凡的事情转化为新事物.

弗					
莱					
明					

FORD福特fu te

Henry Ford

Vision without execution is just hallucination.
没有执行力的愿景只是幻觉.

Worry is the most wasteful thing in the world.
忧虑是世界上最浪费的事情.

You can do anything if you have enthusiasm.
如果您有然情，可以做任何事情.

Quality is doing it right when no one is looking.
没有人注视时，质量就是对的.

Don't find fault, find a remedy; anybody can complain.
不要发现错误，请寻求补救措施任何人都可以抱怨.

If you've never failed you've never tried anything new.
如果您从未失败过，就不会尝试任何新的尝试.

My best friend is the one who brings out the best in me.
我最好的朋友是发掘我最好的朋友.

Those who walk with God always reach their destination.

与上帝同行的人总能利达目的地.

Education is pre-eminently a matter of quality not amount.

教育首先是质量而不是数量的问题.

Whether you think you can or you think you can't your right!

无论您认为自己有权利还是认为自己没有权利

Life is a series of experiences, each one of which makes us bigger.

人生是一系列的经历，每一次经历都使我们变得更大.

If everyone is moving forward together, then success takes care of itself.

如果每一人都一起前进, 那么成功就取决于自己.

The secret of a successful life is to find out what is ones destiny to do, and then do it.

成功人生的秘诀是找出自己, 该做的事, 然后再去做.

Thinking is the hardest thing there is, which is probably the reason why so few engage in it.

思考事最困难的事情, 这可能是很少有人参与其中的原因.

Even a mistake may turn out to be the one thing necessary to a worthwhile achievement.

即使是错误, 也可能是成就有价值的成就的一件事.

Coming together is a beginning; keeping together is progress; working together is success.

在一起是一个开始; 团结是进步; 共同努力就是成功.

Anyone who stops learning is old, whether at twenty of eighty.
Any one who keeps learning stays young.

停止学习的人都老了, 不管是八十岁.任何不断学习的人都可以保持年轻.

The object of education is not to fill a man's mind with facts; it is to teach him how to use his mind in thinking.

教育的目的不是要用事实充实一个人的思想, 而是要教他如何在思想中运用自己的思想.

When everything seems to be going against you remember that an airplane takes off against the wind, not with it.

当一切似乎都在逆转时, 请记住,飞机是随风而起, 而不是随风而起.

Failure is simply the opportunity to begin again, this time more intelligently. There is no disgrace in honest failure; there is disgrace in fearing to fail.

失败只是重新开始的机会，这次是更明智的选择.诚实的失败是没有耻辱的.害怕失败是可耻的.

FORD福特fu te

福					
特					

FOX福克斯fu ke si

Terrance Stanley "Terry" Fox

I've said to people before that I'm going to do my very best to make it, and I'm not going to give up. And that's true. But I might not make it. And if I don't make it, the Marathon of Hope better continue.

我之前已经对人们说过, 我会尽力做到这一点, 并且我不会放弃.没错.但是我可能做不到.如果我没有做到, 希望马拉松最好继续.

福					
克					
斯					

FRIEDMAN弗里德曼fu li de man

Esther Pauline Friedman (aka Anne Landers)

The naked truth is always better than the best dressed lie.

赤裸裸的事实总是比装腔作势的谎言好.

弗					

里					
德					
曼					

FROBEL弗罗贝尔fu luo bei er

Friedrich Wilhelm August Frobel

The purpose of education is to encourage and guide man

as a conscious, thinking and perceiving being...

教育的目的是鼓励和引导人作为一个有意识的, 思考和感知存在的人这是我的荣幸....

弗					
罗					
贝					
尔					

FREUD佛洛伊德fo luo yi de

Sigmund Schlomo Freud

From error to error, one discovers the entire truth.

从错误到错误, 人们发现了全部真相.

佛					
洛					

伊					
德					

FULLER富勒fu le

Richard Buckminister "Bucky" Fuller

You can't learn less.

你不能少学.

富					
勒					

GAGARIN加加林jia jia lin

Yuri Alekseyevich Gagarin

I looked and looked but I didn't see God.

我看了又看,但没有上帝.

加					
加					
林					

GARLAND加兰jia lan

Judy Garland

Always be a first-rate version of yourself, instead of a second - rate version of somebody else.

永远是自己的一流版本, 而不是别人的一流版本.

加					
兰					

GANDHI 甘地gan di

Mahatma Gandhi

God has no religion.

圣帝没有宗教

~

Be the change that you wish to see in the world.

成为您希望在世界上看到的变比

~

An eye for an eye will only make the whole world blind.

以眼还眼只会使整个世界变得盲目

~

Freedom is not worth having if it does not include the freedom to make mistakes.

如果自由不包括犯错的自由，那么就不值得拥有有自由.

甘					
地					

GEHRIG各日工ge ri gong

Henry Louis "Lou" Gehrig

There is no room in baseball for discrimination. It is our national pastime and a game for all.

棒球中没有歧视的余地.这是我们的民族消遣，也是所有人的游戏.

各					

日					
工					

GOEBBELS 戈培尔 ge pei er

Paul Joseph Goebbels

..the rank and file are usually much more primitive than we imagine. Propaganda must therefore always be essentially simple and repetitious.

...等级和档案通常比我们想象的要原始得多.因此, 宣传必须始终本质上讲是简单而重复的.

戈					
培					
尔					

GOETHE 哥德 ge de

Johann Wolfgang von Goethe

A man should hear a little music, read a little poetry, and see a fine picture every day of his life, in order that worldly cares may not obliterate the sense of the beautiful which God has implanted in the human soul.

一个人应该每天听一点音乐,读一点诗歌, 看一幅美的图画, 以免世宿的关心不能抹杀上帝植入人心中的美丽感。

哥					
德					

GOLD金 jin

Thomas Gold

In choosing a hypothesis there is no virtue in being timid. I clearly would have been burned at the stake in another age.

选择一个假设,没有胆怯的美德.我显然会在另一个时代被火刑柱烧死.

金				

GUATAMA寡头吗 gua tou ma

Siddhartha Guatama [Buddha]

There is nothing more dreadful than the habit of doubt.

没有比怀疑使可怕的东西了

寡				
头				
吗				

GUILEY吉利gui li

Rosemary Ellen Guiley

True healing must come first at the Soul level... prayer aligns our souls with God... By aligning ourselves with God - this highest possible state of unconditional love, joy, and wholeness - we can overcome anything, be healed of all afflictions.

真正的疗愈必须在灵魂层面首先出现…祈祷使我们的灵魂与上帝保持一致…通过使我们自己与上帝保持一致——这是无条件的爱,快乐和完整的最高境界——我们可以克服任何事情,治愈所有的痛苦.

~

Real magic is not about gaining power over others: it is about gaining power over yourself.

真正的魔法不是获得超越他人的权力:而是获得超越自己的权力.

吉				

利					

HAINES海恩斯hai en si

William Lister Haines

Limits exist only in the soul's of Those who don't dream.
限制只存在于那些不做梦的人的灵魂中.

海					
恩					
斯					

HARVEY哈维ha wei

Paul Harvey

and now you know The Rest of the Story.
《现在你知道故事》

哈					
维					

HAWKING霍金huo jin

Stephen William Hawking

Life would be tragic if it weren't funny!
没有乐趣的生活是悲惨的

霍					

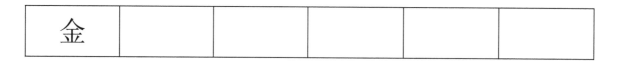

金					

HAY 海 hai

Louise Lynn Hay

If a thought or belief does not serve you, let it go!
某个某个想法或新念不能为您服务，那就放手吧.

The point of power is always in the present moment.
权力的关键始终在当下.

I am in the right place, at the right time, doing the right thing.
我在正确的位置，正确的时间做正确的事情.

Each day is a new opportunity. I chose to make this day a great one.
每天都是新的机会. 我选择让这一天成为美好的一天一.

Love is the great miracle cure. Loving ourselves works miracles in our lives.
爱是伟大的奇迹疗法.爱自己会创造奇迹我们的生命.

I do not fix problems. I fix my thinking. Then problems fix themselves.
我没有解决问题. 我固定我的想法. 然后解决问题他们自己.

It's okay to learn from every experience, and it's okay to make mistakes.
可以从各种经验中习，他可以犯错误.

Remember, you have been criticizing yourself for years and it hasn't worked. Try approving of yourself and see what happens.
请记住，您多年来一直在批评自己，没用 尝试批准自己，看看会 生什么.

No matter where we live on the planet or how difficult our situation seems to be, we have the ability to overcome and transcend our circumstances.
无论我们生活在地球上的任何地方，或者我们有多困难情况似乎是.
我们有能力克服和超越我们的情况.

Each one of us has a three-year-old child within us, and we often spend most of our time yelling at that kid in ourselves. Then we wonder why our lives don't work.
我们每个人中都有一个三岁的孩子，我们经常花我们大部分时间对自己
的那个孩子大喊大叫. 然后我们想知道为什么我们的生活不起作用.

海					

HEARST赫斯特he si te

William Randolph Hearst Sr.

Don't be afraid to make a mistake, your readers might like it.

不要害怕犯错误，你的读者可能会喜欢。

赫					
斯					
特					

HEMINGWAY海明威 hai ming wei

Ernest Miller Hemingway

There is no friend as loyal as a book.

没有像书一样忠诚的朋友.

~

When people talk, listen completely. Most people never listen.

人们说话时，请完全听.大多数人从不听.

~

My aim is to put down on paper what I see and what I feel in the best and simplest way.

我的目标是以最好和最简单的方式在纸上写下不我所看到的和我的感觉.

海					
明					
威					

HENSON很森hen sen

James Maury "Jim" Henson

My hope still is to leave the world a bit better than when I got here.
我的希望仍然是离开世界比我来利这到时更好.

The most sophisticated people I know - inside they are all children.
我认识的最老练的人- 他们内部是孩子.

Life's like a movie, write your own ending. Keep believing, keep pretending.
生活就像电影, 写下自己的结局.　继续相信, 继续假装.

[Kids] don't remember what you try to teach them. They remember what you are.
[孩子们]不记得您想教他们什么.他们记得你是什么.

If you care about what you do and work hard at it, there isn't anything you can't do if you want to.
如果您关心自己的工作并努力工作, 那么就可以做任何事情

很				
森				

HEPBURN赫本he ben

Audrey Hepburn

The beauty of a woman is not in a facial mode but the true beauty in a woman is reflected in her soul. It is the caring that she lovingly gives the passion that she shows. The beauty of a woman grows with the passing years.
女人的美丽不是面部表情, 而是女人的真正美丽反映在她的灵魂中.她充满爱心地给予了她所表现出的热情.女人的美丽随着岁月的流逝而增长.

赫				
本				

HERACLITUS赫拉克利特he la ke li te

The path up and the path down are one and the same.

《向上走的路和向下的路是同一条路.》

赫					
拉					
克					
利					
特					

HERODOTUS希罗多斯xi luo duo si

Herodotus c. 484 – c. 425 BC

The destiny of man is in his own soul.

人的名媛在于他自己的灵魂.

All men's gains are the fruit of venturing.

所有男人的收获都是冒险的结果.

Great deeds are usually wrought at great risks.

通常要冒很大风险.

Neither snow, nor rain, nor heat, nor gloom of night stays these courageous couriers from the swift completion of their appointed rounds.

这些勇敢的信使从迅速完成其指定的巡回检查后, 就不会下雪, 下雨, 也不会热, 也没有夜晚的阴沉.

Some men give up their designs when they have almost reached the goal; While others, on the contrary, obtain a victory by exerting, at the last moment, more vigorous efforts than ever before.

有些人在几乎达到目标时就放弃了设计. 相反, 其他人则在最后一刻通过比以往任何时候都更有力的努力取得了胜利.

希					
罗					
多					
斯					

HEWLETT木利特mu li te

William Redington Hewlett

There is a time and a place for creativity.

有时间和创造力的地方.

木					
利					
特					

HINCKLEY欣克利xin ke li

Gordon Bitner Hinckley

Life is meant to be enjoyed, not just endured.。

生活是应该亨爱的. 而不仅仅是忍受.

欣					
克					
利					

HITCHCOCK希区阿克xi qu a ke

Alfred Joseph Hitchcock

There is no terror in a bang, only in the anticipation of it.

爆炸没有恐怖。只有在期待它的时候.

希					
区					
阿					
克					

HITLER希特勒Xi te le

Adolf Hitler

I use emotion for the many and reserve reason for the few.

我为许多人运用情感，为少数人保留理由.

希					
特					
勒					

HOLMES霍姆斯 huo mu si

Oliver Wendell Holmes Sr.

The sound of a kiss is not so loud as that of a cannon, but its echo lasts a great deal longer.

亲吻的声音不象大跑那样响亮， 但是回声可以持持续更长的时间.

霍				
姆				
斯				

HOMME侯马hou ma

Robert "Bob" Homme

Look up ~ way up!

看上 看恨上

侯				
马				

HOPE霍普huo pu

Bob Hope

I have seen what a laugh can do. It can transform almost unbearable tears into something bearable, even hopeful.

我已经知道笑能做什么.它可以将几乎无法忍受的眼泪变成可以忍受甚至希望的东西.

霍				
普				

HOWARD霍华德huo hua de

Harlan Perry Howard

Country music is three chords and the truth.

乡村音乐是三个和弦与真理

霍					
华					
德					

HOYLE霍伊尔huo yi er

Fred Hoyle

When I was young, the old regarded me as an outrageous young fellow, and now that I'm old the young regard me as an outrageous old fellow.

当我还年轻的时候，老人就把我当成是一个令人发指的年轻人，而现在，我已经老了，那个年经人就把我当成了一个令人发指的老家伙.

霍					
伊					
尔					

HUBBLE哈伯ha bo

Edwin Powell Hubble

Equipped with his five senses, man explores the universe around him and calls the adventure Science.

配备了五种感官的人探索了周围的宇宙，并称之为冒险科学.

哈					
伯					

HUGO雨果yu guo

Victor Marie Hugo

He who opens a school door, closes a prison.

打开校门，关闭监狱的人.

~

People do not lack strength; they lack will.

人不缺乏力量，他们缺乏意志.

~

The future has many names: for the weak is unattainable, for the fearful is the unknown. For the brave the opportunity.

未来有许多名字:因为弱者是无法达到的，因为恐惧者是未知的.为了
勇敢的机会.

雨					
果					

HUME休谟xiu mo

David Hume

Beauty in things exists in the mind which contemplates them.

事物的美存在于恩考它们的恩想中.

休					
谟					

HUXLEY赫胥黎he xu li

Aldous Leonard Huxley

The most valuable of all education is the ability to make yourself do the thing you have to do, when it has to be done, whether you like it or not.

在所有教育中，最有价值的是使自己能够做自己必须做事情，必须完成的事情能为.无论
是否喜欢.

赫					
胥					
黎					

IACOCCA艾科卡ai ke ka

Lido Anthony "Lee" Iacocca

If you can find a better car, then buy it!

如果你能找到更好的汽车，那就买吧!

艾					
科					
卡					

INGERSOLL英格索尔ying ge suo er

Robert Green Ingersoll

Everything is temporary.

切都是暂时的.

英					
格					
索					
尔					

JACKSON杰克逊jie ke xun

Michael Jackson

Just because it's in print, doesn't mean it's the Gospel.

仅仅因为它已经出版了，并不意味着它就是福音书

杰					
克					
逊					

JAMES詹姆斯zhan mu si

William James

A new idea is first condemned as ridiculous and then dismissed as trivial, until finally, it becomes what everybody knows.

一个新的想法首先被指责为荒谬，当候被认为是琐碎的，   直到最后，它变成了大家知道东西.

詹					
姆					
斯					

JESUS耶稣ye su

Jesus the Christ

He that is without sin among you, let him first cast a stone at her.

在你们中间没有罪的他，首先让他向她投石.

John/约翰 8:7

I am ascending to my Father and your Father, to my God and your God.

我升上我的父亲和你的父亲，   升到我的上帝和你的上帝.

John/约翰 20:17

But I say unto you, Love your enemies, bless them that curse you, do good to them that hate you, and pray for them which despitefully use you, and persecute you.

但是我对你说，爱你的敌人，祝福那些诅咒你的敌人，恨你的人行善，并为那些尽管利用率你，迫害你的人祈祷。

Matt 5:44

JOBS贾伯斯jia bo si

Steve Jobs

I want to put a ding in the universe.

我想在宇宙中摆个钟声

~

Your time is limited, so don't waste it living someone else's life.

您的时间是有限的，所以不要浪费时间过别人的生活。

贾					
伯					
斯					

JOPLIN加普林jia pu lin

Janis Joplin

On stage I make love to twenty five thousand people; and then I go home alone.

在舞台上，我与两万五千人做爱，然后我一个人回家。

加					
普					
林					

JUNG荣格rong ge

Carl Gustav Jung

Show me a sane man and I will cure him for you.

给我看一个神志清醒的人，我会帮你治好他的.

荣					
格					

KALAM卡拉姆 ka la mu

Avul Pakir Jainulabdeen (A.P.J.) Abdul Kalam

Man needs his difficulties because they are necessary to enjoy success.

人需要他的困难，因为他们必须亨受成功.

Dream is not that which you see while sleeping it is something that does not let you sleep.

梦不是你睡觉时看到的东西，而是不让你睡觉的东西.

I firmly believe that unless one has tasted the bitter pill of failure, one cannot aspire enough for success.

我坚信，除非有人尝过失败的苦果. 否则就无法向往成功.

卡					
拉					
姆					

KANT坎特kan te

Immanuel Kant

Dare to think!

敢想!

~

Look closely. The beautiful may be small.
仔细看. 美丽可能很小.

坎					
特					

KARAGULLA卡让古拉ka ra gu la

Shafica Karagulla

There is abundant evidence that many human beings are already expanding the usual five senses into super sensory levels. It is possible that there is already a `mutation in consciousness' taking place.

有充分的证据表明, 许多人已经将通常的五种感官扩展到超感官水平.可能已经发生了"意识突变".

卡					
让					
古					
拉					

KELLER凯乐kai le

Helen Adams Keller

I would rather walk with a friend in the dark, than alone in the light.
我宁愿和朋友在黑暗中行走, 也不愿独自在光明中行走.

凯					
乐					

KENNEDY肯尼迪ken ni di

John Fitzgerald "Jack" Kennedy Elisabeth

Forgive your enemies, but never forget their names.

原谅你的敌人，但不要忘记他们的名字.

肯					
尼					
迪					

KILLGALLEN吉尔喝伦ji er he lun

Dorothy Mae Killgallen

I actually turned down an opportunity for a private interview with Adolph Hitler.

实际上，我拒绝了一个与阿道夫·希特勒进行私人采访的机会.

吉					
尔					
喝					
伦					

KING金jin

Martin Luther King

Our lives begin to end the day we become silent about things that matter.

当我们对重要的事情保持沉默的时候，我们的生活就开始结束了.

~

In the End, we will remember not the words of our enemies, but the silence of our friends.

最后，我们将不再记得敌人的话，而是我们朋友的沉默.

~
We should never forget that everything that Adolph Hitler did was legal.
我们永远不能忘记阿道夫•希特勒所做的一切都是合法的.

金					

KING金jin

Hans Christian King

>*Most people don't live their life. They live their reaction to life.*
大多数人都过不上他们的生活.他们过着他们对生活的反应.

金					

KIPLING吉卜林ji bu lin

Joseph Rudyard Kipling

There is no sin greater than ignorance.
没有罪比无聊更大.

Take everything you like seriously, except yourselves.
认真对得自己喜欢的一切, 除了自己.

He who can reach a child's heart can reach the worlds heart.
可能触及孩子心的人可以触及世界的心.

God could not be everywhere, and therefore he made mothers.
上帝无处不在, 因此他做了每亲.

We have forty million reasons for failure, but not a single excuse.
我们有四千万个失败的愿因, 但没有一个借口.

But no price is too high to pay for the privilege of owning yourself.
但是, 付出任何代价都不不足以拥有自己的特权.

If you do not get what you want, it is a sure sign that you did not seriously want it.
如果您没有得到想要的东西, 那肯定是您不想要的东西.

We are the opening verse of the opening page of the chapter of endless possibilities.
我们是无尽可能性这一章开头页的开头.

I am by nature a dealer in words, and words are the most powerful drug known to humanity.
我天生就是言语交易者, 而言语是人类已知的最有力的毒品.

I had six honest serving men. They taught me all I knew. Their names were: Where, What, When, Why, How and Who.
我有六个诚实的服役人员.他们教会了我我所知道的一切.他们的名字是：哪里, 什么, 什么时候, 为什么, 如何和谁.

吉					
卜林					

KISSINGER基辛格ji xin ge
Henry Alfred Kissinger
Corrupt politicians make the other ten percent look bad.
腐败的政客使其他百分之十的人看上去很糟糕.

基					
辛					
格					

KUBLER-ROSS库布勒•罗斯ku bu le~luo si
Elisabeth Kubler-Ross
Forgive yourself.
原谅你自己.

Beautiful people do not just happen.
美丽的人不只是发生.

I'm going to dance in all the galaxies.
我要在所有星系中跳舞

The truth is that life is risky and dangerous.
事实是，生活充满危险和危险.

The more you learn, the harder the lessons get.
您学得越多，获得的经险就越难.

Education makes you humble, it doesn't make you proud.
教育会让你谦虚，但不会让你骄傲.

You are worthy and lovable, just as you are, on your own.
就像您自己一样，您是值得和可爱的.

We often tend to ignore how much of a child is still in all of us.
我们经常倾向于忽略我们每一个中还有多少孩子.

However healthy you think you are, remember that vegetarians die too.
无论您认为自己有多姜康，都请记住素食者也会死.

We cannot look at the sun all the time, we cannot face death all the time.
我们不能一直看着太阳，我们不能一直面对死亡.

The opinion which other people have of you is their problem, not yours.
别人对你的看法是他们的问题，而不是你的问题.

You may also be angry with yourself that you couldn't stop it from happening.
您也可能会为自己生气，无法阻止它的发生.

Live, so you do not have to look back and say: 'God, how I have wasted my life.'
活着， 所以你不必回头说:"上帝，我是如何浪费我的生命的."

Birth is not a beginning and death is not an ending. They are merely points on a continuum.
出生不是开始，死亡不是结束. 它们仅仅是连续体上的点.

There are no mistakes, no coincidences. All events are blessings given to us to learn from.
没有错误，没有巧合.所有的事件都是给予我们学习的祝福.

Learn to get in touch with the silence within yourself and know that everything in this life has a purpose.

学会与自己内心的沉默报持联系，并知道今生的一动都有目的.

Should you shield the canyons from the windstorms you would never see the true beauty of their carvings.

如果您将峡谷遮挡在暴风雨中，您将永看不到它们雕刻的正美.

It is not the end of the physical body that should worry us. Rather, our concern must be to live while we're alive.

担心我们的不是身体的尽头. 相反，我们的关注点必须是活着而活着.

We need time to move through the pain of loss. We need to step into it, really to get to know it, in order to learn.

我们需要时间来克服损失的痛苦. 为了学习，我们需要深入了解它，实际上是要了解它.

There are only two emotions: love and fear. All positive emotions come from love, all negative emotions from fear.

只有两种情绪：爱和恐惧. 所有积极的情绪都来自爱，所有消极的情绪都来自恐惧.

The ultimate lesson all of us have to learn is unconditional love, which includes not only others but ourselves as well.

我们所有人必须学习的最终课程是无条件的爱，它不仅包括他人. 还包括我们自己.

I've told my children that when I die, to release balloons in the sky to celebrate that I graduated. For me, death is a graduation.

我告诉我的孩子，当我死后，在天空中释放气球以庆祝我毕业. 对我来说，死亡是毕业.

Mankind's greatest gift, also its greatest curse, is that we have free choice. We can make our choices built from love or from fear.

人类最大的礼物，也是最大的诅咒，是我们可以自由选择. 我们可以从爱或恐惧中做出选择.

There is no need to go to India or anywhere else to find peace. You will find that deep place of silence right in your room, your garden or even your bathtub.

无需去印度或其他任何地方寻求和平. 您会在房间，花园甚至浴缸中找到寂静的深处.

It is very important that you do only what you love to do. You may be poor, you may go hungry, you may live in a shabby place, but you will totally live.

仅做自己喜欢做的事情非常重要.您可能很穷,您可能饿了,可能住在破旧的地方,但您将完全活着.

I believe that we are solely responsible for our choices, and we have to accept the consequences of every deed, word, and thought throughout our lifetime.
我相信,我们对自己的选择负全部责任,并且我们必须接受我们一生中,每项兴为,言论和思想的后果.

Today, in our "shut up, get over it, and move on" mentality, our society misses so much, it's no wonder we are a generation that longs to tell our stories.
今天,我们以 "闭嘴,克服困难,继续前进"的心态,对我们的社会怀念太多,也难怪我们这一代渴望讲述我们的故事.

But at the time of transition, your guides, your guardian angels, people whom you have loved and who have passed on before you, will be there to help you.
但是在过度时,您的向导,您的守护天使,您所爱的人以及在您之前已经过时的人都将在那里为您提供帮助.

A ship exists on the ocean, even if it sails out beyond the limits of our sight. The people in the ship have not vanished; they are simply moving to another shore.
即使有船驶出了我们的视线范围,它仍然存在于海洋中.船上的人没有消失.他们只是在搬到另一岸.

The five stages - denial, anger, bargaining, depression, and acceptance - are a part of the framework that makes up our learning to live with the one we lost.
拒绝,愤怒,讨价还价,压抑和接受这五个阶段是构成我们学习与失去的人生活的框架的一部分.

There is within each one of us a potential for goodness beyond our imagining; for giving which seeks no reward; for listening without judgment; for loving unconditionally.
我们每个人都有超越我们想象的善良的潜力.不求回报的付出;毫无判断地听;无条件的爱.

The beautiful people we have known are those who have known defeat, known suffering, known struggle, known loss, and have found their way out of those depths.
我们认识的美丽的人是那些知道失败,知道苦难,知道奋斗,知道损失并找到走出这些深渊的人.

People are like stained-glass windows. They sparkle and shine when the sun is out, but when the darkness sets in, their true beauty is revealed only if there is a light from within.

人们就像彩色玻璃窗.当太阳出来时,它们会闪闪发光,但是当黑暗笼罩时,只有在内部有光线的情况下,它们的真正美才会显现出来.

Learn to get in touch with the silence within yourself and know that everything in this life has a purpose, there are no mistakes, no coincidences, all events are blessings given to us to learn from.

学会与自己内心的沉默保持联系,并这道生命中的一切都有目的,没有错误,没有巧合,所有事件都是给予我们学习的祝福.

It's only when we truly know and understand that we have a limited time on earth -- and that we have no way of knowing when our time is up -- that we will begin to live each day to the fullest, as if it was the only one we had.

只有当我们真正地了解并了解到我们在地球上的时间有限时,并且我们无法知道时间何时结束,我们才能每天开始充实地生活,就像那是 我们只有一个.

The most beautiful people we have known are those who have known defeat, known suffering, known struggle, known loss, and have found their way out of the depths. These persons have an appreciation, a sensitivity, and an understanding of life that fills them with compassion, gentleness, and a deep loving concern.

我们所认识的最美丽的人是那些知道失败,经历苦难,知道挣扎,知道损失并且发现自己脱离困境的人.这些人对生活充满欣赏,敏锐和理解,充满同情心,温柔和深切的爱心关怀.

库					
布					
勒					
罗					
斯					

KURTZMAN库茨曼 ku ci man

Harvey Kurtzman

Teenagers are people who act like babies if they're not treated like adults.

青少年是如果不像成年人那样对待婴儿的人.

库					
茨					
曼					

LAURIER劳里埃lao li ai

[SIR] Henry Charles Wilfrid Laurier

Canada is free and freedom is its nationality.

加拿大是自由的, 自由是它的国籍.

劳					
里					
埃					

LAYTON莱顿lai dun

John Gilbert "Jack" Layton

Canada is a great country, one of the hopes of the world.

加拿大输一个伟大的国家, 是世界的希望之一.

莱					
顿					

LAZARUS拉撒路la sa lu

Emma Lazarus

Give me your tired, your poor, Your huddled masses yearning to breathe free, The wretched refuse of your teeming shore. Send these, the homeless, tempest-tossed, to me: I lift my lamp beside the golden door.

给我你的疲惫, 你的贫穷, 你拥挤的群众渴望自由呼吸, 你丰沛的海岸的悲惨垃圾.把这些, 无家可归的人, 暴风雪扔给我, 我把灯举到金门旁边.

拉					
撒					
路					

LEARY李尔利 li er li

Timothy Francis Leary

turn on, tune in, drop out; think for yourself and question authority

打开, 退出, 为自己着想, 质疑权威

李					
尔					
利					

LEE李li

Stan Lee

Everybody learns differently and everybody gets to a certain point from a different direction.

李				

LENNON蓝侬lan nong

John Winston Lennon

life is what happens when you are busy making other plans.

生活就是当你忙于制定计划时发生的事情

蓝					
侬					

LEONOV列昂诺夫lie any nuo fu

Alexei Arkhipovich Leonov

If we ever travel far from in the universe to another planet with intelligent life, let's just make patterns in their crops and leave.

在他们的庄稼上做图案然后离开.

列					
昂					
诺					
夫					

LI李

Li Bai

生人701~ 762年

In a universe animated by the interaction of yin (female) and yang (male) energies, the moon was literally yin visible. Indeed, it was the very germ or source of yin, and the sun was its yang counterpart.

在一个由阴（阳）能和阳（阳）能相互作用形成的宇宙中，月亮从字面上可以看到阴.的确，它是阴的起源或根源，而太阳是阴的源头.

李					
白					

LIBERACE利巴日记li ba ri ji

Wladziu Valentino Liberace

Nakedness makes us democratic, adornment makes us individuals.

赤裸裸使我们民主，装饰使我们成为一个人.

利					
巴					
日					
记					

LINCOLN林肯lin ken

Abraham Lincoln

Nearly all men can stand adversity, but if you want to test a man's character, give him power.

几乎所有男人都可以忍受逆境，但是如来您想测试一个男人的性格，请给他力量.

林					
肯					

LINKLETTER林克莱特 lin ke lai te

Arthur Gordon "Art" Linkletter

Things turn out best for the people who make the best out of the way things turn out.
对于娜些从事态发展中获得最大收益的人来说，事情发展得最好.

林					
克					
莱					
特					

LOVECRAFT吕卡热法特 lv ka re fa te

Howard Philips Lovecraft

The oldest and strongest emotion of mankind is fear, and the oldest and strongest kind of fear is fear of the unknown.

人类最古老和最强烈的情感是恐惧, 最古老和最强烈的恐惧是对未知的恐惧.

吕					
卡					
热					
法					
特					

LOVELL吕花乐lv hua le

James Arthur "Jim" Lovell

Houston, we have a problem!

休斯敦, 我们有问题.

吕					
花					
乐					

LUXEMBURG罗森博格 luo sen bo ge

Rosa Luxemburg

Those who do not move, do not notice their chains!

她后来会因自己的观点而被处决.

Freedom is always and exclusively freedom for the one who thinks differently.

对于有不同想法的人，自由永远是唯一的自由.

罗					
森					
博					
格					

MACPHAIL马凯法 ma kai fa

Agnes Campbell Macphail

... well I'm no lady, I'm a human being.

我不是女人，我是一个人

马					
凯					

法					

Malcolm X习xi

The man who stands for nothing will fall for anything.

《什么都不代表的人，什么也不会相信》

习					

MALLROY马尔罗伊ma er luo yi

George Herbert Leigh Mallroy

Why do you want to climb Mt. Everest, Sir? ~ Because it is there."

先生，你为什么要攀登珠穆朗玛峰? - 因为它就在那里.

马					
尔					
罗					
伊					

MANDELA曼德拉man de la

Nelson Rolihlahla Mandela

It always seems impossible until it's done.

知道完成，这似乎总是不可能的.

Lead from the back — and let others believe they are in front.

从后面从后面领导=让真他人相信自己在前面.

Resentment is like drinking poison and then hoping it will kill your enemies.

怨恨就像喝毒，然后希望它会杀死你的敌人.

Education is the most powerful weapon which you can use to change the world.
教育是您可以用来改变世界的岁强大的武器.

Do not judge me by my successes, judge me by how many times I fell down and got back up again.
不要以我的成功来评判我. 而要以我跌倒并重新站起来的次数来评判我.

When a man is denied the right to live the life he believes in, he has no choice but to become an outlaw.
当一个人被剥夺享有他所信奉的生活的权利时, 他别无选择, 只能成为违法者.

There is nothing like returning to a place that remains unchanged to find the ways in which you yourself have altered.
没有什么比回到一个不变的放来寻找自己更像了.

For to be free is not merely to cast off one's chains, but to live in a way that respects and enhances the freedom of others.
为了自由, 不仅要摆脱束缚, 耳且要以尊重何增进他人自由的方式生活.

曼					
德					
拉					

MCAULIFFE麦考利夫mai kao li fu

Sharon Christa Mcauliffe

I touch the future. I teach.

我触及未来.我教书.

麦					
考					

利					
夫					

MCCAIN 麦凯恩 mai kai en

John Sidney McCain III

duty, honor, country!

"责任, 荣誉, 国家!"

麦					
凯					
恩					

MCCLUNG 麦克隆 mai ke long

Nellie Letitia Mcclung

They did not know that the day was coming when women … would push back the horizon of their narrow lives and take their place beside the men of the world.

她们不知道有一天, 女人们……会把她们狭隘生活的地平线往后推, 在男人们身边占据一席之地.

~

Never explain, never retract, never apologize. Just get the thing done and let them howl.

从不解释, 从不收回, 从不道歉.把事情做好, 让他们嚎叫.

麦					
克					

隆					

MCCRAE麦克雷mai ke lei

John McCrae

Loved, and were loved, and now we lie in Flanders fields.

被爱，被爱，现在我们躺在佛兰德斯田.

We are the Dead. Short days ago we lived, felt dawn, saw sunset glow.

我们是死者.短短几天前，我们住了，感到黎明，看见日落发光.

Take up our quarrel with the foe: To you from failing hands we throw, The torch, be yours to hold it high.

与敌人争吵：尚我们投掷失败的双手给你，　火炬，成为您的高毛

麦					
克					
雷					

MCKINNEY麦金尼mai jin ni

Louise McKinney

What, after all, is the purpose of woman's life? The purpose of woman's life is just the same as the purpose of man's life: …

毕竟，女人生活的目的是什么? 女人生命的目的和男人生命的目的一样……

麦					
金					
尼					

MCLEAN麦克勒安mai ke le an

Andrew Stuart McLean

I see the good in people, and in things. To me, the glass is always half full.

我看到人们和事物的优点. 对我来说，杯子总是半满的.

麦					
克					
勒					
安					

MEIR梅厄mei e

Golda Meir

You can not shake hands with a clenched fist.

你不能握紧拳头握手.

梅					
厄					

MILNE米尔恩mi er en

Alan Alexandre Milne

Some people care too much. I think it's called love.

有些人太在乎了.我认为这就是爱.

米					
尔					

恩					

MOCKFORD莫克福特mo ke fu te

Frederick Stanley Mockford

"Mayday":"come and help me" ~ repeated three times.

《来帮我!》重复三次.

莫					
克					
福					
特					

MONSON曼森man sen

Thomas Spencer Monson

May we ever choose the harder right instead of the easier wrong.

愿我们选择更难的对而不是更容易的错误.

曼					
森					

MONTAIGNE蒙田meng tian

Michel Eyquem de Montaigne

I do not teach. I relate.

我不教.我联系.

~

The most certain sign of wisdom is cheerfulness.
智慧最确定的标志是快乐.

~

Lend yourself to others, but give yourself to yourself.
借给自己，但献给自己.

~

Happiness involves working toward meaningful goals.
幸福涉及朝着有意的目表努力.

~

Friendship is the highest degree of perfection in society.
友谊是社会是最高完美程度.

~

Ignorance is the softest pillow on which a man can rest his head.
无知是一个最软的枕头，一个人可以靠在软头上.

~

A man who fears suffering is already suffering from what he fears.
一个担心苦难的人已经在遭受他所担心的.

~

The profit we possess after study is to have become better and wiser.
我们学习后拥有的利润将变得更好，更明智.

~

When I quote others I do so in order to express my own ideas more clearly.
当我引用别人的时候，是为了更清楚地表达自己的想法.

~

A good marriage would be between a blind wife and a deaf husband.
盲目的妻子和聋哑的丈夫之健将友一段美好的婚姻.

~

Love is like playing the piano. First you must learn to play by the rules, then you must forget the rules and play from your heart.
爱就像弹钢琴.首先，您必须学会遵守规则，然后您必须忘记规则并发自内心地发挥.

蒙					
田					

MONTGOMERY蒙哥马利meng ge ma li

Lucy Maud Montgomery

In this world you've just got to hope for the best and prepare for the worst and take whatever God sends.

在这个世界上, 您只是希望拥有最好的, 为最坏的事情做准备, 并接受上帝所差的一切.

蒙				
哥				
马				
利				

MORGAN摩根mo gen

Edward Paddock Morgan

A book is the only place in which you can examine a fragile thought without breaking it, or explore an explosive idea without fear it will go off in your face. It is one of the few havens remaining where a man's mind can get both provocation and privacy.

一本书是只有在这里您可以检查脆弱的思想而无需打破它, 或探索一个爆炸性想法, 而不必担心它会在你的脸.它是男人心中剩下的少数避风港之一可以同时获得挑衅和隐私.

摩				
根				

MORSE莫尔斯mo er si

Samuel Finley Breese Morse

What hath God wrought

上帝所做的

莫					
尔					
斯					

MOWAT 莫厄特 mo e te

Farley Migill Mowat

Without a function, we cease to be. So, I will write till I die.

没有功能，我们就不再是. 所以，我会写直到我死.

莫					
厄					
特					

MOZART 莫扎特 mo za te

Wolfgang Amadeus Mozart

When I am traveling in a carriage, or walking after a good meal, or during the night when I cannot sleep; it is on such occasions that ideas flow best and most abundantly.

当我在马车上旅行，跟后顿饭后散步时或夜间无法入睡时;正是在这种情况下，思想才是最好，最丰富的.

莫					
扎					
特					

MURPHY墨菲mo fei

Emily Gowan Murphy

Whenever I don't know whether to fight or not, I always fight.

每当我不知道该不该战斗时，我总是战斗.

~

This is courtship all the world over - the man all tongue; the woman all ears.

这是全世界的求爱-男人全是舌头.女人全耳.

墨					
菲					

NEVILLE那威勒na wei le

Eric Neville

Captain Kirk basically set his phaser on destruct and blew
Popcorn play house off the air.

柯克船长基本上将他的相位器设置为破坏和自爆爆米花播放空中的房子.

那					
威					
勒					

NIETZSCHE尼采ni cai

Friedrich Wilhelm Nietzsche

~

The doer alone learneth.

行动者独自学习.

~

Enjoy life. This is not a dress rehearsal.

享受生活.这不是彩排.

~

That which does not kill us makes us stronger.
没有杀死我们的西会使我们变得更强大.

~

He who has a why to live can bear almost any how.
有生存理由的人几乎可以忍受.
Our greatest experiences are our quietest moments.
我们最大的经验就是我们最安静的时刻.

~

In every real man a child is hidden that wants to play.
每一真正的男人中都有一个想要玩耍的孩子被藏起来.

~

Become who you are. Make what only you can make.
成为你自己.做只有你能做的.

~

Love your enemies because they bring out the best in you.
爱你的敌人,因为他们发掘出你最好的敌人.

~

When you look into an abyss, the abyss also looks into you.
当您看着深渊时,深渊也会看着您.

~

To live is to suffer, to survive is to find some meaning in the suffering.
生存就是受苦,生存就是在苦难中找到一些意义.

~

I know of no better life purpose than to perish in attempting the great and the impossible.
我知道没有更好的人生目的,就是死于尝试伟大和不可能的事情.

~

There will always be rocks in the road ahead of us. They will be stumbling blocks or stepping stones; it all depends on how you use them.
我们前面的道路上总会有岩石.它们将成为绊脚石或垫脚石;这完全取决于您如何使用它们.

~

Our treasure lies in the beehive of our knowledge. We are perpetually on the way thither, being by nature winged insects and honey gatherers of the mind.
我们的宝藏在于我们知识的蜂巢.我们永远在前进的道路上,天生是有翼的昆虫和心灵的采集者.

~

I was in darkness, but I took three steps and found myself in paradise. The first step was a good thought, the second, a good word; and the third, a good deed.

我当时处于黑暗中，但是我走了三个步骤，发现自己陷入了天堂.第一步是一个好主意，第二步是一个好词.第三，是一件好事.

尼				
采				

NOBEL诺贝尔nuo bei er

Alfred Bernhard Nobel

For the greatest benefit to Mankind.

对人类最大的利益.

诺				
贝				
尔				

O'LEARY奥利里ao li li

Brian Todd O'Leary

The truth will set you free,but first it will piss you off!

真理会让你自由，但首先它会让你生气!

奥				
利				
里				

OPPENHEIMER奥本海默ao ben hai mo

Julius Robert Oppenheimer

No man should escape our universities without knowing how little he knows!

任何人都不应该在不知道自己知道多少的情况下逃离我们的大学.

~

The optimist thinks this is the best of all possible worlds. The pessimist fears it is true.

乐观主义者认为这是所有可能世界中最好的.悲观主义者担心这是真的.

~

There are no secrets about the world of nature. There are secrets about the thoughts and intentions of men.

关于自然世界没有任何秘密.关于男人的思想和意图有秘密.

奥					
本					
海					
默					

ORWELL奥威尔ao wei er

George Orwell [pseudonym]

To see what is in front of one's nose requires a constant struggle.

看看自己面前有什么鼻子需要不断地挣扎.

奥					
威					
尔					

PALMER帕尔姆pa er mu

Arnold Daniel Palmer

Always make a total effort, even when the odds are against you!

拼尽全力, 哪拍烦事缠身

~

Concentration comes out of a combination of confidence and hunger.

专注来自信心和饿的结合

~

The most rewarding things you do in life are often the ones that look like they cannot be done.

您一生中所做的最好有意义的事情通常是看起来无法完成的事情.

帕					
尔					
姆					

PARKS帕克斯pa ke si

Rosa Louise McCauley Parks

生人Feb 4, 1913 - Oct 24, 2005年 》92

We will fail when we fail to try.

没有教育就没有未来.

There is no future without education.

如果尝试失败, 我们将失败.

To bring about change, you must not be afraid to take the first step.要实现变革, 您一定不要害怕迈出第一步.

I have learned over the years that when one's mind is made up, this diminishes fear; knowing what must be done does away with fear.

多年来我了解到, 只要下定决心, 这就会减少恐惧; 知道必须做些什么就能消除 带着恐惧.

帕					
克					
斯					

PARLBY帕尔比pa er bi

Mary Irene Parlby

If politics mean … then it mostly assuredly is a woman's job as much as it is a man's job.

如果政治意味着⋯⋯那么,它基本上是一个女人的工作,就像男人的工作一样.

帕					
尔					
比					

PEROT佩罗pei luo

Henry Ross Perot

The activist is not the person who says the river is dirty. The activist is the person who cleans up the river.

活动家并不是说河流很脏的人.活动家是清理河流的人.

佩					
罗					

PHILIP斐里伯fei li bo

(Prince) Philip [Mountbatten]

I am the only man in the country not allowed to give his name to his children.

我是该国唯一不允许给自己的孩子起名字的人.

斐					
里					
伯					

PLATO柏拉图bo la tu

Plato

Wise men talk because they have something to say; fools, because they have to say something.

智者之所以说话,是因为他们有话要说.傻瓜,因为他们不得不说些什么.

柏					
拉					
图					

POLO 波罗bo luo

Marco Polo

You would not believe half of what I have seen.

你不会相信我看到的一半.

波					
罗					

PONTIAC庞体克 pang ti ke [zhang]

[chief] Pontiac

They came with a Bible and their religion stole our land, crushed our spirit … and now tell us we should be thankful to the 'Lord' for being saved.

他们带着圣经，他们的宗教信仰偷走了我们的土地，粉碎了我们的精神……现在告诉我们，我们应该感谢"主"的得救.

庞				
体				
克				

PRESLEY普雷斯利pu lei si li

Elvis Aaron Presley

Truth is like the sun. You can shut it out for a time, but it ain't goin' away.

真相就像太阳.您可以将其关闭一段时间，但不会消失.

普				
雷				
斯				
利				

PRICE普瑞斯pu rui si

Vincent Price

It's as much fun to scare as to be scared.

收到惊吓与受到惊吓一样有趣.

普					
瑞					
斯					

QUESNAY奎尼kui ni

Francois Quesnay

Without the sense of security which property gives, the land would still be uncultivated.

如果没有财产所赋予的安全感，土地仍然是未开垦的.

奎					
尼					

RAMON拉蒙la meng

Ilan Ramon

Jerusalem we have a problem!

耶路撒冷我们有问题

拉					
蒙					

RAVENSCROFT莱文新克格福特lai wen xin ke ge fu te

Thurl Arthur Ravenscroft

Good? They're grreatt!

《好吗? 他们是同性恋!》

莱					
文					
新					
克					
格					
福					
特					

REAGAN雷根lei gen

Ronald Wilson Reagan

Mr. Gorbachev, tear down this wall.

戈尔巴乔夫先生，拆掉这堵墙.

雷					
根					

REDENBACHER热嗯把卡re en ba ka

Orville Clarence Redenbacher

I want to make it clear that I am real.

我想说清楚我是真的.

热					

嗯					
把					
卡					

REE热义re yi

Paul Ludwig Carl Henirich Ree

I have to philosophize. When I run out of material, perhaps it is better that I die.
我必须进行哲学思考.当我用完了材料,也许我死了更好.

热					
义					

RIPLEY里普利li pu li

Robert Leroy Ripley

Their is nothing more stranger than Man.
他们只不过是人而已.

里					
普					
利					

ROCKNE罗克luo ke

Knute Kenneth Rockne

Win or lose, do it fairly.

输赢，公平地做

It isn't necessary to see a good tackle. You can hear it.
没必要看到一个好的解决方案.你会听到的.

Build up your weaknesses until they become your strong points.
建立自己的弱点，直到它们成为您的长处.

Football is a game played with arms, legs and shoulders but mostly from the neck up.
足球是一种用胳膊，腿和肩膀进行的比赛，但主要是从脖子到脖子.

罗					
克					

RODDENBERRY罗顿巴里luo dun ba li
Gene Roddenberry

It isn't all over; everything has not been invented; the human adventure is just beginning.
还没有结束; 一切还没有被发明; 人类的冒险才刚刚开始.

罗					
顿					
巴					
里					

ROGERS罗杰斯luo jie si
Will Rogers

Even if your on the right track, you'll get run over if you just sit there.
即使你走的路是对的, 如果停滞不前, 也会被车压死.

罗					
杰					
斯					

ROGERS 罗杰斯 luo jie si

Fred Mcfeely Rogers

Love isn't a perfect state of caring. It's an active noun, like 'struggle.

爱不是关怀的完美状态.这是一个活跃的名词,例如"奋斗.

~

If you could only sense how important you are to the lives of those you meet, how important you can be to the people you may never even dream of. There is something of yourself that you leave at every meeting with another person.

如果您仅能感觉到自己对遇到的人的生活有多么重要,那么对于您甚至从未梦想过的人们来说,您有多么重要.在与另一个人的每次会面中,您都会离开自己.

罗					
杰					
斯					

ROONEY 如尼 ru ni

Andrew Aiken "Andy" Rooney

We're all proud of making little mistakes. It gives us the feeling we don't make any big ones.

我们都为犯小错误而自豪.这让我们觉得我们没有做什么大的.

如					

尼					

ROOSEVELT罗斯福luo si fu

Franklin Delano Roosevelt Sr.

... a date which will live in infamy.

一个将以恶名为生的日子.

罗					
斯					
福					

ROSE罗索luo suo

Hilly Rose

But that's not what I called about.

但这不是我所说的.

罗					
索					

RUMI如迷ru mi

Mawlana Jala ad-din Muhammad Rumi

Inside you there's an artist you don't know about. He's not interested in how things look different in moonlight.

在你里面, 有一个你不认识的艺术家.他对月光下的事物看起来并不感兴趣.

如					

迷					

SAGAN萨根sa gan

Carl Edward Sagan

No such thing as a stupid question.

没有愚蠢的问题.

~

One glance at a book and you hear the voice of another person, perhaps someone dead for 1000 years. To read is to voyage through time.

当你看一本书的时侯，你可以听到这个人内心的声音，也许这个人已经去世了几千年.阅读就是在时间的长河里遨游航行.

萨					
根					

SANDERS伞得日斯san dei ri si

Harland David Sanders

It's finger licking good.

手指舔得很好.

伞					
得					
日					
斯					

SAXE萨克斯sai ke si

John Godfrey Saxe

Laws, like sausages, cease to inspire respect in proportion as we know how they are made.

法律，像香肠一样，不再像我们知道的那样，按比例激发人们的尊重.

~

Beauty intoxicates the eye, as wine does the body; both are morally fatal if indulged.

美貌能陶醉人的眼睛，就像美酒能陶醉人的身体一样;如果沉溺其中，美貌和美貌在道德上都是致命的.

萨					
克					
斯					

SCHOPENHAUER施盆哈尔shi pen ha er

Arthur Schopenhauer

Every truth passes through three stages before it is recognized. In the first it is ridiculed, in the second it is opposed, in the third it is regarded as self evident.

一切真理都经过三个阶段.首先,它是被嘲笑的.第二,它遭到强烈反对.第三,它被认为是不言而喻的.

施					
盆					
哈					
尔					

SCHULTZ徐拉特思xu la te si

Charles Monroe Schultz

Just remember, once you're over the hill you begin to pick up speed.

只要奇住, 一旦您越过山坡, 您就会开始加快速度.

徐					
拉					
特					
思					

SCHWEITZER施韦策shi wei ce

Albert Schweitzer

Example is not the main thing in influencing others. It is the only thing.

榜样并不是影响他人的主要内容.这是唯一的事情.

~

Success is not the key to happiness. Happiness is the key to success. If you love what you are doing, you will be successful.

成功不是幸福的关键.幸福是成功的关.如果您热爱正在做的事情, 您将会成功.

~

Eventually all things fall into place. Until then, laugh at the confusion, live for the moments, and know EVERYTHING HAPPENS FOR A REASON.

最终所有的事情都会发生.在那之前, 嘲笑困惑, 活在当下, 知道一切发生的原因.

施					
韦					
策					

SENECA 塞内加 sai ni jia

Lucius Annaeus Seneca

Whatever begins, also ends.

如果生活得好，寿命就足够长.

Life, if well lived, is long enough.

如果生活得好，寿命就足够长.

>As long as you live, keep learning how to live.

只要你活着，就要不断学习如何生活.

The whole future lies in uncertainty: live immediately.

整个未来都充满不确定性：立即生活.

It is not that we have a short time to live, but that we waste a lot of it.

不是我们生活时间短，而是我们浪费了很多时间.

We should always allow some time to elapse, for time discloses the truth.

我们应该总是留出一些时间，，因为时间会揭示真相.

They lose the day in expectation of the night, and the night in fear of the dawn.

他们因期望夜晚儿失去了白天，而害怕黎明却失去了夜晚.

The greatest obstacle to living is expectancy, which hangs upon tomorrow and loses today.

生存的最大障碍是期望，它在明天依然存在，儿在今天却失去了.

生存的最大.

塞					
内					
加					

SEUSS苏斯su si

Theodore "Ted" Seuss Geisel

Don't cry because it's over. Smile because it happened.

不要哭了, 因为结束了.微笑, 因为发生了.

~

The more that you read, the more things you will know. The more that you learn, the more places you'll go.

阅读的内容越多, 您就会知道的越多.您学得越多, 您就会去的地方越多.

苏					
斯					

SHAKESPEAR莎士比亚sha shi bi ya

William Shakespear

The soul's joy lies in doing.

灵魂的喜悦在于做事.

莎					
士					
比					
亚					

SHAPLEY莎普利sha pu li

Harlow Shapely

Here is the letter that destroyed my universe!

这是摧毁我的宇宙的信!

莎					
普					
利					

SHAW 肖 xiao

George Bernard Shaw

Life isn't about finding yourself. Life is about creating yourself.

生活不是为了找到自己.生活就是创造你自己.

~

Make it a rule never to give a child a book you would not read yourself.

永远不要给孩子读一本自己会读书的书，这是一条规则.

~

We don't stop playing because we grow old, we grow old because we stop playing.

我们不会因为变老而停止比赛，我们会因为停止比赛而变老.

肖					

SHELLEY 事利 shi li

Mary Wollstonecraft Shelley

The beginning is always today.

永远都是今天的开始.

~

My education was neglected, yet I was passionately fond of reading.

我的教育被忽略了， 但我仍然然非常喜欢阅读.

事					
利					

SINCLAIR辛克莱 xin ke lai

Will the real Gordon Sinclair please stand up!

"请真正的戈登·辛克莱站起来!

辛					
克					
莱					

SNOW斯诺si nuo

Edgar Parks Snow

Do not suppose, first of all, that Mao Tse-tung could be the "saviour" of China. Nonsense. There will never be one "saviour" of China. Yet undeniably you feel a certain force of destiny in him."

首先,不要认为毛泽东可以成为中国的 "救世主".胡说.中国永远不会有一个 "救世主".但不可否认,你在他身上感受到了某种命运的力量."

斯					
诺					

SOCRATES苏格拉底su ge la di

Let him that would move the world, first move himself.
让他感动世界, 先感动自己.

~

I cannot teach anybody anything, I can only make them think.
不要能教任何人任何东西, 只能让他们思考.

苏					

格					
拉					
底					

SOUBIROUS苏比鲁su bi lu

Saint Bernadette Soubirous

I'm happier with my crucifix on my bed of pain than a queen on her throne.

在痛苦的床上钉十字架，我比坐在王位上的女王更快乐.

苏					
比					
鲁					

SPENCER斯宾塞si bin sa

Herbert Spencer

A jury is composed of twelve men of average ignorance.

陪审团由十二个一般无知的人组成.

斯					
宾					
塞					

SPOCK斯帕克si pa ke

Benjamin Mclane Spock

You know more than you think you do.

你知道得比你想象的要多

斯					
帕					
克					

STALIN斯大林si da lin

Joseph Vissarionovich Stalin

The death of a comrade is a tragedy, the death of millions is a statistic.

同志之死是悲剧，百万之死是统计数字

斯					
大					
林					

STEELE斯第尔si di er

[Sir] Richard Steele

Reading is to the mind what exercise is to the body.

读书对头脑来说就像运动对身体一样.

斯					
第					

尔					

STOKER斯特克尔si te ko er

Abraham "Bram" Stoker

We learn from failure, not from success!

德古拉伯爵…我们从失败中学习，而不是从成功中学习!

斯					
特					
克					
尔					

SULLIVAN萨丽芬sa li fen

Anne Sullivan

Education in the light of present-day knowledge and need calls for some spirited and creative innovations both in the substance and the purpose of current pedagogy.

根据当前的知识和需求进行教育，需要在当前教育学的实质和目的上进行一些精神和创造性的创新.

萨					
丽					
芬					

TERESA特蕾莎te lei sha

MOTHER Teresa [pseudonym]

Peace begins with a smile.

和平始于微笑.

>If you judge people, you have no time to love them.

如果你判断别人，你就没有时间去爱他们.

Not all of us can do great things. But we can do small things with great love.

并非所有人都能做得很好. 但是，我们可以怀着极大的爱去做小事.

Kind words can be short and easy to speak, but their echoes are truly endless.

亲切的单词可能简短而易于于说出来，但它们回声确实是无止境的.

Yesterday is gone. Tomorrow has not yet come. We have only today. Let us begin.

昨天不见了. 明天还没有到. 我们只有今天. 让我们开始吧.

Every time you smile at someone, it is an action of love, a gift to that person, a beautiful thing.

每次对某人微笑时，这都是爱的举动，是对那一个人的礼物，是一件美丽的失去.

Do not think that love in order to be genuine has to be extraordinary. What we need is to love without getting tired. Be faithful in small things because it is in them that your strength lies.

不要以为真正的爱情就必须与众不同. 我们需要的是爱而不累. 忠于小事情，因为您的力量在于它们.

I am not sure exactly what heaven will be like, but I know that when we die and it comes time for God to judge us, he will not ask, 'How many good things have you done in your life?' rather he will ask, 'How much love did you put into what you did?

我不确定天堂到底会是什么样，但是我知道，当我们死后，到了上帝审判我们的时候，他不会问："你一生做了多少好事？" 而是他会问："您对自己所做的工作投入了多少爱心？".

特					
雷					

莎					

TESLA特斯拉te si la

Nikola Tesla

I have not failed. I've just found 10,000 ways that won't work.

我没有失败.我刚刚发现了10,000种行不通的方法.

~

Be alone, that is the secret of invention; Be alone, that is when ideas are born.

独自一人，这就是发明的秘密.独自一人，这就是想法诞生的时候.

~

If you want to find the secrets of the Universe, think in terms of energy, frequency and vibration.

如果你想找到宇宙的秘密，就得考虑能量,频率和振动.

特					
斯					
拉					

THATCHER撒切尔sa qie er

Margaret Thatcher

No great goal was ever easily achieved.

没有伟大的目标曾经轻易实现.

Never flinch. Make up your own mind and do it.

永不退缩.下定决心，做到这一点.

Don't follow the crowd, let the crowd follow you.

不要跟随人群，让人群跟随你.

The spirit of envy can destroy; it can never build.

嫉妒的精神会毁灭.它永远无法建立.

You do not achieve anything without trouble, ever.

您永远都不会毫无困难地实现任何目标.

If you set out to be liked, you will accomplish nothing.

如果你开始受到喜欢, 您将一事成.

Plan your work for today and every day, then work your plan.

计划今天和每天的工作, 然后制定计划.

The price of freedom is still, and always will be, eternal vigilance.

自由的代价然是, 并将永远是永远的警惕.

It may be the cock that crows, but it is the hen that lays the eggs.

可能是公鸡在打乌鸦, 但是是在产卵的母鸡.

The first step in calculating which way to go is to find out where you are.

计算走哪条路的第一步是找出您的位置.

Pennies do not come from heaven. They have to be earned here on earth.

便士并不来自天堂.他们必须在地球上获得.

If you want something said, ask a man. If you want something done, ask a woman.

如果您想说些什么, 请问一个男人.如果您想完成某件事, 请问一个女人.

Europe will never be like America. Europe is a product of history. America is a product of philosophy.

欧洲永远不会像美国.欧洲是历史的产物.美国是哲学的产物.

It pays to know the enemy - not least because at some time you may have the opportunity to turn him into a friend.

了解敌人很有意义- 优琪是因为时您可能有机会将他变成朋友.

Disciplining yourself to do what you know is right and important, although difficult, is the highroad to pride, self-esteem, and personal satisfaction.

管教自己去做正确而重要的事情, 尽管困难重重, 但却时骄傲。自尊和个人满足的道路.

Freedom is not synonymous with an easy life. ... There are many difficult things about freedom: It does not give you safety, it creates moral dilemmas for you; it requires self-discipline; it imposes great responsibilities; but such is the nature of Man and in such consists his glory and salvation.

自由不是轻松生活的代名词. …关于自由有许多困难的事情: 它没有给您安全, 它给您带来了道德上的困境; 它需要自律; 它承担着巨大的责任; 但是这就是人的天性, 而这正是他的荣耀和救赎.

撒					
切					
尔					

THERESE特蕾莎te lei sha

[St] Therese of Lisieux

Love needs to be proved by action.
爱需要通过行动来证明

It isn't enough to love; we must prove it.
爱是不够的. 我们必须证明这一点.

When one loves, one does not calculate.
当一个人爱的时候, 他不会计算.

You cannot be half a saint; you must be a whole saint or no saint at all.
你不能成为圣人; 你必须是一个完整的圣人, 或者根本不是一个圣人.

A word or a smile is often enough to put fresh life in a despondent soul.
一个单词或一个微笑通常足以使一个沮丧的灵魂充满生气.

If every tiny flower wanted to be a rose, spring would lose its loveliness.
如果每朵小花都想成为玫瑰, 春天将失去它的可爱.

特					

蕾					
莎					

TOLSTOY托尔斯泰tuo er si tai

Lev "Leo" Nikolayevitch Tolstoy

In the name of God, stop a moment, cease your work, look around you.
奉上帝的名义, 停不片刻, 停正工作, 环顾西周.

~

Everyone thinks of changing the world, but no one thinks of changing himself.
每个人都想改变世界,但没有人想改变自己.

托					
尔					
斯					
泰					

TRUDEAU特如都te ru du

Joseph Philippe Yves Pierre Elliot Trudeau

Just watch me
看着我

特					
如					
都					

TWAIN吐温tu wen

Mark Twain [pseudonym]

Explore. Dream. Discover.

探索.梦想.发现.

~

Don't wait. The time will never be just right.

不要等时间永远不会恰到好处.

~

The world owes you nothing. It was here first.

世界没欠你什么.它首先在这里.

~

When all else fails, write what your heart tells you.

当其他所有方法都失败时，写于您的内心所言.

~

I have never let my schooling interfere with my education.

我从来没有让我的教育干扰我的教育.

~

Never put off till tomorrow what you can do the day after tomorrow.

永远不要推迟明天后天才能做的事情.

~

Life is short, break the rules. Forgive quickly, kiss slowly. Love truly.

人生苦短，打破常规.快速原谅，慢慢亲吻.真正地爱.

~

It's not the size of the dog in the fight, it's the size of the fight in the dog.

不是战斗中的狗的大小，而是战斗中的狗的大小.

~

Kindness is the language which the deaf can hear and the blind can see.

善意的语音，聋人可以听见盲人可以看见

~

Give every day the chance to become the most beautiful of your life.

每天都有机回成为您一生中最美丽的一天

~

Laugh uncontrollably and never regret anything that makes you smile.

不可控制地笑，永远不好后悔让你微笑的任何事情.

~

You can't depend on your eyes when your imagination is out of focus.

当您的想象力不清晰时，您就不能依靠眼睛.

~

Never argue with stupid people, they will drag you down to their level and then beat you with experience.

永远不要与愚蠢的人争论.他们会把你拖到他们的水平，然后已经击败你.

吐					
温					

TYNDALE廷代尔ting dai er

William Tyndale

Lord, open the King of England's eye's!

上帝，打开英格兰国王的眼睛!

挺					
代					
尔					

USTINOV优斯特诺夫you si ti nuo fu

[SIR] Peter Alexander Ustinov

Beliefs are what divide people. Doubts unite them.

信念使人分裂.怀疑他们团结起来.

~

Since we are destined to live out our lives in the prison of our minds, it is our duty to furnish it well.

由于我们注定要在我们的牢狱中过着我们的生活，因此，有责任做好它.

乌					
斯					
季					
诺					
夫					

VAN ANDEL范安得fan an de

Jay van Andel

When you reach your highest goal, choose a new one!

当你达到你的最高目标时，选择一个新的.

温					
安					
得					

VICTORIA维多利亚wei duo li ya

[Queen] Alexandrina Victoria Hannover

We are not interested in the possibilities of defeat; they do not exist.

我们对失败的可能性不感兴趣;它们不存在.

维					
多					

利					
亚					

VOLTAIRE伏尔泰fu er tai

Common sense is not so common.

常识不是那么普遍

伏				
尔				
泰				

von GOETHE玩哥德wan ge de

Johann Wolfgang von Goethe

We do not have to visit a madhouse to find disordered minds; our planet is the mental institution of the universe.

我们不必去疯人院去寻找混乱的头脑.我们的星球是宇宙的精神机构.

玩				
哥				
德				

WALES威尔士wei er shi

Jimmy Donald Wales

Imagine a world in which every single person on the planet is given free access to the sum all human knowledge.

想象一个这样的世界:地球上任何一个人都可以自由的获得人类全部知识的总和.

威					
尔					
士					

WALLACE华勒斯hua li si

Alfred Russel Wallace

Truth is born into this world only with pangs and tribulations, and every fresh truth is received unwillingly..

真理在这个世界上诞生，只有痛苦和磨难，每一个新的真理都是不情愿地接受的.

华					
勒					
斯					

WATSON沃特森wo te sen

James Dewey Watson

Some think there is something wrong about enhancing people.

有些人认为增强人心是有问题的.

~

If your the most intelligent person in the room, your in the wrong room!

如果你是房间里最聪明的人，你就错了房间!

沃					
特					

森					

WATSON沃特森wo te sen

Thomas John Watson

I think there is a world market for maybe 5 computers.

我认为世界上有5台电脑的市场.

沃					
特					
森					

WELK威尔克wei er ke

Lawrence Welk

Dreams do come true, even for someone who couldn't speak English and never had a music lesson or much of an education.

梦想成真, 甚至于那些不会说英语, 从未听过音乐课或没有接受过很多教室的人.

威					
尔					
克					

WOODLAND伍德兰wu de lan

Norman Joseph Woodland

Instead of dots and dashes, I can have thick and thin bars.

我可以用粗条和细条代替圆点和破折号

伍					
德					
兰					

X习shi[xi]

Malcolm X

The man who stands for nothing will fall for anything.

什么都不代表的人，什么也不会相信

习					

YASGUR亚斯古尔ya si ge er

Max B. Yasgur

That's what this country is all about and I am not going to let you throw them out of our town just because you don't like their dress or their hair or the way they live or what they believe. This is America and their going to have their festival. If we join them, we can turn those adversities that are the problems of America into a hope for a brighter and more peaceful future.

这就是这个国家的一切，我不会因为你不喜欢他们的衣服,头发,生活方式或信仰而让你把他们赶出我们的城市.这是美国，他们要去参加他们的节日.如果我们加入他们，我们就可以把美国面临的困难变成一个更光明,更和平的未来的希望.

亚					
斯					
古					

尔					

YOUNG亚嗯ya en

Brigham Young

It is wise for us to forget our troubles, their are always new ones to replace them.
忘记我们的烦恼是明智的，他们总是新的来取代他们

亚					
嗯					

ZAYTSEV柴瑟夫chai se fu

Vasily Grigoryevich Zaytsev

Patiently await the moment for one, and only one, well-aimed shot. 请耐心等待片刻，只有一张，对准目标.

柴					
瑟					
夫					

ZHU 朱

朱熹zhu xi 1130~1200时

Study everything, at all times, everywhere
无论何时何地，都有学习一切

朱					

ZIGLER齐格勒qi ge le

Hilary Hinton "Zig" Zigler

Where you start is not as important as where you finish.
从哪里开始并不像从哪里结束那么重要.

Expect the best. Prepare for the worst. Capitalize on what comes.
抱最大的希望, 做最坏的打算, 从结果中学习.

Positive thinking will let you do everything better then thinking negative will.
积极思考会让您做的更好, 然后消极思考.

You can have everything in life you want, if you help enough people get what they want.
如果你帮助足够多的人得到他们想要的, 你可以拥有生活中你想要的一切.

Getting knocked down in life is a given. Getting up and moving forward is a choice.
在生活中被撞倒是必然的. 起床并向前迈进是一种选择.

Lack of direction not lack of time, is the problem. We all have twenty - four hour days.
方向不足而不是时间不足, 就是问题所在. 我们都有二十四小时的工作日.

F-E-A-R has two meanings: Forget Everything And Run or Face Everything And Rise. The choice is yours.
F-E-A-R具有两个含义:忘记一切奔跑或面对一切奔腾.这是你的选择.

齐					
格					
勒					

* *coming soon ~ Voices From the Past is an in-depth look at the quotes of many individuals from this book as well as additional people that I have researched. Feel free to contact me with your favourite historic person of interest.

EXAM PORTION

~ 试题~ looking back over history.

The Eiffel Tower contains 72 names with 18 names on each face.

1. Find and write one name for each of the faces: NW-NE-SW-SE.

2. How many people are mentioned only using their pseudonym?
3. How many people were involved in the development of the sewing machine?
4. Who had the longest name?
5. What is the real name of Mr. Twain?_____ _____ _____
6. What was the birth name of Mother Therese?_____ _____ _____
7. Who often said "I get no respect"_____
8. Who said "God has no religion"._____
9. Who wrote 'on Flanders Field?_____

10. What was the name of the political group in early Canadian history...."The Famous _____?

11. What year and date was Alberta Canada born._____

12. Who said "Houston, we have a problem"?_____

13. Finish the sentence.... "This is one small .... "_____

14. Who said "Dream is not that which you see while sleeping, it is something that does not let you sleep." _____

15. Which two men did 毛泽东[mao ze dong] admire the most? One American, one Canadian. _____ _____

16. Who said "Education is not something you finish". _____

17. Who coined the term "Fossil Fuel". _____

18. Who coined the term "Big Bang". _____

19. How many men formed Harley-Davidson? 2,3, 4, 6.

20. The family name of Queen Elizabeth II.

21. How many living people are mentioned at the time of printing?

------------------------------- finished * have a nice day -------------------------------

MISCELLANEOUS ~ RETRO

1935 circa King George V before his passing Jun 3, 1865 - Jan 20, 1936 (age 70). The Grand Father of Princess Elizabeth.

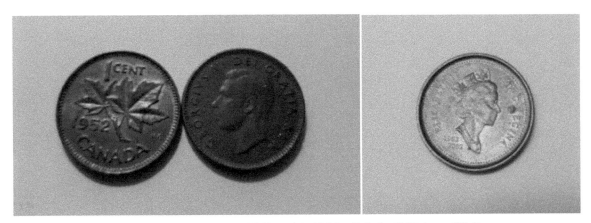

Final year of King George VI,Dec 14, 1895 - Feb 6, 1952 (age 56) then his daughter begins her reign as Queen Elizabeth II in 1952.

The Canadian penny went out of circulation in 2013; three faces include
[no crown, large crown and small crown] and two obverse.

Canadian Centennial 100 year anniversary penny: 1867~1967
Photo by Forest L.

Canadian 5 cent coin: prior to 1999 the Monarch with crown, post 2000 no crown.
The national animal the beaver by J.K. Gray sculptor

Canadian 10 cent coin: 50 years of monarch from 1952 to 2002 with Royal Crown. Golden jubilee
Bluenose schooner had won many competitions. Emmanuel Hahn.

.25 cent coin: designed by Emmanuel Hahn. These are the standard coins of Canada today.

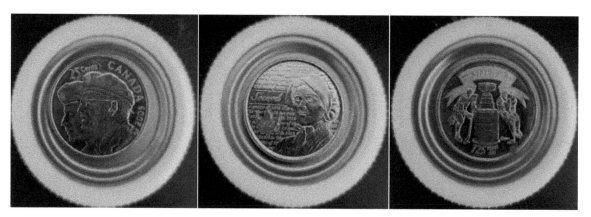

*L-R; War veterans~Secord~ Stanley cup

The old one dollar note. The Queen and the parliament building
and the logging boats of Canada and the

one dollar coin with a Canadian Loon.

Old two dollar bill with the Queen and obverse with two robins

The new two dollar coin. The Queen and the polar bear.

The Canadian 5 dollar note. Prime Minister Wilford Laurier, holographic window
with parliament building; opposing ~ The Canada Arm in space.

The three faces of the $10 dollar Canadian bill

First Prime Minister of Canada, Prime Minister MacDonald

Second addition: MacDonald, Cartier, Macphail and Gladstone.

Desmond; first to challenge the government that 'Black people' have rights within Canada.

Top, 20.00 dollar note~The Queen. Middle, from 2004 to 2012 on the reverse of
the Canadian 20 bill.The sculptor of 'The Spirit of Haida Gwaii by Bill Reid.

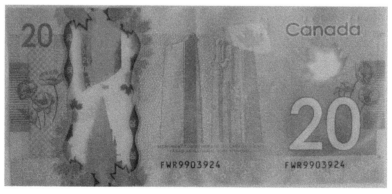

Vimy Monument and Red Poppies.

50 dollar note [red] with Prime Minister McKenzie King on the
face, with braille; opposing with the SS Amundsen.

Prime Minister Robert Borden on the Canadian 100 note; medical achievements on
the opposing side. Women in science, discovery of insulin and the double-helix.

Canadian National Anthem ~ English version ~ Robert Stanley Weir

O Canada! Our home and native land!

True Patriot love thou dost in us command.

We see thee rising fair, dear land,

The True North strong and free;

And stand on guard, O Canada,

We stand on Guard for thee.

Chorus:

O Canada! O Canada!

O Canada! We stand on guard for thee

O Canada! We stand on guard for thee

O Canada! where pines and maples grow,

Great prairies spread and lordly rivers flow,

How dear to us thy broad domain,

From East to Western sea!

Thou land of hope for all who toil

Thou True North strong and free!

Chorus

O Canada, Beneath thy shining skies

May stalwart sons and gentle maidens rise

To keep thee steadfast though out the years.

From East to Western seas

Our own beloved native land

Our True North strong and free.

Chorus

Ruler Supreme, Who hearest humble prayer,

Hold our dominion within Thy loving care.

Help us to find, O God in thee,

A lasting, rich reward,

As waiting for a Better Day,

We ever stand on guard

chorus

Forest Leigh Littke - 634

Top left; D Day, Top Right....daddy don't leave
Bottom L) old and new veterans from past wars. R) 1994 memorial.

Remembrance Day
11 NOVEMBER

In Flanders Fields
poem by Lieutenant Colonel John McCrae, 3 May 1915

In Flanders fields the poppies blow
Between the crosses, row on row,
That mark our place; and in the sky
The larks, still bravely singing, fly
Scarce heard amid the guns below.

We are the Dead. Short days ago
We lived, felt dawn, saw sunset glow,
Loved and were loved, and now we lie,
In Flanders fields.

Take up our quarrel with the foe:
To you from failing hands we throw
The torch; be yours to hold it high.
If ye break faith with us who die
We shall not sleep, though poppies grow
In Flanders fields.

lest we forget

LEST WE FORGET

OUR ANCESTORS PAST

Breton Museum.
L~R cream can container going to market to make butter, old style school classrooms,
cream separator using centrifugal force to remove cream from the milk. [hand crank].

Courtesy The Antique Store [Edmonton].
Top L~ kerosene lamp, clothes wheel spindle.
Bottom ~ single sheet typewriter, sewing machine with foot power peddle.

Childhood home in North Alberta 1959~1975. No running water, no toilet.

BIBLIOGRAPHY - PHOTOS.

1. KJV- King James version
2. READING AND WRITING CHINESE CHARACTERS-陈维琪，王涛.2014
3. 中文e.n: This guide has been very instrumental in teaching me Chinese.
4. wikipedia
5. Baidu 翻译; is the Chinese equivalent of Google. Translator tool.
6. Bing search engine.
7. Most photos in this book were taken by me either in China or around Alberta Canada. Eiffel tower was taken by Rebecca Littke (daughter) on her 2019 trip to France

Lightning Source UK Ltd.
Milton Keynes UK
UKHW050704081120
373029UK00003B/57

9 781663 200280